MW00574221

The Rise of Majority Rule in Early Modern Britain and Its Empire

This expansive history of the origins of majority rule in modern representative government charts the emergence of majority voting as a global standard for decision-making in popular assemblies. Majority votes had, of course, been held prior to 1642, but not since antiquity had they been held with any frequency by a popular assembly with responsibility for the fate of a nation. The crucial moment in the global triumph of majority rule was its embrace by the elected assemblies of early modern Britain and its empire. William J. Bulman analyzes its sudden appearance in the English House of Commons and its adoption by the elected assemblies of Britain's Atlantic colonies in the age of the English, Glorious, and American Revolutions. These events made it overwhelmingly likely that the United Kingdom, the United States, and their former dependencies would become and remain fundamentally majoritarian polities. Providing an insightful commentary on the state of democratic governance today, this study sheds light on the nature, promise, and perils of majority rule.

WILLIAM J. BULMAN is Associate Professor of History and Global Studies in the Department of History at Lehigh University. His articles on the intellectual, religious, political, and cultural history of England and its empire have appeared in *Past and Present*, *Historical Journal*, and *The Journal of British Studies*. His previous publications include *Anglican Enlightenment* (2015) and, as co-editor with Robert G. Ingram, *God in the Enlightenment* (2016).

The Rise of Majority Rule in Early Modern Britain and Its Empire

William J. Bulman

CAMBRIDGE
UNIVERSITY PRESS

CAMBRIDGE
UNIVERSITY PRESS

University Printing House, Cambridge CB2 8BS, United Kingdom

One Liberty Plaza, 20th Floor, New York, NY 10006, USA

477 Williamstown Road, Port Melbourne, VIC 3207, Australia

314–321, 3rd Floor, Plot 3, Splendor Forum, Jasola District Centre, New Delhi – 110025, India

79 Anson Road, #06-04/06, Singapore 079906

Cambridge University Press is part of the University of Cambridge.

It furthers the University's mission by disseminating knowledge in the pursuit of education, learning, and research at the highest international levels of excellence.

www.cambridge.org
Information on this title: www.cambridge.org/9781108842495
DOI: 10.1017/9781108909648

First published 2021

A catalogue record for this publication is available from the British Library.

Library of Congress Cataloging-in-Publication Data
Names: Bulman, William J., 1979- author.
Title: The rise of majority rule in early modern Britain and its empire / William J.
  Bulman.
Description: Cambridge ; New York, NY : Cambridge University Press, 2021. |
  Includes bibliographical references and index.
Identifiers: LCCN 2020042675 (print) | LCCN 2020042676 (ebook) |
  ISBN 9781108842495 (hardback) | ISBN 9781108829205 (paperback) |
  ISBN 9781108909648 (epub)
Subjects: LCSH: Great Britain. Parliament. House of Commons–History. |
  Representative government and representation–Great Britain–History. |
  Majorities. | Democracy–Great Britain–History. | Parliamentary practice–
  Great Britain–History. | Legislative bodies–America–History. | Legislative
  bodies–Ireland–History. | Great Britain–Colonies–Administration. | Great
  Britain–Politics and government–1485-
Classification: LCC JN900 .B85 2021 (print) | LCC JN900 (ebook) |
  DDC 328.4109/03–dc23
LC record available at https://lccn.loc.gov/2020042675
LC ebook record available at https://lccn.loc.gov/2020042676

ISBN 978-1-108-84249-5 Hardback

To my parents

Contents

Figures

Tables

Acknowledgments

Writing this book and launching the ongoing project of which it is a part required years of additional training outside my original areas of expertise. At the same time, this book is the product of general interests in social science history and political decision-making that I have had the privilege to nurture since graduate school. I am therefore especially grateful to the scholars who have encouraged and supported this nurturing and training over the years. My graduate advisors at Princeton, Peter Lake and Anthony Grafton, did so without reservation, despite the fact that my curiosity on this front ranged far from their own core scholarly commitments and took significant time away from my dissertation. This testifies to their open-mindedness, intellectual range, and confidence in their students. Lake, in particular, has encouraged and engaged with my work on political decision-making without interruption for over fifteen years now. It would be hard for me to exaggerate the benefits I have accrued from our exchanges. At the same time, four scholars with agendas more closely aligned with this strand of my scholarship were more than happy to guide and encourage me. Early on, Christopher Achen and J. Andrew Harris pointed me to the right tools and asked good questions. Steve Pincus has encouraged and engaged with my work on this front for as long as Lake has. His commitment to a fruitful dialogue between history and the social sciences continues to inspire. Finally, Jason Peacey exhibited patience, humility, and enthusiasm as I became acquainted with parliamentary history and overcame my own doubts about this project. I have benefited immensely from both his input on my work and his scholarly example.

This book also draws on the knowledge, insight, encouragement, and generosity of many other scholars and technical experts, including Julian Ball, Alex Barber, Alexander Bick, Carolyn Biltoft, Ann Blair, Michael Braddick, Megan Cherry, Thomas Cogswell, Jeffrey Collins, David Como, Nandini Deo, Robert Flowers, Scott Gordon, Philip Gorski, Karl Gunther, Tim Harris, Simon Healy, Amanda Herbert, Derek

Hirst, Khurram Hussain, Richard Huzzey, Robert Ingram, Joanna Innes, Brendan Kane, Mark Knights, Janet Laible, Naomi Lamoreaux, Nitzan Lebovic, Rick Matthews, Monica Miller, Rupali Mishra, Philip Morgan, Ziad Munson, Kevin Narizny, Uğur Peçe, Mark Pegg, Markku Peltonen, Mark Philp, Michael Raposa, Sophia Rosenfeld, Alexander Russell, Paul Seaward, Ethan Shagan, Scott Sowerby, Philip Stern, Laura Stewart, Christopher Thompson, Philippe Urfalino, James Vaughn, Amy Watson, Rachel Weil, Nicholas Wilson, Benjamin Wright, and Keith Wrightson. At the end of this long list Noah Millstone, Nicholas Popper, and Corey Tazzara deserve special mention. My intellectual kinship with them has been an inspiration and a challenge from before our collaboration to the present. I hope they see this book as a step in the right direction, even if there is still a long way to go.

Some of my discussions with other scholars about this project occurred in and around talks I gave on my research at Harvard, Johns Hopkins, Lehigh, Miami, UConn, Vanderbilt, Warwick, Yale, and the North American Conference on British Studies. I am grateful to all of these sponsoring institutions and organizations for their invitations and support, and to the participants for their thoughtful responses to my work. I owe Yale and Lehigh a particular debt on the institutional front. This project may have seemed too risky and time-consuming a venture were it not for a two-year postdoctoral fellowship at Yale's European Studies Council and the constant stream of funding and research assistance I have received at Lehigh since my arrival in 2012. Special thanks go to Rob Weidman and the rest of Lehigh's Digital Scholarship Team, who provided much of the technical backbone for this project before, during, and after the year I spent as Lehigh's inaugural Digital Scholarship Faculty Fellow; Patricia Ward and Brigit Gray at Library Circulation Services, who fielded innumerable and obscure requests with good cheer; the Humanities Center, where the digital and interdisciplinary aspects of this project were strengthened in three successive faculty seminars; my formal academic homes, the Department of History, the Program in Global Studies, and the College of Arts and Sciences; and, last but not least my graduate research assistants Cal Parks, Blake Michaels, Jay Donis, Austin Stewart, and Samuel Dodge. My final acknowledgment on the institutional front goes to Cambridge University Press. Liz Friend-Smith showed keen interest in this project from the moment I mentioned it to her, and she took care to send the manuscript to two excellent external reviewers, for whose insights I am also grateful.

My deepest gratitude, as always, goes to the members of my family in Pennsylvania, Colorado, and California – especially to Andrew and Liam

Bulman, for respecting my work, even when it meant less playtime; to Eric and Susan Busch, for giving me time to do my work and to play; to Catherine Bulman and William Bulman III, for offering love, encouragement, and support of every kind; and to Kathryn Bulman, for all of the above and more.

Note on the Text

In quotations, orthography has usually been modernized. Dates are rendered in Old Style, with the year beginning on 1 January. The footnotes contain short title and author or editor references. Full references appear in the Bibliography, where the titles of early modern printed books have often been abbreviated. In references to the journal of the English House of Commons, the journal of the English House of Lords, *Proceedings in Parliament 1624*, Townshend's *Historical Collections*, and Anchitell Grey's *Debates*, dates have been listed (in the format "month/day/year") instead of page numbers, in order to facilitate location in both digital and print versions of these sources. In references to Sir Simonds D'Ewes' Long Parliament diary, a reference to the original manuscripts (British Library MSS Harley 164-6) is normally followed by a parenthetical reference to page numbers in a nearly complete transcript (Yale University Archives MS 1987).

Abbreviations

Aston	Maltby (ed.), *Short Parliament Diary*
BL	British Library, London
Bodl.	Bodleian Library, Oxford
Burton	Rutt (ed.), *Diary of Thomas Burton*
CD 1629	Notestein and Relf (eds.), *Commons Debates for 1629*
CJ	House of Commons, *Journals*
Dering	Henning (ed.), *Parliamentary Diary of Sir Edward Dering*
D'Ewes	Coates (ed.), *Journal of Sir Simonds D'Ewes*
D'Ewes MS	British Library MSS Harley 164–6, Yale University Archives MS 1987
Grey	Grey, *Debates of the House of Commons*
Harington	Steig (ed.), *Diary of John Harington*
LJ	House of Lords, *Journals*
LMA	London Metropolitan Archives, London
Milward	Robbins, (ed.), *Diary of John Milward*
NA	National Archives, Kew
PJLP	Coates et al. (eds.), *Private Journals of the Long Parliament*
POSLP	Jansson (ed.), *Proceedings in the Opening Session of the Long Parliament*
PP 1610	Foster (ed.), *Proceedings in Parliament 1610*
PP 1614	Jansson (ed.), *Proceedings in Parliament 1614*
PP 1624	Baker (ed.), *Proceedings in Parliament 1624*
PP 1625	Jansson and Bidwell (eds.), *Proceedings in Parliament 1625*
PP 1626	Bidwell and Jansson (eds.), *Proceedings in Parliament 1626*
PP 1628	Johnson et al. (eds.), *Proceedings in Parliament 1628*
PSP	Cope and Coates (eds.), *Proceedings of the Short Parliament of 1640*
Verney	Bruce (ed.), *Verney Papers*

1 Introduction

In today's democracies, the nation's elected representatives normally make important decisions by enumerated majority vote. The vote is a procedure, of course, but it is also the defining feature of these systems. It is how democracies decide. They decide in this way largely because we live in a world of ideological conflict and vested interests in which the consistent production of consensus through debate and deliberation is presumed to be impossible. While mundane decisions made by legislatures are still commonly reached by means of consensus or unanimity, decisions of political import are usually meaningfully majoritarian. This institutionalized practice is in symbiosis with another institution – the party system – whose rich history has been exhaustively documented. In short, parties exist to secure majorities. Yet despite the importance of this relationship, scholars and citizens alike have tended to assume that, unlike partisan organization, majority voting has no history. It is taken to be either natural or automatic in politics, at least when people are making collective choices under conditions of ideological diversity. As a result, when we think about the turn to modern political life, we think above all about parties and very little about the majoritarian politics they presuppose.

This is short-sighted. Prior to the modern era, humans mostly made important political decisions by entrusting them to superiors or by forging consensus. Whatever conflict existed was suppressed at the moment of decision. Majority voting, by contrast, acknowledges conflict at the core of the political process. And whatever its merits or demerits, allowing one group to decide for another simply because of strength in numbers is hardly a natural way of securing the common good. The dominance of majority decision-making as a global standard for political decision-making is therefore something to be explained, not assumed. This task is of central importance. After all, majority rule is as much *a rule* for deciding as it is *the rule* of the greater part. Indeed, one might even argue that the turn to majority voting is more essential to the history of majority rule than the gradual attainment of universal suffrage.

1

The former certainly preceded (and had to precede) the latter. In this sense, at least, the rise of majority voting was the most important aspect of the rise of majority rule. And this makes the transformation of pre-democratic decision-making foundational to the history of democracy.

None of this, of course, ought to be taken to suggest that the history of the rise of majority rule is a history of triumph. Indeed, part of what makes the sudden emergence of majority voting in the English Revolution so interesting is that it immediately exposed what would become some of the central dilemmas of democratic life. Majority rule is no anodyne synonym for democracy. As an idea and a practice, it lies at the heart of a series of scholarly and public debates about the viability of democratic polities and the meaning of democratic citizenship.[1] While today these debates tend to center on a particular set of salient topics – campaign finance, partisan rancor, civic education, and, above all, populism – it is important to recognize that a profound unease about majority voting has always been embedded within representative democracies. Among the variety of institutional responses to this unease, the most direct are worth special mention: some decisions faced by representative democracies are simply considered too important to be left to a simple majority. Some actions are deemed so momentous that they can be taken only either with the consent of a supermajority or after an expression of outright unanimity. In the legislative realm, this can be seen everywhere from the supermajority requirement for constitutional amendments to the expectation of unanimity in declarations of war.

Both the character of majority voting and our deep discomfort with it have roots in the world of political decision-making from which majority rule initially emerged. This was a world in which consensus was prized, in part for good reason. This book is therefore premised on the basic historical and social-scientific insight that institutions are path-dependent. They carry with them, as it were, the moment of their creation. It is impossible, therefore, properly to address the promise and pitfalls of majority rule today without a history of its rise at the ready. This book is the first such history. It describes and explains the crucial moment in the majority's global rise to power: its embrace by the elected assemblies of Britain, Ireland, North America, and the Caribbean in the

---

[1] A representative sampling of this voluminous and diverse literature from recent years might include Urbinati, *Democracy Disfigured*; Urbinati, *Me the People*; Achen and Bartels, *Democracy for Realists*; Mounk, *The People vs. Democracy*; Runciman, *How Democracy Ends*; Van Reybrouck, *Against Elections*; Rosenfeld, *Democracy and Truth*; Kloppenberg, *Toward Democracy*; Maloy, *Colonial American Origins of Modern Democratic Thought*; Schwartzberg, *Counting the Many*; Novak and Elster (eds.), *Majority Decisions*; Bourke and Skinner (eds.), *Popular Sovereignty in Historical Perspective*.

age of the English, Glorious, and American Revolutions. The crucial turning point occurred in the fall and winter of 1642–3. As the people of England faced each other in battle, their representatives in Parliament were waging civil war by other means. The House of Commons had found itself deadlocked over the excruciating question of how to deal with an anointed monarch who had taken up arms against his subjects. To get on with governing, the members of Parliament accepted their differences. They abandoned their cherished tradition of consensual decision-making and turned to the dark arts of majoritarian maneuver. Within months the proportion of decisions they made with recourse to enumerated majority votes had approached that of a modern legislature. Enumerated majority votes – "divisions" in the English lexicon – had been permitted in the early modern House of Commons since at least the early sixteenth century, but this procedural option was hardly ever used to make important decisions. In the 1640s, however, party and preference had apparently replaced wisdom and deliberation as the engines of government. Majority votes had been held prior to 1642, of course, in England and elsewhere. But not since antiquity had they been held with any frequency by a popular assembly tasked with the fate of a nation.

To make important decisions in this way was to hazard radical innovation in a society that abhorred it. Yet the House of Commons never turned back. England's body politic continued to act by ritually splitting itself in two even after the English Revolution had been crushed and the monarchy restored. A majoritarian pattern of political decision-making became institutionalized years before the emergence of what many consider the world's first party system. Even if one dates the advent of Whig and Tory politics to the late seventeenth century, it is hard to argue that party politics was thoroughly institutionalized by the time majority voting was. In fact, because of the lack of regularity and structure in the Whig and Tory politics of the late seventeenth and eighteenth centuries, historians usually date the emergence of the British party system to the nineteenth century, not the seventeenth. Assuming that this convention for dating the advent of party politics in Britain is a reasonable one, majority decision-making may be the only institutionalized transition to modern political practice before the nineteenth century, or at least the most important. Almost as significantly, by 1776 – and usually long before – every elected assembly in Britain's Atlantic empire had followed suit. This provided, among other things, the institutional basis for the party politics of the early United States.

As both an institutional reality and a profound conundrum, the rise of majority voting in early modern Britain and its empire turned out to be a pivotal event in world history. It ensured that the two greatest powers of the modern world – the United Kingdom and the United States – would be majoritarian powers. And this ensured that when the former colonies, dependencies, and vanquished enemies of Britain and America took their own democratic turns in the half-century after World War II, they were overwhelmingly likely to take majoritarian turns as well. The globalization of the majority and the globalization of democracy went hand in hand. The benefits and dangers of one were transferred to the other. Yet we know almost nothing about the former, more fundamental development.[2] We may therefore have much to learn about the underpinnings of modern politics from describing and explaining the initial emergence of this institution. We certainly have much to learn about a fundamental shift in the history of political practice in Britain and its empire that rivals the importance of any other such change in the early modern period.

Over 120 years ago the famed legal historian F. W. Maitland remarked that "one of the great books that remain to be written is The History of the Majority." He observed that because "our habit of treating the voice of the majority as equivalent to the voice of an all is so deeply engrained," we "hardly think that it has a history. But a history it has."[3] It is particularly ironic that Maitland's advice has gone unheeded for so long in the British context. The most important source for studying the rise of the majority in British politics is perhaps the most commonly cited document in the field of early modern history: the official journal of the English House of Commons. Availability, however, does not imply legibility. Manually examining each of the 30,000 formal decisions made by the Commons in the seventeenth century alone, without any idea that there would be a story worth telling, is a gamble with time that scholars have understandably avoided. In recent years, however, the methods of digital history have made it possible to get a bird's-eye, *longue durée* view of the story before examining particular moments and decisions. This makes it possible to confirm the story's fundamental interest, reveal its broad contours, and pinpoint focal points for archival and interpretive analysis. The present study is based on a unique database of over 150,000 formal decisions recorded in the Commons journal between the reigns of Elizabeth I and Elizabeth II, and tens of thousands of formal decisions made in the colonial lower assemblies in the century and a half prior to the American Revolution.

---

[2] The pioneering studies that highlight the central importance of early modern England in the history of majority rule are Baty, "History of Majority Rule"; Heinberg, "History of the Majority Principle"; Edwards, "The Emergence of Majority Rule"; Kishlansky, "Emergence of Adversary Politics"; Kishlansky, *Rise of the New Model Army*; Mansbridge, *Beyond Adversary Politics*, 3–16.

[3] Maitland, *Township and Borough*, 34.

There are also basic historiographical reasons why scholars have neglected this subject. Persistent national, regional, and chronological hyper-specialization is perhaps the most obvious. More interesting, perhaps, are the thematic commonalities in all of the research subfields this study brings together. Students of both British and American politics in both the seventeenth and eighteenth centuries have long been pre-occupied by searching for the causes of the period's great constitutional and ideological watersheds – the English Revolution, the Glorious Revolution, and the American Revolution – to the exclusion of equally important transformations in institutions and mundane patterns of political practice.[4] As a result, they have paid far more attention to the struggles between monarchs and representative assemblies than to changes internal to those assemblies. In this sense, both Parliament and the colonial legislatures have somehow sat neglected at the center of British and American historiography. Historians have long recognized the pivotal role of their increasing power in the political history of the seventeenth- and eighteenth-century British Atlantic world.[5] But they have not seriously considered the long-term importance of fundamental changes in the way the House of Commons and the lower assemblies managed to get on with political life over the course of this period.

Recently, there has, in fact, been something of a turn to political practice and temporal breadth in early modern British and colonial American historiography, as these fields escape the once-productive dialectics of Whig narratives, revisionisms, and post-revisionisms, and a limiting focus on the analysis of semiotic or communicative action.[6] Newer histories of politics, many of them centered on the so-called public sphere, which in fact emerged from semiotically focused approaches to political history, have shown how the focused study of political practices and institutions can expose the way in which the very nature of the political process changed over the course of the early modern period. This, in turn, has provided the basis for novel accounts of the same constitutional and ideological upheavals that have always

---

[4] Accordingly, this book does not directly address the general, ambiguous, and contested question of whether or when early modern England became, in general, a divided or conflictual society or polity in advance of the outbreak of the Civil War. For a discussion of how the following account of the pre-revolutionary House of Commons should be read in light of revisionist and post-revisionist scholarship on early modern English politics, see Bulman, "Consensual Conflict in the Early Stuart House of Commons."
[5] The important works on colonial America most relevant to the present study are Greene, *Quest for Power*; Bailyn, *Origins of American Politics*; Morgan, *Inventing the People*.
[6] The most prominent and controversial call for a return to long-term perspectives that appeared during the research and writing of this book is Armitage and Guldi, *The History Manifesto*.

engaged the attention of scholars across the disciplines. The idea is that changes in the structure of politics altered the probability and the character of conflict and creativity. This book provides the same sorts of insights and adds to this emerging body of scholarship, while at the same time trying to shift its focus. To date these pioneering histories of practice have understandably remained centered on both the discursive dimension of political action and a series of topics central to earlier phases of historiography: the advent of opposition, resistance, parties, popular participation, public spheres, and competitive elections.[7] But the independently significant narrative of political practice and institutions emerging from this work suggests the possibility of moving beyond these familiar themes to study less well-known but equally important and closely related transformations in the nature of politics.

This book clarifies the remarkable extent to which majority voting in elected assemblies often made possible and amplified many of the important developments in political practice already studied in detail by other scholars. It also clarifies the fundamental reason why historians have neglected the rise of majority voting: they have yet to develop a thoroughly historical approach to early modern politics because they retain ahistorical assumptions about the decision-making at its core. Drawing on a small body of existing scholarship that has attempted to historicize the individual and collective decision-making of political actors in the seventeenth century, this book provides a crucial through line for what promises to become a unified historiography of political practice in the early modern British Atlantic world.[8]

It is also worth specifying what this book is not meant to accomplish and why. Doing so will also provide a sense of the broader context in which the following pages ought to be read and appreciated. First of all, this book is a history of practices and institutions. It is not a history of ideology, ideas, discourses, or norms. Accordingly, the terms

---

[7] For an extended discussion of the relationship between the "post-revisionist" approach to British political and religious history and recent scholarship on religious and political practice, see Bulman with Dominguez, "Introduction." For recent work on British political practice that treats both familiar and less familiar topics, see, for example, Lake and Pincus (eds.), *Politics of the Public Sphere*; Bulman, "Practice of Politics"; Peacey, *Print and Public Politics in the English Revolution*; Millstone, *Circulation of Manuscripts*; Popper, "An Information State for Elizabethan England"; Weil, *Plague of Informers*. For recent work on North America and the wider Atlantic world, see, for example, Beeman, *Varieties of Political Experience*; Smolenski, *Friends and Strangers*; Roney, *Governed by a Spirit of Opposition*; Sharples, "Discovering Slave Conspiracies"; Perl-Rosenthal, "Atlantic Cultures in the Age of Revolution."

[8] Different takes on the need more deeply to historicize the political in the early modern period include Bulman, "Practice of Politics"; Kishlansky, *Parliamentary Selection*, ix; Millstone, "Seeing like a Statesman."

"majoritarian" and (occasionally) "majoritarianism" are employed here to describe the character of institutionalized practices. These terms are not meant to refer to the ideologies, ideas, or norms surrounding those practices. Decision-making in the House of Commons and the colonial lower assemblies became practically majoritarian long before the members of these bodies were in general ideologically, intellectually, or normatively majoritarian.[9]

There are other limits to the scope of this study as well. It is not concerned with the place of early modern Britain and its empire in the vast history of collective decision-making in all social contexts. Nor is it concerned with Britain's place in a comprehensive history of either majority decision-making or majority rule in particular. Indeed, it does not even approach the gargantuan task of identifying the many realms in which political decisions were made by majority vote throughout the complex institutional landscape of the early modern British world, from the Privy Council to parish vestries in North America. Instead, it concentrates on decision-making within England's only elected, representative, national body, the House of Commons, and its colonial counterparts, the lower assemblies, which later served, along with the British House of Commons, as the basic models for the US House of Representatives. Any historian of majority rule must begin with these institutions because of their uniquely pivotal role in the globalization of majoritarian and democratic government.

There is nothing definitive to be said, in any case, about the first political institutions to feature consistent group decision-making by majority rule. This is due to the paucity of evidence concerning the political history of antiquity. There are, for instance, scattered and ambiguous indications of majoritarian voting in Mesopotamian assemblies from the third millennium BCE onward, but nothing to support remotely firm conclusions about first instances.[10] Ancient Athens is of course the traditionally referenced site for the emergence of majority

---

[9] For brief remarks about the relationship between the history recounted here and the history of political thought, see the Conclusion (Chapter 8). The broader intellectual-historical, political-historical, social-scientific, and political-theoretical ramifications of the revolution in practice described here will be examined in a series of future publications. For arguments about the importance of the seventeenth century to the history of democracy that focus on political thought, see Maloy, *Colonial American Origins of Modern Democratic Thought*; Cuttica and Peltonen (eds.), *Democracy and Anti-Democracy in Early Modern England*.

[10] Jacobsen, *Toward the Image of Tammuz*, 132–70, 372; Evans, "Ancient Mesopotamian Assemblies"; Evans, "Ancient Mesopotamian Assemblies: An Addendum"; Larsen, *Old Assyrian City-State and Its Colonies*, 161–91, 304, 319–26; Martin and Snell, "Democracy and Freedom."

rule, but we know too little about other societies before and during the fifth century BCE to make ironclad claims about Athenian exceptionality. Even the evidence we do have on other societies threatens to undermine such conclusions. Buddhist sources from India, for instance, indicate the use of majoritarian procedures in monasteries by at least the fifth century BCE, if not earlier, although there is no clear evidence that such procedures were followed in the so-called Indian republics of the same period.[11] The archival difficulties at play imply that there is no story to be told whatsoever about "the invention of the majority" in politics (or in democracies, for that matter). They also imply that the spirited inquiry and debate surrounding the Western or non-Western origins of democracy is largely a nonstarter.[12] Neither majoritarianism nor any other democratic value or institutional element can be definitively attributed to a particular society or region of the world.

The only stories we can tell about majority rule and democracy are stories about their incidence in recorded history. The larger story behind this book – the story of a turning point beyond which majoritarian political institutions followed the global exportation of Western democratic governance to become the overwhelming worldwide norm for collective decision-making in politics – is arguably the most important of those stories. Remarkably, this story is an early modern one, not an ancient one. Despite all the attention lavished upon them by generations of historians and political theorists, ancient precedents for majority rule simply did not have the same lasting, continuous, or direct significance for modern practices of governance as the developments of the early modern era.

Early modern elites were nevertheless well aware of ancient Greek and Roman majoritarianism. It is important to register this if only to emphasize the ambiguity and limited afterlife of these precedents, and to contextualize the early modern world's initial, utter distaste for them. The Spartan *gerousia* (council of elders) and *apella* (popular assembly), as well as the Athenian Areopagus (aristocratic council) and *ekklesia* (popular assembly), may have employed enumerated majority voting upon their founding. But there is no unambiguous evidence relating to any of these institutions that survives from prior to the fifth century

---

[11] *Vinaya Texts Translated from the Pali: The Kullavagga*, esp. 24–7; Muhlberger, "Republics and Quasi-Democratic Institutions in Ancient India"; Sharma, *Republics in Ancient India*, esp. 200–2.

[12] For this debate, see Goody, *Theft of History*, esp. 49–60; Isakhan and Stockwell (eds.), *Secret History of Democracy*; Isakhan and Stockwell (eds.), *Edinburgh Companion to the History of Democracy*.

BCE.[13] By then, at least on some occasions, the Spartan *apella* appears to have made decisions consensually with recourse to various forms of acclamation. On at least on one occasion in 432 described by Thucydides, when the result of an acclamation was unclear, the assembly apparently made use of a division procedure similar to the one used by English House of Commons two millennia later.[14] The Spartan *gerousia*, alternatively, may have proceeded much like the House of Lords. In judicial cases, at least, it appears to have held enumerated votes via roll call or consecutive voting by individuals when called upon. The similarity between the Spartan and English procedures is remarkable, but no account of the origin of the English variant has ever been given. In Athens, by contrast, the massive citizens' assembly voted by a show of hands. It is unclear whether and with what frequency hands were counted one by one instead of being estimated. The Athenian Council of Five Hundred followed suit. Ostracisms in the Athenian assembly were conducted with tile or potsherd ballots. Votes on the status of individuals were also conducted by ballot (pebbles or olive leaves were used) in the Council.[15] The Athenian precedents clearly have little connection to early modern British practices.

Much more is known about voting in ancient Rome, where a two-level form of majoritarian voting was institutionalized in the Republic's three popular assemblies. In each assembly social groupings, not individuals, were the voting units in final decisions. Each social grouping itself voted in accordance with an enumerated majority of the votes of the grouping's individual members. This procedure would later appear, for instance, in the Continental Congresses of revolutionary British North America. In one of these assemblies, the *comitia centuriata*, voting units were of variable sizes. This weighted the vote in such a way that the wealthiest citizens could secure a majority of unit votes without attracting wider support. According to Cicero, who defended this practice, such arrangements were anti-majoritarian in principle: those who had the most to gain from a healthy state (and the most to lose from a failed state) were

---

[13] Staveley, *Greek and Roman Voting and Elections*, 18–27.

[14] Thucydides, *War of the Peloponnesians and the Athenians*, 52–3 (I.87). Spartan practices were also attested in Pausanias' *Description of Greece* (second century CE), another text known to early moderns.

[15] Staveley, *Greek and Roman Voting and Elections*, 73–8, 83, 86, 88–9, 93–4, 96–8. The Athenians made extensive use of sortition in place of election. Mansbridge, *Beyond Adversary Democracy*, 14, 336–7, emphasizes the fact that the Athenians may have mostly voted consensually, despite the availability of majoritarian procedures, as was the case in England before the Civil War.

properly given disproportionate voting power.[16] Deliberation in advance
of votes appears to have been limited and, in many cases, nonexistent.
Originally, votes were probably conducted by acclamation, but this practice appears to have been abandoned in the first half of the fifth century
BCE. Until the third quarter of the second century BCE, individual
members of each social unit filed past a *rogator* (questioner) to vote by
voice, and the vote was recorded on a wax tablet. This method was then
replaced by written ballots (wax-covered wooden tablets) placed in a
large urn. The majority decision in each unit was calculated as that unit's
vote, and then the majority of all units' votes determined the final
decision.[17]

For all their striking characteristics and their legibility in later periods,
the most salient point about practices of majority rule in the ancient
world is their apparent abandonment in the political realm for about
one thousand years following the fall of the Roman Empire. Because of
limited evidence, we know very little about the specifics of decision-
making within any political (not to mention "national") assemblies in
the medieval period before 1300. What can be said is that while majority
votes did occur in urban communities, in all contexts unanimity and
consensus were highly valued and apparently widely practiced. Up to the
thirteenth century, at least, political assemblies in Europe were primarily
ritual in nature, shunning and avoiding open expressions of conflict or
disagreement. They were part of cultures in which people were generally
unable to express conflict or opposition in a controllable, nonviolent
form. Opposing or contradicting someone in public was to insult that
person. What little conflict or disorder transpired was to be resolved in
ritual. This of course did not mean there were no private political
calculations or conflict-laden arguments. It meant that those arguments
were not to be conducted in public.[18]

The central assembly that emerged in medieval England exemplified
the consensual politics that prevailed elsewhere in Europe. Two developments in particular provided the underpinnings for the political practice of the early modern House of Commons: first, the emergence of
Parliament as a powerful, national, representative institution; and
second, the formation of a distinct "house" of commoners. Like its early
modern counterpart in the Tudor and early Stuart periods, this socially

[16] Staveley, *Greek and Roman Voting and Elections*, 121–8; Cicero, *On the Republic*, 75–6
    (2.39–41).
[17] Staveley, *Greek and Roman Voting and Elections*, 143, 153, 157–60, 177–8.
[18] Reuter, *Medieval Polities and Modern Mentalities*, 196–7, 199, 203–4; Reynolds, *Kingdoms
    and Communities in Western Europe*, 30–3, 45–56, 99–100, 144–6, 187–92, 196, 212–14,
    302–19, 336. On late medieval assemblies, see Hébert, *Parlementer*, esp. 416–30.

subordinate grouping within Parliament was characterized by consensual interaction supported by both deliberation and status interaction.

National conciliar assemblies can be found in England over a century before the Norman Conquest, in the witans of the reign of Aethelstan. Considered in terms of frequency, regularity, attendance, business, control of lawmaking, and royal investment, the tenth-century witans were national assemblies that played a central role in English politics and government. Described as "the witan of the English people" by the early eleventh century, these assemblies appear to have been understood as a national and representative institution. Like their continental counterparts, the witans were consensual, ritualized affairs whose proceedings were characterized by feasts, deliberations, gift exchanges, petitions, and patronage. This held true even in moments of crisis and amid bargaining between kings and assemblies. In such situations, deliberation, in particular, served to avert violence. The consensualism of these English councils only intensified after the Conquest, when the operation of the assemblies was subsumed by feudal structures.[19]

Assemblies of *witan* (wise men) met throughout the medieval period to discuss crucial business that concerned the realm. These meetings were transformed between the tenth and thirteenth centuries into parliaments, slowly acquiring many of the characteristics that parliaments would exhibit in the sixteenth and early seventeenth centuries, before the House of Commons took its majoritarian turn. The assemblies were known immediately after the Conquest as *concilia*, and the French term *parlement* was in use as early as the 1170s. Not long after the Conquest, the king's greater and lesser tenants-in-chief were formally distinguished and summoned separately. *Concilium* attendees sought to influence the king's decision-making and to accrue honor, prestige, and confirmation of social rank. The quality of one's speech in the *concilium* was thought to maximize these benefits, tying skillful deliberation to personal status. Moreover, an appreciation of the assembly as virtually representative, as "the community of the realm," strengthened in the late twelfth and thirteenth centuries. This occurred along with the implicit (and in Magna Carta, explicit) embrace of the principle of parliamentary consent to direct taxation. These intertwined notions of representation and consent account for much of the primacy later placed in the Tudor and early Stuart parliaments upon the achievement of internal consensus in grants of taxation. In a representative institution, consensus implied the consensus of the entire populace. In the early thirteenth century, knights of

---

[19] Maddicott, *Origins of the English Parliament*, 3–4, 12, 14, 23–7, 37, 50–6, 61.

the shire were for the first time summoned to central assemblies and described as representatives of their counties. Meanwhile, magnates in council were coming to be seen as national representatives. Eventually, the magnates came to be regarded as representative not simply in discussions of taxation but also in matters they chose to discuss. These trends were reinforced by the minority of Henry III (1216–27), after which use of the Latin term *parliamentum* became common.[20]

In the mid-thirteenth century Parliament emerged as an essential government institution dealing with a variety of business. By the 1270s kings seem to have felt bound to consult a parliament even in times of no particular financial exigency, and the profile of the knights of the realm in the assemblies was growing. As early as the Montfortian parliaments of the 1260s, the knights were described with some frequency as representative figures. The knights' local and national representative status – and perhaps, on occasion, the status of the burgesses who began more frequently to attend parliaments – continued to be clarified. On occasion the knights, as a unit, were even described as "the community" or "the community of the realm."[21] In the later thirteenth century, knights were explicitly invited to parliaments in order to bind their local communities to taxation. The summoning of knights and burgesses became still more common in the early fourteenth century, even if their power remained minimal. This period also witnessed frequent reelection of the same commoners to increasingly long and frequent parliaments. The continuity created an esprit de corps, evidenced and supported by the emergence of the common petition, which would be issued by a separate "house" as the sole representative of the broader commons of the realm. Noncommoners, of course, had no need for representation, since they attended Parliament in person. The peers were also now commonly referred to as occupants of a "house" and treated as an order separate from the knights. From the thirteenth century, then, power in English government was distributed to a striking extent between assemblies and the ruler. Both this division of power and the extent of central authority generally set England apart from continental states. The prominence of the medieval English assemblies is especially vivid in comparison with France, whose assemblies exhibited a relative lack of power, local representation, and national unity.[22] A series of medieval developments therefore ensured that the early modern Parliament was a distinctively powerful, national, representative, and consensual body.

---

[20] Ibid., 75, 82–5, 92–4, 97, 108–9, 119–26, 132–4, 137–44, 148, 157–8.
[21] Ibid., 267–70, 274–6, 289.   [22] Ibid., 316, 335–40, 350–2, 376–453.

For a time, at the beginning of the early modern period, the consensualism of the English Parliament also set it apart from some continental assemblies, as a variety of subnational European councils appear to have embraced majoritarian decision-making. Yet Parliament is most aptly compared not to all these bodies, but rather to those continental assemblies that can in some sense be considered nationally representative. Here it is essential to observe that the early modern institutional trajectory of these councils, to the extent that they ever adopted majority decision-making, was the opposite of the English trajectory. These assemblies gradually turned away from anything resembling national representation by means of majoritarian decision-making. They did so either because they reembraced consensual practices or because they succumbed to absolutist or foreign domination, decentralization, or destruction.[23]

By surveying some of these comparable examples from early modern continental Europe it is possible both to highlight how exceptional English developments were and to qualify what can be said with certainty on this front. This will again help to clarify the limits, nature, and scope of the present inquiry. In France, central, provincial, and local estates revived during the reign of Charles VII, after having fallen into abeyance in the late fourteenth and early fifteenth centuries. The estates' position in French politics was inconsistent over the following century and a half. In general, central and national assemblies played little role in consenting to taxation. The activity of provincial and local assemblies varied immensely, despite an overall development of representative institutions at those levels. Under the Bourbons, central representative institutions collapsed entirely, amid attacks on the provincial estates.[24] Notoriously, the Estates General ceased to meet at all after 1614. Until the Revolution of 1789, this absolutist arrangement utterly precluded developments in national, representative institutions that paralleled English ones.[25] In any case, votes in the early modern Third Estate – the nearest equivalent to a national, popular assembly in pre-revolutionary France – appear to have always been cast by administrative units, not by individuals.[26]

---

[23] See, for example, Myers, *Parliaments and Estates in Europe*; Koenigsberger, *Politicians and Virtuosi*, 1-61; Koenigsberger, *Estates and Revolutions*, 1–93, 125–43, 176–210.

[24] Major, *Representative Institutions in Renaissance France*; Major, *The Deputies to the Estates General in Renaissance France*; Major, *Representative Government in Early Modern France*.

[25] For post-absolutist developments in France, other European countries, and their colonies, see the Conclusion (Chapter 8).

[26] Rothrock, "Officials and King's Men," 508; Hayden, "Deputies and *Qualités*," 514 (both referring to 1614).

A better comparison might be made with the Cortes of Castile, the primary national body in Spain. Here meaningful majority votes by individual members were procedural options in most situations, as they were in England by at least the early sixteenth century. Such votes did apparently occur in the Cortes with some frequency during the early modern period, but their frequency has never been studied with any precision. What we do know for certain is that various types of consensual decisions were extremely common and prized in particular situations, including taxation.[27] Whatever the nature of decision-making in the later sixteenth- and early seventeenth-century Cortes, a century of institutional vitality ended in 1665. At that point the Cortes was rather suddenly stripped of all political importance in favor of decentralized government, and it never met again.[28] Other Spanish representative assemblies of a semi-national (if not popular) character had broadly similar trajectories to that of Castile's Cortes, including those of Aragon, Catalonia, Navarre, and Valencia. In the Cortes of Aragon, for instance, members of the estate of the towns voted by town, not as individuals, and when each estate deliberated by itself, the most important decisions had to be unanimous. This Cortes met only five times between 1600 and 1711, the year in which it was abolished.[29] In the Catalan Corts, to take another example, subsidies could only be granted with unanimity in each estate. And while decisions on grievances required only a majority, rules enabling dissenters to stall proceedings ensured that a strong consensus was typically required for deciding matters of any importance.[30]

The diets of the Holy Roman Empire often used some sort of majoritarian mechanism in the sixteenth and seventeenth centuries. But even they came to require consensus for decisions on religion and taxation in

---

[27] De Dios, "El funcionamiento interno de las Cortes de Castilla," esp. 259–74. See also Lorenzana de la Puente, *La representación política en el Antiguo Régimen*, which includes some comparative discussion.

[28] Manuel de Bernardo Ares, "Parliament or City Councils." See also Thompson, *Crown and Cortes*, esp. chapters 6 and 7. A ceremonial Cortes, Spanish not Castilian in nature, met occasionally in the eighteenth century.

[29] Gil, "Crown and Cortes in Early Modern Aragon," 111. Some decisions did evidently fail to precisely meet the unanimity requirement. See also Baydal Sala, "Voting in the Parliaments of the Crown of Aragon," which discusses multiple Iberian assemblies. On the lack of comparable institutions in Spanish America and the preference for municipal representation there, see Borah, "Representative Institutions in the Spanish Empire of the Sixteenth Century."

[30] Elliott, *Revolt of the Catalans*, 218–20. For other Cortes, see, for example, Puy Huici Goñi, *Las Cortes de Navarra*, esp. 201–10, 237–42; Vázquez de Prada and Floristán, "The Relationship of the Kingdom of Navarre to Central Government"; Casey, *Kingdom of Valencia*, esp. 225–46.

1648, at the very moment when consensual decision-making was collapsing in the English House of Commons.[31] Between 1648 and their dissolution in 1806, the largely impotent *Landtage* (representative assemblies) of the Empire became even more dramatically consensual bodies working under absolutist regimes. Their typical mode of operation was broadly similar to the workings of the pre–Civil War House of Commons. Deliberation was a theater of oratory and debates were primarily sites for the affirmation of status. Members cherished the political utility of unity and harmony. Debate was seen as a means of securing the representative, unitary character of the institution and thereby celebrating political community.[32]

The broader European history of national representative assemblies and their decision-making in the age of absolutism serves to highlight how remarkable it is that England's representative assemblies turned *toward* majority decision-making in the same period. The main exception to England's apparent peculiarity one might cite would be the Dutch Republic, whose States General, an assembly of delegates chosen by the States of the seven sovereign provinces, appears to have engaged in majority voting on matters of defense and foreign affairs. But in the States General, as in the French Estates General, votes were cast in Roman fashion by provincial units, not by individuals. Moreover, given the strong independence of the seven provinces and their provincial States throughout the early modern period, as well as the power of the Stadholder in the early seventeenth century, the States General (an unelected body in any case) was by no means a powerful, national, representative institution in the sense that Parliament (or the House of Commons in particular) was.[33]

The fundamental point here, however, is not about firsts in the history of majority voting in representative national assemblies. To an extent any such determination is impossible to verify, and meaningful comparison with England is often difficult. A case in point is the Scottish Parliament, which was neither a popular nor a wholly elected assembly. It was mixed in social composition, since it included both noble and nonnoble

[31] Schulze, "Majority Decision in the Imperial Diets." These assemblies were in any case not elected, representative, or national in character.
[32] Neu, "Rhetoric and Representation." For a broader introduction in English, see Carsten, *Princes and Parliaments in Germany*. There were a series of similar, less central examples throughout Europe. See, for example, Baker, "Discursive Republicanism in Renaissance Florence," esp. 49, 55, 57, 61, 63, 72; Russocki, "De l'accord commun au vote unanime" (on Poland).
[33] Grever, "Structure of Decision-Making in the States General"; Grever, "Committees and Deputations in the Assemblies of the Dutch Republic."

members; it was led by the nobility; and its practices were relatively uninstitutionalized. Prior to the Restoration era the Parliament's estates often met separately, but official acts of Parliament were made by the estates assembled as one. In the seventeenth century, this Parliament seems to have normally conducted formal votes in a manner similar to the English House of Lords. Individuals stood when called in order of estate and voted by voice, with the majority of all votes determining the outcome. Dissent from the majority was often noted for the record. But because of the nature of the records, there is nothing certain or precise to be said about the process of deliberation or the frequency of enumerated majority voting either before or after the Civil Wars. The final and perhaps most important consideration here is that the Scottish Parliament, devolution notwithstanding, was an institutional dead end, due to its extinction in 1707.[34] For all these reasons it has been excluded from further discussion in this book.[35] The English Parliament and Britain's colonial assemblies are ultimately the proper focus of concern in an account of the rise of the majority not because they were definitely the first national, representative assemblies to institutionalize majority voting, but because of their uniquely influential, long-term position in the global history of majority rule.

Decision-making within the House of Commons in particular deserves pride of place in this history for a variety of reasons. It is tempting to think that elections to the Commons, for instance, might be an equally important topic of discussion, especially given the painstaking research that has

---

[34] For relevant work on the early modern Scottish Parliament, see Rait, *Parliaments of Scotland*, esp. 402–18; Thomson, *Parliament of Scotland*, esp. 83–8; Brown and Mann (eds.), *Parliament and Politics in Scotland*; MacDonald, "Voting in the Scottish Parliament before 1639"; MacDonald, "Deliberative Processes in Parliament"; Brown and MacDonald (eds.), *History of the Scottish Parliament*. For evidence of early enumerated majority votes, see Rait, *Parliaments of Scotland*, 407–9; *Records of the Parliaments of Scotland*, A1648/3/4–8. On a ballot box experiment, see MacIntosh, *Scottish Parliament under Charles II*, 45.

[35] Similarly, there is hardly any point in asking whether the English Parliament was an outlier among political institutions within England itself. Too little is known, for instance, about the nature of decision-making in English corporations. In most trading, livery, and urban corporations, the exact nature of non-electoral decision-making normally cannot be discerned from the records, while in other corporations there is stronger evidence of commonplace majority voting. For ambiguous examples, see, for example, Mishra, *Business of State*, 38, 86, 88, 94–5; BL IOR B/13 (East India Company); NA SP 105/148 (Levant Company); LMA microfilm X109/072 (London Common Council); Stevenson (ed.), *Records of the Borough of Nottingham*, vol. IV; Salter (ed.), *Oxford Council Acts 1583–1626*; Hobson and Salter (eds.), *Oxford Council Acts 1626–1665*; LMA Ms 5257/4–5 (Barber-Surgeons); LMA Ms 16967/4 (Ironmongers). See also Chapter 6 for the Atlantic colonial trading companies. For a seemingly majoritarian example, see Bateson (ed.), *Records of the Borough of Leicester*, vol. III; Stocks (ed.), *Records of the Borough of Leicester*, vol. IV.

been conducted on the topic over the past fifty years. The emergence of contested elections has rightly been associated with the rise of political division, political consciousness, majoritarianism, and representative democracy itself. More intriguingly, the chronology of developments in the electoral sphere also generally matches the chronology of the rise of majority voting in the Commons. Contested elections were unusual before 1640 and indeed until after the Restoration, because local elites normally decided on a single candidate in advance of the election itself. This pattern was rooted in social relationships of hierarchy, honor, reciprocity, and deference, again somewhat like consensual patterns of decision-making in the House of Commons. Contests and related competition that did not lead to contests on election day appear to have increased dramatically in frequency during the early Stuart period, and especially in the 1620s. This was related to an expansion and politicization of the electorate driven by inflation, communicative developments, and heightened political conflict. But no one would deny the novelty of the Short and Long Parliament elections of 1640, in which the number of contests spiked again. In a pattern very similar to changes within the Commons examined in the following chapters, the majoritarian structure of elections, both contested and uncontested, solidified after the Restoration, even though traditional values, structures, and dynamics persisted alongside novel patterns of practice.

The underpinnings of this institutional transformation on the electoral front also seem to have been similar to what we will see were those of the majoritarian turn in the Commons. In the traditional institution of parliamentary "selection," competitive elections and the tactics associated with them were thought to dishonor those competing for the seat. Uncontested elections, by contrast, were sources of honor. Contests and attendant maneuvers were traditionally considered, like divisions in Parliament, to signal faction, disunity, and corruption. In the new, majoritarian institution of the Restoration era, however, both competing and succeeding in elections were sources of social credit and political reward; traditional considerations of status were sidelined. The gains to competing had somehow surmounted the costs of competing.[36]

Yet for all their importance in the history of early modern English political practice, contested, majoritarian elections have limited significance

---

[36] For this and the previous two paragraphs, see Hirst, *Representative of the People?*; Hodges, "Electoral Influence of the Aristocracy"; Kishlansky, *Parliamentary Selection*; Thrush and Ferris (eds.), *House of Commons 1604–1629*, vol. I, 94–154; Cogswell, "Canterbury Election of 1626." For a social-scientific analysis that corresponds in many ways to the analysis of Commons deliberation conducted below, see Ferejohn, "Rationality and Interpretation."

in the global history of majority rule. This is because their eventual institutionalization implied nothing about whether national decision-making would at some future point be based on the will of a majority. Even though elections are taken in popular theories of democracy to be fundamental to democratic politics, in representative systems their real impact on national decision-making is far from clear.[37] They certainly do not determine whether national decision-making is patterned along majoritarian lines. Elections only begin the decision-making process, at a local level, with the choice of those who will make national decisions with other representatives. What ensures the majoritarianism of representative democracies is the majoritarian decision-making of representative institutions themselves. A system in which a majoritarian electoral process is paired with a consensual representative assembly is still a system in which the political nation decides and acts in a consensual manner; conversely, a system of consensual elections and majoritarian decisions in assembly is still a majoritarian system.

This point about the primacy of decision-making in representative assemblies in determining the character of national decision-making also clarifies the essential difference between the advent of majority rule in the ancient world and the advent of majoritarianism in those modern societies that would eventually become democracies. In direct democracies like ancient Athens, the decision-making practices of ordinary citizens were indeed the defining feature of national decision-making. But in representative democracies, because it is representatives who make national decisions, majority voting by those representatives is the necessary condition for majoritarian decision-making by "the people." This book accordingly focuses on the internal workings of the House of Commons. This was where the people's representatives – and in theory, the people themselves – made decisions for the nation.

The representative character of the Commons is also important for understanding why its decision-making, as opposed to the decision-making of the Lords or Parliament as a whole, was essential to the eventual emergence of Britain as a majoritarian democracy. As Thomas Hooker explained in 1572, "in the knights, citizens, and burgesses are represented the commons of the whole realm, and every of these giveth not consent only for himself but for all those for whom he is sent." The representative function of the Commons was so crucial, in Hooker's view, that only the presence of the king and the Commons was necessary for making a Parliament. "The king," Hooker continued, "with the

---

[37] See, most recently, Achen and Bartels, *Democracy for Realists*.

consent of his Commons, had ever a sufficient and full authority to make, ordain and establish good and wholesome laws for the commonwealth of his realm." This implied that if the Lords were summoned, "yet refusing to come, sit, or consent," they could not "by their folly abridge the King and the commons of their lawful proceeding in Parliament." The Lords were unnecessary because in early parliaments "the king and his Commons did make a full Parliament," and because "every baron in Parliament doth represent but his own person, and speaketh in the behalf of himself alone."[38]

From the Tudor period onward, the Lords themselves had no representative function whatsoever. By contrast, while the Commons was not perfectly representative in territorial terms, it did effectively represent the English political nation.[39] This implied that the character of decision-making by the English political nation was overwhelmingly defined by the character of decision-making in the House of Commons. The unanimity of king, Lords, and Commons required for legislation was of limited significance as a description of national decision-making if the body that represented the political nation was itself meaningfully divided in its decision-making. Moreover, the Commons made many important decisions on its own, and in these cases it was, in a sense, working independently as a national representative. As we will see, in these cases the maintenance of consensus was both more symbolically significant and more difficult.

This understanding of representation, established in the sixteenth century, remained in place under the Stuarts.[40] The first statute passed in the reign of James I described Parliament as England's high court, in which "all the body of the realm, and every particular member thereof, either in person or by representation (upon their own free elections), are by the laws of this realm deemed to be personally present."[41] The statute explicitly distinguished between the representation occurring in the Commons and the character of the Lords. The House of Commons described itself in its journal as "the representative body of the commons," and James referred to "the lower house" as "representing the commons of this realm." The Lords, on the other hand, represented "themselves only."[42] Like other political bodies in which individual

---

[38] Snow (ed.), *Parliament in Elizabethan England*, 181–2. See also Dewar (ed.), *De Republica Anglorum*, 79.

[39] Elton, *Studies in Tudor and Stuart Politics and Government*, vol. II, 38–9, 47, 58.

[40] Thrush and Ferris (eds.), *House of Commons 1604–1629*, vol. I, 441.

[41] Kenyon (ed.), *Stuart Constitution*, 24.

[42] CJ, 5/17/1604, 2/9/1621, 6/29/1641, 5/4/1641, 12/3/1641, 5/7/1642; Kishlansky, *Rise of the New Model Army*, 123; Adamson, *Noble Revolt*, 459.

dignity was a primary consideration, the House of Lords appears to have always conducted enumerated majority votes.[43] But the manner of the Lords' decision-making did not have considerable symbolic import for the state of the political nation. In this sense, the Lords' decisions were of much the same character as decisions reached in local elections: they were the decisions of a small number of individuals.

By now the rationale for this book's focus on the House of Commons and its colonial counterparts should be abundantly clear. To be sure, any broader history of majority rule would include elections and upper assemblies. Both are important aspects of modern majoritarian politics, especially following the emergence of elected upper chambers and elected heads of state in so-called presidential systems. But in this book the aim is simply to pinpoint and explain the initial rise of the majority as the central decision-making agent in the two political systems that would, after becoming democracies themselves, provide the two most important blueprints for the world's other majoritarian states. The proper focus of study, with this aim in mind, is the moment when the most important decisions affecting the English population were for the first time routinely made with the support of only a majority of the political nation.

---

[43] This is at least true from the earliest period for which plentiful records survive. See Graves, *House of Lords in the Parliaments of Edward VI and Mary I*, 164–6.

2   Consensus in the Commons, 1547–1642

Understanding the origins of majority rule in the English House of Commons first requires understanding the consensual regime that preceded it. By the later sixteenth century, the House appears to have established fairly consistent procedures for making decisions, and beginning with the reign of James I, the House's formal activities were documented in detail. At that point, at least, the House followed a clear if complex set of rules and conventions for acting and deciding as a body. If the House was going to conduct any sort of business, a member had to make a motion to engage in it, and that motion had to be seconded and then formally relayed to the House by the Speaker. The House was now in possession of the question. Members were free to debate the motion, each of them speaking no more than once. At any juncture during debate, the motion could be laid aside by the Speaker or superseded by another member who successfully made a motion that was a direct response to the current motion. A member might, for example, move to have a committee examine the matter. Alternatively, if the original motion remained live, it was subject to no dissent, and there was no request for a formal vote, that motion could simply be "ordered" or "resolved" by the House, in accordance with what was often called the House's "general voice" or "common consent."[1] This was an unusual manner of proceeding when motions of any political importance were under consideration. Normally, debate continued until no additional members wished to speak. At this point, the Speaker would put a

---

[1] A bill could be committed if there was no debate on a motion for committing it, and it could be passed (or rejected) if, after it was read, someone spoke on either side of the question and was not contradicted by anyone (BL MS Harley 1058, f. 49). The House also often held voice acclamations without formally putting the question. For this and more conventional, nonvoted resolutions and orders, see inter alia CJ, 3/27/1604, 3/29/1604, 4/2/1604, 4/5/1614, 2/7/1621, 3/12/1621, 5/29/1621, 5/31/1621, 6/22/1625, 11/19/1669; *PP 1628*, vol. II, 446, 521; *CD 1629*, 240, 256–7; *POSLP*, vol. II, 410; D'Ewes MS 165, f. 172v. (851–2); Marvell, *Poems and Letters*, vol. II, 90; Grey, 2/9/1678. For evidence suggesting that if even one member spoke against a motion, a formal question had to be put, see Sims (ed.), "'Policies in Parliaments,'" 49.

question related to the current motion that reflected the present state of deliberation. This initiated the formal voting process. Questions were formally phrased and posed by the Speaker, although in debate other members often suggested content and phrasing for the Speaker to employ. Questions put by the Speaker were "yes or no" questions.

On a formal level, the putting of the question was always a majoritarian procedure. When the Speaker put a question, he initiated a voice vote. He first asked for "yea" voters to call out, and then for "noe" voters to do so. Debate was permitted between the "yea" and "noe" votes. After hearing the acclamations, the Speaker would assess whether a louder chorus of voices favored one side or another. He then either declared that the question had been answered in the affirmative or the negative, or he declared the voices doubtful. In the latter case, he was supposed to put the question once more.[2] If the Speaker offered a positive estimate of the voices on either occasion and that estimate went unchallenged, the Speaker would proceed to report the House's collective resolution of the question.[3] If the Speaker declared the voices doubtful after a second voice vote, or if any member spoke up to challenge his positive estimate of the voices (and this member was not unanimously shouted down by his fellow members), the House would "divide," unless at that moment the member who made the initial motion withdrew it.[4] In a division, members on one side of the question – usually the one considered to be innovatory – would process out of the chamber. Two tellers for the side remaining within the chamber would each count those present, and if the tellers agreed in their count, the total would constitute the vote tally for that side. Then those who had left the chamber would return, and as they passed back through the entrance to the chamber, another two tellers would count them. The four tellers would then report both tallies to the Speaker, who would announce the House's collective resolution of the question. In matters of importance, this process of making motions, putting questions, holding acclamations, and, if necessary, holding enumerated votes was the means by which the House of Commons engaged in collective decision-making and action.

[2] See, for example, *PP 1626*, vol. II, 227; vol. III, 53, 84; D'Ewes MS 164, ff. 343r. (381), 330r. (445). It is unclear how consistently second voice votes were conducted.

[3] For members' ability, on occasion, to estimate the proportion of voice votes on each side, see, for example, *POSLP*, vol. IV, 10; *PP 1610*, 319; *PP 1614*, 41, 78; below, 69, 82, 148, 174.

[4] In the quantitative measures used in this study, situations where divisions were called but one side yielded before the telling are counted as divisions, since they indicate a meaningfully majoritarian episode. These votes are a tiny percentage of the total division counts. They are not counted in Snow, "Attendance Trends and Absenteeism in the Long Parliament," in accordance with the goals of that study.

Since both acclamations and divisions were formally majoritarian, any shift in frequency of usage between the two available decision methods might be said to have no broader significance whatsoever.[5] But the seventeenth-century House of Commons is a vivid reminder of why neither formal organizations nor formal rules of conduct should be mistaken for the institutional realities that prevail alongside them. In other words, it is important to depart here from both the casual usage of the term "institution" by historians and the more self-conscious understandings of institutions as sets of formal organizations or rules that prevail in the social sciences. If formal rules, procedures, and organizations are dismissed or ignored, they are of little importance to social life. They merit attention only to the extent that they are employed by individuals in ways that serve to coordinate social interactions. For this reason an institution is better understood as an array of elements – including rules, beliefs, organizations, and norms – that consistently enables a central transaction among social actors. In other words, institutions are systems of social factors that together serve to generate a regularity or pattern of social practices.[6] Votes by members of the Commons were important social transactions supported by a formal organization, a set of institutionalized procedural rules, a set of expectations about possible outcomes and members' behavior, and a set of shared, internalized norms.

From this perspective, the key question about institutionalized decision-making in the Commons is not whether the House's rules *permitted* meaningfully majoritarian voting (or enumerated majority voting, in particular), but whether its members regularly made use of this procedural option. In other words, what was the nature or patterning

---

[5] For this view see Edwards, "Emergence of Majority Rule."

[6] For this understanding of institutions, see Greif, *Institutions and the Path to the Modern Economy*; Greif and Laitin, "Theory of Endogenous Institutional Change"; Greif and Kingston, "Institutions: Rules or Equilibria?" Studies of early modern English politics influenced by the new institutional social sciences have tended to employ rule-oriented or organization-oriented understandings of institutions and have not engaged with Greif's insights. See, for example, Pincus and Robinson, "What Really Happened during the Glorious Revolution?" For criticism of the typical approach, see Hoppit, *Britain's Political Economies*, 31–3. The present study conceptualizes institutions and institutional change in a manner that is also largely compatible with William H. Sewell, Jr.'s theory of structural transformation, part of which involves an adaptation of the practice theory of Pierre Bourdieu. The discussions to follow therefore often blend a vocabulary of practices and structure drawn from Bourdieu and Sewell with a vocabulary drawn from the work of certain new institutionalists. See Sewell, *Logics of History*, esp. 124–51, 225–70; and the work of Pierre Bourdieu, starting in this context with Bourdieu, *Outline of a Theory of Practice*. On the compatibility of certain versions of rational choice and practice theory, see Ermakoff, "Theory of Practice, Rational Choice, and Historical Change."

of the actual transactions at the heart of the House's decision-making and action? With what relative frequency did members choose to vote in a meaningfully consensual or majoritarian manner? Determining this, of course, requires a clear sense of what ought to count as consensual and majoritarian voting in this period. A formal perspective fails to illuminate anything on this front. It would lead us to count as majoritarian any decision reached by determining which side of the question appeared to have the most individual votes (as measured by volume of voices) or in fact had the most votes (as measured by the tellers in divisions). This would amount to an argument that even in practical terms, every decision in the Commons was inevitably majoritarian. But how meaningful is it to say, for instance, that a voting system in which historically all or nearly all decisions have been unanimous is a majoritarian system, simply because the rules permitted non-unanimous decisions? To do so ultimately tells us only about organizational rules and nothing about the historical record of practices. Even a slightly less strict formulation, in which one equated consensus with unanimity (even in enumerated voting situations) and equated majority decisions with the existence of any minority vote, however small, is mostly devoid of meaning. For how informative is it to say that a 500-member assembly in which most decisions are made with a single dissenter is a majoritarian body and not a consensual one?[7] Both entirely consensual and exclusively majoritarian political assemblies are largely unknown. What is of interest is the shifting, overall balance between consensual and majoritarian decisions, measured against a modern benchmark for majoritarian politics.[8]

It is far more meaningful to define majoritarianism and its opposite, consensus-based decision-making, in nonabsolute, nonformal terms. In what follows "consensus" will not be taken to denote only expressions of unanimity (enumerated or nonenumerated) and instances of apparent consensus (when no opposition to a decision is voiced but may still exist).[9] Instead, "consensus" will be construed more broadly. It will be taken to denote an overwhelming, expressed, collective preference for one option over another. A pattern of consensual decision-making in the Commons would therefore be indicated over time by a distribution of vote differentials that was heavily weighted toward lopsided votes and away from close votes. Institutions are often appropriately considered in

---

[7] For a similar view in an early study, see Baty, "History of Majority Rule," 14, 19. Commons voting was not, of course, a consensual system in the sense that individual members possessed veto power.

[8] Mansbridge, *Beyond Adversary Democracy*.

[9] On apparent consensus, see Urfalino, "La décision par consensus apparent."

distributional, nonabsolute terms because they are characterized by regularities in behavior to which there are feasible alternatives and therefore occasional exceptions.[10] Decision-making patterns are a clear example of this sort of institution.

It is equally ill-advised to adopt an extreme standard for a majoritarian voting pattern. A reasonable and in fact rather demanding standard for such a pattern would be a distribution of recorded vote victory margins that implies that members were not at all reluctant to end debate when victory (or defeat) seemed probable, to vote according to their preferences, and to risk close votes. In such a legislature, we might assume (all other things being equal) that vote margins would be equally distributed everywhere between unanimous and tied votes. After all, even in representative institutions today, which are dominated by majoritarian patterns of decision-making, close votes are unusual. In the nineteenth century, following the First Reform Act, the British House of Commons divided less than one quarter of the time a question was put. And in the twentieth and twenty-first centuries, the Commons has divided less than one third of the time.[11] These benchmarks confirm the reasonability of using a uniform distribution of vote differentials as a basic model of majoritarian voting.

The Consensual Tradition

These commonsense assumptions provide a clear and useful perspective on Commons voting data for the early modern period and beyond. The basic evidence we have for the incidence of meaningfully majoritarian decisions is data on the frequency of divisions, as recorded in the Commons journal and other sources. As we have seen, while there is no precise information on the decision-making activities of the medieval parliaments, they appear to have been largely consensual affairs.[12] The Tudor parliaments, which continued this tradition, are far better documented. It is clear that from 1523, when a division procedure was apparently used for the first time in the Commons, these enumerated, meaningfully majoritarian votes were rare and usually of little political significance. While the division evidence for parliamentary sessions held prior to the accession of Elizabeth I is certainly scattered, it is clear that

---

[10] Greif, *Institutions and the Path to the Modern Economy*, 33.

[11] These estimates are derived from basic natural language processing of complete digital texts of the Commons journals for the years between 1835 and 2012. Processing of the Hansards was also used to confirm the accuracy of the Commons journal findings.

[12] See 10–12 above.

acclamation was almost exclusively the way in which the House made decisions on legislation, even in cases of serious political and religious conflict. Only eleven divisions have been found for the entire period up to 1558.[13]

For the period between 1559 and 1581, only twenty-one divisions were recorded in either the Commons journal or unofficial sources. This would amount to a division about every twenty-five days in session, making it a very unusual event.[14] In the Commons journal entries for the years between 1547 and 1581 (after which point the Commons journals do not survive until 1604), divisions were also recorded on average only about once every twenty-five recorded days in session.[15] In unofficial journals of proceedings in Elizabeth's reign after 1581, twenty-five divisions were recorded, or one for about every fifteen recorded days in session (Table 2.1).[16] The frequency of divisions over a given period of time in session is a measure that bears a strong relationship to the experience of the House's members. In essence, it describes the extent to which divisions were "everyday" occurrences.[17] From this vantage point, at least, the insignificance and rarity of divisions in the Elizabethan period is fairly clear.

However informative the available data on the Tudor period might be, it does not approach the level of detail available for the Stuart period. James I's parliaments of 1604–7 and 1610 are much better documented than their Elizabethan predecessors (for the purposes of the analysis here), even though there are still serious limitations to the data that prevent the type of quantitative analysis possible for 1614 and thereafter. This is because questions put were inconsistently recorded. It is nevertheless clear that in James I's first two parliaments, the House divided about once every seven days in active session. This matches the daily frequency of divisions in the entire period between 1604 and the outbreak of the Civil War. The divisions that did occur in this period were also overwhelmingly related to private bills and other relatively trivial

---

[13] Hayward, *House of Commons 1509–1558*, 331–8. There is considerable evidence that these early divisions before Elizabeth's reign were usually initiated by minorities. See also Edwards, "Emergence of Majority Rule," 179. On the importance of "minoritarian" divisions, see below, 82–4, 93, 189, 192, 252.

[14] Elton, *Parliament of England 1559–1581*, 89, 122–3, 179, 183; D'Ewes (ed.), *Journals of All the Parliaments during the Reign of Queen Elizabeth*, 1–310.

[15] Since questions put were not recorded regularly for this period, this is the best frequency measure.

[16] D'Ewes (ed.), *Journals of All the Parliaments during the Reign of Queen Elizabeth*, 311–418; Townshend (ed.), *Historical Collections*.

[17] Because of its experiential relevance, the frequency of divisions per day in session will also be considered when appropriate in the discussion that follows, even in sections that discuss periods for which more precise figures can be computed.

Table 2.1 *Mean division frequency, 1547–1699*

Period	Per question put	Per day in session
1547–81	N/A	0.040
1584–1601	N/A	0.070
1604–10	N/A	0.142
1614–24	0.027	0.074
1625–9	0.028	0.082
1640–2	0.036	0.178[a]
1643–9	0.102[a]	0.298
1650–9	0.153	0.451
1660–9	0.115	0.413
1670–89	0.230	0.350
1690–9	0.204	0.500

[a] Greatest percentage change from previous period in direction of overall trend.

matters. This strong impression of consensus decision-making patterns corresponds closely with the far more precise measurements obtainable for the following years.

From 1614 onward it is possible to measure the frequency of divisions as a proportion of the total questions put to the House over a given period of time. Divisions per questions put is the most precise means of measuring the frequency of divisions over a given period because this measurement describes the incidence of divisions relative to the number of occasions on which it was possible to divide. The data for the early Stuart period are very striking. From 1614 to 1640, only 2.6 percent of voice votes resulted in divisions. They occurred about once every ten days in active session. Their frequency increases to only 3.4 percent if 1641 and 1642 are included in the data (Table 2.1 and Figure 2.1).[18]

[18] These data and others like them throughout the present study are derived from basic natural language processing of complete digital texts of the printed, early modern Commons journals. The primary measure used in this study is computed by dividing the total of divisions held by the total of questions put over a given period. A less precise, and sometimes misleading way of measuring division frequency, used by Kishlansky – simple counts of the number of divisions in a given period – fails to alter significantly the story told here. Measures for question totals are derived by counting explicit mentions of a question being put. There are a tiny number of divisions missing from the Commons journal for the period between 1614 and 1640 because some days' proceedings were entirely omitted. Dates missing from the journal for which divisions are recorded in other sources include 24 March and 17 April 1624. A full record of these sessions would not alter the conclusions of this study.

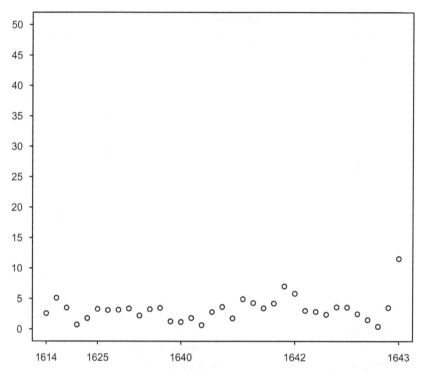

Figure 2.1 Mean division frequency as percentage of all questions put, 1614–42. Each dot represents a period of thirty days in session. Tick marks are located on the thirty-day unit that includes the beginning of each year.

This gives a dramatic initial impression of a representative assembly that was firmly consensual in its decision-making practices prior to the outbreak of the English Civil War.

Yet even once we have settled on qualitative definitions for majoritarian and consensual patterns of voting behavior, studied detailed data on division frequency, and observed the extreme rarity of divisions before 1643, there is a possible problem with our tentative conclusion that needs to be addressed. Data on divisions do not allow us directly to assess the character of most of the voting that went on in the Commons during the Elizabethan and early Stuart periods. We have precise information on divisions, but hardly any direct evidence on the character of voice votes, the normal practice in the House. Voice votes, after all, are inherently imprecise, and early moderns did not measure decibel levels. Indeed, they recorded hardly any information whatsoever about what actually tended to occur during these acclamations, presumably because like most mundane, repeated occurrences, they were unworthy of comment.[19] The journals of the House usually report only the putting of questions and the holding of divisions, noting, in the latter case, the vote tally and the names of the tellers for each side. As a result, it is impossible to be absolutely certain that conclusive voice votes that were nevertheless meaningfully majoritarian did not occur throughout the early Stuart period and even earlier.

Again, the general lack of contemporary commentary on conclusive voice votes strongly suggests that they were unremarkable affairs, devoid of divisiveness. Even more importantly, voice votes do seem, in general, to have been true acclamations, not genuine contests over an issue. This is revealed by the fact that voice votes that did not lead to divisions were almost always resolved in the affirmative.[20] This does not mean, of course, that disagreement and conflict were absent from all of these situations. But it does imply that that persistent disagreement, to the extent it existed, was normally resolved by the capitulation of the presumed minority. The preponderance of affirmative voice votes also suggests that questions tended not to be put unless they were expected to be resolved in the affirmative. The few votes that were persistently contested appear to have normally resulted in divisions. Nevertheless, we ought to more firmly rule out, if feasible, the possibility that Tudor and early Stuart Commons proceedings featured frequent voice votes that were meaningfully majoritarian but not close enough to lead to divisions.

Fortunately, there is a systematic way of not only accomplishing this but also recovering patterns of voice voting in the early Stuart Commons. The trick is to leverage the indirect evidence we have on voice voting by considering the observable implications of voice voting patterns. It is possible to infer the level of majoritarian activity in early Stuart voice voting from the complete time series of data on questions put, divisions held, and votes counted. The first step in constructing this inference is to

---

[19] The limited amount of available, direct evidence on voice votes is ambiguous. The journals often noted when a question was resolved unanimously or *nemine contradicente* (the latter phrase is a description of apparent consensus). But it is extremely unlikely that they did so consistently, and it is unclear how one would interpret the information if they did. The only clear suggestion that emerges from direct evidence is that the House was reluctant to record close voice votes that did not result in divisions. For a question resolved by voice vote on 27 March 1604, a Commons scribe actually wrote in the manuscript version of the journal that "it was resolved by the major part, that they should not" confer with the Lords in the matter under discussion. The clerk then crossed out "by the major part," and this part of the sentence did not appear in the printed journal. Compare CJ, 3/27/1604 with Parliamentary Archives, HC/CL/JO/1/3, f. 63r.

[20] Kishlansky, *Parliamentary Selection*, 62, makes an analogous argument about elections.

realize that the data on vote tallies provide strong if indirect evidence for the usual threshold of competition at which a voice vote was deemed inconclusive and a division initiated by the Speaker. The mean margin of victory in divisions held across the seventeenth century was 16 percent of the total votes cast, which translates, for the average turnout in a division (158), to a typical vote of 92 to 66. This mean vote margin remained remarkably consistent across subsections of the seventeenth century. A vote margin of 16 percent of the total voice votes cast might therefore be taken to refer to a rough threshold of disagreement at which a division tended to be forced, usually because the Speaker could not discern the outcome of a voice vote that was closer than this, at least without facing plausible dissent from other members, which would itself result in a division.

Once this information about victory margins has been derived, we can then ask what frequency of divisions we would expect to see if voice voting, overall, was meaningfully majoritarian, according to the definition given earlier. In such a House, where there was no hesitation to force divisions in situations where no consensus had been achieved but a majority opinion had emerged, the incidence of divisions would simply indicate the proportion of voice votes that were too close to be determinate. We would expect that a large proportion of other voice votes were simply less close, but still meaningfully majoritarian. Vote margins in such a House would, again, be uniformly distributed everywhere between unanimous and tied votes, or between margins of 100 percent and 0 percent of the total votes cast. Given that the mean threshold beyond which voice votes usually led to divisions was 16 percent of votes cast, we would expect such a House to hold divisions 16 percent of the time a question was put to it. Yet as we have seen, before 1643, only 3.4 percent of voice votes resulted in divisions. It is therefore extremely improbable that voice voting in the early Stuart Commons assumed anything approaching a majoritarian pattern.

In order further to ascertain the nature of voice voting in the House prior to 1643 we should also pose the opposite question: What division frequency would we expect in a strongly consensual legislature? One such body would be an assembly in which the median victory margin in voice votes was 95 percent of the total votes cast (i.e., a vote of 154 to 4 with the average House turnout). This conservative measure easily accords with both modern and early modern norms for a decision that would not be viewed by participants as signifying meaningful division or conflict. In this model, if we assume an even distribution of the votes that were closer than the median vote differential of 95 percent, we would expect a division frequency of 8.4 percent. This is more than twice the frequency we actually find. It is therefore very probable that voting practices in the House of Commons were *extremely* consensual before 1643.[21] Despite the presence of regular procedures that enabled and even invited majoritarian decision-making, the members of the early Stuart House of Commons almost completely avoided making decisions that were meaningfully majoritarian.

Even if one does not accept the notion that division frequencies can be used as indirect indicators of patterns in voice voting, it is worth appreciating that the data on division frequency are independently significant. An almost total lack of divisions certainly implies the rarity of close, competitive, and glaringly divisive votes, just as a high frequency of divisions would imply the opposite. Moreover, when the Commons were able to record decision after decision reached without recourse to enumerated votes, even during the resolution of divisive issues, they dramatized, ritualized, publicized, and inscribed their unity and that of the nation they represented. They buried and concealed whatever disunity had been present prior to each vote. By the same token, when the House began to conduct divisions and formally note them in the journal with increasing frequency, they were more regularly dramatizing, ritualizing, publicizing, and inscribing disunity. As members left and returned to the chamber during a division, they were more easily identified by fellow members and more easily associated with factional groupings than during voice votes, when it was more difficult to discern who was voting which way. As we will see, these symbolic effects only deepened in significance once divisions were being illicitly reported outside Parliament.

The Institutional Framework

The regularity of decisions by acclamation in the pre–Civil War Commons strongly suggests that consensual decision-making was fully institutionalized. This did not mean, of course, that serious conflict was alien to the House during this period or that members were genuinely being brought into agreement with each other on every matter at hand.[22] As we will see, divisions were tactfully avoided, compromises were hatched, capitulations were made, and serious ideological and constitutional conflict was at times a regular phenomenon. Nevertheless, even under the most

---

[21] For accounts of lopsided voice votes where those voting in the minority were counted by observers, see *PP 1610*, 319; *PP 1614*, 41, 78.

[22] Again, in historiographical terms, this means that the claim about consensual decision-making here is consistent with both revisionist and post-revisionist understandings of the politics and political culture of the period.

trying conditions, nearly all politically significant, final decisions made by the House were made by means of acclamation. This amounted to a symbolically significant pattern of ritualized unity that is mostly foreign to modern democratic politics.

In order to identify this consensual institution, understand its workings, and explain both its persistence and its eventual collapse, we must first identify the factors that could possibly determine the frequency of consensual and majoritarian decisions in the House. In other words, it is necessary to specify the conditions under which the House could find itself debating issues that were politically significant, divisive, irresolvable, incapable of being set aside, and therefore bound to result in a division. Some of the most important factors were external to the House itself. Parliament was called and adjourned at the pleasure of the monarch, which meant that the monarch had a negative form of agenda control. The act of proroguing, dissolving, or simply not calling a parliament could limit the incidence of divisive decisions there. Monarchs also had a positive form of agenda control: they usually expressed the intent behind their calling of Parliament and often outlined what matters were fit for discussion and in what order they ought to be discussed. To the extent that the monarch effectively exerted this form of agenda control, the monarch limited the extent to which issues could come to the floor that were so divisive and unavoidable that a division on them might have been inevitable.

Elections, similarly, could either inject division into the House or shut it out. They produced a membership that was more or less willing to raise divisive issues, more or less politically divided, more or less pre-committed to specific policies, and more or less comfortable with divisions as a decision-making procedure. As we will see, there is little evidence that early Stuart members were at all comfortable with divisions. There is also little evidence that members in the seventeenth century were pre-committed to positions on national issues to a degree that would have precluded them from reaching consensus decisions in Westminster. When they received instructions from constituents, which could in theory pre-commit them to certain positions, these instructions were normally local in nature and issued in ignorance of what specific decisions would eventually have to be made in a session.[23] The Long

---

[23] Thrush and Ferris (eds.), *House of Commons 1604–1629*, vol. I, 456–8; Hirst, *Representative of the People?*, 160–6. The local nature of instructions might be another reason why private legislation was more prone to divisions in the pre-revolutionary period. For discussion of pressure on members related to national issues in the early Stuart period, aside from Hirst, *Representative of the People?*, 178–90, see Cust, "Politics and the Electorate in the 1620s," 161–2; Peacey, "Sir Edward Dering." The earliest

Parliament would only be an extreme example of this broader reality, despite the fact that instructions from 1640 often dealt with national issues. Moreover, members commonly insisted that their election itself signified assent to their future actions.[24]

There is, however, considerable evidence that the Short and Long Parliaments, for instance, had memberships that were unusually politicized and divided. In addition, public pressure, including constituent pressure, could hypothetically result in agenda shifts. It could also make members relatively unwilling to change their minds in the course of debate with their peers and thereby depart from the wishes of their constituents. This could make them less likely to reach a consensus on politically divisive issues. There is of course evidence, in the 1620s and in 1640 especially, of wide public discussion of ideological issues relevant to parliamentary business. This leads to one final consideration: on the most general level, the House could be indirectly subject to whatever level and diversity of political division was present in the country as a whole at any given time, to the extent that its members reflected that division or public pressure introduced it.

Whatever the mechanisms responsible, divisive issues did regularly reach the floor of the House in the Elizabethan and early Stuart periods. This makes all the more remarkable the fact that even in the Short and Long Parliaments, prior to the Civil War, when the political process was more conducive to promoting divisions than it had ever been, divisions remained extremely rare. The persistence of consensual decision-making across these dramatic changes in external conditions strongly suggests that none of the factors outlined thus far was an element of either this institution or its eventual demise. Instead, it is clear that the institution of consensual decision-making was supported by phenomena internal to the business of the Commons. In other words, it appears that consensual decisions were the norm in the House primarily because its members willingly refrained from putting the question until the existence of a consensus ensured that a vote could be conducted by way of acclamation

evidence of the large-scale use of instructions on national issues dates to the third Exclusion Parliament of 1681, long after majority voting had been institutionalized in the House. See below, 200, 201, and Henning, *House of Commons 1660–1690*, 39. The practice appears to have been uncommon for the rest of the century and into the eighteenth. See Hayton, *House of Commons 1690–1715*, 187–8; Kelly, "Constituents' Instructions to Members of Parliament in the Eighteenth Century." If anything, therefore, the use of instructions solidified (but did not cause) the institutionalization of majority voting in the English Commons. In any case, for most of the seventeenth century, constituents would not have known the details of how those they elected voted, making their instructions unenforceable in future elections.

[24] Hirst, *Representative of the People?*, 182–3, 185.

and without a division.[25] As the diarist member Sir Simonds D'Ewes put it in 1641, using standard language for the time, the Commons normally did not end debate until the House was "ripe for a question," which appears to have meant that the question had been sufficiently debated and, in nearly all cases, that a consensus had been reached.[26]

Once a motion came to the floor of the House, in order for a consensual decision to be made, the question had to be put only when members were in a position willingly to vote in a consensual manner. This could, of course, be true at the time of voting because members were sufficiently agreed on the matter of hand. But it could also occur under conditions of persistent disagreement if those evidently in the minority considered forcing a division to be so undesirable that they decided to refrain from expressing their views when the question was put or somehow avoided the putting of the question altogether. On some occasions, proceedings for a division would begin and one side would simply yield in order to avoid the division.[27] Alternatively, proponents of a given motion might simply drop the motion once they realized they remained in the minority after considerable debate.[28] In other words, there were a number of routes to the achievement of consensus or the avoidance of divisions under conditions of persistent disagreement and conflict. None implied an ideal deliberative environment. Yet as a whole these routes to consensus and routes away from divisions were what enabled the institutionalization of consensus politics under conditions of ideological difference and political controversy.

Debate on motions was, of course, the primary means by which consensus was regularly formed – and the putting of the question temporarily avoided – when consensus on a motion did not already exist. In James' reign, for instance, the House explicitly called for and entered into a filibuster on the union with Scotland, apparently after a doubtful voice vote, in order to hold off a division.[29] Longer speeches in the House were in formal terms a hybrid of rhetorical introductions and other techniques combined with structures traceable to the teaching of dialectic (logic) and the conduct of formal disputation in the universities. Most speechmaking and debate on the question at hand, however, to the extent that it

[25] Russell, *Parliaments and English Politics*, 5. Russell's largely undocumented claims on this front are similar to the ones documented here.
[26] *POSLP*, vol. VI, 20.
[27] For example, *PP 1624*, 4/17/1624; CJ, 6/7/1610, 6/17/1610, 6/26/1610, 5/27/1624, 5/6/1626, 5/21/1628.
[28] *PJLP*, vol. II, 98.
[29] Russell, *King James VI and I and His English Parliaments*, 64; Wilson (ed.), *Parliamentary Diary of Robert Bowyer*, 190–1.

had a formal character, was derived exclusively from dialectic, not rhetoric. A speaker would summarize points made by the previous speaker and answer each in turn. He would then offer his position on the question and sometimes include an argument.[30] On countless occasions, force of argument seems to have changed members' opinions and created unity, even on controversial public matters.[31] In June 1625, for instance, during a debate on articles of religion and after prolonged discussion of the first article in a committee of the whole, the member John Pym reported that "in this variety the House being like to be divided, Sir Henry Marten propounded a form of entry for that article which for the present settled the debate."[32] Conversion, compromise, or acquiescence was the assumed end point of prolonged argument.[33] This was indicated, for instance, by the common use of the rhetorical device *insinuatio*, which involved claiming that one was expressing a contrary view only to be brought genuinely into consensus.[34] Debate also served an informational purpose, since it allowed members to indicate their current preferences and the basis of those preferences. This made it possible for other members to decide how the House should proceed at each moment. Both of these functions were limited, however, by the requirement that when the House was debating a motion, each member could speak only once.

The fundamental goal of both rhetoric and dialectic in the parliamentary context was to persuade or, in the case of dialectical disputation, to convince hearers that the case one was making was the better one, which amounted to a particular form of persuasion. As a result, neither the often adversarial nature of parliamentary rhetoric nor the oppositional nature of dialectic led naturally to nonconsensual decisions.[35] While in a modern, majoritarian political setting debate might function to pinpoint matters of disagreement in order to put them to the vote, in this setting

---

[30] Mack, *Elizabethan Rhetoric*, esp. 215, 232; Thrush and Ferris (eds.), *House of Commons 1604–1629*, vol. I, 302.

[31] For examples aside from those below, see Neale, *Elizabeth I and Her Parliaments*, 289–90; *PP 1625*, 275–80.

[32] *PP 1625*, 259–60, 265. See also Townshend, *Historical Collections*, 3/5/1593.

[33] Peltonen, *Rhetoric, Politics and Popularity*, 212.   [34] Ibid., 145.

[35] Mack, *Elizabethan Rhetoric*, esp. 215, 232; Peltonen, *Rhetoric, Politics and Popularity*. Mack's conclusions on the predominant role of dialectic clearly apply to later periods. Peltonen focuses exclusively on rhetorical content and predominantly on longer speeches. Neither author considers the ultimate consequences of their analyses for formal decision-making in the Commons. For this reason, these analyses, despite Peltonen's historiographical positioning of his work, are in fact mostly parallel to the broader debate about consensual and adversarial politics in early Stuart historiography. For a 1620s description of parliamentary debate as "disputing," see BL MS Add 36856, f. 28r.

the goal was not to specify disagreement but to eliminate it.[36] When this failed and debate resulted in a divisive vote, the Commons had implicitly admitted the existence of a divided set of national representatives, and thus a divided political nation. It had admitted that the process of debate – a process that captured the essence of parliament as event or institution – had produced neither wisdom nor truth. This was often taken to have occurred because the process itself had somehow become corrupted and had consequently failed to provide the House with an opportunity to resolve its differences in a genuine manner. In particular, divisive votes were often taken to suggest that freedom of speech was somehow being suppressed, either because members were coming to the House with preconceived, unmalleable preferences that may have been formed by the mechanics of partisan organization, or because their speech was being restricted by new public pressures coming from without the chamber. Such results were, accordingly, often associated with sin, and read in terms of biblical injunctions against division.[37]

To avoid such disastrous outcomes, members engaged in a process of argument on each side of a question. They were convinced that this process, which was consistent with the dictates of both dialectic and rhetoric, would result in members yielding to the better argument and thus to wisdom or truth. By 1593 debate *in utramque partem* (on both sides of the question) was essentially a standing order of the house.[38] In what might seem a paradox to those immersed in debates over whether early Stuart politics were primarily characterized by conflict, adversarial practices led to agreement around what was thought to be an emergent wisdom. If there was in fact some erosion of rhetorical or political ideals of persuasion and unity in the early Stuart period, or if speech in the Commons was increasingly too informal and poorly organized to achieve the goals of rhetoric or disputation, the unintended consequences of debate gone wrong did nothing to change the ultimate orientation of decision-making.[39]

[36] Russell, *Parliaments and English Politics*, 40.

[37] See, for example, 1 Corinthians 1:10. For similar claims about a similar context, see Kishlansky, "Consensus Politics and the Structure of Debate at Putney," 50–69.

[38] Peltonen, *Rhetoric, Politics and Popularity*, 138–9.

[39] Kyle, *Theater of State*, 16, 21, 30; see generally 13–35. Kyle emphasizes the departure of most early Stuart parliamentary speech from "fully fledged classical oration" (20), but as Mack explains, this was never the norm, nor was it intended to be. In any case, as Kyle observes (30), while even the more complete records of the 1620s do seem to reflect an increasingly informal style of debate, apparent changes over time in the nature of parliamentary debate may very easily in fact be changes in the manner of recording by diarists and other recorders. For this reason, it is also impossible systematically to

The ability of debate to produce consensus or simply delay voting was amplified when debate occurred in a committee of the whole. Motions for these committees could in theory serve as a direct response to any other motion. Committees of the whole provided a way of continuing House debate indefinitely because members could speak more than once. These committees, like select committees, were accordingly seen as a way of avoiding divisions.[40] It will come as no surprise, for instance, that debates on subsidies, which were often controversial and a setting for indirect debate on foreign policy, were the most common topics in committees of the whole. These debates nearly always continued in committee until leaders of what appeared to be the losing side were prepared to rise and say that they had been converted.[41] This form of extended debate allowed for both the process of conversion or capitulation and the signaling of that conversion or capitulation. At the very least, it delayed votes and thereby opened the House to still further interruptions of its progress toward a decision.

Inside and outside committees of the whole, once remarks had been made on behalf of a particular view, members could indicate consent either through speaking in favor of the same position or by remaining silent.[42] This is clear, for example, from the end of a debate on Mary, Queen of Scots, in May 1572. The Speaker attempted to bring debate to a conclusion with the following comment:

You have heard the effect of the Queen's message, you have heard diverse very learnedly show cause why her disposition in the same is misliked. I have heard none show any liking thereof, so as by silence they have all confirmed that which hath been said by others. It remains you grow to resolution for the order of your proceeding.[43]

Alternatively, the decision to continue speaking to a motion was sometimes a signal of remaining disagreement either on the part of the member speaking or on the part of others of whose disagreement the member speaking was somehow aware. These conventions of course

discern differences between debate in the pre–Civil War period and debate in the revolutionary era.
[40] See, for example, *POSLP*, vol. III, 582.
[41] Russell, *Parliaments and English Politics*, 40–1.
[42] For other examples of silence, see *CD 1629*, 240, 256. A negative indication of the importance of the debating process is that in the very few politically salient divisions from the pre–Civil War period that seem to have occurred without extended debate preceding them, the issues at play were ones on which clear lines had already been drawn and the distribution of views was probably well understood.
[43] Hartley (ed.), *Proceedings in the Parliaments of Elizabeth I*, vol. I, 378; CJ, 5/23/1572. After this, debate ended with a successful motion to confer with the Lords before moving forward.

implied that not all members would speak in any given debate. In fact, in a typical debate most members remained silent. This was also due in part to the fact that a few members clearly wielded power – rhetorical, dialectical, or material – over others. This reality was even more acute in committees of the whole. Even under James I, when participation in debate was unusually widely distributed, only about half of members would normally speak even once in an entire session of Parliament.[44] Debate was thus a complex struggle to determine (in both senses of the word) other members' preferences. Inflected by inequalities, it was a signaling exercise in which members strove both to direct and to discern "the sense of the House."[45]

Beyond persistence in debate, there were a number of other ways in which the House could successfully avoid putting the question.[46] These measures provided more time for consensus to emerge, initiated additional procedures in which such a consensus could emerge, or simply provided an additional means of deferring a final decision. When appropriate, the subject of a motion could be entrusted to a committee. In other cases, a conference with the Lords or the monarch could be initiated.[47]

Both committees and conferences displaced the burden of forming a consensus onto other groupings that were either not coextensive with the House's membership or not the House in a formal sense (in the case of committees of the whole). Committees could also simply be used to displace the reality of persistent division onto a less symbolically important stage. Although they were not consistently recorded, divisions were clearly held in committees. Business moved forward (or halted) as a result, and members gained some information on the balance of opinion among members. This could allow for capitulations and consequent acclamations in the final stages of the process. Divisions in committees of the whole were particularly useful in this regard. A successful, majoritarian vote in committee of the whole on a motion usually resulted in a

---

[44] Kyle, *Theater of State*, 21–2. Consensual decision-making institutions are often supported by inequalities among the members, which induce silence both in debates and in votes by those who fear ridicule or conflict. There is considerable evidence of these sorts of dynamics in the early Stuart parliaments. More generally, see Mansbridge, *Beyond Adversary Democracy*, 59–68, 149, 164. On more extreme occasions, dissent within the House was actually simply silenced by the expulsion of a member. See Zaller, *Parliament of 1621*, 42–3.

[45] See, for example, *CD 1629*, 189.

[46] While it is largely invisible in the historical record, prearrangement of Commons proceedings, involving both deliberation and compromise, probably also led to less open conflict on the floor of the House.

[47] *PP 1625*, 259–60, 265; *POSLP*, vol. III, 582.

consensual vote on that motion in the House itself. The committee of the whole, in these instances, had failed to produce a consensus by means of extended debate, but it had nevertheless succeeded in making it possible for the Commons to avoid a majoritarian vote in the House proper. Divisions in committee did not, apparently, have the same negative significance as divisions of the House.

Of course, it was not always possible to resort to either committing or conferencing. If a matter was being considered by the House immediately following a committee report on it, it was unlikely to be returned to committee; and if the matter under consideration was the proper concern of neither the Lords nor the monarch, it could not become the subject of a conference.[48] If responsibility for the decision at hand could not be rerouted in these ways, the entire House itself had somehow to be brought together on the issue.

A more technical but extremely important device for avoiding a question being put on an important matter that would be divisive was to put the "previous question" instead. The previous question was a question about a question: members were asked whether or not a specific question should be put.[49] It could take a number of precise forms. As one procedural tract put it,

it happens many times, especially in matters which are debated upon motions, that diverse will move to have the question deferred until the next day or some longer time, and sometimes they will move not to have it to be put at all to the question, especially if it be a matter which they desire should either pass with an unanimous consent, or not at all.

In such cases, the Speaker was "to make the question, whether they will have it then put to the question, or defer the putting thereof till some other time: or whether they will have any question at all to be put as he finds the inclination of the house, either to the one or the other."[50] The previous question was often used as a means of achieving capitulation on one side when the balance of opinion in the room remained in doubt. Members were given an opportunity to divide on an ostensibly procedural matter in order to avoid dividing on the substantive issue. If the previous question passed, it indicated that a majority favored the

---

[48] As one member put it in 1671, it was "an indisputable rule of Parliament, that you cannot confer upon a thing not depending between both Houses" (Grey, 4/10/1671). For an unusual early Stuart example of a matter returning directly to the committee from which it came in order to avoid a division, see Russell, *Parliaments and English Politics*, 96.
[49] For perhaps the first instance, see CJ, 5/25/1604. That day there was "much labour to keep the bill from the question at that time."
[50] Sims (ed.), "Speaker of the House of Commons," 92.

measure under consideration. If it failed, of course, it indicated insufficient support and the measure was automatically dropped. After a successful previous question, members could respond to the clear evidence of majority support for the measure that the previous question had provided by voting in unison on one side of the (ostensibly) substantive question when that question was finally put. On those second votes, losers in the procedural vote normally capitulated.[51]

The previous question was clearly a crucial device for avoiding divisions in trying situations. It highlights how tightly members clung to the fiction of ritualized consensus on matters of significant public import. The previous question was also clearly a rather desperate measure, especially when it was used frequently. As we will see, the frequency of its use closely tracked the weakening and eventual deinstitutionalization of consensus decision-making. This technique was notably similar in function to a division in committee of the whole. It allowed for an enumerated vote that was not, technically, a vote on a matter of major political substance in the House proper, which is what members of the Commons clearly tried to avoid. In the case of a division in committee, the vote was not taking place in the House, and in the case of the previous question, the vote was not being held on a matter of substance. Both safeguarded the sanctity of consensus in formal votes of the House on matters of national, public significance.

Other tactics for sidestepping the challenge of forging consensus were considered illicit because of their normative implications.[52] The Commons instituted limited measures to ensure that an apparently consensual vote of all members present was not in fact a factional coup or an accident made possible by the absence of an unusual number of members. Such proceedings in what was called a "thin House" would violate the fiction that votes of the Commons represented a unified decision of the political nation. Members normally insisted that public matters (or at least bills) should not be put to the question (or in the case of bills, passed) in thin Houses. This is why public business usually began

---

[51] See, for example, *POSLP*, vol. VI, 21: on 20 July 1641, according to D'Ewes, "the second question passed without difficulty because we were loath to make a second division of the House."

[52] In this sense early Stuart members did indulge in rare (and normally condemned) acts of "policy" like those that P. G. Thomas and others have shown to be commonplace from the later Stuart period onward. See Thomas, *House of Commons in the Eighteenth Century*, ch. 13; and below, Chapter 6. Again, since these tactics were logistically possible alternatives to routine behavior, the fact that they were employed on occasion is to be expected in a grouping of strategically aware political actors. This fact is in no way inconsistent with the existence of a consensual decision-making institution.

no earlier than nine o'clock in the morning.[53] Additionally, in early 1641 the House formally established a quorum of forty members for the Speaker to go to his chair and begin the day's business.[54] These were minimal safeguards for the claims of representation and unification that the House made about its decisions.

Members also shut down affronts to the House's custom of avoiding divisive votes. On the rare occasion that a member attempted (consciously or inadvertently) to force a question to be put before the House was ready, he would often simply be overruled by others. The overruling members would normally indicate that they were "wary of putting this to the question," either because they possessed more information on "the sense of the House" or because they were more committed than the offending member to avoiding a division. Members who opposed a motion to put the question could resort to any of the delaying motions described above, including motions for the continuance of debate.[55] This happened occasionally, for instance, during debates in the 1620s on supply when individual members tried to force the question.[56] On even rarer occasions, votes in which reasonable dissent had been registered could apparently be reversed on further scrutiny. According to one procedural commentator,

if upon putting of the question in the negative there be but one that is heard to say no, it has been seen that he being a man of special note, has been desired by the house to discover to them the reason of his differing in opinion from the whole house. And upon his voluntary declaration thereof, the whole house hath changed their former resolution.

The commentator referenced an episode of this sort from 1571.[57] This type of incident shows how strong an association members made between consensual decisions and sound decisions. The House's keen attention to a lone minority voice in such episodes also clarifies the depth of members' anti-majoritarian and inegalitarian assumptions about truth and political wisdom.

This reflection on the House's strong commitment to consensual deliberation brings us to the crucial point of our institutional analysis. Once we have established *how* divisions were normally avoided in this

---

[53] Hakewill, *Manner How Statutes Are Enacted in Parliament*, 35.   [54] CJ, 1/5/1641.
[55] For example, *PP 1610*, 336–7; *PP 1625*, 444, 446, 450–1, 453; *CD 1629*, 157, 171.
[56] Russell, *Parliaments and English Politics*, 189, 250, 251, 258, 308; *PP 1625*, 114–22, 440, 450–1. On 18 March 1606, royal counselors clearly forced two divisions, aided by a partisan speaker, when other members were calling for further debate. See Wilson (ed.), *Parliamentary Diary of Robert Bowyer*, 84–5. For a similar attempt in 1614, see *PP 1614*, 444.
[57] Sims (ed.), "Speaker of the House of Commons," 94.

period, we must move to the question of *why* they were avoided, even under conditions of serious conflict. If we rely on commonsense, ahistorical assumptions about political decision-making, the answer is elusive. Majoritarian behavior has a familiar rationale for both majorities and minorities. Why would members in the majority ever refrain from forcing a vote at the moment their majority status had been revealed through debate or other means? If members in the majority were only concerned with securing their favored result in the matter at hand, forcing the vote would be an obvious choice. Allowing further debate or other extensions of the decision-making process would risk only a change in the tide of opinion, a shift in the set of members present to vote, or the sudden termination of the process by a prorogation, a dissolution, or an emergency. The rationale for minorities supporting a majoritarian routine is only slightly less strong. Why did members apparently in the minority after thorough debate sometimes capitulate (either by joining in an acclamation or by accepting a voice vote) when they could easily register their disagreement with what they considered an unwise decision and possibly even win a division? It is remarkable that minorities forced divisions as rarely as they did prior to the 1640s when House procedures made it so easy to do so. The initial answer to these questions about why neither majorities nor minorities supported majoritarian decision-making must be that for both groups, something other than the simple prospect of an enumerated vote or majoritarian voice vote was at stake in the decision about whether or not to force or risk a division. Members must have had some sort of intrinsic preference for making consensual decisions over majoritarian decisions, a preference that trumped their interest in a particular outcome.[58]

Members actively expressed strong distaste for meaningfully majoritarian votes. They typically registered concern with divisions in particular, as opposed to any and all meaningfully majoritarian decisions, including close voice votes. But it is easy to see how distaste for divisions would lead to both a low frequency of divisions and a low frequency of meaningfully majoritarian voice votes: allowing anything approaching a

---

[58] There was, to be sure, one realm of practical considerations that influenced members' willingness to force divisions. If information on a secure majority was scarce, a motion risked rejection if a vote was pushed at the time. See, for example, Hartley (ed.), *Proceedings in the Parliaments of Elizabeth I*, vol. I, 369; *PP 1614*, 440; Russell, *Parliaments and English Politics*, 189, 250, 251, 258, 308; *PP 1625*, 114–22; Sims (ed.), "Speaker of the House of Commons," 93. The other presumptive logistical advantage of acclamations – speed – probably applied only to cases where there was little disagreement, since extended debate aimed at the production of consensus could take much longer than a division.

close voice vote risked a division. In other words, the fundamental antipathy current among members might best be expressed as an antipathy to putting the question before it could be resolved consensually. Members in fact regularly made pleas not to put the question on divisive issues. In the heated atmosphere of 1628, for instance, Sir John Coke explicitly reminded his fellow members that they ought not put the question when it seemed likely that the House would be divided.[59] These pleas were especially common during debates on supply, in which consensus was often both difficult to achieve and highly valued.[60] Avoiding divisions was clearly a means of symbolically expressing unity, just as the division was a transparent display of division. But what exactly was the basis of members' utter distaste for divisions? Whatever it was, the distaste was conditional, not absolute. After all, divisions on matters of public importance did sometimes occur.

The key to solving this puzzle is to observe the widespread evidence that House members took very seriously considerations of status when they went about making decisions. Members' deep concern about matters of status is evident enough in the successful, impressive efforts they made to avoid divisions in trying situations. But it is most evident on the rare occasions when their efforts failed and a division resulted.[61] It is well known that early modern elites were nearly preoccupied with the acquisition and maintenance of status.[62] The specific status considerations that were central to decision-making in the antebellum House of Commons were the closely related notions of honor and privilege. Honor was and is a capacious, contested, and discursively variable concept. But these characteristics were simply the marks of its deep significance. It was one of the primary concepts that English elites used to contemplate and acquire power and to establish and maintain order.[63] Its role in parliamentary politics is best understood with reference to specific instances of use. But these specific contextualizations do correspond with a general definition of honor, one that applies to wide variety of usages, admits the contested nature of the concept, and suits the parliamentary context in particular. This definition was offered with typical concision

---

[59] *PP 1628*, vol. II, 319; see also 324, 329. For other examples of attempts to prevent the question from being put, see *PP 1614*, 123, 125, 146.

[60] Russell, *Fall of the British Monarchies*, 118, 121; Russell, *Parliaments and English Politics*, 185; *PP 1625*, 446.

[61] The primacy of status interaction in Commons decision-making, as we have seen, sits well with available explanations for the general lack of majoritarian behavior in elections to Parliament prior to the 1640s. See Kishlansky, *Parliamentary Selection*.

[62] A recent, vivid account is Sternberg, *Status Interaction during the Reign of Louis XIV*.

[63] Kane, *Politics and Culture of Honour*, 6, 10–11; Smuts, *Culture and Power in England*, 7–17. See also Thomas, *If I Lose Mine Honour*.

on the eve of the Commons' departure from consensus decision-making by England's top political thinker, Thomas Hobbes, in *De Cive* (1642). "Properly speaking," he wrote, honor "is nothing other than the opinion one has of the union of power and goodness in another person."[64] In other words, honor was the recognition of an external entity's power and moral worth. That which was honorable was anything that elicited this recognition; that which was dishonorable was anything that detracted from this recognition. As we will see, the dominant understanding of what behavior merited recognition of "the union of power and goodness" could change over time, and appears to have done so in Parliament.

The classic formulation of early modern honor in modern historiography complements Hobbes'. It associates early modern honor with "competitive assertiveness" or "preeminence," but also with "consistency in standing by a position once taken up." This moral quality of fidelity to an adopted position was commonly described by early moderns as "resolution." By the early Stuart period, honor had been largely accommodated to both Christian morality and the state, and in particular, state service. In the process it became associated with morally upright public conduct (in addition to violence and other aggressive action) and contrasted with cowardice.[65] Traditionally, honor had been a pretext for resistance to royal authority, and this understanding was revived in the 1620s and 1640s. There were important changes in the social valence of honor in this period as well: the increasing social and political importance of the gentry limited the exclusive association of honor with nobility, and thus potentially made the gentry-heavy Commons and its members sites of honor.[66] In other words, in the early Stuart period, it became possible to associate honor with both violence and the restraint of violence, and with both nobility and gentility. All these aspects of honor identified by Hobbes and modern scholars turn out to have been operative in "the honorable House of Commons," as contemporaries called it, and in Parliament more generally.

Privilege was a closely related status concept operative in Parliament, but also a more formal one. The two basic, interrelated privileges of House members, ordinarily requested by the Speaker at the beginning of each parliament, were freedom from arrest and freedom of speech. The two privileges were closely related. Without freedom of speech,

---

[64] Hobbes, *On the Citizen*, 175–6 (XV.9). See also Hobbes, *Leviathan*, vol. II, 136, 137, 140, 141, 142, 143.
[65] James, *Society, Politics and Culture*, 309, 313, 316, 320, 328, 333, 339, 376, 380, 392–3.
[66] Ibid., 341, 400–10, 358.

members could not independently make wise decisions for the public good. And without freedom from arrest, members could not speak freely without fear of retaliation. In addition, if arrests by external entities were permitted when the House was in session, the House could be purged with specious charges against particular members.[67] Breaches of privilege were thus taken to implicitly legitimate broader attempts to destroy Parliament and its power. This is why they were so closely related to affronts to parliamentary honor, and so fiercely resisted. Actions of a wide variety were described as breaches of privilege on the same general grounds.[68] Privilege, like honor, was by no means a codified notion in this period. It was expansive, ambiguous, and contested in application. Understood as a collection of historical precedents, it was subject to interpretation and debate within Parliament. It was inconsistently invoked, often for political reasons. In other words, it was both an internalized norm and one regularly subject to manipulation. Freedom of speech within the House was a crucial instance of this. While Parliament was reluctant to allow the monarch to restrict free speech, its members regularly punished and intimidated fellow members when they voiced unpopular opinions.

The general principle of privilege – as well as the closely aligned and for our purposes synonymous notions of rights and liberties – was the idea that all members had to be protected from any disturbance that might inhibit their attendance at and independent participation in Parliament. Such principles obviously had a close relationship to parliamentary and royal power more generally, and therefore to honor. Parliamentary privilege, in particular, was inseparable from parliamentary power. As a matter of privilege the Commons demanded, for instance, that taxation took place only with parliamentary consent and that subsidy bills, in particular, had to be initiated by the lower house. Correlatively, any attempts to undermine privilege, including sermons or publications of an absolutist bent, could themselves be understood as breaches of privilege or threats to it. Making a formal statement of these privileges and having them confirmed by the monarch was a regular concern in the 1620s parliaments, especially since the Stuart kings had intimated that parliamentary privilege was a free grant from the monarch, not a stable possession. In part because privilege was so closely related to parliamentary honor and power, it was central to the constitutional conflicts of the early Stuart period. By 1642, privilege had become

[67] For commentary and dispute in 1642, see *PJLP*, vol. I, 19, 42.
[68] See, for example, ibid., vol. I, 44; vol. II, 15.

synonymous with the control of the Houses over their own business and, to an extent, with their control of business outside the chamber.[69]

The close relationship between honor and privilege is particularly evident in debates over supply. These were, again, probably the most politically important debates that recurred in nearly every parliamentary session. This makes them particularly worthy of close attention and interpretive weight. Consensual agreements on supply were made possible by free speech on often sensitive matters of international significance, and by recognition of the Commons' central position in these taxation grants. In this sense consent to taxation was intrinsically honorable: it projected the unity and power of the nation and its representatives, while also projecting the unity of the king in Parliament in defense of the common good. All of these effects were thought best achieved by consensual or even unanimous votes. The presence of negative votes in a decision in favor of supply might be taken to imply that some members of the political nation were being forced to give up their property without their consent, and that English military action was not backed by the full support of the kingdom's substantial inhabitants.

Accordingly, in a 1614 supply debate, Sir Edwin Sandys recalled a 1606 division on supply that was decided by a single vote and observed that if James I "should now gain diverse subsidies with so many negative voices," it would be "not honorable." Elizabeth, he claimed, had never carried a subsidy with even a single negative vote. William Hakewill added after Sandys' remarks that it was "not fit to put this now to the question, but that the honorable persons about the chair may, as voluntarily of themselves, inform the king that generally all that have spoken (which are many) have, *una voce*, agreed in their thoughts and speeches to relieve his Majesty."[70] Honor was clearly being invoked here in association with both unanimity and the consensus of "generally all" of those debating a motion (if not all of those present). Similarly, on the final day of the 1625 session, in a debate about supply, John Glanville remarked that in cases where "the disputes against supply are greater in number, and weightier in reason," the House tended not "to rush so far as to a question, until it be seen to be granted; for as it will be a dishonour to the king if it be denied, so to pass with difficulty by numbering our voices will take away the merit from us." Edward Alford added that he "would not have the matter decided by question, for whether carry it or lose shall reap dishonor." This strong association between close votes and dishonor was the dominant interpretation. But the related point made here,

---

[69] Sommerville, "Parliament, Privilege, and the Liberties of the Subject."
[70] *PP 1614*, 153–4. For a later example, see *Aston*, 143. See also *PP 1624*, 3/19/1624.

that the king reaped dishonor from a denial of supply, was occasionally deemed more important than the costs of a close vote. In the same debate from 1625, the duke of Buckingham's ally Sir Robert Killigrew argued in favor of putting the question by insisting that "it is a greater disgrace to be denied by a few than by all." This more unusual argument was typically made unsuccessfully, and it sidestepped entirely considerations regarding the honor or merit of the Commons.[71] Moreover, even this position was founded on a strong preference for positive, consensual action among the House's members. Divisions on matters of political importance were avoided, it appears, because they were dishonorable.

Institutional Failures under Charles I

The primacy of unity and honor in the Commons ensured the forceful direction of members' debating and procedural repertoires toward the production of consensus. The basis of this routine practice in internalized norms was of course rarely worthy of remark when the routine was being successfully maintained. As the comments of Sandys in 1614 suggest, the historical record is far more informative and often explicit on the role played by norms of honor and privilege in cases where the application of those norms *failed* to produce the routine result. For this reason, the moments in which divisions did occur prior to the Civil War are worthy of detailed consideration. These incidents are unusually informative about the institution of which they constituted a failure. In fact, they quite clearly reveal the underlying basis for the institution of consensual decision-making.

The best way to assess whether the frequent references to honor and other forms of status in Commons debates are in fact indicative of the underpinnings of this institution is to consider the observable implications of this conjecture. Two considerations deserve particular attention. First, if concerns about the public status of the House and its members were indeed determinative of the House's reluctance to divide, we would expect its members to be *willing* to divide on private bills, and on other matters of merely private or logistical significance. Doing so would presumably allow the House to save time in debate and hasten other business, and it would allow majorities to seize a moment of perceived advantage. This, it turns out, is exactly what the data show: the overwhelming majority of divisions held between 1614 and 1642 were private

---

[71] *PP 1625*, 452, 463, 470. See also *PP 1628*, vol. III, 141.

or logistical in nature.[72] In these situations, the status of the House was not at stake in the manner in which it made decisions, so there was no normative barrier to deciding by majority vote.

Second, and more importantly, if status considerations governed the operation of this decision-making institution, we would also expect another species of division to occur occasionally. These would be divisions on disputed matters of public significance whose status significance outweighed the status significance of making a single decision by means of majority vote. These divisions would, in a sense, constitute institutional failures. Although they were exceedingly rare, they too can be found in the data for the early Stuart period. They occurred after prolonged debate on questions of serious public significance, in situations where a division was eminently undesirable.[73] It is this portion of the early Stuart division data that requires closer inspection. For it was these divisions, which came to proliferate only after the outbreak of the Civil War, that ultimately destroyed the consensual decision-making conventions of Parliament's lower house.

These moments of serious institutional failure were clearly considered disastrous, awkward, and embarrassing. In general, they were ritualized instances of national disunity – and thus dishonor, since unity projected power and righteousness – and they were appreciated as such. The only politically important division of the 1624 session, a 28 May vote on the duke of Buckingham acquiring York House, followed three hours of debate. During the division, seven of the members present, "refusing to give voice one way or other," tried to creep into an adjacent committee chamber in order to avoid taking part. The vote, which according to the diarist John Hawarde included "a strong opposition," was so divisive that when the ayes returned to the chamber, William Noye suggested that the House engage in a ritual of reunification. He moved that "the no [voters] should go now out and bring in the bill, which is the ancient use of the House." But "in regard of the multitude of business and shortness of time" (at least ostensibly), the ritual "was now forborne."[74] The suggestion itself nevertheless implied that divisions were considered to be serious symbolic expressions of national disunion, and the rejection of the suggestion might be taken to indicate the suggestion's futility.

---

[72] Baty, "History of Majority Rule," 26–7, argues that the English became majoritarians by absent-mindedly extending their practice of dividing on trivial matters to nontrivial matters.

[73] See, for example, Russell, *King James VI and I and His English Parliaments*, 56, 84–5, 107.

[74] CJ, 5/28/1624; *PP 1624*, 5/28/1624. For other examples, see *PP 1626*, vol. III, 53; *POSLP*, vol. II, 589–90.

As Noye had noted, there were precedents for his motion. During a division in 1597, it was resolved "that according to the ancient custom of this House, all the members of the same which did speak against the passing of the said bill, should go forth of the House to bring in the bill into the House again, together with the residue of the members of this House which went out before with the passing of the said bill." The idea here was that after the votes had been counted, the House's entire membership would leave the chamber and process back into it together, bill in hand, registering their unified endorsement of it. Accordingly, on that occasion, "all the members of this House being gone forth, saving Mr. Speaker and the clerk, Mr. Controller brought in the bill in his hand, accompanied with all the members of this House, and delivered the same bill to Mr. Speaker according to the ancient former use of this House."[75] An early seventeenth-century procedural commentary offered an interpretation of this ritual. "Upon the division of the House," the commentator stated, "it has been seen that those which have been the lesser part, against the bill have made a recantation of their error." In situations where this did not happen, "if they have been against a bill which by the greatest number is past, they are to come down all out of their places and jointly to present it to the Speaker, saying they affirm it."[76] Such unity gestures and rituals were taken to enable the House to affirm the wisdom of their decision with unanimous consent after a moment of disunity. They were premised on a strong association between consensus and truth. As another procedural tract put it, "the ancient course has been, if those for the bill are the greatest number, that those which sat in the negative should go forth, and bring in the bill, and present it to the Speaker, thereby to acknowledge their consent to it, and their error in being against it." This early Stuart commentator nevertheless noted that the ritual "has not been used of late times."[77] Normally, the House did not consider it possible or worthwhile to attempt to undo the damage a division had done.

Indeed, it is unclear how often anything like this actually happened. On 25 June 1604, according to the Commons journal, "upon motion, such as sat against the bill, went forth of the House, and brought in the bill in their hands, which is according to ancient order, and was now moved, and done (once in a parliament) for preserving memory of the order; and so expressed by the mover."[78] By the seventeenth century, it

---

[75] Townshend (ed.), *Historical Collections*, 12/15/1597. That year this apparently became a standing order (BL MS Add 36856, f. 55v.). See also *PP 1624*, 3/9/1624.

[76] Sims (ed.), "'Policies in Parliaments,'" 48–9.

[77] Sims (ed.), "Speaker of the House of Commons," 95.   [78] CJ, 6/25/1604.

seems, this ritual was less an attempt to reverse the effects of a specific division than it was a rather empty memorialization of an outdated performance of unity. However often the ritual was in fact used in the early seventeenth century, its main importance lies in the information it provides about the sort of event divisions – with or without the unity ritual tacked on – were taken to be. Because unity rituals seem to have been enacted (to the extent they were enacted at all) in cases where a bill was passed, initiatives in favor of unity rituals at the very least betray the sentiment that *positive* action by a divided body was particularly alarming. Yet divisions resulting in positive action were just as common as divisions resulting in inaction or negative action, both across the seventeenth century and prior to the 1640s. The Commons seems to have deplored the spectacle of national disunity involved in any division on an issue of major public significance.

Aside from indirectly dishonoring the House by performing disunity, politically important divisions were also apparently thought to result in the transfer of the honor of the House and its members onto the subject of the division. One can see this in the only division of the Short Parliament, which occurred as part of the prosecution of an absolutist sermon delivered in 1635 by the Arminian William Beale at Cambridge, where he was vice chancellor. Beale had apparently denied parliamentary power in matters of taxation, stated that the king could "constitute laws what, where, when, and against whom he would," and left the calling of parliaments to the King's "mere grace." Such a sermon was, by its very nature, understood by many to dishonor Parliament.[79] In a debate over whether the House must proceed to a division after a close voice vote on how to deal with Beale, Sir Henry Mildmay suggested the gravity of the impending division by noting that "we should do too much honour to this unhappy man to divide the house about him." The puritan John Wray added to admissions of the seriousness of the matter by stating that it was "no wonder that he that made a division in the church should make a division in the house."[80] The House's conduct, these members suggested, was making it possible for Beale to continue to dishonor Parliament just as his Laudian initiatives had helped to divide and dishonor the church.

As this example indicates, the most important information conveyed by the politically important divisions of the early Stuart period is precisely that which confirms the specific workings of the institution of consensual

[79] *Aston*, 112. On Beale, see Burgess, *Politics of the Ancient Constitution*, 183–6; Hoyle, "A Commons Investigation of Arminianism and Popery," 419–25.

[80] *Aston*, 114, 115. For more on this division, see below, 70.

decision-making: information about how the honor considerations that normally determined the decision-making procedure in these situations were trumped by other considerations tending to division. Those considerations were in fact *other* status-related considerations. These examples show that the primary way in which divisions occurred on politically significant issues during the antebellum period was that there was disagreement on the question at hand, and one or both sides to the debate decided that a greater dishonor to the House or some of its members (and, by extension, the House as a whole) would result from agreeing to the opposite side of the question than from the dishonorable act of dividing. In other words, the status stakes of the particular decision itself were higher than the status stakes involved in the choice between a consensual or majoritarian means of making the decision. As we will see, this is exactly the same mechanism that would produce an explosion of majoritarian decisions in the 1640s. We will also see that in many of these incidents, the likelihood of a division was higher than usual because some of the common procedural means of avoiding a division were unavailable. This could occur because these tactics were impossible, exhausted, or inappropriate to the matter at hand. The unavailability of consensual tactics ought to be considered a secondary cause of politically important divisions.

The role of status considerations as the fundamental trigger for important divisions is abundantly clear when we turn to specific examples from the 1620s, during the reign of Charles I. This is a particularly well-documented period in which, despite extreme political conflict, divisions remained very rare – occurring only 2.8 percent of the time a question was put (Table 2.1 and Figure 2.1). Both of the divisions in the 1625 parliament concerned the status of the House. On 22 June, before the House divided on whether to confer with the Lords about joining in their petition for a general plague fast, Sir Edward Coke "vouched a precedent" from the Elizabethan period "wherein the like petition was by the Commons alone." This concern was enough for a minority in the House to submit to a division that they lost, 195 to 172.[81] The second division, on 5 July, was part of a controversy over a contested election for Yorkshire. In the election, a close voice vote had been held, according to normal procedure. But after the voice vote, the sheriff, Sir Richard Cholmley, had chosen not to proceed to a poll but instead

---

[81] *PP 1625*, 217, 221.

simply to return Sir Thomas Wentworth and Sir Thomas Fairfax.[82] Elections with contested legitimacy, of course, strongly concerned the honor and legitimacy of the House and Parliament, and often the honor of the members involved in the dispute. Wentworth urged that a proper legal hearing of counsel for him concerned the House's honor. And after the division, at a point when Wentworth had again taken his place in the House, despite concern about the propriety of his place there, Sir John Eliot accused Wentworth of attacking the privileges of the House. He alleged that "a greater dishonour and contempt this House has at no time suffered than what does now affront it."[83] Concerns over status were at the forefront of the controversy from start to finish.

In the following year, 1626, a dozen divisions were held. Most of the politically important ones centered on the Commons' attempt to destroy the duke of Buckingham. They again make clear the primacy of status considerations in the provocation of institutional failures in the early Stuart Commons. In a conference on 7 March, the Lords urged the Commons to take up (after a month's neglect) what Archbishop Abbot called "that which most mainly concerns the honour and safety of the king and kingdom": prosecuting and funding the war with Spain. On the following day the conference was reported in the Commons, and the House divided over whether to consider an answer to the Lords' request. They agreed, 226 to 166, to do so. The basic political issue at play here was the House's insistence on proceeding with an attack on Buckingham before granting supply. But this issue, for all its ideological significance, was not sufficient for causing a division. Indeed, the fact that the division occurred on the question of whether even to answer the Lords makes clear that what was at issue was a perceived affront to the Commons. After all, the Commons could have answered the Lords with a refusal. The real dilemma was over whether even answering them would be a mistake.[84]

The question of whether to consider an answer had serious status implications for those on both sides of the question. Abbot, of course, had identified the status concern that would have motivated proponents of proceeding with supply. But other members were concerned with the implications of answering the Lords for the status of the Commons itself. In particular, they were concerned that the Lords appeared to be

---

[82] See Thrush and Ferris (eds.), *House of Commons 1604–1629*, vol. VI, "Wentworth, Sir Thomas (1593–1641)," 709. There was also a division in committee about this election: *PP 1625*, 300.

[83] *PP 1625*, 513–15.

[84] *PP 1626*, vol. II, 221, 227–32. In a newsletter this division was described in adversarial terms as a victory "won" for the "affirmative part" (BL MS Harley 390, f. 24r.).

initiating the process of granting supply, when this customarily happened in the Commons. Some had concluded from this that the Lords should not be answered at all, because to do so would be to dishonor the Commons with respect to their power over the initiation of taxation. Still others probably believed that a refusal was a sufficient and appropriate way of maintaining the Commons' supply privileges. The decision clearly entailed rather subtle considerations regarding the status consequences of particular actions by the Commons, ranging from prosecuting the war to acknowledging the request of the upper house.

The next division of the 1626 session, which occurred three days later, concerned Buckingham's re-arrest of a French merchant ship, the *St. Peter*, after it had been released by order of the Court of Admiralty. The ship had originally been arrested for carrying goods to Spain.[85] The House had been investigating this matter since late February, and the investigation eventually led to a second and a third division over the following months, as the Commons debated whether they ought to pursue the re-arrest as a formal grievance. These divisions were perhaps the only important ones in the period that may not have primarily concerned the honor of the Commons or its members but were rather more squarely centered on the politics of supply and grievances. Yet maintenance of the Commons' ability to pursue both grievances and supply was itself a matter of privilege, since it pertained to freedom of speech and conventions of representation. Moreover, in the debates that preceded these divisions, members explicitly noted that the honor of the English state and, by implication, the honor of the Commons and its members were at stake in the *St. Peter* controversy. As William Noye put it on 1 May, the second time the issue surfaced, the concern was that "if we determine that this stay was unjust, we shall condemn ourselves and be stopped to say the French did us unjustice" in responding to the *St. Peter* incident with the seizure of English ships. In other words, as John Bankes described it, such a course "will tend to the dishonour of our state." The need to oppose Buckingham's abuse of power was seen to be at odds with the need to maintain the honor of the monarchy and Parliament in particular with respect to France.[86]

The Commons' attack on Buckingham became more tightly tied to the defense of the House's own status after Charles I's order on 29 March to end their "unparliamentary" proceedings against the duke, which the king clearly viewed as an attack on his own honor. In response to the

---

[85] This division was also reported in the same newsletter as "won" by "the negative part," if only "with very little difference of voices" (BL MS Harley 390, f. 27r.).

[86] *PP 1626*, vol. III, 109, 114.

royal order, the Commons drew up a Remonstrance defending their actions. Presented with this on 4 April, Charles said that he would not respond to it and added that he expected the Commons to adjourn for Easter for only seven days, as the Lords had, so that "we may redeem the time we have lost." The Commons divided over whether to adjourn for the brief period suggested by the king. Opponents of this measure would have seen it as a specific affront within the broader struggle over the appropriateness of the Commons' prioritization of grievances over supply, which was clearly a matter of privilege and status more generally.[87]

After the recess, there were another two important divisions. On 24 April, the Commons divided on whether to allow a select committee to continue investigating the duke on new fronts not already identified in the House or in a committee of the whole. This vote was so contentious that a number of members tried to get permission to go into the committee chamber instead of participating in the division, after having refrained from participating in the two voice votes that were taken. Proceeding with a select committee was seen by its opponents as unparliamentary – a violation of privilege and a source of dishonor to the House and to the members excluded from the committee's secret meetings.[88] The committee, once formed, looked into Buckingham's possible role in the death of James I and reported to the House on 27 April about the testimony of the king's physicians. A division then occurred over whether to debate this report in a committee of the whole. Here again the issue may have been the appropriateness of the committee's proceedings, in addition, of course, to the reluctance of Buckingham's clients to allow such serious proceedings against him to continue.[89]

A division more indirectly related to Buckingham occurred on 3 May. The House voted narrowly, 114 to 105, not to have the Speaker write a letter to the High Commissioners (of which the duke was one) annulling the Commission's 1624 proceedings against Sir Robert Howard, who had been excommunicated for adultery while sitting in the House in 1624. While on an ideological level this case certainly related to the constitutional status of the High Commission, it also involved multiple dimensions of concern over privilege and the status of the House as a whole. Howard's excommunication was taken by some to threaten the status of all members.[90] The House had resolved without a vote that

---

[87] Russell, *Parliaments and English Politics*, 291, 293; *PP 1626*, vol. II, 431, 434.
[88] *PP 1626*, vol. III, 53, 55, 56.
[89] Ibid., vol. III, 84–6; Bellany and Cogswell, *Murder of King James I*, 228–9.
[90] Russell, *Parliaments and English Politics*, 277.

the Commission's proceedings in 1624 were void and should be vacated, and it also resolved after the division that the Commons would inform members of the Commission whom they were interviewing of the Commons' view of the matter and what they expected to be done. It was the question of what further vindication of privilege and means of erasing the proceedings to pursue that was in dispute, amid general concern over what Sir Nathaniel Rich called "the injury done to the House." Even the case against writing to the Commission was made, in the view of John Lowther, "both because it is against our dignity to entreat and not prevail, so likewise not to command because we cannot enforce." The centrality of the honor and privileges of the House to this division is clear.[91]

The 1626 divisions that concerned Buckingham culminated in a 226 to 106 vote on 9 May to move the Lords to commit the duke to prison. The motion under consideration here was seen by many as a vindication of Parliament's honor and privileges against the greatest single threat to them. Ideological and status considerations were partly merged. In the division itself, the noes yielded when the yeas processed out of the chamber, but the yeas refused to accept their submission and insisted on being counted. As John Lowther described it, the yeas, "to have honour in it, would not take it." At this point the noes apparently offered to go out of the chamber as well, in order to initiate a unity ritual. But "the greater number opposed and did make a terrible contest-ation."[92] The yeas clearly wanted to perform their honorable defense of the House against Buckingham. And they were perhaps even more eager to expose the dishonorable conduct of those who voted against the motion to call for Buckingham's imprisonment. These considerations had outweighed their concerns over the negative status effects of a division. When the yeas chose to insist on being counted and to reject the noes' offer of a unity ritual, the division was, in any case, already underway, and much of the damage done. The noes, in turn, may have been employing their submission and request for ritual as a means of exposing the divisiveness of the yea voters. Episodes like this one would first become common during the Long Parliament.

The initial desire for action against Buckingham on 9 May, as well as opposition to swift action against him, were clearly prompted by status concerns. Discussion of the duke's imprisonment had commenced on the previous day, after presentation of charges against Buckingham had begun. The duke had reportedly slighted the members of the Commons

[91] *PP 1626*, vol. III, 141–52, esp. 142, 145, 150.   [92] Ibid., vol. III, 201, 216.

as they spoke to the Lords, prompting members' desire to imprison him. The House resolved to continue debate on 9 May and spent considerable time arguing over precedents, in part because, as Sir John Finch put it, "it is the honour of our House to go the same way that our predecessors have done." Moving too hastily against the duke for "an uncertain crime," Sir Richard Weston argued, "behooves not the gravity of this House," and thus restraint was "for the honour of this House." The final, politicized division of the session, again indirectly related to Buckingham, completed the theme. The Buckingham client and Commons member Sir John Savile's February letter to allies in Leeds attacking the Commons' proceedings against Buckingham was introduced to the House on 22 May and condemned as an insult. Savile responded by accusing two members of trying to defame him and denying authorship of the letter. Again both sides cited dishonor to the House or its members as the basis for their position. On 13 June the House divided over whether to hear Savile's side of the case the following day.[93]

The pattern evident in 1626 is also clear in a series of divisions from the next parliament, in May and June 1628, during controversy over the Petition of Right.[94] In the 1628 election for Cornwall, Lord John Mohun and his political allies, including deputy lieutenants and justices of the peace, tried to persuade, intimidate, and coerce John Eliot and William Coryton into not standing for election. They failed and both Eliot and Coryton were elected. Evidence of these tactics – in the form of letters sent to Coryton that he presented to the House – was taken into consideration by the Commons committee on privileges in March, soon after the opening of the session. After the letters were read, members immediately indicated that these actions were a grave threat to parliamentary privilege and liberty. Sir Edward Coke called them "a way to purge the fountain of the freedom of this House." The next day all those whose names appeared on the letters were summoned to the House. The offenders refused to come with the sergeant at arms and petitioned the Commons. They asked to delay their appearance because they were busy enforcing martial law in the county. This response, in part because of its inappropriate mode of address to the Speaker, further slighted the House. Sir Thomas Hoby exclaimed that the petition was "the greatest contempt that I ever saw."[95]

[93] Ibid., vol. III, 202, 204, 207, 208, 210, 211, 212, 215, 301, 303–4, 306–8, 392–401, 433. There was a politically important division in committee of the whole the previous day (BL MS Harley 390, f. 77r.; *PP 1626*, vol. III, 428).
[94] Two earlier divisions in the 1628 sessions were on politically trivial matters, one a private bill.
[95] *PP 1628*, vol. II, 33–4, 38, 41; vol. III, 4, 5, 26, 29.

The committee examining the letters read to the House in March reported in mid-May, registering among other threats to the status of Parliament the aspersions cast on Eliot and Coryton in the letters. The committee described the letter writers' behavior as "but a scorn to the House." On 13 May, after four men from the county finally appeared before the House and answered questions through their counsel, the House divided on whether to conclude the matter by compelling them to make recognition of their offenses at the next assizes in Cornwall. Sir Thomas Wentworth expressed the stubborn anger of many members at the slights received by the House that led to the division, stating, "I will never show mercy when the offense is so great against this House." John Selden reinforced the importance of maintaining parliamentary honor beyond Westminster by arguing that "this House cannot right itself without an acknowledgment. What we do here will not be known in Cornwall." Opponents of the measure such as Sir John Coke replied in vain that "moderation is the honour of this House."[96] In the background of this conflict was a matter of constitutional significance that would be taken up in the Petition of Right: the letter writers' enforcement of martial law. But the key, common feature of this and other politicized divisions in 1628 was the presence of perceived threats to the status of the House and its members.

The division on the following day, 14 May, was directly concerned with the Petition of Right and again entailed status considerations. The dispute concerned a conference with the Lords about the Petition and, in particular, the problem of the king's letter sent to the Lords and read to the Commons on 12 May. It stated that he would not allow his power of committing men to prison without cause to be circumscribed. There was also the question of whether this and recommendations on revisions to the Petition from the Lords relayed the same day required amendments to the Petition. This situation was of course of profound general significance to the status of Parliament and its members. On this level, ideological and status considerations overlapped. Sir John Eliot had said on 12 May after the reading of the letter that "upon this resolution" on how to respond to the letter "depends all that is called ours." But there were also more specific status considerations that caused the division on 14 May. The question was how to deal with the propositions from the Lords and the king's letter "with regard to the honour of this House and the safety of the cause," as Eliot put it in debate on the previous day, 13 May. The House first discussed alterations to the Petition and then

[96] Ibid., vol. III, 368, 386, 389, 392, 393; see generally 365–401.

returned to the letter, which, it was successfully argued, was to be laid
aside and returned to the Lords without debate. This was done in part
because the letter was addressed to the Lords and also because dealing
with it would be against parliamentary custom (and thus dishonorable):
the king was in effect answering the Petition before it had been
delivered.[97]

It is clear from debate after the conference with the Lords at which the
king's letter was presented that at least some members saw the transfer of
the letter by the Lords as an attempt to get the Commons to back down
from their claims about imprisonment in the Petition. On this view, the
matter was an important occasion for the lower house's vindication of
both privilege and broader constitutional principles. The division on
14 May was over whether to signify in a message to the Lords about
the House being ready for a conference the reasons why the Commons
was going to disregard the king's letter. (The alternative course of action
was to raise the issue at the conference itself.) In other words, the
question at hand was whether the Lords were owed an explanation, or
whether the more honorable course would be to ignore the letter as
part of the Commons' decision to accept the Lords' invitation to confer.[98] In this context, once again, the Commons' decision-making was
overwhelmingly influenced by subtle but serious status considerations.

The final important division in 1628 occurred on 30 May.[99] It concerned a monopoly held by the courtier Sir Thomas Monson, which
again entailed considerations relevant to the status of the House. The
matter had come out of committee and presumably could not be recommitted. Members noted that Monson's patent had been previously
condemned by the House in James I's reign, and on this basis they
considered its resurrection an affront to the Commons.[100] The division
was over whether to consider the patent with a single question over
whether it was a grievance, or to divide the issue into more than one
question on different aspects of the case. Opponents of subdividing the
question presumably feared that this would dilute the strength of their

---

[97] *PP 1628*, vol. III, 373, 394, 404, 406, 408, 409, 411, 412, 417.

[98] Ibid., vol. III, 411, 413. It is possible if unlikely that this specific issue was not a
significant matter of honor. But in that case it was of only procedural significance,
and, as a trivial matter, it was subject to a division, especially when time was of the
essence, as many members said it was during this discussion.

[99] The context for a division on 20 May on whether the House was to rise or not for the
day is unclear. It was most likely either insignificant or wrapped up with ongoing debate
and exchanges with the Lords on the Petition of Right, and in that way related to the
proper means of protecting the House's status in those exchanges and in the petition.
The division is not mentioned in diaries.

[100] *PP 1628*, vol. IV, 23.

response. As Sir Robert Phelips put it, a major aspect of the issue was "what concerns the House in point of honour," which meant that it was "needful and commendable for us to vindicate our honour." Others argued against Phelips that they "would have no touch upon Sir Thomas Monson, being of honour." When successful in the division, Monson's opponents were able to move on to a successful voice vote that the patent was a grievance.[101] The House had again been overwhelmingly concerned with the vindication of its honor while confronting an issue of undoubted ideological and constitutional significance.

The Parameters of Consensus and the Path to Division

By this point, the common element among the politically significant divisions of the later 1620s should be clear. These enumerated majority votes were rare but revealing spectacles of disunity: status considerations were central to every one of them. It is important, however, to be clear about what this means, in order properly to understand what occurred when Parliament was summoned again in 1640. The rarity of politically significant, status-related divisions in the early Stuart period should not be taken to imply a lack of status-related *decisions* made by the House at that time. The Commons, of course, did not divide when they confronted status-related issues but were able to reach an agreement by means of thorough debate and standard procedural maneuvers. Disagreement was a necessary condition for divisions on issues with serious status implications. But it was not a sufficient condition for divisions, which were in fact regularly avoided on subjects that were sites for serious ideological and constitutional conflict.

Indeed, the incidence of divisions in the early Stuart period was not even coextensive with the incidence of motions on the floor of the House with profound status implications that were subject to significant disagreement. Meaningfully majoritarian divisions that were nevertheless resolved by voice votes probably occurred on occasion. More importantly, the House had a series of maneuvers at its disposal for avoiding

---

[101] Ibid., vol. IV, 22–3, 27, 29, 30. The last division of the session, on 11 June, occurred amid the political climax of the session after Charles' calculated assent to the Petition of Right, and a last effort to save Buckingham from a specific condemnation within a Commons' Remonstrance concerning linked religious and political threats. Despite the fact that this general context certainly involved the status of the House, the specific issue on which the House divided – whether to make report from the committee on the Remonstrance at a specific time – appears to have been of only procedural significance. It was not mentioned in any of the extensive diary entries covering the debates of this day. See ibid., vol. IV, 236–77. In the 1629 session, no divisions were held.

divisions that could even be successful in situations of persistent disagreement on status-related issues. The status component of such issues certainly meant that members were more *willing* than usual to force divisions in order to resolve them. The presence of concerns over status may also have meant that forging consensus on these issues was intrinsically more difficult than forging consensus on other issues, because honor politics were not normally a realm of compromise. But none of this should be taken to imply that divisions resulted automatically when differences on matters of status were being addressed. Members still made efforts to forge a consensus and often attempted to forestall divisions in hopes of reaching a consensus, employing the usual array of tactics.[102] And while such efforts were being made, contingencies such as the ending of a session by the monarch could often intervene to make an otherwise likely division impossible. The point is simply that divisions were far more *likely* in situations where members were in persistent disagreement on a status-related issue, and this specific form of disagreement, unlike ideological or constitutional disagreement, appears to have been a necessary condition for the incidence of meaningfully majoritarian decisions.

The honor and privilege of the House and its members were so jealously guarded, it seems, because once compromised, they were hard to regain. Honor and other forms of status had to be constantly demonstrated, defended, and acknowledged in practice in order to be maintained. In a discussion during the only division in the Short Parliament – a lopsided vote in which members of the losing side refused to yield – one member made this point clearly. He remarked that "though the particular" was "of no moment," in the sense that it concerned the offensive but not particularly damaging actions of an individual, "yet we must divide, for maintaining the privilege of the House, lest we feel it in other occasions."[103] Most significant divisions before 1642 or so occurred on this basis.[104] The status of the House and its members, and, if possible, Parliament as a whole, was to be protected and maintained whenever possible.

Pinpointing the conditions under which the Commons' institution of consensus decision-making failed clarifies why that institution was so

---

[102] Examples of such situations are presented at the beginning of Chapter 3.

[103] *Aston*, 115. A fairly detailed newsletter account of parliamentary proceedings in the final days of the Short Parliament does not mention this division or the issue it concerned (BL MS Add 11045, ff. 114r. –115v.).

[104] On occasion, divisions were provoked by divisive religious issues, which as we will see in Chapter 3 were usually subordinated to struggles over political authority that had a status component. See, for example, *POSLP*, vol. IV, 601–18.

remarkably stable before the outbreak of the Civil War. Consensus decisions resulted in this period under specific strategic conditions that nearly always prevailed. Normally, the status implications of dividing were so grave that even if all the tactics for avoiding a vote had failed, members of a minority would simply capitulate, by voice-voting with the other side, remaining silent, or simply not insisting on a division. A division would be forced only when the status implications of the highly contested question at hand were grave enough to demand it. This could include situations in which being seen on one side of an issue, even if one was sure to lose the vote, was considered to be more important, in status terms, than avoiding a division. There were secondary triggers to divisions as well. In many of the situations that led to divisions, at least one common means of avoiding them – conferencing – was not an option, because the matter at hand was an internal problem that the House had to solve by itself. Matters of privilege were one such class of situations. As Sir Simonds D'Ewes put it in 1642, "in matter of privileges of this House we are the judges ourselves."[105] There were also probably other situations in which debate or the passage of time was thought to endanger the prevalence of one's side, or simply to constitute a waste of time, because the agreement was thought incapable of resolution, precisely because of the grave matters of status involved. In this sort of predicament, it was possible for members to choose, despite the status costs entailed, to forego thorough debate altogether in favor of a snap vote that they believed would best protect their status given the available alternatives.

It is important to understand that this chapter's claims about the underpinnings of the consensual decision-making institution that prevailed in the pre–Civil War House of Commons do not require the assumption that in individual instances members were normally and consciously making the relevant strategic calculations about status identified here. Like most practices, consensual decision-making was almost certainly so routine that the maintenance of this pattern of conduct normally required little conscious, cognitive effort, and perhaps so fast-moving that pondering the procedural choices available in every situation would have been a waste of valuable cognitive resources. Yet none of this contradicts the notion that this institutionalized practice had an underlying strategic logic. That logic could certainly be violated on occasion by individual actors for a host of contingent reasons. Institutions induce patterns of behavior; they do not lay down universal, inviolable rules.

[105] *PJLP*, vol. II, 11.

Even more importantly, if novel circumstances repeatedly put before even the least strategically nimble members tangible evidence that consensual decision-making was no longer logical, those members would gradually grow more conscious of the strategic underpinnings of such repeated situations and become more open to a practice that deviated from past routine.[106]

With this understanding of the Commons' institutionalized, consensual form of decision-making in place, it is easy to see what one would expect to lead to the increasing incidence of divisions over time in an otherwise consensual body that members witnessed to their dismay in the Long Parliament. The key determinant would likely be the increased incidence of motions on the floor of the Commons that could not be deflected, that provoked serious disagreement, and that concerned serious matters related to the status of the members, the House, the Parliament, or the monarchy as a whole. The institution that normally produced almost exclusively consensual decisions in the Commons would cease to do so to the extent that these destabilizing conditions were present, because these were the parameters under which the institution had always experienced failure. With enough consistent disruption of this sort, the institution itself could be fundamentally compromised and ultimately transformed. This was precisely what occurred after the outbreak of the Civil War.

---

[106] Greif, *Institutions and the Path to the Modern Economy*, esp. 18–23; Bourdieu, *Outline of a Theory of Practice*, esp. 72–82; Bourdieu and Wacquant, *Invitation to Reflexive Sociology*, 131; Bourdieu, *Practical Reason*, 75–6, 79–83; Bourdieu, *Logic of Practice*, 60–4; Ermakoff, "Theory of Practice, Rational Choice, and Historical Change."

3   Consensus Imperiled, 1640–1641

The Tudor and early Stuart pattern was permanently altered over the course of the 1640s. But the shift did not occur immediately. In the entire Short Parliament, which met for three weeks in April and May 1640, and in the first five months of the Long, between early November 1640 and early April 1641, the House held only six significant divisions. Enumerated votes were held only every twenty days and only after two out of every hundred questions put. This meant that divisions were significantly *less* frequent in this period than during the earlier Stuart parliaments. Issues related to the constitutional, religious, and military crisis already under consideration by the House in these months included supply for war with the Scots, prerogative taxation, church reform, the actions of royal judges, monopolies, the earl of Strafford, other royal counselors, and the future of parliaments. But not even the presence of this series of difficult problems and decisions was sufficient to prompt a majoritarian pattern in the Commons' decision-making. Indeed, the division frequency per question put in the Commons remained remarkably stable until the very end of 1642 – months after the outbreak of civil war (Figure 2.1 and Table 2.1). There could hardly be a greater demonstration of the ability of the Commons' consensual decision-making institution to absorb an onslaught of severe political discord within and without the House and an unprecedented level of public pressure on its work.

The general reason for the lack of divisions between April 1640 and early April 1641 was not an absence of status-related issues under consideration, but rather a basic agreement in the House of Commons on how to *begin* opposition to the recent actions of Charles I's regime that had significant status components. The Commons of the Short Parliament was by no means dominated by the godly or the constitutionally radical, but its membership was overwhelmingly opposed to the policies of the Personal Rule.[1] This ground for agreement, combined

---

[1] On the Short Parliament, see Russell, *Fall of the British Monarchies*, 94–121.

with the successful use of consensual tactics, including committees and conferences, ensured that divisions in this session were rare, despite its high political temperature. The only truly difficult issue was a constitutionally loaded and familiar matter of process: the question of whether the House should compromise on some of their grievances in order to comply with the king's request for supply. There were status elements to both the grievance and the supply sides of this question. Grievances were often centered on the privileges and authority of Parliament, while denials of supply, as well as any divisions on supply, were commonly thought to hazard dishonor to the king, the nation, and its representatives in the Commons. Indeed, the House's very ability to order its own proceedings, speak freely on grievances, and initiate supply was itself understood in terms of privilege.

In 1640 and 1641, business related to violations of privilege was conducted on a daily basis. Other proceedings were regularly interrupted when perceived threats to the House's status suddenly emerged. Normally, members agreed on how to proceed, but even in situations where they were at variance on these status-related problems, they usually managed to avoid dividing on them. During an 18 April 1640 debate on possible violations of privilege at the end of the 1629 session, one diarist noted that "after long debates" the House was "not able to come to the question." In response, a subcommittee was formed to examine violations of privilege on the final day of that session. At the Commons' next meeting, on 20 April, the committee made its report, and "after a long and various debate," according to the journal, it was resolved on the question, without a division, that the Speaker's manner of adjourning the 1629 session had been a breach of privilege.[2] This was a charged debate about a perceived threat to the status of the House. The ability to avoid a division here is remarkable but clearly attributable to the effective use of debate and the committee system.

Alternatively, in two other trying situations on 22 and 23 April, the House made use of a conference with the Lords to channel persistent dispute. On the 22nd it agreed on the question to resolve an extended debate about Convocation and religious innovation by moving to a conference. The next day the Commons debated in committee of the whole an entire host of grievances with an eye to the question of whether to pursue supply or grievances first. After extensive discussion the House resolved by acclamation to pursue a conference on the grievances under discussion. On the 24th it agreed by voice vote to a series of heads for that

---

[2] CJ, 4/20/1640; *Aston*, 13–22; *PSP*, 161–3.

conference. And on the following day, at the conference itself and at the king's urging, the Lords pressed the Commons to prioritize supply. Two days later, in the Commons, the House resolved by voice vote that the Lords had violated their privileges in the conference by pressing them on supply, which was taken to be the preserve of the Commons. This occurred after considerable debate, strong consensus among members who were not royal spokesmen, and requests by some members to refer the matter to committee.[3] Consensual decisions like these ones were of a piece with others from the Short Parliament that were less centrally concerned with status.[4]

Recourse to committees and conferences was certainly an important means of delaying decisions and building consensus, but these practices were probably also appealing to many members because they bolstered the Commons' efforts to prioritize grievances over supply in the face of the king's demands. This introduces what will be a recurring theme of the 1640s and later periods as well: the techniques of consensus politics often served as effective political tactics. The initiation of committees and conferences commonly diverted the House's business and precious time away from the consideration of supply and toward grievances, a widely popular course of action in general. At the same time, the House was still managing to avoid firm statements on these grievances and thereby forestall internal conflict. By agreeing to either committing or conferencing, members were merely consenting to the House taking up more time with grievances without entering into potentially more divisive discussions about the specific stances the House might take on those grievances and the most acceptable means of redressing them.

Parliament did not, however, have full control of these dynamics in the spring of 1640. While in late April the Commons had successfully stalled on supply without clearly declaring for or against it, the king was unwilling to let matters rest there. As a result, the Commons came to the brink of a very significant division that seems to have been averted only by Charles' dissolution of the Short Parliament. On 2 May Sir Henry Vane senior relayed a message from the king that called out the Commons on their tactics: "[D]elay of supply," he said, "is as destructive as denial" because it threatened "great danger" to "the whole state, upon his own honour, and the honour of this nation." Grievances, the king reminded his subjects, were not the only pressing threats to the status and authority

---

[3] CJ, 4/22/1640, 4/23/1640, 4/24/1640, 4/27/1640; *Aston*, 30–44, 49–59, 67–76; *PSP*, 168–80; Russell, *Fall of the British Monarchies*, 113.

[4] See, for example, Russell, *Fall of the British Monarchies*, 114–16; CJ, 4/30/1640; *Aston*, 99–109; *PSP*, 184–5.

of the nation's representatives. The Commons debated Charles' message at length into the evening but at last resolved not to put it to a question and to continue debate in a subsequent meeting. Here again a common means of consensus-building was being used for a secondary purpose as well: it delivered a sharp message to the king.[5] On 4 May Vane returned to the Commons with a new message from Charles, who offered to abandon ship money as a source of revenue in exchange for twelve subsidies. By setting the terms of debate so narrowly, the king made it difficult for those willing to grant supply under different conditions to appear supportive while continuing to delay.

Debate went on until six at night, with many urging the House to put the question whether "the legality or illegality of ship money be first debated and voted, before we give an answer to the king's business." Again members were justifying politically motivated inaction with reference to consensual norms of procedure. They argued for delay "by reason of the difference of opinions" and because "no motion that was not either for a peremptory 'I' or 'Noe' would please the one side, nor the other were pleased with any that might imply any consent till first their grievances were voted." Charles Jones argued for "the question of legality [to be] waived" because the House "would not have a question to which they must say noe. We would not have a question put with which we must say 'noe' to the king." The House thus resolved to adjourn for further discussion the next day, "which the king took for a delay."[6] He responded by immediately dissolving Parliament.

In the spring of 1640, high political stakes, controversy, and ideological conflict were in themselves unable seriously to damage the institution of consensual decision-making. Such damage could occur only under more specifically trying conditions. Similar conclusions emerge from a survey of some of the important business done in the first five months of the Long Parliament, between early November 1640 until early April 1641. In this period, again, the Commons were largely united in their desire publicly to expose and repudiate the policies and machinations of the Personal Rule on all levels – political, fiscal, judicial, and religious.[7] This unity prevailed despite members differing in their specific views on the nature of royal policies, the reasons for opposing them, the best means of opposing them, and the best means of replacing them. The cause was largely taken up by the Commons in the form of

---

[5] CJ, 5/2/1640; *Aston*, 121–7; *PSP*, 188–93, 206–8.

[6] *Aston*, 128–44; *PSP*, 193–7, 208–10; Russell, *Fall of the British Monarchies*, 119–21.

[7] In addition to Adamson, *Noble Revolt*, see for analysis Millstone, *Manuscript Circulation*, 275–315.

the investigation of innumerable cases of abuse. The investigations were conducted both by the House as a whole and by a proliferation of small committees. The House thus became clogged with business that proceeded slowly but largely consensually. Significant bills were few and slow to progress. For the most part, latent tensions among members became clear only after January 1641, partly because the leading reformist member, John Pym, and his allies had taken a self-consciously moderated approach up to that point. Here again conflict grew more likely once the Commons, and in particular the Bedford House group – which included Pym, the earl of Bedford, and their allies in both houses – returned to the problem of addressing the financial needs of a monarchy whose fiscal apparatus had now been largely decimated. Pym and his allies yoked the satisfaction of the king's demands to the satisfaction of the Commons' demands for a reversal in Charles' counsels, a broader set of royal concessions, or a new political and religious settlement.

Eventually, this situation, which lasted until March, raised the difficult issue of precisely what concessions would be required of the king in exchange for funds. Once negotiation with the king became the order of the day, the Commons was bound to come into internal conflict over questions of how exactly to move forward. Nearly two years later, in the winter of 1642–3, precisely the same sort of predicament would cause majoritarian decisions to become commonplace for the first time in parliamentary history. Early in 1641, differences among members emerged over a series of interrelated issues: the treatment of Catholics, the reform of the English church, the treatment of the earl of Strafford, and negotiation with the Scots.[8] Yet in general, even under these conditions, the lower house managed to handle a long series of grave and potentially controversial matters in the traditional way. Since most of this business concerned the status of the House rather directly, its members were able to avoid divisions only because they tended to agree or came to agree on how to deal with the problems that emerged. A host of difficult issues was resolved without recourse to divisions, including taxation for funding the northern armies, religious reforms, condemnations of the policies of the Personal Rule, prosecutions of its agents, aspects of the Scottish settlement, and the Triennial Act.

On 30 December 1640, for instance, a bill for annual parliaments was read for the second time. This bill was obviously an initiative to protect and even enhance the status of Parliament after it had not been permitted to meet for over a decade. In debate, Sir Simonds D'Ewes urged the

---

[8] For this and the previous paragraph, see Russell, *Fall of the British Monarchies*, 219–73; Adamson, *Noble Revolt*, 95–214.

House to withdraw the bill and draft another one. "Many," he reported, "cried 'well spoken'; and Sir John Wray seconded my motion. But the greater part of the House were much set upon the allowing of the bill; and so it was ordered to be committed."[9] In this case, members' sense of a strong majority on one side of the question apparently led most in the minority, including D'Ewes, to capitulate and thereby avoid a division. The bill that emerged from this committee, rewritten and retitled, was the triennial bill. It was debated thoroughly on 19 January 1641 after an initial speech in favor by Oliver St. John and a speech in opposition by the king's solicitor, Edward Herbert. Herbert argued that by guaranteeing triennial parliaments independently of the monarch's wishes, the bill took from the king one of his chief prerogatives. In a committee of the whole, "a number of objections and doubts," according to D'Ewes, were thrown at the bill, "which when they could not be satisfied with reason they were allowed upon the question by the multitude of voices." After this forced compromise, Sir Thomas Peyton reported, "the bill was put to the question" in committee "and the yeas were many. The noes were not many." After this vote in committee of the whole, the Speaker retook the chair. "Diverse spoke against the said bill" at this point, too, according to D'Ewes. But on a voice vote the bill was nevertheless ordered to be engrossed. It was read for a third time the following day and passed without a division.[10]

Another example of the House's successful use of traditional mechanisms in difficult situations comes from two days later, on 21 January. Members were reiterating concerns raised during the Short Parliament about the Commons' right to control the provision of subsidies and paying close attention to the symbolism of their actions on this front. Accordingly, the House debated at length whether their subsidy bill should address the king as "your Majesty's most humble subjects the Commons in this your High Court of Parliament," or whether "the Commons" should be left out, in order to indicate that in this area the Commons spoke for Parliament as a whole. The status of the Commons was again clearly at issue. "Myself and others desired to have it put to the question, so to determine the dispute," D'Ewes wrote in his diary. "But it growing late, it was rather desired that we should forbear to put the question and to defer the determination of this dispute till tomorrow, when it was possible we might be more united in our opinions

---

[9] *POSLP*, vol. II, 62, 65. The bill was committed by putting the question.

[10] Ibid., vol. II, 222–5, 228, 229, 231. In taking the final vote the Speaker asked if the bill should pass "for a law" or "as a law." This language, according to Peyton, was unprecedented and understood as such "by most."

by conference with one another." D'Ewes and a few others, at least, were apparently willing to endorse a slightly majoritarian way of proceeding here, although they may have assumed that the weaker side would simply capitulate in the voice vote. Whatever their intent, their suggestion was overruled on traditional grounds. Given more time to deliberate, other members assumed, the Commons would emerge with a genuine consensus. The issue was in fact apparently resolved informally in between sittings (this is apparently what D'Ewes meant when he referred to "conference with one another") and addressed with no further debate the following day.[11]

In a final important example from the early months of the Long Parliament, on 10 March 1641 the House debated a matter central to Parliament's institutional composition. This was the first head of the ministers' remonstrance, which concerned the secular employment of clergy. The House first turned to address the role of bishops in the House of Lords, Star Chamber, commissions of the peace, Privy Council, and temporal offices. After an extensive debate with many differences expressed on the role of bishops in Parliament, the House voted without a division – "but four gainsaying it," D'Ewes said – to draw up a bill to take away the legislative and judicial power of the bishops in the House of Lords because it was "a great hindrance to the discharge of their spiritual function" and "prejudicial to the commonwealth." The second part of the first head of the proposed bill was addressed the following day, and with very little debate and unanimous voice votes, the other secular functions of bishops were also voted to be removed by bill.[12]

Even in cases where divisions occurred in this period, the overall maintenance of consensual decision-making was notable. One example comes from perhaps the most contentious debate in the Commons before April 1641: the discussions on 8 and 9 February concerning the famous London root and branch petition for the abolition of episcopacy, the ministers' remonstrance, and other related issues. These debates involved one division, which will be discussed later. But more than anything these debates indicated the general persistence of traditional deliberation, and the ingenuity that was so often employed in maintaining traditional norms. After a tactful reframing of the question by the Speaker, the issues raised in the ministers' remonstrance and the London petition were committed, with the exception of the thorny problem of episcopacy, which was reserved for debate by the full House at an

---

[11] Ibid., vol. II, 85, 89. The bill was finally passed on 18 January: "[A]ll or most ... cried aye," according to D'Ewes (ibid., vol. II, 216).
[12] Ibid., vol. II, 693, 695–7, 699–701, 702–3, 710–11.

undetermined time in the future. On 20 February, the House was unable to reach a consensus on whether to grant a further two subsidies to support the northern armies on the Scottish border. In addition to noting the usual honor considerations involved in discussions of supply, some members framed the issue in terms of resolution. They argued that the House could maintain its honor in this situation only by remaining true to its prior assurances of support for the northern forces. As D'Ewes put it in one of his speeches, "we were bound both in honour and necessity to make this grant ... to supply the necessities of the northern parts and the king's army, for the maintenance and relief of both, which we had engaged ourselves, so as in us the word and promises of the whole kingdom was also plighted and voted." The House resolved the impasse by dividing on a previous question in a committee of the whole, 195 to 129, in favor of subsidies. This vote in committee, which did not have the same significance as a vote in the House, conveyed the information needed for capitulations to occur. The members were able to hold two successful voice votes on the substantive issue (the granting of the subsidies themselves) – one in committee, and one in the House proper. The Commons thereby avoided both dividing on the substantive issue and recording a division in the journal.[13]

By contrast, the significant divisions that did occur between early April 1640 and early April 1641 prefigured the sorts of situations that would trigger a constant flow of majoritarian decisions a few months after the outbreak of civil war. The division that occurred four days before the end of the Short Parliament, on 1 May 1640, has already been described briefly in the previous chapter. Pym led an attack on a sermon by William Beale that had belittled the legal authority of Parliament. Pym insisted on sending for Beale simply on information but without proof. The House was packed for the debate over how to proceed. A large minority appears to have thought the House would reap more dishonor by haste, especially when proceeding against a cleric who could claim privilege as both a member of Convocation and a royal chaplain. The conflict here was clearly one in which the status of Parliament was stake for members on both sides of the debate. The ostensible issue at hand, however, was not a general matter of constitutional principle, but an individual case and its procedural details, which made a division, at least on the surface, less significant.[14]

---

[13]   Ibid., vol. II, 390–3, 396–401, 496–502.

[14]   *Aston*, 112–13; *PSP*, 185–6, 205; Russell, *Fall of the British Monarchies*, 116; CJ, 5/1/ 1640. It is in fact unclear how serious this division was taken, aside from the fact that it cost the House time at a moment when the Lords were requesting a conference.

The first important division of the Long Parliament occurred on its first day of business, 6 November 1640. It too was triggered by the question of how to respond to an individual, absolutist threat to parliamentary authority and longevity. But on this occasion, the threat was that posed by the ultimate symbol of Charles' supposedly malign counsels, the earl of Strafford. Before dividing the Commons agreed in a voice vote to set up a Committee for Irish Affairs that would spearhead the prosecution of Strafford. This was itself a constitutionally aggressive move, since it assumed English parliamentary authority over Ireland. The House then divided very closely, 165 to 152, with a strong turnout, over the ostensibly procedural question of whether this committee would be a select committee or operate as a committee of the whole. In substance, however, the Commons was dividing over the question of whether this committee would be a slow-moving one, burdened by the need to develop consensus among a large group of members but saved from suspicion of faction, or whether it would be a swiftly moving committee of the more like-minded that might easily be seen as partisan. The majority preferred the former course. This demonstrated widespread opposition to the procedures advocated by the most committed anti-Straffordians and was probably rooted in considerable opposition to the constitutional assumptions underlying their efforts.[15] This decision about committee work, of course, was not one that could be avoided with recourse to committee or conference. It was therefore more likely, for procedural reasons, to be made with recourse to a division. Finally, in such a close and well-attended division, discernment of a clear majority and consequent yielding by the minority before the enumeration of votes was impracticable.

The second division of note called in the Long Parliament concerned taxation, an issue on which consensus was usually at a premium. On 13, 16, and 19 November the House had agreed after long debate but without a division to raise a lump sum of £100,000 for the armies in the north. On 10 December, they debated further the means of doing so, and in particular, whether traditional subsidies were in fact the best course, thus reconsidering a vote from 19 November in favor of a lump sum. In arguing for the lump sum, Pym wanted to avoid an

---

"It was," one witness wrote, "thought a small matter for the house to be divided about." The best interpretation of this vote is either that it was a status-significant division of an ostensibly personal nature or that it was simply insignificant. Both interpretations fit with the previous chapter's general account of the incidence of divisions under an institutionally consensual regime.

[15] Russell, *Fall of the British Monarchies*, 214; Adamson, *Noble Revolt*, 95–8; *POSLP*, vol. I, 20, 22.

underassessment in order to convince Charles to trade this guaranteed revenue for a change in his counsels. His position was strengthened by the urgent need to pay off the Scottish army. He and D'Ewes also considered backtracking to vote subsidies to be inappropriate because, in D'Ewes' words, it was "against the honour and greatness of this House to change their order," and according to Pym, "contrary to all former precedents to alter what we have done and agreed on." Resolution, again, was the honorable course. Pym, D'Ewes, and others also opposed voting subsidies before grievances had been redressed.[16]

The king's ministers, however, preferred the traditional method of taxation. Debate eventually turned to whether the House would put the question to consider the topic in a committee of the whole or put the question to alter their former order and provide two subsidies. The opponents of a subsidy preferred a committee of the whole because they wanted a chance to delay and to persuade more members of their position. The previous question was put for a committee of the whole but it failed on a division in which the yeas yielded before votes were actually tallied. This set up a question on whether to switch the raising of funds to subsidies, which was then predictably carried without a division, since it had been substantively resolved in the previous vote.[17] This was a confrontation between figures like Pym and D'Ewes and those who were relatively unconcerned with the possibility that following the king's preferred course posed a threat to the House's status. When that confrontation came to settle on a specific procedural move, there was no justification for avoiding it with recourse to the usual tactics. In a sense, the House was dividing on whether to engage in one such tactic, from which only one party to the vote could see itself benefiting. The vote was in this sense similar to the division on 6 November.

The third important division of the Long Parliament occurred, as noted earlier, during the famous debate on religious reform in early February 1641. Yet its significance was mostly political, not religious. Many members were well aware that Charles would be unwilling to assent to the triennial bill if Parliament continued to meddle with the abolition of episcopacy. They had agreed to entrust further discussion of the London root and branch petition, the ministers' remonstrance, and a series of county petitions to a committee of twenty-four on church affairs, which was dominated by episcopalians. They divided over whether six

---

[16] *POSLP*, vol. I, 129–41, 154, 156, 158, 159, 160, 186, 188, 189, 191, 193, 198, 552–5; Russell, *Fall of the British Monarchies*, 242; Lambert, "Opening of the Long Parliament," 268–9.

[17] *POSLP*, vol. I, 555–8.

new members, most of them strong advocates of extensive church reform, including two supporters of root and branch, should be added to the committee. This change would jeopardize the committee's status as a sign that Charles no longer had to worry about the Commons considering root and branch legislation. In other words, the ultimate issues here were the triennial bill, the fundamental means of protecting Parliament's status in this moment; the question of what specific tactics best conduced to that end; and the question of whether religious concerns superseded institutional concerns.[18] In this situation, too, it is obvious that the decision at hand – on committee membership – could not have been referred to another setting.

The first of two significant divisions from March featured the largest turnout of the entire Long Parliament. This division was over whether to imprison Thomas Chaffin for a 1634 sermon that reflected "in an ill and scandalous sense upon parliaments." Chaffin had allegedly said that in his litanies he would always use the supplication "from lay puritans and lay parliaments good Lord deliver us." Once again the question was too specific to be deferred for a superficial reason. At least one member found the process of division here – the only one from this period not ostensibly concerned with an internal procedural question – unbearable. Richard Shuttleworth, "sitting still saying nothing," refused to engage in the process. "Some said he must be an aye, some said a no, but it was concluded that he must be a no." His was the deciding vote in a 190 to 189 division. Sir Thomas Peyton observed in his diary that "herein is to be seen the danger of admitting infants into the House, when it may come to a single vote to overthrow any law."[19] The predicament posed by such divisions apparently exhausted the nerves of some of the House's least experienced members, and for more experienced members, the inability of the Commons to reach a consensus rendered it subject to the will of infants.

All four of these divisions from 1640 and early 1641 exhibit a series of important characteristics. Each division was in part driven by important ideological differences but also dealt with an ostensibly procedural matter, usually one internal to the work of the House. This meant that while the House could maintain a veneer of consensus on underlying matters of constitutional principle and the Commons' relationship with the king, it could not successfully defer a decision on the procedural

---

[18] *POSLP*, vol. II, 396–402; Adamson, *Noble Revolt*, 184–5. See also Glow, "Manipulation of Committees in the Long Parliament," 41–4. On the heated, adversarial tenor of interaction in the Commons at this point, see also BL MS Add 64922, ff. 3v.–4r.

[19] *POSLP*, vol. II, 583, 585–6, 588–90; Russell, *Fall of the British Monarchies*, 279.

matter at hand, because these decisions were fit for neither committee nor conference. In addition, these divisions clearly dealt, in substantive terms, with serious disagreements over perceived slights to Parliament or threats to its status that had legal or broader constitutional significance. They also involved disagreements over what it meant to respond and proceed in such situations in an honorable manner in order to preserve the authority and legitimacy of the Lords and Commons alike. These considerations were what forced divisions to occur.

In all of these incidents, conflicts over status overlapped with ideological dilemmas. Ideological differences probably did make such debates more likely to end in a majoritarian decision. But only disagreement over the status dimension of these decisions was a necessary condition for the divisions that resulted. This was the fundamental source of these decisions' intractability. Ideological and confessional conflicts and disagreements were neither necessary nor sufficient causes of divisions. Countless decisions in which such conflicts and disagreements played a role were resolved in a nonmajoritarian manner when they did not also involve conflicting positions on the maintenance of status. Majoritarian decisions of political import nearly always had a clear status dimension, but they did not always have a clear ideological or confessional dimension.

In the early 1640s, conflicts over the fundamental issue of honorable conduct were eventually manifest in frequent confrontations between royalist and parliamentarian members. These episodes confirmed the increasing entanglement of matters of status and matters of ideology and constitutional principle. An early indication of this entanglement was the only other publicly significant division held before early April 1641. The House was voting on whether it should commit (and therefore at least delay) discussion and determination on a Scottish treaty article proffered in March that would have sent the Scottish army back over the border. This was plainly part of Charles' struggle with Parliament over the Scottish crisis, and it reflected Parliament's use of the presence of the Scots army in England as a negotiation tool. Here again, the key circumstance that led to a division was the fact that the specific decision at hand was about internal procedure and could not itself be deferred by conventional means. When divisive episodes like this one became routine over the next few years, the maintenance of the Commons' status would gradually become attached not solely to consensus decision-making but to allegedly honorable responses to external circumstances that could justifiably (if regrettably) be preceded by a division and the recognition of internal conflict. Every time such a rupture occurred, the House's status was potentially becoming less consistently (and less plausibly) maintained solely through the production of consensus. The strong association between status and consensus was being disrupted, if only occasionally, for actors and observers alike. The implicit dilemma here was that either one esteemed Parliament despite its internal dissension because of the honorable but divisive actions in which it was engaged or one rejected its status outright on the grounds that it had been taken over by a faction, thus insisting on the traditional association between consensus and legitimacy. This dilemma was in no way acute or systematic in effect early in 1641. But even the earliest divisions held during the mounting constitutional crisis reveal the essential tension that would help produce both royalism in the coming months and revolution later in the decade.

There is also a final, related way in which these early divisions were proleptic in nature. All three of them were precipitated by the desire of a group in the Commons – a group in which Pym figured prominently – to work aggressively against threats to the Commons' status in ways that many considered to be legally dubious or at least rash. The problem of defending parliamentary honor thus became bound up with Parliament's increasingly novel assertions of constitutional authority. Other members, however, viewed these assertions themselves as threats to the House's honor. The tension here was difficult to resolve. Similar scenarios would come to dominate the breakdown of consensus decision-making in the thirty months to follow.

The intractability of this tension also had a personal dimension. Arguably, by December 1640 a recognized, distinct group of peers and commoners – which in the lower house included Pym, Oliver St. John, Nathaniel Fiennes, Denzell Holles, Henry Vane, Jr., William Strode, Sir Walter Earle, Sir John Hotham, and John Hampden – was beginning regularly to initiate confrontations over parliamentary authority with a significant degree of coordination, aided by the relatively unfettered circulation of ecclesiastical and political print. In most cases, these men's concern for the status of the House was intimately bound up with the more basic question of their own survival. This limited their ability to seek consensus with those who favored a less aggressive approach to dealings with the king. Most of these men had been involved with the Petition of the Twelve Peers and the treasonous collusion with the Scots in the summer of 1640. This predicament made them violently averse to even the possibility of being exposed to royal justice. This in turn narrowed the space for compromise with Charles.[20] The mere presence of organized attempts to augment the power of Parliament in early

---

[20] Adamson, *Noble Revolt*, 138–40; Como, *Radical Parliamentarians and the English Civil War*, 88–9 (on the connections of this group to the radical press).

1641 did not in itself, however, lead to further divisions. It had to be combined with even-sided conflict on a specific problem with an important status dimension. In addition, we do not see for this period, as we do for later periods, any strong evidence that Pym, his allies, or others willingly engaged in majoritarian tactics to achieve their ends, even if their ends contributed to a few majoritarian outcomes.

Mounting Failures: April 1641–December 1642

Between April 1641 and December 1642 the Commons' traditional decision-making regime was significantly weakened. The House held more divisions in this eight-month period (107 in total) than in the entire period between 1604 and 1629 (ninety-one in total). From late November 1641 these divisions were also regularly reported, without vote tallies, in printed newspapers.[21] While the frequency of divisions per question put remained largely consistent with early Stuart levels in this period (Table 2.1 and Figure 2.1), the Commons was dividing at a rate of once every five days in session between April 1641 and December 1642, as opposed to once every fourteen in the period between 1614 and March 1641 (Table 2.1 and Figure 3.1). From 7 May onward, one possible limiter of the incidence of divisions was removed when Charles assented to Parliament being dissolved only by its own consent. The House's stream of business could no longer be interrupted or delimited by the directives or initiatives of an external entity. The king's basic means of agenda control had evaporated.

It is worth recalling too that divisions in earlier periods had dealt overwhelmingly with private and other insignificant issues. Division frequency figures from those periods, as low as they are, actually exaggerate the frequency of institutional failures. Divisions in the 1640s, in stark contrast, were almost always of public significance, and therefore almost always institutional failures. In addition, a number of important voice votes during this period can be confirmed to have been meaningfully majoritarian: they were not close enough to cause a division, but they nevertheless represented a partial failure of consensual processes and, sometimes, a striking willingness among members to proceed with divisive votes.[22] All this suggests a rather significant increase in meaningfully

---

[21] On the role of print in the widening circulation of information on and factional analysis of Parliament in this period, see Peacey, *Print and Public Politics in the English Revolution*, esp. 125–228.

[22] For relatively clear examples, see *POSLP*, vol. IV, 10, 76, 417; vol. V, 206; vol. VI, 584; *D'Ewes*, 47, 92, 101–2, 281; *PJLP*, vol. II, 185, 350, 357; vol. III, 96. When appropriate, the transcriptions of Sir John Holland's parliamentary diary (Bodl. MS Rawl. D.932)

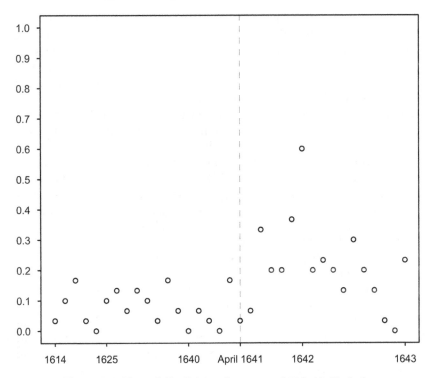

Figure 3.1 Mean daily division frequency, 1614–42. Each dot represents a period of thirty days in session. Tick marks are located on the thirty-day unit that includes the beginning of each year.

majoritarian decisions between spring 1641 and the end of 1642. While there is no precise way of measuring it, members were at least coming considerably closer to a point where divisions on matters of national importance would no longer be seen as rare and anomalous failures of normal parliamentary conduct, but rather as somewhat common – if still regrettable – episodes.

Traditional practices nevertheless continued in important situations. The House regularly managed to reduce disagreement through debate and avoid divisions with recourse to the usual tactics of commission and conferencing. On 22 April 1641, for instance, after extended debate, an aggressive bill for excluding clergy from secular employments, which did not directly touch on the status of Parliament, was "at last committed to

available in the footnotes of *D'Ewes* have been cited as *D'Ewes* in place of references to the original.

avoid further dispute." The bill was ordered to be engrossed without any apparent further debate the following day and passed unanimously a week later.[23] On 3 May, the Army Plot was revealed and the Protestation taken. The genesis, drafting, and approval of the Protestation, which explicitly involved a defense of the privileges of Parliament, is a revealing example of the persistence of consensual decision-making. Pym's initial motion to draft an oath of association for the defense of Crown and Church in the morning was greeted by a chorus of nearly unanimous approval in the speeches that followed, and a committee was named to draft the document he proposed. Dispute emerged only after the committee presented a protestation in the afternoon and the wording and nature of the document were debated. After about two hours' debate the document was recommitted and some of its critics were added to the committee in order to absorb dispute on the religious language of the Protestation and the extent to which protesting would be obligatory. When a redrafted version was presented in the evening, the Commons resolved apparently with no further debate to have the Protestation sworn by all 379 members present. Everyone had apparently taken the Protestation by seven o'clock.[24]

The House was in agreement on the matters of status related to the Protestation and it had successfully managed a series of non-status-related, specific disputes about the wording and use of the document. This case is all the more remarkable because the purpose of this initiative seems to have been in part to identify Parliament's enemies and unify its true friends. Its ideologically radical implications and its origins in the agenda of Pym and his allies were in themselves insufficient for provoking any meaningfully majoritarian decisions on the matter, even when the entire deliberation was crammed into a day's business. The connection between consensus and honor was in fact crucial to the Protestation's perceived effectiveness: it was intended, as Pym had put it, "for the better evidence of their union and unanimity, which would be the greatest discouragement to all who wished ill to them."[25]

Similarly, effective use of committees of the whole enabled the consensual resolution of numerous debates on various forms of taxation (including subsidies and tonnage and poundage) that either did not concern the status of Parliament or benefited from a consensus about how to approach the issue in this particular context. On 26 June, for instance, the House debated whether to specify poll tax rates for peers before sending a poll tax bill to the Lords. D'Ewes spoke in favor,

---

[23] *POSLP*, vol. IV, 60, 74, 160.   [24] Walter, *Covenanting Citizens*, 14–28.
[25] *POSLP*, vol. IV, 180. On the ideological character of the Protestation, see Walter, *Covenanting Citizens*, esp. 36–49.

stressing that the House's right to do this was implied by their control over supply and had ample precedent. Edward Hyde, according to D'Ewes, "spoke what he could against my advice but without any effect, for I was seconded by two or three and had wholly convinced the rest of the House, so as when the Speaker put it to the question it passed without a negative."[26] In this case there was indeed disagreement over a status-related issue, but the minority was either tiny and yielded or it became genuinely convinced of the alternative position.

The divisions that did occur, meanwhile, continued to be overwhelmingly related to perceived threats to the honor, privilege, existence, or authority of the House of Commons, the Parliament as whole, or its members in particular. Even on a conservative interpretation, well over half of the divisions in the 1640–2 period concerned status-related issues. These sorts of divisions occurred more than three times as often as the next most prominent issue: religion. Even apparently religious divisions were in this period normally driven by connections to overwhelming political (and honor-bound) considerations. There were a few situations in which divisions occurred before the outbreak of the Civil War on public issues that were not ultimately related to status. But for all the importance of ideological and confessional considerations in many individual instances, there were hardly any non-status-related divisions in 1641, before clear conflicts between royalists and parliamentarians and among parliamentarians had begun to emerge and became an underlying source of many divisions that was itself, of course, related to the status of Parliament. These emerging factional or partisan divisions even apparently helped to provoke a few early, unambiguous examples of members willingly pursuing enumerated votes.[27] In other words, the turn to majoritarian decision-making clearly began with and continued primarily to be driven by considerations of status. But this development was soon reinforced by the wider constitutional, ideological, and religious crises of the day.

It is therefore no accident that divisions became more frequent during and after the trial, attainder, and execution of the earl of Strafford. The Strafford controversies exposed conflicts between loyalists and those seeking to undermine monarchical power, but they also exposed conflicts among reformists. The divisions in the Commons directly related to Strafford's fate highlight most of the emergent, majoritarian patterns of decision-making that would characterize the period from April 1641 to

---

[26] *POSLP*, vol. V, 368.
[27] See, for instance, *D'Ewes*, 181–7; *PJLP*, vol. I, 268–9; vol. II, 294. These situations will be addressed in more detail in the next section.

the outbreak of civil war in August 1642. The Strafford trial was of course closely tied to a series of other politically significant issues. The first important division to occur during the trial was held on 9 April 1641, when the House voted on whether to extend for a fortnight England's truce with the Scots, which was set to expire in a week's time. The day before, the Commons' leaders had presided over a disastrous session of the trial, in which the earl had humiliated his enemies. At the same time, the Scots remained unwilling to complete a treaty and withdraw their forces until the trial was concluded and the earl destroyed. As the Scots waited, the cost to Parliament of maintaining their army in England mounted. These fiscal burdens and the apparent collapse of the trial combined to weaken support in the Commons for the Scottish-friendly agenda of Pym and his "Junto" allies. It amplified sentiment in favor of risking the lapse of the truce and England's reentry into a state of war with the Scots. In other words, the pro-Scots leadership of the prosecution of Strafford was being forced to advocate fiscally unpopular measures that their critics believed were also dishonorable. D'Ewes argued against these critics that a continued truce and union between the kingdoms was the honorable course. The debate lasted until seven at night. When the question was put for extending the truce, the Speaker stated that the ayes had clearly carried the voice vote. "Yet the negatives," D'Ewes recalled, "would not so rest satisfied." They forced a division and lost by nearly forty votes.[28]

The next division during the trial was held a week later, on 16 April. A bill of attainder against Strafford – which now competed with the trial as a possible means of proceeding effectively against the Earl – had just been read a second time. Members differed over whether to abandon the impeachment proceedings and focus on the attainder. A committee met to prepare heads to propose for a conference with the Lords about further trial proceedings. The heads included the Commons' desire to "send a committee of this House only to hear what his [Strafford's] counsel shall say" in matters of law. This head was subject to dispute. Pym argued that "if we did not go this way to have it heard publicly in matter of law as well as it had been heard for matter of fact, we should much dishonour ourselves, hazard our safeguard, and put upon ourselves the impossibility

---

[28] *POSLP*, vol. III, 477–8, 480–2; Adamson, *Noble Revolt*, 233–4. The official tally was 167 to 128. Other sources report wider margins, including "about 140 being against it and 240 for it" and 187 to 128 in favor (*POSLP*, vol. III, 480, 481). See also Bodleian Tanner MS 66, f. 50r., for another 140 to 240 tally and reflections on importance of honor to the debate. It was considered "dishonourable to move from that House (the representative body of the kingdom) unless either the Scots or the Lords Commissioners of the upper house should move it as formerly."

ever to bring it to pass." Others also framed the matter in terms of honor. The question was put twice because the first voice vote was doubtful. After a second doubtful voice vote tellers were appointed, but the noes yielded to the yeas. This all occurred in between a series of far more lopsided voice votes resolving that Strafford had endeavored to subvert the laws and was therefore guilty of high treason.[29]

The final division of this crucial period in the spring of 1641 was the 21 April vote on Strafford's attainder. D'Ewes' anxiety at this moment was acute: he wrote a large proportion of his diary entry for the day in cipher, and he noted the tenor of votes in more detail than usual. The attainder bill was first taken up in a committee of the whole. The members present voted to incorporate into the preamble of the bill alterations and additions voted by a subcommittee, "there being only some three or four noes," according to D'Ewes. Afterward the members voted on some other provisos moved to be added to the bill. In the middle of the process, the Speaker suddenly resumed the chair. At this point, many members rose to leave the chamber. In response, at one moment the door was locked and no one was permitted to go in or out without license. Apparently, members were already trying to avoid the looming final decision, which would likely involve a division. Once the proviso debates in committee were concluded, Gervase Holles had in fact asked to be excused from the House. "He declared," D'Ewes wrote, "that he knew we did nothing but in truth and justice, yet being in a case of blood, his conscience being not satisfied, it would be murder in him which was but justice in the House. And therefore desired to be excused in that he did not give his assent to the bill." His request appears to have been denied, because he was among the "noe" voters in the final tally. The Speaker then put the question for engrossing a revised bill. "Many more said aye than no," according to D'Ewes. The House rose at this point, intending to reassemble at three o'clock for the final reading of the bill of attainder.[30]

When the Speaker returned to the House at three, many members were "in the Court of Requests and other places near adjoining," so "the sergeant was sent with his mace to fetch them in." A final debate followed the third reading of the attainder bill. In his controversial speech at the beginning of this debate, Lord Digby revealed some other aspects of the situation. "Away with personal animosities, away with all flatteries

---

[29] *POSLP*, vol. III, 579–80, 582–3, 588; vol. IV, 5, 10; *Verney*, 49–50; Adamson, *Noble Revolt*, 247. For a description of the vote as majoritarian, see BL MS Add 11045, f. 139r.

[30] *POSLP*, vol. IV, 36, 39–41, 44–5. Perhaps by asking to be "excused" Holles simply meant to plea for the forgiveness of his peers.

to the people, in being the sharper against him because he is odious to them," he pleaded. "Away with all fears lest by the sparing his blood they may be incensed." He continued: "Of all these corruptions of judgment, Mr. Speaker, I do, before God, discharge myself to the uttermost of my power. And do with a clear conscience wash my hands of this man's blood by this solemn protestation that my vote goes not to the taking of the earl of Strafford's life." Digby was suggesting that popular pressure was playing a powerful (and in terms of privilege, entirely inappropriate) role in members' decision-making. Around six o'clock, the bill passed 204 to 59. While "the number of ayes was in the very sound of them five or six times at the least more than the number of the noes," D'Ewes observed, "yet some amongst the noes would have the House divided." As the division proceeded on the insistence of the "noe" voters, "Mr. John Moore and one or two other members of the House took their names." D'Ewes himself recorded the names in his diary.[31]

One report from that day noted that "near 200" members had "declared themselves not there at the reading of the cause" and therefore abstained from voting on the attainder bill by citing a technicality. Others reported that many opponents of the bill left the House or withdrew from the chamber before the final division. Indeed, there is strong evidence that the basic cleavage in the final vote was not between nascent parliamentarians and royalists, but between those enemies of Strafford who had been convinced of the need for an attainder, especially given fears of an imminent dissolution of the parliament, and those reformists who joined future royalists in opposing the attainder because it would dash their hopes of a settlement with Charles.[32] The division was obviously the result of the minority's desire to have their votes against the attainder counted and recognized, perhaps even as protests against the House's decision. There is also some evidence that the division was forced to make clear that the vote was in some sense illegitimate because the votes in favor of attainder were those of a minority of the members eligible to vote. Even the total number of votes, Sir Edward Nicholas later wrote in his history of the Long Parliament, was "little exceeding half the House." In his view, the vote was in essence that of "the factious party of this parliament."[33]

---

[31] *POSLP*, vol. IV, 36–7, 41–2, 45–6, 50–1. Other reports described this division as going "to the pole" and mentioned taking down the names of "noe" voters (BL MS Add 47145, f. 85r.; Durham UL MS MSP 30, f. 31r.).

[32] BL MS Add 4180, f. 170r.; Adamson, *Noble Revolt*, 254–5; Fletcher, *Outbreak of the English Civil War*, 13–14; BL MS Add 64922, ff. 22v.–23r.

[33] BL MS Add 4810, f. 170r. See also Add MS 31954.

Many members feared reprisals from fellow members and the populace for voting against the attainder, and from Strafford and Charles (should both men escape their current predicaments and the parliament be successfully dissolved) for voting in favor. The popular element, in particular, was certainly a factor in the attainder bill debates. News of an impending dissolution seems to have been widely circulated in London that day. This in itself, along with popular agitation in previous weeks, brought immense pressure upon members to approve the attainder bill quickly. In the afternoon of 20 April, the day of the vote, City allies of Strafford's enemies assembled a crowd to physically prevent a commission of dissolution from being read, and by dusk, on D'Ewes' estimate, 10,000 people, including many aldermen, followed three City militia officers to the Palace of Westminster in order to present a petition demanding Strafford's death. They presented the petition once the members had returned from bringing their attainder bill up to the Lords. In addition, the list of "noe" voters in the attainder division was posted in the Old Palace Yard in Westminster on 3 May after having circulated immediately in print and manuscript on the day of the vote.[34]

The attainder division and the other episodes examined earlier in this section exhibit a number of commonalities that prefigured the divisions of the rest of 1641 and 1642. The clearest is by now familiar: the way in which conflicts over what course of action best conduced to maintaining the status of the House led to divisions. We see more here, though, than the simple inability of the House to come over to a single side of the question when such difficult issues were at stake. None of these votes was consensual, of course, but two of them were remarkably lopsided. In each case, with little or no hope of victory, the minority had forced a division to be called. The willingness of minorities to do this had the potential greatly to increase the incidence of divisions. Even more importantly, these groups were so concerned to dissociate themselves from what they took to be the gravely dishonorable actions of a faction that they were willing to use a division not to secure a desired, honorable result, but simply to disavow responsibility for a dishonorable result and, perhaps, to shed some of the attendant dishonor to themselves. This was a graphic rejection of the traditional norms of unitary decision-making, albeit under unusual conditions. Most significantly, perhaps, it showed

---

[34] *POSLP*, vol. IV, 42–3; Adamson, *Noble Revolt*, 252–3. On 4 May, Edward Kirton, who appeared on the list, moved that a committee search for those responsible for making the vote public. Moore prepared an apology for his involvement in publishing the vote but apparently never delivered it.

the potential for members to see the very act of *dividing* as an honorable one, at least in particularly grave circumstances.

The minority's action in the attainder vote was likely part of a wider effort by many members to dissociate themselves from the House's fateful decision on Strafford. As noted earlier, this effort included avoiding the vote in the first place with recourse to a variety of tactics. Yet by forcing a division instead of merely dodging the vote, members were doing something distinctive. They appear to have been visibly protesting the House's decision and suggesting its factional origins, as Digby had done in explicit, spectacular form with his speech earlier in the day. Forcing the division also compelled more reluctant members on both sides of the question to make clear to observers where they stood.

Finally, as Digby had emphasized, these "minoritarian" protests were clearly connected to the perceived and actual role of external pressure in the House's decision-making – pressure both from the populace at large and from Charles, Strafford, and his other powerful defenders in particular. Those who forced the division and the others who voted against the attainder with their feet performed their loyalty to the king while their opponents were forced and seen gravely to affront him. At the same time, observers complained that popular pressure had compromised freedom of speech in the Commons at this moment. This, they alleged, had the effect of pushing the majority of members toward attainder and intimidating those who opposed it. As if to confirm the validity of this viewpoint, the negative attainder votes were ultimately made public. As a precedent, the circulation of this list threatened to erect a permanent barrier to freedom of speech in the Commons, and it raised the specter of the corrupt use of public politics to influence parliamentary business. Under these conditions the House might be forced into still more frequent divisions, both because members would be inclined to maintain certain positions dictated to them from beyond the walls of the chamber and because other members would be inclined to oppose any major decision made by the Commons when its freedom was compromised by popular pressure. All of these problems evident in the period of the Strafford attainder vote would be increasingly prominent themes of parliamentary politics in the years to come.

For a month after the vote, amid fears of dissolution and the revelation of the Tower plot, the House was largely unified. It agreed on a series of extremely important measures – including attacks on episcopal power, the Protestation, and the dissolution bill – without dividing. The Protestation oath, which bound every member to "maintain and defend ... the power and privilege of Parliament," undoubtedly caused the House to center its activities more than ever around protection of Parliament's status. It also meant that members might be loath to change their opinions or capitulate in a case where Parliament's power or privileges appeared to be at stake, which would in turn increase the likelihood of majoritarian votes. Repeatedly cited in Commons debates in the following years, the Protestation probably helped precipitate more and more frequent divisions on matters of status.[35]

When divisions again grew more frequent, from the end of May onward, they concerned honor-related aspects of Parliament's competition with the king for legal authority, allegiance, and military security. The first three questions in a series of divisions on 21, 22, and 24 May concerned the treaty with the Scots. They followed a series of consensual decisions on the same topic. Debate on the treaty in the Commons had begun in earnest after the execution of Strafford on the 12th. The reformers were focused on continuing to satisfy the Scots and divert them from any thoughts of reconciliation with Charles. The king wanted to work with the Covenanters to have a treaty completed quickly under favorable terms, the armies disbanded, and an end put to the threat of northern incursions, as he planned for a visit to Scotland in July in order to cement support there. His enemies wanted to keep the Scottish army in play and address the Scots' financial (and, eventually, their religious) grievances.[36]

Debate on the 17th featured a testy exchange between D'Ewes – joined by those he called "all the honest men of the House" – and Hyde, Digby, Falkland, and others who wanted to disregard the Scots' demands for religious uniformity. The deliberations that day nevertheless resulted in a unanimous vote for an encouraging response to the Scots' demands. On the 18th the House agreed (without dividing) on an act of oblivion and on fundraising details. These resolutions on financial details continued into the following day, when the House also took up the second and third articles under the second head of the Scottish peace provisions. D'Ewes, Pym, Hampden, Marten, and others engaged in debate with Sir John Culpepper, Edmund Waller, Edward Kirton, and Sir Ralph Hopton – all future royalists who wanted to drop or slow consideration of these articles. Action was eventually taken on the articles by means of voice votes. The House took up the

---

[35] Walter, *Covenanting Citizens*, 38. For the different versions of the Protestation that circulated in Parliament during the process of its drafting, taking, and printing (none of which contained significant variants on the language quoted here, which is from the manuscript Commons journal), see Walter, *Covenanting Citizens*, 36–49. For an example of the citation of the oath in later business, see CJ, 1/3/1642.

[36] Adamson, *Noble Revolt*, 312–13, 320–1.

fourth, fifth, sixth, and seventh articles in like fashion the following day. Many of these articles were thought to have serious constitutional ramifications and relevance to the status of Parliament. There were some differences on them, but these differences were confronted, if not wholly resolved, by means of both debate and procedural channels that enabled the postponement of any final decision.[37]

Matters did not proceed quite so smoothly on 21 May. The House first agreed via voice vote, again using the usual tactics, on a series of motions related to the financial aspects of the peace. In committee of the whole, they agreed to a response to the eighth and final article of the second heading, and to responses to all articles under the third heading, which dealt with trade. Once out of the committee of the whole, though, members differed over whether the committee chair should report in a thin House. D'Ewes, the committee chair, and the Speaker argued in favor. "I confessed the House was thin," D'Ewes recalled, "but that was no fault of ours who had stayed. The matters had been thoroughly debated and I conceived all were here that desired to give their votes to it." D'Ewes warned against delaying and forcing the House to repeat the entire process the next day and suggested that everyone with no excuse for absence be fined. He could not secure agreement and the House divided and voted against a report from the committee of the whole, 53 to 48. This was a victory for those who wanted to delay work on a treaty with articles that seemed to damage the king's authority and perhaps secure better numbers on their side in a future vote in a full House. After this division a debate ensued over whether the House should be called (i.e., a roll call of those present conducted) and whether (with or without this motion) those currently absent were to be fined. The House eventually agreed that the House would be called the following day at five o'clock. Again D'Ewes and others found themselves in debate against Culpepper here.[38]

The committee report was made the following morning, and the House fell into dispute over whether the committee votes should immediately be put to the question. The members agreed to continue debate in the afternoon. The House then consented to the committee's votes on the first ten articles under the third head, but ran into conflict on the eleventh and final article. This article stated that delinquents and incendiaries wanted in one kingdom could not be allowed to simply

---

[37] *POSLP*, vol. IV, 416–17, 437–9, 459–66, 488–9. The debate on the second article under the second heading occurred after a chaotic scene in which members, nerves on edge, heard cracking window laths and supposed them to be a gunshot.
[38] Ibid., vol. IV, 502, 505–6, 508–12.

escape into another. The article had occasioned debate on the 21st, and it obviously related to the status of both the English and Scottish Parliaments. The committee had assented to the first part of the article and agreed that the second part should be referred back to commissioners. On the 22nd, debate on the article was vigorous, with D'Ewes, Denzil Holles, and other important members arguing in favor of ratifying the committee's voting. When the House finally voted on ratifying the committee's assent to the first part of the article, it divided twice. On the first vote, "the noes not resting satisfied," according to D'Ewes, a division was apparently forced by the minority. But the vote was close enough that this was not necessarily a strongly "minoritarian" move. The issues of parliamentary status and authority in relation to that of the king and the Scottish Parliament raised by this article were so significant that they led to another two divisions on 19 June. Debate featured very clear parliamentarian and royalist sides with relation to policy on Scotland.[39]

The final division in this series in late May occurred on the 24th, when the House was presented with votes from a committee investigating corruption among the king's customs officials in the 1620s and 1630s. This issue had previously led to debates about the legality of specific royal customs and impositions.[40] The House considered voting the customers delinquents, but decided instead, with a voice vote, to continue discussion the next day. The intense debate then turned to whether or not those who had collected tonnage and poundage, in particular, were able to do so without consent of Parliament or legal warrant. The Commons divided in a fairly full House, 146 in favor and 177 against, over whether to put this question.[41] This was another division that ostensibly dealt with a procedural matter but in substance determined whether the House would explicitly vindicate the authority of Parliament with respect to that of the king.

In the period leading up to the outbreak of war, there were many similar fronts on which the Commons divided frequently over attempts to bolster its authority or debase the king's. Perhaps the topic most commonly at issue was Parliament's efforts to identify, punish, or deny royal appointments to those they deemed or suspected to be delinquents,

---

[39] Ibid., vol. IV, 509–10, 523–4, 530–2; vol. V, 234–5, 237–41, 243–6; Adamson, *Noble Revolt*, 660–1, n. 180. "Delinquents" were men who served the king with arms, money, or personal service potentially involved in the making of war against Parliament. This included refusing to contribute to Parliament or otherwise showing opposition to its measures, as defined in an order of 27 March 1643.

[40] *POSLP*, vol. IV, 110, 114, 117, 523, 526–30, 533–7, 540.

[41] Ibid., vol. IV, 545–6, 548–53.

malignants, traitors, or royalists.[42] The questions of loyalism and royalism, from the Strafford vote onward, became closely associated with vindications of parliamentary status and authority, since loyalist and royalist members of Parliament had clearly dishonored Parliament with their actions and could be taken to have rejected its legitimacy. But because identifying and punishing opponents of Parliament were such fraught actions, they frequently led to divisions, some of which were accompanied by markedly majoritarian behavior.

One prominent example was the attack on Lord Digby in the Commons for his speech against Strafford's attainder on 21 April and its printing, which was taken to be a violation of parliamentary privilege.[43] The most revealing incident here was not recorded in the Commons journal. According to a newsletter account, on 8 June Digby "was accused to have caused that speech of his made in favor of the earl of Strafford to be printed, and had sent copy thereof to the said Earl." On a motion to form a committee to investigate the charge of violating the privacy of parliamentary proceedings, the question was put and "there was heard a mixed cry of yeas and noes of different judgment. Yet the Speaker pronounced it for the yeas. Whereupon the contrary side demanded that the House should be divided, and upon the division the noes carried it." The "anti-Digbians" nevertheless pressed on, urging "that there might be some time appointed further to consider of it, but the number of the noes was so loud in the House that they durst not divide the House, who moved it." At this point Digby's enemies appeared to have acquiesced. But Digby, concerned to vindicate himself, then stood up and requested "that which my adversaries could not just now obtain, that there may be a day set apart for the examination thereof." The discussion was set for three days later. At this point another member rose and observed that "there are threescore of us which have been pested and much traduced for uttering our minds in the same cause." Here the member was again referring to "noe" votes on Strafford's attainder. "I must in the name of all," he said, "protest against the hearing of this business of my Lord Digby, until we have been righted for [being pested and traduced]: for if I may not have

[42] Ibid., vol. IV, 523–4, 532, 546, 548–9, 551–3; vol. VI, 90, 94, 675, 678, 685, 690; CJ, 10/29/1641, 12/17/1641, 1/3/1642, 1/24/1642, 1/27/1642, 2/2/1642, 2/15/1642, 2/22/1642, 3/10/1642, 5/3/1642, 5/9/1642, 6/11/1642, 6/16/1642, 8/17/1642, 8/27/1642, 9/2/1642; D'Ewes, 50–1, 302, 304–5; PJLP, vol. I, 1, 5, 143, 150–1, 155, 158, 188–91, 198, 200, 204, 253–5, 261, 264, 391, 393, 442; vol. II, 23–4, 267, 271, 294, 298; vol. III, 61–4, 87, 90–1, 320–1.
[43] For later developments on this front that led to another division and clearly concerned the status of the House, see POSLP, vol. V, 611–22.

liberty securely to speak my conscience here, let me beg your leave, and I will go to my house whence I came." All parties to this dispute, then, saw violations of privilege at stake, in the form of various restrictions on free speech and privacy in the House. They were willing to engage in extraordinary actions to vindicate their privileges and their honor, forcing divisions and even explicitly protesting the House's decisions and the legitimacy of its ongoing business.[44]

Royalism and the First Lurches into Majoritarianism

It was mostly in these votes concerning incipient royalism that divisions were for the first time forced on a regular basis. Hyde later described this development in his *History of the Rebellion*. Writing about Commons proceedings in October 1641, but offering a more general reflection on the behavior of his regular opponents in the House, he complained that

> in all debates of this nature, where the law, reason, and common sense were in diameter opposite to what they proposed, they suffered those who differed from them in opinion and purposes to say what they saw fit in opposition, and then, without vouchsafing to endeavour their satisfaction, called importunately for the question; well knowing that they had a plurality of voices to concur with them in whatsoever they desired.[45]

There could hardly be a clearer diagnosis of the utter corruption of consensus decision-making and its replacement by a majoritarian tyranny. On Hyde's reading of the situation, when Pym and his allies wanted the House to make indefensible decisions, they traded genuine deliberation (a process in which they faced certain defeat) for a game of numbers. They allowed a veneer of normal debating procedure to persist, but they had no intention of taking their fellow members' opposing arguments seriously. While making a hollow gesture to parliamentary tradition, they were forcing through the objects of their desire by counting heads.

Hyde's commentary was of course a partisan one, but in factual if not explanatory terms his remarks correspond with evidence from other sources concerning particular instances of majoritarian activity in this period. A revealing example comes from the day before Parliament adjourned itself on 9 September 1641. That day D'Ewes, certainly no royalist himself, recorded a series of brazenly majoritarian tactics that members employed under time pressure. The House was debating the

---

[44] BL MS Sloane 1467, ff. 71v.–72v. See also *POSLP*, vol. V, 30, 36, 41, 46.
[45] Clarendon, *History of the Rebellion*, vol. I, 402; see also vol. I, 428–9.

content of a letter to be sent from the Speaker to the earl of Holland, Lord General in the north, about disbanding the English army there. The members disagreed about whether the Commoner army plotters John Ashburham and Hugh Pollard should be paid as part of the disbandment. Neglecting to pay them would of course be a means of vindicating the House's authority against members who were thought gravely to have threatened Parliament's existence. These payments had in fact been ordered in June. But the order was reversed in a morning division that day about the content of the letter before Pym was ordered to draft it. Only ninety members participated. Low vote turnouts, as we will see, were increasingly drawing suspicion as the possible product of factional, majoritarian maneuver.[46]

Pym's draft letter to Holland was read between six and seven at night, while candles were brought into the chamber. Edmund Waller moved to reverse that morning's order on payments and he was seconded by William Strode and others, who argued that it was inconsistent to deny Ashburham and Pollard personal pay when "greater offenders than these" – Henry Percy, Sir John Berkeley, and Henry Wilmot – had already been paid. D'Ewes and others spoke in favor of the former order, arguing that "it having been ordered in the daytime this very day that they should not receive their said pay when the House was reasonably full, that we might not proceed to the altering of that order thus late at night when the House was thus thin but that we might defer the question until tomorrow morning." According to D'Ewes, "the other side pretended that there was great haste of the letter to be finished presently and to be sent away early in the morning." Pym argued against them. "He confessed that himself and others were over-voted in the morning, but he desired that the rule of the House might be rather to carry matters by strength of reason than by number of voices. And therefore he desired that someone of the contrary party would give him some satisfaction for what he had desired." Pym was clearly insinuating that his opponents were engaged in a deplorably majoritarian ploy.[47]

D'Ewes responded at length, casting his own position as reasonable and returning the anti-majoritarian favor. "Notwithstanding what I had alleged," he complained in his diary, "the other party would not rest satisfied though no man could rationally and fully contradict that which I had affirmed. But guessing themselves to be the major number some of them spoke very earnestly that the said Mr. Ashburham and Mr. Pollard might have their pay, calling so long upon the Speaker to put the question

[46] *POSLP*, vol. VI, 675, 685.   [47] Ibid., vol. VI, 678, 689–90.

that at length he performed it." D'Ewes then lost a 29 to 23 division, in an extremely thin House. Even after the division, around eight o'clock, "some of those who were of the noes began to speak against the carrying of the business at this time of the night," casting suspicion on the legitimacy of the vote. D'Ewes, however, "prevented this device" and substituted it with a more clever tactic: a different last-minute motion, "which the other party, ere they were aware, yielded unto." This was a blatantly majoritarian riposte. D'Ewes, on his own account, "stood up and moved that though I were a negative yet seeing the greater number of voices had over-ruled it otherwise I rested satisfied therewith." He then "desired that the clerk might get it copied out fair against the morning that it might be read in the House as was usually observed in matters of this nature." His opponents "readily assented, never considering that the House might then call the same matter in question then again, which was the true scope of my motion and as it fell out accordingly on the ensuing morning." D'Ewes was shrewdly manipulating procedure in order to reopen discussion at a time when the voting conditions were again more likely to work in his favor.[48]

Sure enough, the debate began anew the following day, when the new version of the letter was read. Robert Goodwin "said that he desired we might renew our former orders made in the daytime which were that the pay of those two gentlemen might be suspended for a time, and that the order made yesternight might not stand, in which the House was surprised, for otherwise he should for his part protest against it." Pym, alarmed by this open threat of a protest against the previous night's vote, "said that he desired such protestations might be forborne in this House" and "wished to hear no more of this manner of protesting in the House." D'Ewes concurred with Pym's point about protestation, which he said had been "seldom or never seen" in the House. Such attempts to explicitly protest a vote of the Commons would become increasingly common and controversial in the coming months. D'Ewes again took a more tactful route than some of his allies, remarking that he was "also glad that we have the day to succeed the night, that we may this morning call into question again what so late and so unseasonably [was] ordered yesternight." The debate was renewed, and at one point Sir Henry Heyman claimed that Pym had "stretched the order in his drawing the letter" and was forced to apologize. The debate was derailed by this altercation and a message from the Lords, and the letter was apparently

---

[48] Ibid., vol. VI, 690–1. There were six divisions in September 1641 as the Commons tried to hurry through business before the adjournment. In general, during the 1640s, time pressure was a complicating but insufficient factor leading to divisions.

voted to be sent in its current form.[49] This had been an extremely volatile tactical battle over a perceived matter of parliamentary vindication. Votes were challenged and protests threatened because the votes were conducted in a thin House, which was itself indirect evidence of members using timing to construct effective majorities on intractable issues.[50] A slow movement toward majoritarian politics had begun amid the same sorts of dilemmas that would, within a little over a year, turn the lurching and creeping into a sprint. What began as no more than a series of ruptures in 1640 and early 1641 would soon become a profound structural dislocation.

[49] Ibid., vol. VI, 710–12, 718.
[50] Timing tactics were certainly used throughout the consensual era in the Commons, but not in a majoritarian fashion. See, for example, Hartley (ed.), *Proceedings in the Parliaments of Elizabeth I*, vol. II, 113.

4   Consensus Destroyed, 1641–1643

Two of the majoritarian tactics occasionally employed by members of the Commons in the late spring and summer of 1641 – the manipulation of House attendance and the initiation of protests – manifested themselves repeatedly in the coming months. These tactics, which featured in a number of very important votes, are properly understood as majoritarian because they were actions known to hazard majoritarian outcomes. They implied a willingness to cause and benefit from majoritarian spectacles even when they were unnecessary. These tactics violated consensual norms and entailed the temporary neglect or abandonment of consensual tactics. The ruptures they caused were not, however, driven by a normative, general commitment to majoritarian tactics or by an outright rejection of consensual politics. Members who employed these tactics at the time clearly considered them to be emergency measures that enabled those members to engage in effective status interaction under extremely trying circumstances.[1]

The strongest general indication that House members were manipulating attendance to their advantage is the frequency with which important divisions were held in thinly attended houses. Between the late spring of 1641 and the summer of 1642, fewer than 100 members were counted in about one out of every seven divisions. In some instances there is evidence that these divisions in thin houses were purposely arranged. There is also evidence for the negative equivalent of this tactic: members trying to avoid debate on specific issues when the House was full and this would put them at a voting disadvantage.[2] At the same time, incipient royalism was increasingly accompanied by what in the previous chapter were termed "minoritarian" divisions: moments when a minority

---

[1] On contemporary print analysis of the tactics described here, see Peacey, *Print and Public Politics in the English Revolution*, 131–62.

[2] Adamson, *Noble Revolt*, esp. 148, 330, 406–7. For other comments on thin houses, see *PJLP*, vol. II, 174; vol. III, 102, 310–11, 351; Clarendon, *History of the Rebellion*, vol. I, 381–4, 420, 428–9.

demanded that a division be held even when the result was not in doubt. Minoritarian divisions became very frequent in the lead-up to civil war. In these situations the Commons was not dividing because debate had failed to bring an overwhelming majority to one side of the question. Instead, small minorities who had clearly lost a voice vote were simply ignoring the fact that in such cases, as D'Ewes put it, "it [was] usual" to yield to the Speaker's judgment.[3] The status implications of these decisions were simply too high for some members of the minority to submit to being identified with them in the same way members of the majority were.

Minoritarian divisions accounted for more than a quarter of the divisions held between April 1641 and September 1642.[4] In many of these episodes, members were essentially adopting a royalist pose: they were not permanently abandoning Parliament, but they were openly dissociating themselves from votes of the Commons. Their actions make even clearer than in typical divisions that the willingness to undergo a division resulted from a sense that the status considerations at stake in the specific decision the House was making were thought to be greater than the status considerations entailed in the way that decision was made. The members of the minority who initiated and participated in minoritarian divisions were engaged not only in dissociation but also in a form of protest. The fact that they viewed a division as a way to accomplish these two things confirms yet again that divisions were rituals of disunion. Normally, divisions were regrettable failures, but in these situations they were being willingly provoked for partisan advantage. However extreme and novel this behavior was, it could be justified by traditional norms. From these minorities' point of view, Parliament's authority – properly rooted in the nation as a whole – had already been usurped by a faction, whether or not that faction was able to carry important votes with ease. In the case of minoritarian divisions forced by royalists, one might even extend this observation to speculate that divisions were knowingly being used to damage Parliament's status or legitimacy.

---

[3] *POSLP*, vol. VI, 635.

[4] Ibid., vol. IV, 606, 614; vol. V, 235, 239; vol. VI, 90, 94, 242, 635; *D'Ewes*, 50–1, 54, 295, 304; *PJLP*, vol. I, 15, 191; vol. II, 120, 294, 298, 344; vol. III, 6, 91, 191, 193, 255, 260, 321; CJ, 6/27/1642, 7/26/1642, 7/28/1642, 8/17/1642. This is a fairly conservative proportion estimate. Most divisions that featured margins of victory above the mean were not clearly commented on as minority divisions. These clear victories for which we have no record of commentary have been counted only in cases where the margin was particularly wide and the voice vote could not have been doubtful. In those cases, it is impossible to tell whether the decision to call the division was the Speaker's or another member's (the former is very unlikely). For minoritarian dynamics not involving divisions, see *PJLP*, vol. III, 58.

Both the manipulation of House attendance and the forcing of minoritarian divisions were first graphically evident in spring 1641 divisions ostensibly centered on matters of religion. These divisions were of course driven in part by differences over episcopacy and other pivotal religious issues, but with respect to the purposes of the present chapter, they were fundamentally about politics. This is because they were almost all clearly anchored to aspects of Parliament's struggle over a favorable political settlement with the king and, in particular, to Parliament's desire to remain in the good graces of the Scots and remove royalist voters (the bishops) from the Lords. In this sense matters of religion were for practical purposes being subsumed by the Commons' confrontation with nascent royalism. Removing bishops from the Lords threatened fundamental alterations to the constitution of the upper House, and appeasing the Scots entailed enraging Charles and decreasing the possibility of an accommodation.[5] This strategic context is perhaps the first one in which the House fell into a pattern of majoritarian behavior for a sustained period of time.

The richest evidence for this behavior appears in accounts of House proceedings following the introduction of the root and branch bill for abolishing episcopacy. In a 27 May debate over whether to read the bill a second time, Sir Charles Williams (according to D'Ewes) "stood up and said that if they were but six that were noes, yet he would divide the House though many that were noes did yield." Williams did not quite have to carry out his threat, but the House did divide, with 108 voting against and 139 in favor of a second reading. After the vote William Strode, noting that Williams "was a young parliament man," requested "that hereafter such words might be forborne that any would cause the House to be divided for six voices' difference only." Williams responded by standing up and acknowledging that "those words were spoken rashly by him."[6] Despite its evident impropriety, the thinking behind this dramatic minoritarian gesture was probably not simply the sort of gaffe one might expect of inexperienced members in troubled times. In at least a few other cases, minoritarian divisions followed the basic pattern Williams had outlined in his threat: most members of a minority believed they had lost a voice vote and chose not to challenge the Speaker's

---

[5] See *POSLP*, vol. IV, 602, 716; vol. VI, 632, 648; *D'Ewes*, 25, 30, 52–4; CJ, 2/17/1642, 4/23/1642, 5/31/1642; Adamson, *Noble Revolt*, 355, 394. For a possible exception to the subsumption of religion by politics in this moment that was nevertheless closely related to the politics of the Irish Rebellion, see CJ, 12/11/1641.

[6] *POSLP*, vol. IV, 606, 614.

estimate, but a single person or subset of the minority nevertheless forced a division to be held.[7]

The early debates over episcopacy provide even better evidence of members paying close attention to the balance of opinion in the House at specific moments in order to time (or to avoid) votes accordingly.[8] On 3 June "the House was so full," a newsletter writer reported, "that many were forced to stand for want of place, which being for the [ad]vantage of episcopacy, the enemies thereof purposely avoided the question" for passing the root and branch bill. Since the majority of members would apparently oppose the bill and it could pass only in a thin House mostly attended by committed opponents of episcopacy, the writer continued, "the fall of episcopacy is deferred until Monday next, that is to say till they find an opportunity who would have it down." While Monday had by order of the House been "appointed for episcopacy," it turned out that "two things diverted that business from being fallen upon: first, a too full House, not for the advantage of those abolishers; and then hope of a greater party, if the Lords should not remove [the bishops] out of Parliament." Here the writer, a supporter of episcopacy, was referring to the expectation that abolition would find more favor in the Commons if the upper house proceeded to dash a separate bill, already passed by the Commons, that would have removed bishops from the Lords.[9]

These tactics were employed on both sides of the conflict. "Our men," the writer continued, "insisted to have it then put to the question (a strange riddle that they that are for episcopacy should desire to put it to votes, whether it should down or not, and the enemies thereof plead against their proposal) but it was strongly opposed." The defenders of episcopacy then moved to schedule a vote in order to be able to make plans for full attendance on a specific day. "They then proposed that a day should be set for it," the writer explained, "but the Speaker would not be induced to propose that (the reason of their not appointing a day is because they would make use of the first occasion of an empty house, whence they are sure never to be absent for their advantage)." These brazen attempts by episcopalians, countered by the Speaker, brought the House to a high pitch of acrimony. "Some words upon this occasion being interchanged," the writer continued, "they began to call one another to the bar, and rescue one another from it, spending the whole morning in this kind of courseing, whilst the Lords were examining their reasons for the removing the bishops from their house."[10]

---

[7] Ibid., vol. VI, 94, 242.

[8] For an example in addition to those discussed below, see BL MS Sloane 1467, ff. 70r.–v.

[9] Ibid., ff. 96r.–v., 98r.   [10] Ibid., f. 98r.

In his commentary on this struggle the news writer also outlined a tripartite relationship among Lords, Commons, and populace that had grave implications for parliamentary privilege. His analysis was suffused with majoritarian assumptions. Popular pressure on parliamentary business was raising concern about freedom of debate, while also subtly encouraging the intransigence and desperation evident in some members' tactical behavior. In his description of the 8 June session the writer observed that "it is thought there is no other way of preserving episcopacy but by their [the bishops'] voluntary yielding of their right in Parliament." The idea was that this would satisfy moderates in the Commons, who would then oppose the outright abolition of episcopacy. This was considered a necessary if desperate move because if the Commons voted for abolition, it would spell doom for the bishops: they would be compelled by an emboldened populace to concur. "If the House of Commons votes them [the bishops] down (as it is feared they will)," the writer continued, "the multitude will again press upon the Lords to pass the bill against them as they have done formerly in the case of my Lord of Strafford." The alternative way of thinking current at the time, the writer continued, was that "there is yet hope that the enemies of episcopacy may come short of numbers when it comes to votes" on abolition in the Lords.[11] From this perspective, the bishops and their allies in the Lords were best served by standing firm on the matter of bishops' voting rights. That day, in accordance with this latter point of view, the Lords rejected the Commons' initiative to remove bishops from their secular employments and awaited the lower house's vote on root and branch.

"Certainly," the writer admitted, this move by the Lords would "deprive [the bishops] of some votes in the House of Commons for the main matter of episcopacy, which now must be expected to be pursued with vigor." Yet sound tactics might still save episcopacy. "If warning can be given," he wrote, "I hope that a full House will make a prevalent side for episcopacy against the opposers thereof." On 11 June, after debate in committee of the whole on the preamble to the root and branch bill, the Commons "resolve themselves into a house, make the report, vote, and carry it by so visible a number of voices, that it is apparent that whatsoever they will have to pass, cannot want a plurality to countenance it." With such evidence of a clear majority in the Commons, the writer concluded, "the last refuge is upon the Lords' refusal to pass the same. And in case of that refusal, no little apprehensions of a confusion.

[11] Ibid., f. 72v.

Thus we stand in jeopardy between Silla and Charibdis."[12] At this moment, the writer suggested, the entire logic of parliamentary strategy was premised on the specter of popular violence. Concerns about popular pressure were inducing and even legitimating majoritarian tactics.

The manipulation of House attendance was again evident during a series of important incidents in the fall. When Parliament reconvened in late October after a short recess, attendance was, for a time, minimal. Pym and his allies seem to have taken advantage of the situation.[13] On 23 October, for instance, the House began proceedings with only forty-one members present. After discussion of a petition and a scandalous pamphlet, the sergeant went with the mace into Westminster Hall to call up the members who were walking there. After a motion by Sir Edward Dering to draft an act for a national synod, Cornelius Holland moved that a bill against clergy in secular employments first be read for a third time. Hyde opposed this, declaring that "he did not think it fit that it should be read at that time, by reason of the thinness of the House." Holles seconded Holland's motion to read the bill a third time, remarking "that was not reason for what if men would neglect their duties there should the business of the commonwealth perish for want of their company, he saw no reason for that." The bill was then read, and Falkland, Hyde, and Henry Lucas spoke against it. Hyde objected that the bill violated the privilege of the Lords. D'Ewes countered by citing precedents and remarking that "I did not doubt but that the most of the Lords would be as willing to be rid of [the bishops] as ourselves" and that since the bishops, in their dual status as spiritual lords and temporal lords in Parliament, were "monster in nature," "for us to take from them their voice in Parliament is no more than to set a man at liberty that is imprisoned with golden fetters." He also responded to Hyde's concerns about a thin House, retorting that "truly, if when men are once elected members of this House, if they have not so much conscience as to attend the service of the House, I know no reason why business of importance should be neglected for their absence." In the end D'Ewes had his way and the bill passed without a division.[14]

Thin houses were even taken by some at the time to cast doubt on the legitimacy of successful parliamentary orders. Expressing those doubts, of course, could itself be a tactic of debate. On 12 February 1642, for instance, the House considered whether to send to the Lords their orders

---

[12] Ibid., ff. 99r., 101v. For other evidence of attention to vote timing and related conflict, see ff. 100r.–v.

[13] For relevant episodes on 20, 21, and 22 October, see *D'Ewes*, 11–16, 21–2, 25, 28.

[14] *D'Ewes*, 29–32.

from 8 and 9 September 1641 (just prior to the recess) against innovations and the admission of lecturers in churches where there was no preaching. According to D'Ewes, Sir William Lewis and Sir John Hotham pointed out "that the former order against innovations was passed in a thin House and therefore desired that we might superview it again." D'Ewes retorted that he "was very sorry to see such a scandal cast upon the proceedings of the House by the members of it as to say that the said order was passed in a thin House, as if such of us who stayed here according to the public trust reposed in us when others took their pleasure and departed away must therefore have our just actions questioned as invalid." The House in fact resolved without a division to draw up bills in accordance with the previous orders, thus dismissing D'Ewes' claim that revisiting these orders would dishonor the House.[15] Under conditions that seemed to indicate a factional or unfree Commons, even its previous decisions were being protested and disputed by past minorities who had hopes to be majorities in the future.

The Protestation of the Grand Remonstrance: November–December 1641

There were only a few minority divisions in 1641 before minority protests took novel forms that broke from existing parliamentary rules. They included an effort to have the dissent of each individual member of the minority formally recognized by the House. These initiatives failed in the end. They would have brought Commons procedure more in line with that of Lords, but they were so controversial that they brought the House to the brink of armed violence.

In advance of the 22–3 November 1641 marathon debate on the Grand Remonstrance, D'Ewes was told by Sir Christopher Yelverton that "those who wished well to the declaration did intend to have it pass without the alteration of any one word." This attitude would of course have encouraged a majoritarian outcome by stifling deliberation and compromise. D'Ewes responded accordingly. Because "there were some particulars in the said declaration which I had formerly spoken against and could not in my conscience assent unto," he stayed away from the House that day in order to avoid being part of an unnecessary division.[16] Attitudes were also apparently hardened among those opposed to the Remonstrance. Near midnight, Edward Nicholas assured the king that there were "diverse in the Commons House, that are resolved to stand very stiff for rejecting that

---

[15] *PJLP*, vol. I, 355, 360.   [16] *D'Ewes*, 185.

Declaration, and if they prevail not then to protest against it."[17] Some sort of confrontation appears to have been inevitable.

The Remonstrance itself was carried by only a narrow majority of 159 to 148. This apparently occurred after numerous alterations were made to the original text. George Peard then moved to have the document printed. This of course was a major escalation on the part of the strongest supporters of the Remonstrance: the document was to be used as a public weapon, not simply as an address to the king. In response to the motion, Hyde and Culpepper "and diverse others offered to enter their protestations against the printing of it." But this was "gainsaid," explained D'Ewes, because "no protestation can be entered without the consent of the house." At this point – it was already one o'clock in the morning – members apparently had the impression that the motion to print the Remonstrance had been "laid aside until a further time of debate" because of the evident strength of opposition to it. But this fleeting consensual momentum was suddenly destroyed by Geoffrey Palmer, who "stood up and desired that a protestation might be entered in the name of himself and all the rest." Other opponents of the Remonstrance then "cried 'all, all,' and some waved their hats over their heads, and others took their swords in their scabbards out of their belts and held them by the pumells in their hands, setting the lower part on the ground, so as if God had not prevented it there was a very great danger that mischief might have been done."[18]

Palmer and those who cried out in support of his motion were deeply affronted by the prospect of printing the Remonstrance – so deeply affronted, in fact, that they were signaling that if they could not be formally dissociated from the vote to print it, they would resort to violence to stop the vote. This sentiment may have originated in the conviction that the vote and its likely outcome were themselves the results of the factional corruption of the Commons. As Nicholas understood it, "some resolved that they would no longer stand to be baffled by such a rabble of inconsiderable persons, set on by a juggling junto." These men considered the majority behind the Remonstrance to be a faction mostly composed of ignorant members of low social standing and led by the "Junto." Such a group was completely unsuited to making such a monumental decision. The only proper response was to "oppose

---

[17] *Evelyn*, vol. IV, 133.
[18] *D'Ewes*, 186–7; Clarendon, *History of the Rebellion*, vol. I, 419–20; Parliamentary Archives, HC/CL/JO/1/21, p. 704; BL MS Add 4180, f. 174. On the revolutionary significance of the prospect of the printing of the Remonstrance, see Millstone, *Manuscript Circulation*, 313–15.

their attempts by open protestation."[19] In other words, these members demanded to be dissociated from foolish, intrinsically shameful votes in an unfree Parliament. For all the obvious and broad ideological importance of the divisions over the Remonstrance, the honor component of the situation certainly helps explain the threat of violence.

Some members who were opposed to printing the Remonstrance nevertheless thought Palmer had gone too far, and they proceeded to speak against Palmer's motion. John Hampden "demanded of him how he could know other men's minds," which would itself imply factional organization in advance of the House's meeting. Palmer replied that "he having once before heard them cry 'all all' he had thereupon desired to have the said protestation entered in all their names." After the clerk had apparently recorded the names of some of those who had protested and then struck the entry from the record, the members finally agreed to leave the issue of printing unresolved.[20] It was then ordered with a division, as a safeguard, that the Remonstrance should not be printed without a particular order from the House. The House also voted, however, 124 to 101 not to include the word "published" in the provisional order against printing. This allowed manuscript versions of the Remonstrance to circulate. At two in the morning, the House finally rose.[21]

The Commons had courted bloodshed because some of Pym's opponents were ready to do nearly anything to distance themselves from the printing of the Remonstrance, the House's most extreme flirtation to date with the blatant manipulation of public opinion, itself a matter of considerable ideological import. One member, a son of Sir John Coke (either John or Thomas), described the matter explicitly in terms of majorities and minorities. The motion for printing the Remonstrance, he said, "disagreed so much with the sense of those that would have rejected it, that most of them desired that their protestations might be entered against it. This drew it into debate whether the minor part by the orders of the House might protest against the major part by the orders of the House." The actions taken against Palmer after this incident were also described in majoritarian terms. "How the major part will proceed against the rest of the protesters I cannot tell," Coke continued.[22]

---

[19] *D'Ewes*, 187; BL MS Add 4180, f. 174r.

[20] *D'Ewes*, 187. The clerk's actions may have occurred later.

[21] *D'Ewes*, 187; Clarendon, *History of the Rebellion*, vol. I, 419–20; BL MS Add 4180, f. 174r. Hyde apparently viewed the printing of the Remonstrance without leave from the Lords as illegal and popular. He mentioned the dissenting practices of the Lords in conjunction with his protestation request. See Clarendon, *History of the Rebellion*, vol. I, 419–20, 423.

[22] BL MS Add 64922, f. 67r.

The incident was also briefly described in a printed newspaper, which noted that the entire debate was conducted "with the trained band attending the House all the time."[23] The controversy over the Grand Remonstrance was the most severe disruption of consensual politics to date. And the threat of violence within and without the House of Commons was perhaps its most graphic symptom, one appropriate to a sphere of practice suffused with the politics of honor.

Proponents of the Remonstrance and the Junto agenda recognized the fundamental institutional threat posed by the move toward protestations and focused their attention on rendering it an impossibility. Were the Commons to use this procedure with any regularity, their divisions would be additionally dishonorable and delegitimizing, to the point that the House's votes could be plausibly depicted not only as factional but also as the acts of mere individuals, as votes in the Lords were. They would in essence be the opposite of the resolutions of the unitary, honorable representative of the people that they were meant to be.

Accordingly, on 24 November, John Hotham (whether senior or junior is unclear) moved to proceed aggressively against Palmer, the main instigator of the melee on the 22nd. The specific offense Hotham cited was that "when a gentleman [Hyde] offered to make a protestation and another [Culpepper] seconded him, then the said Mr Palmer protested for himself and all the rest." At this motion, "many cried that he said 'all the rest.'" The key point for Hotham, presumably, was that Palmer had not simply repeated the action of Hyde and Culpepper after they had been "gainsaid," but engaged in action that was meant to rally others in a factional manner. "These words," Hotham explained, "did tend to draw on a mutiny." He deduced "that if this were permitted in the House ... anyone might make himself the head of a faction here," destroying the House's status along with its fictions of unity. Hotham was even reported to have said that Palmer had "made himself the head of a party" with his actions. If this continued to occur, "there would soon be an end of the liberty and privileges of Parliament, and we might shut up the doors." In other words, the repetition of such action could prove a threat to free speech and freedom from prosecution. It could not be left alone as a precedent. Peyton added in his diary that Palmer's words "were taken to be factiously spoken and tending to disunion."[24]

Hotham then asked that the House send for Palmer, who was absent. "Others," however, "were against his being sent for, and some took

---

[23] Anon., *Heads of Severall Proceedings in This Present Parliament*, 3 (mispaginated as 5). See also BL MS Add 33468, ff. 73v.–75r.

[24] *D'Ewes*, 192, 196.

exception to the words Mr. Hotham had used, as if a faction were in the house." Palmer's defenders thus revealed another illicit aspect of such situations. The very claim that faction existed threatened the House's fictions of unity; it was considered entirely inappropriate for a member even to suggest that the House was factionalized. As debate proceeded, Palmer entered the chamber and Hotham reiterated his charges. Some moved for Palmer to answer and then withdraw into the committee chamber so that the House could proceed to censure him. But others were opposed to requiring Palmer to answer for his words two days after they had been spoken. As Culpepper explained, "it were dangerous for a man to be questioned for words spoken in this House after the time he should speak them; for then he might be questioned in another Parliament after." Hyde clarified that "this takes away the great privilege of freedom of speech." D'Ewes countered Hyde, pointing out that there were ample precedents for after-the-fact questioning of this sort; indeed, he argued, to disallow it was "to destroy the very ancient liberties and rights of Parliament." Each side of this debate depicted a situation in which the privileges, rights, and liberties of Parliament and its members were under grave threat.[25]

In a debate of this nature, it should come as no surprise that the House divided twice over whether and in what form Palmer should be asked to answer Hotham's charge against him. In the end Palmer was required to answer. He argued that after Peard's motion for printing the Remonstrance, "diverse protested against it and that [he] himself desired also to have his protestation entered." Afterward, he claimed, "it was moved that the names of such as had protested might be entered," and he simply "desired that his own name and the name of the rest who had protested might be entered by the clerk." Discussion continued on the following day. In over three hours of debate, many members concluded that after the House had been pacified following Hyde's and Culpepper's motion on a protestation, Palmer "by his new motion to have a protestation entered in his own name and the name of all the rest, did again raise the flame to such an height as if God had not prevented it, murder and calamity might have followed thereupon: and this Parliament with our posterities and the kingdom itself have been destroyed for upon Mr. Palmer's said motion some waived their hats and others their swords with the scabbards out of their belts and held them in their hands." Others contended that the offense was merely a mistaken attempt to conclude debate and put off consideration of protestations until the

---

[25] Ibid., 192–5; *Verney*, 126.

following day. The House agreed neither on the nature of Palmer's offense nor on the penalty it deserved. They divided twice over the penalty, voting to send Palmer to the Tower but not to expel him from the House altogether.[26] In the debate over Palmer's actions, protestation had been equated by its enemies with an attempt to destroy the Parliament – and, by extension, with outright malignancy or royalism. It had been equated by its proponents with an attempt to save the House of Commons from a slow death by factional corruption.

This issue resurfaced in mid-December, once the printing of the Remonstrance returned as a topic of discussion. In the afternoon of 15 December, William Purefroy moved that in order to raise revenue the Parliament might "cause our declaration to be printed that so we might satisfy the whole kingdom." D'Ewes suspected "that many members were privy to his intended motion" because "they cried 'order it, order it,'" apparently trying to avoid a question from even being put and dispensing entirely with debate. George Peard added that the Remonstrance might be printed along with the petition that accompanied it when it was presented to the king, "to which many also cried 'order it, order it.'" Waller and others then intervened, citing the growing darkness and noting that the issue of printing the Remonstrance had already "bred so much debate before in the night," in reference to the debates of 22–3 November. Yet debate continued until in the House it was "growing so dark as the clerk could not see to write." Many members moved to bring in candles, others opposed the motion, and a minoritarian division was held on this indirect expression of conflict over whether to move toward printing the Remonstrance. "Though the yeas by the very sound appeared to be more than the noes, yet the noes would divide." They predictably lost by a massive margin, 152 to 53. Debate on printing therefore continued in candlelight "with great vehemency pro and con." This led to another somewhat lopsided division, 135 to 83, in favor of putting the question for printing, which itself then passed without a division.[27]

---

[26] *D'Ewes*, 195–9. The debate over Palmer was also reported in the press (Anon., *Heads of Severall Proceedings in This Present Parliament*, 4–5). Members and nonmembers were investigated in this period for merely suggesting that there were factions, sides, or parties in the House. For an incident connected to the Palmer controversy, see *D'Ewes*, 232–4. A manuscript diurnal (BL MS Add 33468, f. 76r.) suggested that the primary issue was whether Palmer was protesting the House's (already passed) vote to publish the Remonstrance or (preemptively) protesting the motion to print it, which would have been a less serious offense.

[27] *D'Ewes*, 294–5.

At this point, however, Sir Nicholas Slanning "and some sixty others desired to protest and that their protestations might be entered if by order of the House they might protest." The following Friday was then appointed for a discussion of protestations in general. Apparently, most opponents of printing the Remonstrance thought the dramatic gesture of forcing two minoritarian divisions was an insufficient response to the gravity of the matter at hand. These members wanted formal notice of their individual dissent entered in the Commons journal, clearly in reaction to an apparently factional proposal meant to curry popular favor and thus enter into a relationship with forces outside the Commons that could compromise freedom of speech within it. At the same time, by proposing this procedure, members of the minority were taking the risk that their efforts to dissociate themselves from the House's actions might be publicized on an individual level, just as votes against Strafford's attainder had been. This would expose Parliament to popular pressure and scrutiny and do public damage to the Commons' traditional fictions of national unity.[28]

On the following day, 16 December, a related exchange occurred before the House returned to the specific issue of protestations. Pym reported votes from a committee of both houses that had been considering breaches of parliamentary privilege. These votes were put to the question in the Commons. On the first question, "that the privilege of Parliament was broken by his Majesty's taking notice of the bill for pressing of soldiers being in agitation in both Houses and not agreed upon," according to D'Ewes, "there were some few noes." Pym then moved for these no voters to be required to give a reason for their voices. "Mr. Waller and Mr. Bridgeman then stood up and desiring to give reasons why they said 'no,' fell upon the debate of the matter, which inconvenience being espied we agreed no reason should be given of any man's vote which ought to be free."[29] Here, apparently, reformists were themselves encouraging a more explicit highlighting (and scrutiny) of the minority, individual views of their opponents. Pym's motion implied that the grounds for these views were unreasonable, rooted in mere preference or outright delinquency. The behavior of both sides, again, was being interpreted as factional and in violation of fundamental privileges and traditional conventions of deliberation.

Discussion of protestations in particular resumed on 20 December. The debate that day was a profound commentary on how the Grand Remonstrance had at least temporarily raised fundamental questions

[28] Ibid., 295.   [29] Ibid., 297–8.

about the nature of decision-making in the Commons. The positions offered on these general issues were consistent with the positions of each member on the Remonstrance protestation controversy in particular. Hyde, who had originally raised the issue of a protestation during the Remonstrance debates, argued that "clearly no man ought to protest when the vote of the house was past, wherein he must needs be involved." Hyde was insisting that members had to associate, include, or "involve" themselves with any vote of the House, and that any post-vote protest nullified such an "involvement," thereby rendering that vote something less than the collective resolution of the nation's representatives. For this reason, protests should be at least technically separated from the Commons' ultimate decisions. A protestation, Hyde argued, could be made only "against a question which was to be put," that is, against the question itself but not the vote that resulted from it being put. In other words, he continued, "a man may ask leave before [a vote] passes that in case the matter be to such a purpose, that then his name may be entered as a dissentient." This, he claimed, was "no more than if the clerk should set down all the assents and dissents, the yeas and noes, which in our numerous house is not used for the labor of it, but in the Lords ever used." For Hyde, then, this pre-vote protest request was simply a request, in accordance with practice in the Lords, to record the vote in a more detailed (individualized) manner than the traditional tally. He added that there was no precedent for or against this in the Commons, just as there had been no precedent for the Remonstrance that had occasioned so many requests for protestations. The Remonstrance, he implied, was of even more questionable legality and appropriateness than the requests for protestation it occasioned.[30]

Hyde was venturing a subtle distinction and suggesting a comparison between the two Houses that partially ignored the representative significance of the Commons. His maneuvers were not well received. Other members countered that it was absurd to allow protests to a nonexistent (hypothetical) vote while disallowing protests to an actual vote, protests that they agreed with Hyde were inappropriate. D'Ewes added that there must have been an original reason for the Lords' peculiar custom. In any case, he added, "the non-usage of this for so many years of this manner of protestation in the House when there were so many occasions for it, and some great matters carried by the plurality of a few voices only, doth strongly evince that it ought not to be used in this House, and that rather because it hath been constantly used in the Lords' House." D'Ewes was

---

[30] Ibid., 320.

making a conventional distinction between the nature of decision-making in the two Houses. He added that "though the Lords protest, which they have often used to do, it is for their own indemnity, sitting in personal capacities." Members of the Commons, by contrast, sat there in a representative capacity.[31]

Robert Holbourne returned to a position more amenable to borrowing Lords' practices. He suggested that "in point of indemnity we may protest." He went on to turn this specific point into a more assertive and in some sense radical defense of protestations. While "we must submit to a law when it is passed," he admitted, it was also true that "if we may not ask leave to protest, we shall be involved, and perhaps lose our heads in the crowd, when there is nothing to show who was inno-cent." Here Holbourne was openly referring to the threat of popular retribution and arguing, remarkably, that it should influence the House's basic procedures. He provided an example: "A parliament may do a thing unlawful, as to change our religion, etc., and then we are bound to ask leave to protest against it." Holbourne was clearly defending an utter abdication of responsibility by members for parlia-mentary actions they found unlawful. This likely extended, for many members, to the Remonstrance and its publication. Falkland added to Holbourne's support for protestations, disputing the absurdity of pro-testing with regard to an eventuality and noting that this was common practice in the Scottish parliament and other assemblies and synods.[32]

Henry Vane senior retorted that "the liberty of protesting used in all foreign diets and councils is no more to be urged here than the use of the common law there, where they are governed by the civil law." In the English tradition, he argued, minority votes were considered irrelevant to the force and legitimacy of the passed motion, and not to be mentioned. "Until Sir Edward Coke's time," he explained, "*nemine contradicente* was never put into any of our votes and orders," presumably because no difference ought to be acknowledged between the unity or consensus expressed in a unanimous vote and one expressed in any successful voice vote. Hypothetical protests were also threats to free deliberation and the tradition of working toward consensus because they encouraged members to stick to their original preferences or opinions on the matter at hand. "If we may ask leave to protest against a motion made in the house," Vane continued, "we may ask leave to protest against that which, upon debate, perhaps we may be convinced in." Here again protestation

---

[31] Ibid., 320–2.   [32] Ibid., 322; *Verney*, 136. On Scotland, see above, 15–16.

was being contrasted with basic elements of the House's consensual tradition.[33]

Edmund Waller attempted to overturn these arguments about the unique nature of decision-making in the Commons. "The Lords," he insisted, "sit there in sight of their persons and of their whole baronies, of whom held many freeholders who had no voice in the election of knights and burgesses." This was to argue that the lords, too, were representatives of the people. Waller, essentially reiterating one of Hyde's arguments, added that the danger of protestations suggested by other members was overblown because protestations "were of no force to enervate any law made by the greater part." The religious legislation of the first year of Elizabeth's reign, for instance, was "enacted in the name of all the lords spiritual and temporal although the bishops dissented." John Wilde countered that "a protestation in law was a saving of himself from being bound by the act of others, which cannot be admitted." Culpepper also alleged that in 1624 a member, at the passing of a bill, "desired his name might be entered against the bill, that posterity might see, somebody did foresee the great mischief the bill would have upon the commonwealth." Others who had been present for this vote pointed out that the member "received a check for it" and "was neither approved nor seconded by any man." Still other members explained that protestations would make nonsense of traditional assumptions about local representation. "If it be said that the members dissentient may protest, and in their protestation involve all those they represent," one member asked, "then, if in case two members of the same borough differ *in diametro* in any point or matter, which of them shall be said to represent the borough holders? And so of knights, the freeholders, etc." The same logic applied to the entire House when matters of public significance were afoot. "In general cases and republic considerations, that is, in favor of the whole, always the minor part much give way, and forego itself." Self-denial by the minority was seen as crucial to the legitimacy or force of decisions on matters of national concern.[34]

In the end, the House resolved without a division not to permit such protestations to be requested or granted. The prevailing opinion was still the traditional, anti-majoritarian one, which had been voiced in another context by Pym on 3 December. "We being the representative body of the kingdom," Pym explained, "shall join with those Lords who are more

---

[33] *Verney*, 136.

[34] *D'Ewes*, 322–3. This last point also helps clarify why members distinguished between the appropriateness of divisions on public ("republic") and private matters and, relatedly, why capitulations occurred so often.

careful of the safety of the kingdom, they being but private persons, and having a liberty of protestation."[35] But sentiment on the matter was to an extent mixed, and after this debate, minoritarian divisions continued. Diarists ceased to remark on them as unusual, as if they had become a de facto form of protestation that fell within traditional procedural boundaries and unitary fictions. The House was slowly and unwittingly carving out a space for adversarial politics.

External Pressures and Violent Threats: November 1641–October 1642

The controversy over protestations to the printing of the Grand Remonstrance also reflected another crucial, emerging phenomenon first evident during the time of Strafford's trial and attainder in April and May 1641: popular and military pressure on parliamentary deliberations.[36] Both forms of external pressure, of course, were taken to be threats to privilege. On the evening of 24 November 1641, for instance, as the House debated Palmer's attempted protest at length, one thousand apprentices, later alleged to have been sent there at the behest of Palmer's opponents to intimidate his defenders, assembled outside the House.[37] On the next day, as we have seen, the House voted to send Palmer to the Tower. Observers were likely to connect the two events.

But it is important to recall that those in favor of the strongest punishments for Palmer actually lost a division on expelling him from the House. Both vote tallies, in fact, indicated significant willingness to side with Hyde, Culpepper, and other opponents of the Junto in the Commons.[38] After all, opponents of the Remonstrance were also aided in their efforts by external pressure on Parliament. That same day, the 24th, the king had made an ominously militaristic, formal entry into London, accompanied by around one thousand men from the recently disbanded northern army.[39] The earl of Essex's commission as Lord General also expired on Charles' return to the capital. Charles immediately dismissed the guard Essex had placed around Parliament and replaced it with a force of his own choosing. On the following day, 26 November, after Palmer had been committed to the Tower, the Lords requested a conference "touching the guards that attend without."

[35] *D'Ewes*, 228; see also 94, n. 23.
[36] On popular access to Parliament more generally during this period, see Peacey, *Print and Public Politics in the English Revolution*, 163–94.
[37] Lindley, *Popular Politics and Religion in Civil War London*, 95.   [38] *D'Ewes*, 198–9.
[39] Adamson, *Noble Revolt*, 444–6.

According to Pym's report from the conference, the king had sent word to the Lords concerning the guards that "had been set at the desire of the Commons in regard to the multitude of soldiers, and other loose persons." Charles explained that "the guard, that have been set in his absence, perhaps was done upon good grounds; but now his presence is sufficient guard to his people." Clearly attempting to expose Parliament's deep mistrust of his intentions, he added that "if need be to have a guard hereafter, his Majesty will be as glad to have a guard as any other."[40]

On the Commons' request, the Lords agreed to send Warwick and Digby to ask the king, as the Commons put it, that "the guards may be continued, in regard of some information of danger; and that, in a few days, they will present his Majesty with such reasons, as they doubt not but will give his Majesty satisfaction for the farther continuance of them." On 27 November, Charles responded that he would "command My Lord of Dorset to appoint some of the trained bands, only for a few days, to wait on both Houses; in which time, if I shall be satisfied that there is just reason, I will continue them." The Commons had formed a committee that day to draw up reasons for continuing the guard, but on the 29th, after learning that Dorset would be in charge of the soldiers and that their own preferences for the command had been disregarded, they charged the same committee "to consider what reasons are fit to be given for removing this guard newly appointed, and for preserving the privilege of Parliament in that particular."[41] Members of the Commons had clearly begun to suspect that the guard itself was now the primary threat to their safety, or at least their status, despite the fact that crowd demonstrations at Westminster had begun again the same day. As Holland put it in a speech the next day, "the House chose rather to expose itself to a danger for want of a guard rather than to introduce a precedent of such dangerous consequence as to have a guard put upon them."[42]

The military element in Westminster could be seen either as a guarantor of privilege under threat from popular intimidation and violence or as itself a grave threat to privilege. Both perceptions could be taken to imply the illegitimacy of parliamentary proceedings and the undermining of Parliament's procedural traditions. But these threat perceptions also provided a pretext for extraordinary actions in Parliament that themselves violated and destabilized hallowed traditions. They could at least encourage the view that adherence to tradition was in the present moment extremely difficult or even misplaced, because parliamentary procedure had already been compromised and corrupted by others.

---

[40] CJ, 11/26/1641; LJ, 11/26/1641.   [41] CJ, 11/26–9/1641; LJ, 11/26–7/1641.
[42] D'Ewes, 218; Lindley, *Popular Politics and Religion in Civil War London*, 96.

Finally, to the extent that any of this occurred, consensus decision-making in practice became either more difficult or hollow in its significance, because many members believed that consensus, under these circumstances, was actually the result not of freedom but of coercion.

The situation only deteriorated further in the last days of November. On the night of the 29th, in the words of Cornelius Holland's diary, "some hundreds of the citizens came down with swords and staves and accosted some of the members to desire their votes for the putting down of bishops." Coercion was apparently direct and specific. "The Lords hearing hereof sent them words by Maxwell to depart; they still remaining, some were called into the Lords' House and examined and charged to depart." When they neglected to do so, "the Lord Dorset came forth and caused the guard to thrust them out of the Court of Requests, and [the guards] bent their curasses upon them." D'Ewes added in his diary that Dorset "commanded some of the guard to give fire upon some of the citizens of London in the Court of Requests or near it." In the morning, multiple members moved to conference with the Lords about the guard. Pym and Sir Walter Earle reported what Holland and D'Ewes had reported in their diaries the previous day, without naming Dorset but noting that if the guards had opened fire, "no man knew what bloodshed and mischief might have ensued." No one else in the House was ready to name Dorset either, however, and discussion of this particular topic ended.[43]

A royalist version of recent events was offered in turn by Hyde, Kirton, and others. They were led by Sir John Strangeways, who said he had been informed that there was "some design upon this House," led by the City member Captain John Venn, "that did asperse some members of this House, which on his judgment did amount to high treason." He added that "some of the members of this House in this design were either guilty of the consent, or the contriver thereof." The design, he said, was "to force the votes" for the abolition of episcopacy, because the reformers were otherwise likely to be outvoted. He then reported, in order to corroborate this statement, that last night he "was encompassed by above two hundred sworded and staved, to whom he asking what was their meaning, they told him that they came to him for his vote for the putting down of the bishops." He warned that "the privilege of Parliament was utterly broken if men might not come in safety to give their votes freely." Strangeways and Kirton were commanded to produce the written relations of the conspiracy that they had received. The written information in

---

[43] *D'Ewes*, 211, 213.

Strangeways' possession stated that "the intent of their going was because they heard that some division was like to be amongst the members of the lower house, and that the best affected party were likely to be overborn by the others." Everyone mentioned in these statements was summoned, along with the statements' authors.[44]

Later that day, the Lords demonstrated that they, too, were primarily concerned about the crowds descending on Westminster, and they requested a conference about them. The Lords "desired us to join with them in a declaration to inhibit and restrain their said coming," D'Ewes explained, because "else it might give a wound to those good laws we had made and should make, to have the validity of them questioned as if we had been compelled to make them." Second, "it would be a great scandal to the Parliament to suffer such unruly assemblies and disorderly multitudes so near them, without taking some timely care for prevention thereof." In other words, this situation "would not stand with the honour of the Parliament."[45]

After the conference, Pym reported from the committee charged with assessing the need to continue the guard. He related a series of threatening circumstances and reports of conspiracies that confirmed "that there is some wicked and mischievous practice to interrupt the peaceable proceedings of the Parliament." This required the maintenance of a guard, "but to have it under the command of any other, not chosen by themselves, they can by no means consent to, and will rather run any hazard, than admit of a precedent so dangerous both to this and future Parliaments." The dismissal of the guard was finally ordered at the end of the day's proceedings.[46] Thus two competing conspiracy theories about the primary threat to Parliament's safety and status competed with one another: one focusing on popular violence, possibly condoned or organized by the reformers, and the other focused on allegedly hostile military forces, who were defended by the reformers' opponents. Again, such perceptions could, on both sides, motivate and legitimate unusual tactical measures to secure favorable outcomes, including divisions. For they stipulated conditions that could in themselves legitimate majoritarian behavior, either out of a desperate desire to protect the status of Parliament under threat or out of a recognition that the Commons was already under the control of a faction backed by external forces.

[44] Ibid., 213–15; CJ, 11/30/1641. On the identification of Venn, see Pearl, *London and the Outbreak of the Puritan Revolution*, 221.
[45] *D'Ewes*, 218, 222.   [46] CJ, 11/30/1641.

The contest continued over the following days, and crowds continued to assemble outside the Houses of Parliament. On 1 December, a crowd roared against bishops and verbally assaulted Strangeways.[47] John Wilde reported from the Lords conference, and Arthur Goodwin presented a petition from some of the inhabitants of London and the suburbs who had come to Westminster on the night of 29 November. The petition alleged that they came "in a peaceable manner" but "the earl of Dorset threatened them and bade some of the guard to give fire and so to shoot them and the pikes to run them through." The matter was put off until the following day, while the Lords went ahead on their own to order an examination of members of the crowd and to order the Lord Keeper to issue writs to local sheriffs and justices of the peace for dealing with "riots, routs and unlawful assemblies."[48]

On 2 and 3 December debate continued in the Commons on the conference report and petition. Waller, Culpepper, and others defended Dorset and condemned the crowd, while D'Ewes, Strode, and others condemned Dorset and defended the Londoners from the charge of tumult. The issue was raised anew on 10 December, when Sir Philip Stapleton reported that "there was a new guard set upon the House of two hundred men with halberds." This, according to D'Ewes, "occasioned great fear and trouble in the House," which turned immediately to investigating it. The guard had apparently followed orders issued by the sheriff and justices of Middlesex, acting on the writ sent to them by the Lord Keeper after the 2 December Lords order. D'Ewes charged that "it was against the privileges of this House to set a guard upon us without our own consent," and he likened it to the June army plot. Under such conditions, he continued, "we shall neither be able to sit safely or to speak freely, and so not only our privileges, but the liberty also of the whole commons of England whom we represent shall be all taken away at one blow." Both Houses began to question the officials involved, and the Lords discharged the guard. On the following day, the Commons threw George Long, a Middlesex justice of the peace whom D'Ewes called "the chief contriver of the business," in the Tower for breach of privilege. Not long after this business was concluded, the Commons received a petition from City merchant John Fowke that was (according to D'Ewes) signed by 15,000 citizens. It protested the Lords' stoppage of legislation coming from the Commons and asked the Commons to request that Charles take away the bishops' votes in the Lords.[49]

---

[47] Lindley, *Popular Politics and Religion in Civil War London*, 97–8.   [48] *D'Ewes*, 222.
[49] Ibid., 223, 225–7, 229–31, 263–5, 268–72, 275–6; CJ, 12/10/1641; LJ, 12/10/1641.

These dynamics of popular and military intimidation came to a head at the very end of 1641 and early 1642. This final phase of the conflict began with an eventually successful popular agitation against the bishops and culminated in Charles I's attempt on the five members.[50] The frequency of and propensity to violence of crowd gatherings at Westminster increased dramatically in the second half of December, following the vote to print the Remonstrance. On 22 December, Charles appointed a new lieutenant of the Tower, the reformado Thomas Lunsford. This alarmed Parliament and encouraged members of the lower house to move forward with a radical militia bill. Violent crowds – some royalist, most protesting the bishops' vote – thronged different parts of London between 25 and 27 December. On the 27th, bishops arriving at Parliament were assaulted in their coaches as they went through Old Palace Yard. The Lords had commanded crowds around the Parliament door and elsewhere nearby to disperse, but members of the crowds complained, according to the Lords' journal, that "they dare not, because there is Colonel Lunsford, with other soldiers, in Westminster Hall, that lie in wait for them, with their swords drawn." They reported "that some of them that were going through Westminster Hall home, have been wounded and cut in their heads by the said soldiers."[51]

The Lords launched an investigation into both the crowds and the deployment of soldiers and held a conference with the Commons, asking for a joint declaration against crowds surrounding the houses of Parliament and a petition to the king requesting a guard. The Commons ordered Lunsford to appear before them after two men reported on him at the bar. Only two bishops made it into Parliament the following day. After two hours of debate on the Lords' requests in conference, according to D'Ewes, "the greater part of the House thought it unseasonable to make any such declaration at this time to discontent the citizens of London our surest friends when so many designs and plots were daily consulted of against our safety." Plainly responding to external pressure but somewhat divided about how to do so, the House resolved not to put a question about joining in a declaration. The House also voted to tell the Lords that they would join them in a petition for a guard, so long as it was commanded by Essex and approved by both Houses.[52]

---

[50] For fuller description, see Lindley, *Popular Politics and Religion in Civil War London*, 101–14; Como, *Radical Parliamentarians and the English Civil War*, 109–11; Russell, *Fall of the British Monarchies*, 431–4. On the mechanisms driving the broader context of popular participation in parliamentary politics and the permanent turn to a "common politics" at mid-century, see Peacey, *Print and Public Politics in the English Revolution*.

[51] CJ, 12/27/1641; LJ, 12/27/1641.   [52] CJ, 12/27/1641; LJ, 12/27/1641; *D'Ewes*, 356.

In the Lords, Digby moved unsuccessfully (by only four votes in a House with only two bishops present) to have the Parliament declared unfree. The declaration would have nullified its current and future actions and suspended the session indefinitely. Members of the Commons viewed this as a partisan move, but it was partly rooted in realistic concerns. The next day, the Commons began investigations to have Bristol removed from the court and Privy Council and to establish that Digby, Bristol's son, had scandalized the Commons by declaring that the Parliament was no longer free and that "the House of Commons had trenched upon the privileges of the Lords House and upon the liberties of the subject." Holles called these "the most dangerous and pernicious speeches that were ever spoken by a subject."[53]

The bishops excluded from the Lords appealed to Charles the next day, alleging that because of the violence the Lords had not been properly constituted since 27 December, thus nullifying all laws, orders, and resolutions passed from that day onward. On the 29th the Commons had complained to the Lords that members of Parliament had been attacked by reformadoes and one member had discovered a group of soldiers near Parliament commanded by the archbishop of York. The Commons urged the Lords to quickly consider placing a guard on Parliament commanded by Essex. Their appeal was rejected. The bishops' protest was reported to the Lords on the 30th and roundly attacked as a threat to the privileges and very being of Parliament. The Lords and Commons quickly agreed on charges of high treason against the signatories and all twelve of them had been arrested by the afternoon. In the Commons, after securing the lobby and committee chamber and bolting the doors, Pym announced that "there was a plot for the destroying of the House of Commons this day" and moved that the House request the aid of the City trained bands. He was talked down and the Commons simply renewed their request to the Lords for a guard.[54] On multiple fronts Parliament was facing a crisis of its legitimacy and very being. Under these conditions, which persisted in some form until the outbreak of civil war, novel and unusual parliamentary tactics were especially likely to be unleashed.[55]

---

[53] LJ, 12/28/1641; *D'Ewes*, 361.

[54] *D'Ewes*, 365–6. The preceding account of events in late December also draws on Adamson, *Noble Revolt*, 470–2, 474–7, 482–4; Russell, *Fall of the British Monarchies*, 439–45.

[55] For D'Ewes' similar allegations of restrictions on parliamentary speech as a result of factional power in July and August 1642, see *PJLP*, vol. III, 256–9, 263–4, 270, 295, 320–2.

Charles famously moved on from these losses to plan the attempt on the five members. On 3 January the Commons authorized its members to defend themselves, which apparently encouraged Charles personally to visit the Commons in order to avoid bloodshed. He set out with the Elector Palatine and the earl of Roxburgh after dinner the next day, followed by a large group of armed men. The Commons had been warned by Essex and the French ambassador. Once Charles arrived, the five members had absconded, and the king left the House in frustration and embarrassment. The House adjourned and voted early the next day, with doors locked, that the king had violated their privileges and they could meet no longer until they had reclaimed them. After a minoritarian vote that led to a division, they adjourned as a committee to Guildhall. In committee the House took resolutions to defend themselves with recourse to the City trained bands and won a battle for control of them. Charles abruptly left London for Hampton Court on 10 January, and the Parliament triumphantly returned to Westminster on the following day, escorted by 2,400 armed men.[56] The House had therefore declared itself unfree with Charles present in London but then agreed that the Commons' freedom had been restored on his departure.

At this point, the imminent military threat to Parliament disappeared, while the improvement of relations with Charles became a near impossibility, even for logistical reasons. When the Commons began to experience serious conflict again at the end of January, their concerns had turned squarely to the identification and punishment of suspected royalists who threatened their freedom and privilege. It is impossible to make precise causal claims about how the decision-making of members of Parliament was affected by working under the often terrifying conditions that prevailed in late 1641 and early 1642.[57] But members' strong perceptions of the institutional effects of these conditions, which persisted until the outbreak of war in the late summer and fall of 1642, very likely opened a space for more unusual parliamentary practices. Whether the status of the House had been merely threatened or utterly compromised, the effect on behavior was much the same: tactics aimed solely at securing majorities and otherwise confronting threats to institutional and personal honor had been legitimated.

---

[56] Russell, *Fall of the British Monarchies*, 449–52; Adamson, *Noble Revolt*, 494–9.

[57] For more on the political effects of petitioning and crowd action in the late winter, see, inter alia, Como, *Radical Parliamentarians and the English Civil War*, 114–22; Brenner, *Merchants and Revolution*, 435–45. None of this material, however, relates directly to majoritarian moments in the Commons, because it was not popular mobilization per se that was causing divisions.

These tactics were regularly in evidence as the Commons began the slow march to civil war. On 21 May the Commons began the day's business by debating a draft of a declaration justifying John Hotham's actions at the Hull garrison, to which he had denied Charles I access. The declaration had been presented by a committee charged with amending it. An earlier draft, first presented and read on 18 May, had on the 19th been the subject of a minority division pitting royalists against parliamentarians. On the 21st, according to D'Ewes, the declaration was about "to be put to the question without any man's speaking to it." He intervened to urge further revisions on a specific section. Debate continued, and some members "desired that what [D'Ewes] had objected might receive some answer or that this matter might be recommitted." But those responsible for the initial attempt to rush passage of the declaration earlier in the day were apparently eager to proceed with their preferred wording without securing a consensus. "Some hot and violent spirits," he alleged, "which were likely enough to bring the kingdom to a speedy combustion, with such honest-minded men who were misled by them, would admit of no amendment or recommitment, and so it passed."[58] The rest of the declaration was approved in much the same manner.

A similar episode occurred on 8 June, when the clerk read to the Commons a declaration of propositions for the defense of the kingdom that had been drafted by a newly created committee. A debate ensued for and against different parts of the declaration. In particular, members disputed the first section, which asked men to make contributions of horse, money, and plate for war against the king. D'Ewes argued that this section would unnecessarily "fill men's hearts with the fear and expectation of a civil war." Nevertheless, he alleged, "in the issue those hot earnest men, who either feared or knew more danger than I [did and] had at first promoted this declaration with those who commonly followed their example as a rule, carried this part of the declaration affirmatively." This dynamic continued through debate on the other sections of the declaration.[59]

In both of these episodes, D'Ewes was describing meaningfully majoritarian voice votes forced by a "war party." This group, composed of skillful leaders and unthinking followers, in his view, would do whatever it took to move forward with aggressive action against the king, even if it meant bringing the nation to the brink of calamity. They did so, he alleged, in the belief that the nation was already there. We need not

---

[58] *PJLP*, vol. II, 340, 343–9, 354–8.   [59] Ibid., vol. III, 42–5.

suppose, of course, that at this point only D'Ewes' opponents were making use of such tactics. After all, there was usually a coincidence in these discussions between the traditional procedures D'Ewes was defending and the course of action that would give D'Ewes the best chance of outdoing the proponents of aggression by convincing his audience of the need for moderation. Here again consensual practices were likely being espoused, at least some of the time, in a tactical manner. It is more reasonable to imagine that when he described the machinations of "hot earnest men," D'Ewes was capturing only a portion of the majoritarian activity underfoot at this moment than it is to imagine that he was concocting them out of whole cloth.

By the summer D'Ewes was regularly describing this style of desperate partisan maneuver. It would come to typify his account of parliamentary politics in 1643 and beyond. On 12 July, for instance, the committee for the safety of the kingdom reported their votes to name a general, to raise an army, and to petition to prevent a civil war. The committee then moved to have these questions put to the House. D'Ewes argued against putting the first two questions at all, and he urged further debate on all of them, whether or not the first two questions were ever put. "Many allowed of what I had moved," he reported in his diary, "but the greater number being carried along by an implicit faith to assent to whatsoever some hot spirits should propose, the two first propositions were put to the question and voted affirmatively, and then was the third voted also."[60] Later that day, the Commons resolved to live and die with their general, the earl of Essex, which in effect turned them all into traitors in the eyes of the king, further narrowing the possibilities for honorable compromise on either side.

On 20 August, some members argued that the House should order a number of suspected royalist members to appear before them and explain their actions. "But Mr. Henry Marten and some other violent spirits," according to D'Ewes, "being the major number (for we were not above sixty in the house) cried to have the question put for expelling them out of the house," and they prevailed.[61] Here Marten and his allies were reported to have timed the vote for a thin House, which according to D'Ewes benefited their agenda. Just over a week later, on the 27th, the House fell into a debate about whether it should immediately expel Sir John Culpepper, who had been absent from the House but was now waiting outside the chamber with a message from the king and requesting

---

[60] Ibid., vol. III, 202–3; see also 351.   [61] Ibid., vol. III, 310–11.

admission. The Speaker argued against expelling him in this situation, but "Mr. Henry Marten, Mr. Strode, and the other fiery spirits in the House (fearing, I think, lest this gracious message might beget some right understanding between his majesty and the House) would have had the question put for expelling him out of the house presently." The Speaker then put the previous question, and a division was requested, even though the eventual vote was 67 to 29 against putting the question. A meaningfully majoritarian voice vote followed, in which it was "strongly moved by those fiery spirits" that Culpepper be required to deliver his message at the bar or send it into the House. Culpepper delivered the message and it was read by the clerk. Marten and others then went on from here to further motions meant, in D'Ewes' view, to prevent the formal reception of the king's message. They succeeded in blocking it.[62]

By October, D'Ewes was complaining of factional tyranny in the House. He alleged that all important matters before the Commons were being referred with little or no debate to the committee of safety, which his adversaries led "by a kind of fatality and implicit faith." On his view the committee, "commonly called the Council Chamber," sat almost every morning and "dispatched all the great business of the kingdom which concerned that woeful and fatal civil war into which we were unfortunately fallen." As a result, "the House had little or nothing to do till they came amongst us and communicated as much to us as they thought it fitting for us to know; and then commonly they had power to carry by voices whatsoever they pleased."[63] This, of course, was an exaggeration, but it betrays at least the perception that majoritarian activities were becoming common and well coordinated. It is also worth emphasizing at this point that the Commons still usually operated in its traditional way between the spring of 1641 and the early months of the war in 1642. The division frequency remained very low. But the structural framework in which consensual decision-making had been institutionalized was clearly becoming dislocated. This opened the door to increasingly frequent, intentional behavior of a radically different nature.

---

[62] Ibid., vol. III, 320–24. For other evidence of majoritarian assumptions driving conduct in this period, see ibid., vol. II, 143, 153–4, 166, 169–70, 318; vol. III, 17.

[63] D'Ewes MS 164, ff. 9r. (24), 10r. (27). On the committee, see Glowe, "Committee of Safety." This is precisely the sort of majoritarian committee work that Kishlansky identified exclusively with the later 1640s in "Emergence of Adversary Politics" and *Rise of the New Model Army*.

Turning Point: December 1642–April 1643

D'Ewes' angry cataloguing of conflict within the Commons during the spring, summer, and fall of 1642 was the first sign of a turn away from a struggle between proto-royalists and parliamentarians and toward a struggle for the Revolution. The reasons for the timing of this turn are obvious. In 1642, prior to 4 December, sixty-two members were expelled from the House. Among them were many of those who had spoken powerfully against the king's opponents in the previous year. By spring 1642, however, they had largely ceased to figure in the Commons' deliberations. With very few exceptions, from early 1642 onward future royalists no longer served as tellers in divisions or as members of committees. Many other future royalists who were not expelled prior to 4 December had simply stopped attending the House at some point over the past year. They were formally expelled at a later point in the conflict. Individual expulsions continued throughout 1643, and in February of that year the House disabled from service in the Commons anyone who had "actually levied war, or voluntarily contributed to the forces raised against the Parliament."[64] Majoritarian decisions in the Commons therefore necessarily began to revolve around intra-parliamentarian conflicts. These conflicts would prove decisive in spurring the disintegration of the House's consensual decision-making institution.

The year 1643, it appears, was the most important moment in the emergence of majoritarian politics (Figures 4.1 and 4.2).[65] The frequency of divisions jumped suddenly from 3.4 percent of questions put between 1614 and 1642 to 13.6 percent.[66] A division occurred about

[64] These included Sir Edward Dering, Lord Digby, Sir Ralph Hopton, Sir Nicholas Slanning, Edward Hyde, Edward Kirton, Gervase Holles, Sir John Strangeways, Geoffrey Palmer, and Lord Falkland. See Davies and Klotz, "Members Expelled from the Long Parliament"; Kershaw, "Recruiting of the Long Parliament," 169–79; Snow, "Attendance Trends and Absenteeism in the Long Parliament"; Glow, "The Manipulation of Committees in the Long Parliament," 35.

[65] Contrast Kishlansky, "Emergence of Adversary Politics," and Kishlansky, *Rise of the New Model Army*, 131.

[66] The notation "resolved, &c." was often used in this period to denote decisions reached after a question put on routine matters. (On rare occasions, "ordered" was used for the same purpose.) This might be thought to artificially inflate division frequency counts by concealing questions put, thereby creating a false impression of a departure in 1643. This was clearly not the case. This notation was not used prior to 20 April 1641. It was then used 175 times between that day and the end of 1642, or slightly more than once every three days in session. Over that period the division frequency (with mentions of "resolved, &c." not counted as questions put) was still 3.8 percent. In 1643, the notation was used 246 times, or slightly less than once per day, and the division frequency jumped to 13.6 percent. It is unclear how often this notation concealed questions put, but it did not normally do so. Even if we count all instances of this notation as evidence of

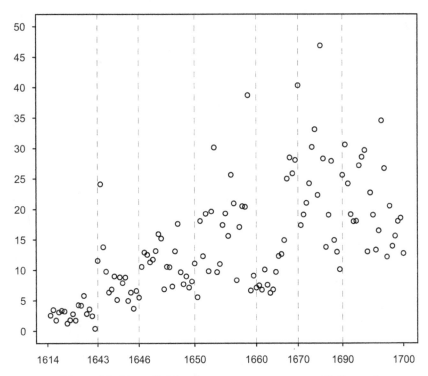

Figure 4.1 Mean division frequency as percentage of all questions put, 1614–99. Each dot represents a period of sixty days in session. Tick marks are located on the sixty-day unit that includes the beginning of each year.

every three days in session in 1643, after occurring only once every ten days before 1640 and once every five days in 1640–2. Even more importantly, the trend evident in 1643 was never reversed. Between 1643 and 1699, an average of 14.4 percent of voice votes resulted in divisions, and divisions occurred about every two or three days in session. These figures are not by-products of temporary, revolutionary conditions, either. The House actually divided more frequently (17.7 percent of the time) after the restoration of the monarchy than in either 1643 or the period between 1643 and 1660. The figures for both 1643 and the rest of the seventeenth century represented a fourfold increase in division frequency from the

questions put, the division frequency in the earlier period is 3.5 percent (remarkably consistent with all previous periods), and in the latter period, 9.9 percent (nearly a threefold increase from the earlier period).

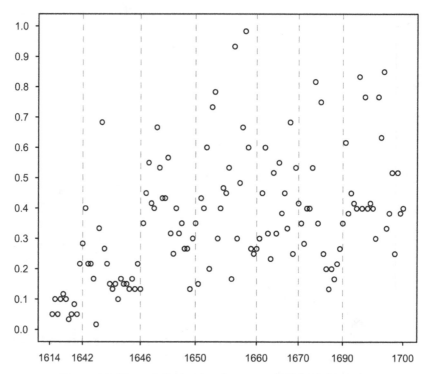

Figure 4.2 Mean daily division frequency, 1614–99. Each dot represents a period of sixty days in session. Tick marks are located on the sixty-day unit that includes the beginning of each year.

early Stuart period. The figure for 1643–99 was also equal to the frequency of divisions in the eighteenth century (14 percent), and it was nearly two thirds the frequency in the nineteenth-century, post–Reform Act House of Commons, which divided less than a quarter of the time. These data render it improbable that even a weak form of consensual politics – say, a situation in which at least half of all voice vote differentials were above 60 percent (an 80 to 20 vote in a 100-person assembly) – prevailed in or survived revolutionary England. If such a minimally consensual regime had remained in place, less than 14 percent of voice votes would have resulted in divisions.

We can in fact be more specific about the way in which the period between late 1642 and spring 1643 was a turning point by considering the data from a few other angles (Figure 4.1). Between 1614 and November 1642, there was no 120-day interval in which the mean division frequency exceeded 5.5 percent. From December 1642 until the end of the seventeenth century, only 6 percent of all 120-day intervals of division frequency ever fell *below* 5.5 percent. Another clear indicator comes from the fact that in the Long Parliament, between November 1640 and December 1642, the Commons had divided only 3.4 percent of the time, and after Charles raised his standard at Nottingham, divisions became even more infrequent until the last month of the year. In fact, between 1 October and 18 November, the Commons did not divide a single time. But over the final weeks of the year, the House divided 11.4 percent of the time, and from the beginning of 1643 to 8 April, the frequency of divisions was a whopping 22 percent of questions put. Finally, while the Commons had divided just 196 times in the entire period between 1604 and November 1642, they divided sixty-one times over the following five *months*. The period between December 1642 and April 1643 was clearly pivotal.[67]

This spike in division frequency followed the first few months of civil war and coincided with the first peace negotiations between Charles I and Parliament, which began in January 1643. After the failure of negotiations in mid-April 1643, England descended into nineteen months of bloody conflict. Negotiations with Charles only began again with a parliamentary commission's visit to Oxford on 20 November 1644 and formal negotiations at Uxbridge on 30 January 1645. The peace negotiations were obviously central to the destruction of consensus politics. Between January and 8 April 1643, 60 percent of the fifty divisions held in the House concerned negotiation with the king. No other single category of dispute was nearly as important, and most of the other divisions concerned integrally related, status-saturated issues. The most common were the funding of the war effort and the identification and treatment of suspected royalists.[68] The breakdown of consensual decision-making in the Commons was clearly a direct result of the wrenching dilemmas posed by the breakdown and destruction of the English polity and Parliament's concomitant assumption of executive functions and authority.

---

[67] On petitioning and other forms of popular action surrounding Parliament in this period and their links to the formation of "war" and "peace parties" in Parliament, see Como, *Radical Parliamentarians and the English Civil War*, 131–55. Again, clear, specific links between this activity and the emergence of majoritarian decision-making practices, as opposed to heightened ideological conflict, are not evident for this period.

[68] The legal problems involved with ordinances were by no means as divisive as one might expect. See, for example, CJ, 11/25/1642, 12/6/1642, 2/4/1643. Hexter, *Reign of King Pym*, was in this sense right about how money bills were successfully managed in this parliament. This may have been related to the primacy traditionally placed on consensus in matters of taxation.

Members of the House of Commons believed that specific aspects of the Oxford Treaty negotiations had incalculably momentous consequences. The divisions over negotiations make clear that the House's institution of consensus decision-making was fatally weakened by the pull between two impulses: members' desire to save the kingdom and its people from mass death and ruination, and their need to protect the honor, privileges, and legal standing of Parliament. Both imperatives could easily surmount the desire of members to avoid the dishonor incurred by meaningfully majoritarian votes, even though in the long run, these same votes would destroy Parliament's legitimacy. Charles himself recognized this problem as early as the summer of 1642. He interpreted majority rule as the essence of parliament's usurpation and illegitimacy. Just as Parliament was "still mis-applying the word Parliament to the vote of both Houses," he wrote in his *Answer* of spring 1642, in another "phrase of the time, the vote of the major part of both Houses, and sometimes of one, is now called, the resolution of the whole kingdom."[69] Yet while majoritarian tactics were often seen as a corruption of parliamentary traditions, they simultaneously served, intentionally or not, as a means of reinventing parliamentary legitimacy under revolutionary conditions. As the Commons continued to act as the representative of the people, increasingly acted as a sovereign entity (with and without the Lords), and resorted to divisions in order to do so, it automatically yoked its authority and legitimacy to majoritarian decision-making, despite the fact that the authority and legitimacy of that mode of governing was deeply suspect to all concerned.

The opposing demands on members that led them to resort to majoritarian decision-making were encapsulated in the commonly agreed goal of Parliament's negotiations. As D'Ewes put it on 9 February 1643, "the work therefore we are now to do is to advise how to make a safe and honourable peace." Settling with security and honor required that "the true religion ... be established, his majesty's person and honour secured, the liberty of the subject asserted, and the privileges of Parliament vindicated."[70] D'Ewes' constant appeals to honor in this period make clear that honor was not merely the preserve of those most committed to war or constancy. Instead, its proper application was disputed, and it could easily be attached to pleas for conciliation and moderation.[71] Yet for many, and in particular members of the so-called war parties in the Commons and among the royalists, honor was closely related to

---

[69] Charles I, *His Majesties Answer*, 6.
[70] D'Ewes MS 164, ff. 293r.–v. (207), 268v. (117). See also ff. 300r. (230–1), 314v. (287).
[71] Braddick, *God's Fury, England's Fire*, 300–2.

constancy or resolution.[72] Since a resolute politician might often prefer to arrange commitments to action before deliberation in Parliament, this style of politics could make majoritarian decisions more likely. If there were fixed views on each side of the question held by significant numbers of members, debate would still occur, but it would be capable of forging only a majority, not a consensus.

Divisions over peace negotiations, royalism, and revenue in this period all resulted from differences between those who wanted to proceed more or less aggressively with Charles. Some believed that relatively assertive negotiating positions, legally dubious revenue measures, and the active identification and punishment of royalists were most consistent with an honorable peace. It is certainly worth recalling here as well that many of the men who adopted this stance would likely face death if Parliament made a generous settlement with the king.[73] As D'Ewes put it on 11 February 1643, after a division on treating with the king in which the noes prevailed, "I know that there were many honest, well-meaning men [who] gave their noes, but they were misled by Pym, Hampden, Strode, Marten and other fiery spirits, who accounting their own conditions desperate did not care though they hazarded the whole kingdom to save themselves."[74] As the conflict escalated, more and more people found themselves in a similar situation. Insisting on strongly favorable peace terms and continuing the bloodshed in hope of a decisive victory were ironically consistent with their self-preservation.

Others, including D'Ewes, believed that conciliatory negotiation, close attention to legality, and sympathy for those who struggled with the vexing question of allegiance was the surer route to an honorable peace. One group was marginally more concerned with peace than with honor, while the other group reversed these priorities. But both were arguably politicizing the entire issue of honor by using it as a byword for their grave concern for either self-preservation or societal preservation. Whether we take the members of the House at their word or not, the effect is the same: either status considerations trumped the honor of consensus, as members normally alleged, or preservational priorities forged in desperation did so. In this moment many aspects of negotiation with Charles could still be resolved consensually.[75] But on the margins of various settlement and war-making schemes, where different forms of

---

[72] Thomas Hobbes argued in the portions of *Leviathan* cited above (44) that resolution was intrinsically honorable. See Hobbes, *Leviathan*, vol. II, 140–1, and, more generally, Bulman, "Practice of Politics."

[73] Scott, *Politics and War in the Three Stuart Kingdoms*, 41–2.

[74] D'Ewes MS 164, f. 269v. (218).

[75] See, for example, CJ, 12/22/1642; D'Ewes MS 164, f. 273r. (128–9).

desperation and concern for status came into conflict, institutional failure was bound to become a regular phenomenon. Parliament was making increasingly aggressive status claims at the same time that its most basic claims to status were perceived to be under the gravest threat. This environment was extremely conducive to a proliferation of majoritarian decisions. The exceptional circumstances under which divisions had occurred in the past were becoming everyday realities.

Competing understandings of what constituted an honorable peace were closely related to the basic differences in political strategy so evident in debate during this period. "War party" argumentation proceeded from the assumption that aggressive vindication of the House's status and relentless prosecution of the conflict were the best means of inducing Charles to accept favorable peace terms. Honorable and resolute behavior was intrinsically valued, but it was also taken to be strategically optimal with an eye to a favorable peace.[76] This was also the view of those royalists who were urging Charles I to practice resolute politics in his struggle against Parliament.[77] Indeed, on 8 April 1643, D'Ewes likened the two groups to one another, speaking of "the violent spirits here and the violent spirits at Oxford."[78] While "peace party" positions, by contrast, were driven by an ethical commitment to act to avert further bloodshed, peaceniks also thought that such conduct, by establishing trust and enabling compromise, was the only feasible means to a respectable peace. The centrality of these partisan differences to negotiations with Charles is abundantly clear.[79] The situations that broke the House in early 1643 were fundamentally the same sorts of situations that had episodically led to divisions in earlier periods. But the problems of status they posed were often far more grave. Considerations of honor and privilege became entwined with broader questions concerning the legal and constitutional status of Parliament and the appropriateness and legality of its increasingly revolutionary acts and assertions.[80]

---

[76] D'Ewes MS 164, ff. 99r.–v. (48–9), 177v. (70–1), 178v. (71–2), 291r.–293r. (198–205), 295r. (213), 296v. (218), 299v.–302r. (229–36).

[77] Bulman, "Practice of Politics."   [78] D'Ewes MS 164, f. 361v. (448).

[79] For examples from the period between mid-November 1642 and early April 1643 aside from those presented in the following discussion, see BL MS Add 18777, ff. 64r.–65v.; CJ, 11/21/1642, 12/29/1642, 12/30/1642; D'Ewes MS 164, f. 99 (48–9). On the relationship between the struggle in Parliament and political mobilization elsewhere in London in the winter of 1642–3, see Downs, "Attempt on the Seven Londoners." Here again there is no clear connection between popular petitioning in this period and the rising incidence of divisions.

[80] For earlier examples of this transition, see POSLP, vol. V, 433–506, 613–22; vol. VI, 89–96; PJLP, vol. I, 14–17, 143–58 (for royalism as the concern here, see BL MS Add 64807, f. 33v.), 187–205 (again on royalism, see BL MS Add 64807, f. 37r.), 254–7, 383–93, 437–46; vol. II, 21–5, 267–71, 293–9, 343; vol. III, 5–12, 61–3, 85–91, 191,

In this sense the conflicts over status that deinstitutionalized consensual decision-making in the House of Commons were integrally related to the broader ideological struggles developing within it, even though these ideological struggles, in themselves, were clearly insufficient conditions for majoritarian decision-making. While it is difficult to establish a precise relationship between behavior and ideas in this context, the resolute politics of the "war party" appear to have been related to an emergent constitutional radicalism among some members. At the very least, the party's practices and aggressive stances drew some argumentative support from the radical discourse of the winter of 1642–3. Some writers seemed willing to countenance popular sovereignty and the deposition of the king on the basis of fundamental laws of nature and equity that trumped English law and vows of obedience. Others clearly asserted Parliament's constitutional supremacy. They rejected the customary assumption that the king was part of Parliament and could veto parliamentary legislation. And they declared that Parliament was bound by neither precedent nor (in the opinion of some) existing law. These positions could be taken to justify parliamentary action that other members deemed illegal and dishonorable. There was also another possible relationship between action and constitutional goals here. Those who rejected compromise with the king may have done so because only total victory would provide the conditions for the dramatic alterations to church and state they desired.[81] Others with more conventional constitutional and religious views, by contrast, were generally more inclined to compromise with the king. Their critics took their inclinations to be pusillanimous and dishonorable.

The struggles over status that broke the House of Commons in 1643 were regularly manifest from the beginning of the year. The 8 February debate over whether the king had actually answered Parliament's peace propositions, for instance, was clearly in part a debate over whether he had dishonored them by not responding properly and instead presenting alternative demands, demands whose relevance to the future status of Parliament was itself at issue. Pym also addressed an underlying problem with the king's demands that related to both status and ideology. He asked "whether we shall put our rights to treaty"

234–7, 266–8, 303–5, 320–4, 330. *PJLP* should be read with the corresponding entries in CJ.

[81] Wootton, "From Rebellion to Revolution," 654–69; Como, *Radical Parliamentarians and the English Civil War*, 132, 150–2, 159–64; Peacey, "'Fiery Spirits' and Political Propaganda." As Wootton notes, on this front, too, the period following the outbreak of civil war seems to have exhibited phenomena traditionally seen (by Kishlansky and others) as first emerging in 1646.

and stated that "the undoubted rights of parliament cannot be put to a treaty without yielding up our rights and privileges." This meant it was necessary "to desire from the king a fuller answer to our propositions: and to treat of such things as are doubtful." Holles concurred.[82] Concern about status was so acute at this point that on the same day, the House was driven to divide over whether to accept a Lords' invitation to discuss the peers' recent votes on a response to Charles. Sir Arthur Haselrig stated the problem in blunt terms: "[T]he House of Commons," he said, "had ability enough to consult amongst themselves and not to receive direction by the votes of the Lords."[83] Even the smallest perceived slight was deemed by many, if not all, to be worthy of a firm repudiation.

The next day, 9 February, Sir Henry Vane junior argued that to have a cessation of hostilities and a treaty before demanding that the armies be disbanded "trenches upon the liberty of the house."[84] Walter Long made a similar argument on the 10th against this manner of proceeding. He pointed out that the basis for treating on propositions with the king was the same as when Parliament had refused to treat with Charles at Nottingham. "Seeing his Majesty had proclaimed the earl of Essex and all his adherents traitors," Long noted, "we could not treat with him till that proclamation was recalled and his standard laid down." This was for Long partly a matter of honor: Parliament could not be seen in any way to acquiesce in the king's denunciation of its members, and it could not contradict its previous commitments. Claims about the need for Parliament to maintain its honor were frequently made in terms of the need to project power and remain resolute. These claims regularly featured in debates that ultimately led to divisions. In his riposte to Long's argument on the 9th, D'Ewes could only suggest that his opponents were adhering too rigidly to their previous and now obsolete resolutions. "We are," D'Ewes reassured the House, "masters of our own resolution." Their honor was no longer at stake in the way they believed it was. In hopes of convincing his fellow members that their honor would be secure if they treated with Charles now, D'Ewes went on to remind them that many of "the greatest princes in the world" had made difficult decisions against former resolutions that were similar to the one they now needed to make.[85] Honor imperatives were the underlying principles on both sides of this debate.

Similar concerns surfaced on 11 February, when the House voted not to treat on peace propositions before demanding that the armies be

---

[82] BL MS Add 18777, ff. 146v.–147r. See also f. 151r.
[83] D'Ewes MS 164, f. 291v. (200).   [84] BL MS Add 18777, f. 147v.
[85] D'Ewes MS 164, f. 294v. (211–12).

disbanded. Sir Henry Vane junior would "have no mediators between us and the king." He warned that "if we admit of an umpire between the king and us and the king's council shall alter and add what they think fit, what will become of the Parliament?" Cornelius Holland "would not have us treat upon the king's five propositions because they overthrow our right and security." Sir John Holland added that "we have a proposition that delinquents may be left to the law. We see this will not be granted yet we are engaged to disband. The king will have them tried *per pares* which is against the privilege of parliament." In a debate on 17 February concerning the Lords' votes for a cessation, a treaty, and a disbanding of the armies within thirty days, Sir Henry Ludlow summarized this status-sensitive situation when he reminded the House that "we took up arms for the defense of the privileges of parliament and calling of delinquents to justice."[86] Henry Marten, for his part, said that the Lords' response to the Commons' former votes on the questions of cessation, peace, and disbandment "slighted us" and therefore had to be rejected.[87]

Parliamentary honor, considered within the wider ideological contestation of Parliament's constitutional status, continued to be the dominant context for differences within the House in March. On the 6th, when Charles responded to Parliament's new peace overtures with his own demands, the Commons declared with the Lords, without a division, that they were "willing to give his Majesty all due satisfaction, in such things as might not be destructive to the privileges of Parliament, or liberty of the subject." They added that they were "resolved (if a just peace, with the security of religion and liberty, cannot by fair means, be obtained), to go on in such a way as may evidence unto the world their constancy in the cause."[88] This statement highlighted the role of institutional and personal status in the situation, and it implicitly underlined the connection between hard-line stances and a resolute, honor-bound political practice.

The following month, on 6 April, the Lords asked the Commons to concur in their statement that "whereas his majesty had in his last message touching a cessation let slip some passages which trenched upon the honour of the two houses of Parliament, they thought it not fit to return any answer thereto in respect that it might beget but greater distaste." The Commons divided over how to proceed beyond sending this non-answer to the king. The Lords wanted to extend the period during which the commissioners at Oxford were permitted to treat with Charles, but many in the Commons were opposed. On the next day, Marten also spoke against concurring with the Lords on another detail of

---

[86] BL MS Add 18777, ff. 151r.–v., 152r.–v., 158r.   [87] D'Ewes MS 164, f. 300r. (231).
[88] CJ, 3/6/1643.

Parliament's response to Charles, "lest by that [we] should seem to submit our judgment to their opinions." D'Ewes accepted Marten's premise and countered that with this concurrence the Commons did in "no way recede from our resolution." D'Ewes thereby confirmed the centrality of considerations of honor and resolution to the debate while contesting their proper application.[89] Under these conditions, the stability of the meaning and referents of resolution and honor had been weakened to the point that they were no longer reliable operative principles in supporting consensual decision-making in the Commons.

The other major issues that caused divisions in this period – royalism and revenue – also had prominent honor components. The question of royalism was of course integrally tied to negotiation and to the legitimacy of Parliament and, in particular, to the honor-bound question of delinquency. On 21 November 1642, for instance, a number of members made reference to the May 1641 Protestation in arguing that Parliament should demand that Charles hand over delinquents. For according to the Protestation, all members had vowed to "maintain and defend" "the power and privilege of Parliaments" and "to bring to condign punishment all such as shall ... do anything to the contrary of this present Protestation."[90] On 29 December, as Parliament was preparing to reopen formal negotiations with the king, it set out to complete the propositions for the occasion by naming those delinquents against whom it would proceed. It divided on whether to name anyone other than Digby, and then divided twice – on a previous question and the question itself, in a clear breakdown of consensual mechanisms – about whether to extend nominations beyond Digby and Newcastle.[91] On the following day, the House divided on a previous question regarding a similar proposition: whether to demand that the king remove Bristol from court and office (this time the main question was put and resolved without a division).[92] Again and again, the need to defend parliamentary honor was in conflict with the need to make concessions that might lead to peace.

Similar issues surfaced in isolated considerations of royalists under parliamentary control. On 19 November the Commons divided on a petition for bail by a royalist, Sir Robert Hatton, and rejected his petition.[93] This decision pitted the appeal of conciliatory gestures against the need to vindicate the House's authority with respect to a man who had

---

[89] D'Ewes MS 164, ff. 359r.–360r. (440, 444–5).
[90] BL MS Add 18777, ff. 64r.–65v.; CJ, 11/21/1642; D'Ewes MS 164, ff. 99r.–v. (48–9); Gardiner (ed.), *Constitutional Documents of the Puritan Revolution*, 156.
[91] CJ, 12/29/1642.   [92] Ibid., 12/30/1642.   [93] Ibid., 11/19/1642.

helped to execute a commission of array and ignored a summons from the House to attend it. Those voting "no" were overwhelmingly concerned with vindicating the honor or legal authority of the House.[94]

As the House repeatedly protected its status by *dividing* and rose in power in the process, its status gradually became less strongly attached to the maintenance of internal consensus. Repeated ruptures made future ruptures more likely. The Commons' regular failure to maintain consensus made consensus a less plentiful source of status. And the defense of status by means of division diluted the very legibility of consensus as a sign of status. In turn, the assertion of status became increasingly dependent on the successful defense of Parliament, the Commons, and its members against external threats, and on Parliament's mounting claims to authority and assertions of power. The *means* by which these defenses, claims, and assertions were made was increasingly a matter of secondary importance. The more the House found itself divided, the less members would have found it reasonable to invest in claims to authority, unity, and legitimacy that were rooted in the achievement of consensus, and the more reasonable they would have found it to do whatever was needed to repel external threats and vindicate Parliament's honor. Once the hold of consensual practices on the Commons was weakened, more frequent divisions were bound to result. This was especially true as the level of ideological conflict within the House increased, because this increased the frequency with which the House was dealing with questions on which there was deep disagreement.

The shift from means-oriented practices to ends-oriented decisions in this moment was profoundly consequential. In circumstances of structural dislocation and desperation, members were more free than ever before to develop fluid, instrumental calculations about how best to ensure that decisions in the House went their way, without worrying as much about how those decisions were reached. This did not imply that majoritarian politics had become institutionalized. But it did imply that new patterns of behavior would emerge, because preexisting structures related to collective decision-making were less able than before successfully to enable or constrain behavior.

Under these conditions the partisan organization of voting partly replaced vociferous debate as the mechanism of decision-making. Parliamentary tactics reflected an implicit acceptance of decision-making

---

[94] On Hatton, see Keeler, *Long Parliament*, 208–9. For other examples, see CJ, 12/3/1642, 12/26/1642, 12/29–30/1642, 1/28/1643, 1/30/1643; *D'Ewes*, 70–2; D'Ewes MS 164, ff. 284r. (171–2), 342v. (380).

by division.[95] This occurred as a response to conflict between two imperfectly defined groupings in parliament: the "war" and "peace" groups. Both of them made appeals to a wider group of active members who regularly appeared on both the "peace" and "war" sides of questions put to the House. The existence of such patterns in voting and debate confirms the underlying prioritizations driving divisions when they occurred. Partisan members were debating in order to form a majority, but not always to form a consensus. The available data on tellers provides an inkling of the leadership behind these activities. Tellers consistently told for the side they supported in a division, and during this period, tellers consistently appeared on either the "war" or "peace" side of questions. These patterns in telling correspond well, in turn, with the record of debates, the contemporary analyses of diarists, and the later analyses of modern historians.[96]

To a limited extent, members may have even begun debating in a "violent" manner, not seriously intending to convince anyone not already in their side.[97] Such debate would have obviously been especially prone to causing divisions. But for the most part, the frequency of

[95] The analysis of majoritarian tactics in what follows is based largely on evidence from print, parliamentary diaries, and the Commons journal. While each source is problematic in one way or another, it is remarkable that they all point toward the same generalizations. As S. R. Gardiner and Jack Hexter showed long ago, D'Ewes' presentation of clearly demarcated parties of men of peace ("sober spirits") and men of blood ("fiery," "hot," and "violent" "spirits") was misleading, and his attribution of motives cannot, of course, be accepted. But his diary is still immensely useful for our purposes here. As suggested earlier, D'Ewes was probably not so much fabricating evidence about the partisan tactics of his enemies as he was neglecting to describe similar behavior by his allies. Denzil Holles, after all, was central to the reemergence of intensely majoritarian politics in 1646, but largely escaped censure from D'Ewes in this earlier period because the two became politically aligned with one another. D'Ewes believed that Holles' early experience of the war had converted him to a peacenik stance. See D'Ewes MS 164, f. 302r. (237–8).

[96] Over the course of this period D'Ewes named Holles, Bulstrode Whitelocke, John Glynn, William Pierrepont, James Fiennes, Francis Rous (just once, ambiguously), John Maynard, and himself as "honest" proponents of peace. The "fiery spirits" he named in this period were Marten, Strode, Pym, Peter Wentworth, Hampden, Dennis Bond (of Dorchester), Alexander Rigby (Gray's Inn), William Ashurst, Vane junior, Rous, Gilbert Millington, Miles Corbet, and Cornelius Holland. Teller data for this period confirm the position of certain members of both groups: in particular, Holles, John Evelyn (Surrey), Waller, John Holland, and Pierrepont as members of a peace party; and Marten, Strode, Hampden, Stapleton, and perhaps Purefroy and John Clotworthy as war party leaders.

[97] D'Ewes MS 164, ff. 99v. (49), 101v. (50), 264r. (102), 271r. (122), 295v. (215). D'Ewes' interpretation here must, however, be used with caution, since he was only describing the speech of his opponents. Relatedly, there were a number of outright altercations between members in the House during this period, which of course signified a breakdown of usual debating conventions. See ibid., ff. 106r., 108v. (52–3), 254v. (97), 292v.–293r. (205–7), 317v. (297).

divisions appears to have simply reflected the fact that members were strictly adhering to their original positions on issues under consideration by the House in accordance with a desperate logic of status and preservation. More importantly, perhaps, members were clearly manipulating the course of debate in ways calculated to secure a political advantage.[98] Opponents of peace, for instance, moved to table or delay discussion of peace propositions, motioned to discuss other topics when the orders of the day prescribed consideration of peace negotiations, introduced alterations to treaty articles under consideration in order to disrupt support for them or delay their passage, and used committees as venues for filibustering.[99]

One dramatic example of this array of tactics comes from 11 March 1643. Opponents of peace tried to delay debate on articles for the cessation of hostilities by first arguing that debate ought to be put off for another time. When this failed, they argued that because it was time for dinner, the house should rise. And when this failed, they urged that the House should be resolved into a committee of the whole, purportedly in order to more thoroughly debate a matter that they had been trying to avoid considering at all. D'Ewes rose to argue against the motion, saying, "I did not allow of the motion of turning the house into a committee at this time because I conceived the modifications which the Lords offered to us upon the king's propositions would not require any long debate." He added, though, that he "especially dislike[d] the reason that was given on the other side … that we should therefore turn the house into a committee because some members used to speak often. For this lays a scandal upon the house."[100] D'Ewes also accused his enemies of colluding with citizens of the City in order to alter the course of debate, disrupt peace negotiations, and even begin a process by which peace-friendly members might be ejected from the House.[101] There is

---

[98] In addition to the examples in the following discussion, see ibid., ff. 99v. (49), 101v. (50–1), 274r. (133), 276r. (144), 276v. (146), 284r. (171), 295r. (213), 305v. (252).

[99] Ibid., ff. 270v. (121), 271r. (122), 275r. (137), 302r. (237), 300v. (232), 301v.–302r. (236), 323r.–v. (313–14). For an earlier example from 1642, before the war began, see *PJLP*, vol. III, 176. Very often the diversion of Commons business was attempted, contrary to the orders of the day, by pushing for the identification and punishment of suspected royalist members who had not pledged loyalty to Essex or made sufficient war contributions. See, for example, D'Ewes MS 164, ff. 291r. (198), 292v. (205), 317v.–318r. (296–8). These controversial attempts to vindicate the honor of the House and Parliament's proceedings in the war themselves often led to divisions.

[100] D'Ewes MS 164, ff. 321v.–322r. (308–10). He continued: "[T]he reason for the most part of turning the house into a committee doth arise upon the experience of difficulties that shall arise upon our debate of a business in the house."

[101] Ibid., ff. 303r. (241), 324r. (316).

also evidence to suggest that peaceniks like D'Ewes manipulated debate in ways similar to the better-documented tactics of their opponents.[102]

As members became aware that divisions were an increasingly regular aspect of decision-making in Commons, they became more attentive than ever to assessing and managing who was in the House at any given time. It was, again, a traditional norm in the Commons that important votes were not to be taken in a thin House and that questions for a bill's passage were to be coupled with questions for other bills and not put early in the day.[103] "It would be some dishonor to the passing" of a bill in a thin House, D'Ewes was wont to say.[104] Whatever the norms and whatever one's attitude toward them, it was nevertheless crucial to be sure that one's allies were in the House when divisions were called. Both sides in the debates of this period clearly paid attention to who was present in the House at a given time and what the balance of opinion was.[105] D'Ewes accused his enemies of using or forcing divisions to pursue their warlike aims at carefully chosen moments when they had superior numbers in the House, thus acting against the traditional norms of consensus.[106] His comments are consistently corroborated by turnout numbers for votes in which his adversaries succeeded.[107]

On 7 March, for instance, "the house being thin between one and two of the clock in the afternoon because so many were gone out to dinner," D'Ewes' opponents moved for a controversial revenue ordinance "with an intent to surprise the house." Warned that this was an important measure that should be debated by a full House at some other time, but "perceiving that they had [at] least ten or twelve voice odds in the house, as it afterwards proved," they refused to delay. A number of members then registered grave objections to the ordinance and tried to have it recommitted, but they were defeated in a division. The ordinance

[102] Ibid., ff. 292v. (203), 312r. (278), 324v. (317). There is no clear evidence of minorities forcing divisions in this period, although there were some fairly lopsided divisions (see, for example, CJ, 2/4/1643, 4/4/1643). There is limited evidence for such minoritarian voting for the rest of the 1640s as well, but see, for example, CJ, 7/15/1647, 5/24/1648, 11/23/1648. The rarity of such voting might be taken further to imply the implicit acceptance of majoritarian practices.
[103] See, for example, BL MS Add 26644, f. 13r.
[104] D'Ewes MS 164, f. 282v. (166). See also, for example, D'Ewes MS 164, ff. 280r. (155–6), 297v. (222), 315v. (289).
[105] Ibid., ff. 99b (49), 324r.–v. (316–17), 334r. (349–50). Turnouts were, as a result, particularly high during the most important peace negotiation debates in 1643.
[106] See also, for example, ibid., ff. 292v. (203), 300v. (232), 311r. (274), 315r. (288). For a royalist account of the same maneuvering, see Mercurius Aulicus (16–22 April 1643; Nelson and Seccombe, British Newspapers and Periodicals, 275.116), 279.
[107] Aside from what is presented below, see D'Ewes MS 164, ff. 270v. (121), 331v.–332r. (341), 350v.–351r. (410–11), 352r.–v. (415–17).

then passed on a second question, without a division.[108] On other occasions, precise timing itself was not the issue, but rather the composition of the members attending the House over a longer period of time. On 28 March, the war party again pressed for members to be taxed further in support of the war, and "knowing their number in the house to be greater (because divers honest men, well-wishers to the peace of the kingdom, were gone out to the kingdom), [they] pressed upon Serjeant Wilde to have the question put." They successfully pushed the measure through in a committee of the whole.[109]

D'Ewes explained these episodes as the results of exploitative, corrupt manipulation of speech and voting in the House, repeating the terms of his accusations of partisan organization from July 1642. "The mean or beggarly fellows on the other side were those who undid us," he wrote about 28 March, "for they commonly, as [Alexander] Bence, [Dennis] Bond, [John] Lowry, [Thomas] Hoyle, and others, having been mechanics and being men of mean fortune, were not so sensible of the destruction of the kingdom as we who had estates to lose, and besides they were so silly as for the most part they followed Mr. Pym and some others which way soever they went as if they had voted by an implicit faith."[110] D'Ewes observed a convergence between the desperation of "fiery spirits," who could save themselves only through military victory, and the lack of concern for the destruction of property in war that was natural among men of no property. But he also believed that the cement in this relationship had been Pym's ability to dupe his more socially humble allies.

As a result of structural dislocation and the consequent emergence of partisan tactics, in the most sensitive settings the House, as the earl of Holland related to D'Ewes in April 1643, had simply abandoned "their old way of advising and debating."[111] They operated instead as a partisan, majoritarian institution regularly burdened with executive decisions. At the very beginning of the unraveling of consensual politics in late 1642 and early 1643, an anonymous Oxford pamphleteer, probably Hyde himself, offered an analysis strikingly similar both to remarks that appeared later in the *History of the Rebellion* and to the many accounts offered by D'Ewes and other parliamentarians in 1642 and 1643. He did so in the course of explaining to his readers why so many moderate

---

[108] Ibid., ff. 315r.–316v. (289–93), 339v. (373). Only fifty-two voted in this division.

[109] Ibid., f. 345v. (391).

[110] Ibid., ff. 345v.–346v. (391–3). The members D'Ewes identified here were a shipper, draper, chandler, and clothier, respectively. See Keeler, *Long Parliament*, 106, 111, 259, 224.

[111] D'Ewes MS 164, f. 361r. (448).

royalists like himself had been turned out of the House since the beginning of the Long Parliament. "Clean contrary to the use, yea and the
honour of Parliaments," he wrote, "things were not debated by reason
and strength of argument, but by putting it to the question, and carrying
it by most voices." In such episodes, the writer continued, factional
organization and manipulation, combined with the tactic of purging,
had replaced free speech, debate, and deliberation. "The greater
number," he sneered, "were so far from understanding many times the
force of arguments, that they did not after the vote was past conceive the
state or sense of the question, but thought it was enough for them to vote
with Master Pym, or Master Hampden by an implicit faith."[112] Both
Hyde and some of his political opponents were observing – and condemning – a majoritarian revolution. In their eyes, the free exercise of
reason in a spirit of national unity had been successfully replaced by the
desperate pursuit of private interest by any means necessary.

The period between December 1642 and April 1643 certainly
exhibited a flurry of majoritarian thinking and action, whatever its underlying character. An exogenous shock to parliamentary institutions – the
outbreak of civil war – had clearly undermined the effective operation of
consensual norms. Humanistic and dialectical debate was failing to
produce consensus around emergent wisdom on matters related to the
status of the House. As a result, consensual practices were failing to
reinforce the status of the Commons and its members in the way they
traditionally had. As beliefs about the effects of consensual decision-
making were repeatedly undermined, the rationale for using debate with
an eye to consensus formation was weakened. At the same time, the
status-related issues confronting the House put immense pressure on
members to use debate to secure desperately desired ends. Both patterns
conspired to make it more desirable for members to use logic and
rhetoric as partisan weapons aimed at the securing of majorities. As this
rationale took hold and divisions became more and more commonplace,
the unity of the body politic as a whole and the Commons in particular
was being destroyed. The utility of consensus decisions for patching
up traditional forms of unity, status, and legitimacy approached irrele-
vancy, and other means of securing the status of Parliament appeared far
more realistic by comparison.

---

[112] [Hyde], *A Complaint to the House of Commons*, 8–9. Multiple versions of the tract
circulated in January 1643. For bibliographical discussion, see Madan, *Oxford Books*,
vol. II, 199–200; Roebuck, *Clarendon and Continuity*, 75–9. For later, strikingly similar
descriptions of the early Long Parliament in printed polemic, see Anon., *Declaration of
the Lords and Commons of Parliament Assembled at Oxford*, 6–7; [Chestlin], *Persecutio
Undecima*, 59–61.

In the end, the same institutional elements that had enabled the self-reproduction of consensus decision-making – norms of honor and honorable practices – were also what caused it both to fail in a new set of circumstances and strategic parameters and to cede ground to a specific set of new practices. The remarkable success of consensus decision-making before the Civil War had evidently bonded the notion of honor so strongly to parliamentary decision-making that when, for exogenous reasons, the Commons experienced an explosion of divisions, it began willingly to undermine its own consensual traditions by defending its honor in a new way. The majoritarian defense of honor would help Parliament win the war, but it would ultimately lead to Parliament's demise. The destruction of consensus politics had simply done too much irreparable damage to the Commons' status, legitimacy, and independence. It emerged from the era of consensus politics internally divided and externally threatened. The interaction between these two weaknesses would ultimately prove fatal.

In this sense the collapse of consensus decision-making in the House of Commons was closely related to an array of remarkable developments in English political culture between 1641 and 1643 that aided the parliamentary cause in many ways while also contributing, over the long run, to a profound crisis in Parliament's authority and stability. In each case, preexisting political practices were altered in consequential ways. A political public sphere that had been episodic in operation prior to this moment in post-Reformation politics rather suddenly became an institutionalized feature of the political process.[113] A series of traditional modes of political practice – including news, petitions, lobbying, protestations, covenants, and oaths of association – were becoming powerful weapons of both elite-led mobilization and broad and inclusive popular-political action, driven in part by a dramatic expansion of print culture and political know-how after 1641. This all resulted in a remarkable practical extension of the political nation and the emergence of a "common politics" – popular and shared albeit inegalitarian and broadly centered on Parliament. Crucial early examples from this particular period abound. It is no coincidence that many of the most important examples have featured prominently in this chapter: the Grand Remonstrance,

---

[113] Lake and Pincus, "Rethinking the Public Sphere"; Raymond, *Pamphlets and Pamphleteering*; Raymond, *Invention of the Newspaper*; Peacey, *Politicians and Pamphleteers*.

the Protestation, the crowd action against the Lords in 1641, and the radical petitioning and addresses of 1642 and 1643.[114] Each aspect of this remarkable convergence of practical transformations would pose profound problems for Parliament by the end of the decade, and had indeed already begun to do so.

[114] Walter, *Covenanting Citizens*; Como, *Radical Parliamentarians and the English Civil War*, 89–155; Peacey, *Print and Public Politics in the English Revolution*, 402; Zaret, *Origins of Democratic Culture*, esp. 174–265; Braddick, *God's Fury, England's Fire*, 113–207; Walter, *Understanding Popular Violence in the English Revolution*; Leng, "'Citizens at the Door.'"

5   Revolutionary Decisions, 1643–1660

Despite the dramatic upsurge of majoritarian votes and tactics in the early months of 1643, it would probably be going too far to say that majoritarian politics was institutionalized in the year following the outbreak of the Civil War. It is more accurate to describe decision-making in the Commons at this point as deinstitutionalized and structurally dislocated. Traditional norms apparently remained in place, but so did a set of circumstances in which these norms were insufficient for consistently maintaining a consensual pattern of decision-making on important political issues. To be certain that members were actually disregarding the status consequences of the way in which they made decisions, one would have to observe them regularly dividing on politically important decisions that *did not* have a significant and possibly countervailing status component. This would imply that members no longer recognized significant status costs in hazarding divisions, because they were willing to hazard them even in the absence of countervailing status concerns. These sorts of votes, however, do not appear to have occurred. This makes it very unlikely that the House had institutionalized majority rule.

A series of other considerations reinforces this impression. There is clear evidence, especially for 1646 and later years, that frequent divisions in the House affected both participants' and observers' views of Parliament's legitimacy.[1] This suggests that consensual norms remained internalized throughout the 1640s. Even more telling on this front is the House's regular use of the previous question. As we have seen, this procedure was recommended in commentaries on parliamentary practice as a way to prevent putting a question that ought to receive a consensus vote in a situation where a division was likely.[2] Use of the

---

[1] For a critique of majoritarian decisions and tactics in 1646, see BL MS Add 24667, esp. ff. 4r., 5r.

[2] For another early example see *POSLP*, vol. VI, 21. Of course, there were other ways of preventing such questions, and divisions did not need to be explicitly related to politically important issues to be politically important. For a later acknowledgment of the

previous question was extremely rare before the outbreak of the Civil War, but very common up until the Restoration, when it again fell into relative disuse. This chronology of the use of the previous question follows what is for a host of reasons the most reasonable chronology of the deinstitutionalization and reinstitutionalization of decision-making in the Commons.

The previous question was used throughout the Civil War period to avoid dividing on nationally important issues. On a formal level, the previous question allowed the House to hold countless divisions in the 1640s on a procedural step – whether or not to put the question – instead of engaging in an explicit ritual of national disunity centered on a pivotal political question. When the previous question succeeded, the following votes on matters of national importance hardly ever led to divisions. The veneer of business as usual, and the semblance of national cohesion and parliamentary wisdom, was being maintained with more than a little desperation and superficiality. But the elaborate effort to do so suggests the persistence of traditional norms. In one case, for instance, Sir Simonds D'Ewes explicitly suggested a previous question because the direct question impinged on the honor of a military officer, and was therefore very likely to lead to a division amid any significant difference of opinion on the matter.[3] Predictably, in some of the most politically unstable years of the 1640s and 1650s, divisions on whether to put the question accounted for the overwhelming majority of the divisions that were held. In some cases, successful motions for the previous question were clearly intended to end debate on a particular motion, while technically addressing it directly, as required by the rules of the House. More rarely, the previous question was actually used to force a division, as is common in modern politics. But even in these cases, the effect of the use of this procedure was to distance the substantive issue from the division itself.

A still more obvious indication of deinstitutionalized decision-making is the fluctuation in data on division frequency over the course of the Civil War era (Figure 5.1). It suggests that majoritarian outcomes mostly remained dependent on the presence of the same parameters for decision-making that had caused the Commons' consensual institution to fail in the past. The severe dilemmas caused by crises of status in 1643 were less commonplace for the remainder of the first Civil War. As a result, divisions were much less frequent in this period than in late

significance and ubiquity of the tactical use of previous questions, see Anon., *A Test, Offered to the Consideration of the Electors*, 22.
[3] D'Ewes MS 166, f. 181r. (1660).

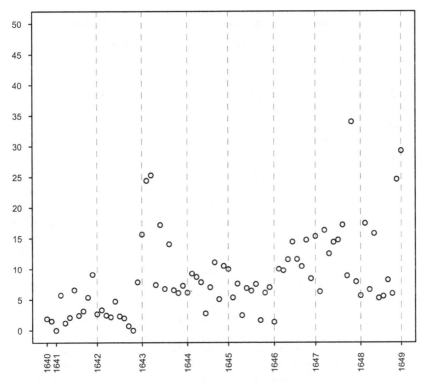

Figure 5.1 Mean division frequency as percentage of all questions put, 1640–9. Each dot represents a period of thirty days in session. Tick marks are located on the thirty-day unit that includes the beginning of each year.

1642 and early 1643. Between the end of the Oxford Treaty negotiations on 14 April 1643 and the end of 1645, the division frequency was only 7 percent. It remained at 9.4 percent between May and December 1643 (a division every five days in session), dropped to 8.2 percent in 1644 (a division every six or seven days), and fell to only 5.1 percent in 1645 (a division every seven days). The division frequency rose again, and did so suddenly, only in the spring of 1646, just before Charles' surrender to the Covenanters on 5 May and the beginning of settlement negotiations. The incidence of divisions was clearly still dependent on moments in politics that were saturated with problems of status. These moments disrupted the House's decision-making traditions for contingent reasons without completing a transformation in the structural environment that constrained and enabled members' behavior.

Structural Dislocation and Civil War: 1643–1645

During the remainder of 1643, following the collapse of the Oxford Treaty in April, the House made numerous important decisions consensually. Many of these decisions were reached on issues that provoked significant disagreement, including the impeachment of Henrietta Maria, the Commons' response to the Waller plot, the creation of the Westminster Assembly, and the establishment and implementation of an excise tax. Ideological conflict continued to be an insufficient cause for majoritarian decisions. And when peace was not a live option and distrust of the king was amplified by the Waller plot and Charles' efforts to arrange a cessation of hostilities in Ireland, the House was relatively united in pursuing unrelenting belligerence and strong assertions of status. At the same time, issues that had been central to the explosion in divisions after the outbreak of civil war, such as the treatment of suspected royalists, had ceased to be central to Parliament's work. Under these conditions, there were fewer occasions on which the House was at risk of failing to make decisions consensually. A drop in the frequency of divisions was the predictable result.

Yet the picture is less clear than these generalizations might suggest. There are a number of striking if ultimately ambiguous signs that many members at least temporarily adopted an aggressively majoritarian approach in this period. It is arguable that the pressing issues and conflicts of this period were so commonly loaded with status implications that the Commons had hardly any opportunities to divide on politically important issues that did not have such implications. If this were true, and the Commons was in fact no longer taking seriously the status benefits of consensual decisions, we would see no direct evidence of it, because on no occasion would the Commons be able to reveal its majoritarianism by considering political issues with no significant status component and dividing on them anyway. Whatever the underlying institutional reality, during this period the Commons certainly continued to resort to divisions in the face of status-related issues on which they disagreed. And between late 1643 and 1645, members also continued to pepper vigorous debate with aggressively and self-consciously majoritarian tactics and considerations.[4]

A vivid example of this continuing majoritarian activity in familiar contexts comes from the next time the Commons was charged with considering negotiations with the king, in August 1643. They divided

---

[4] See BL MSS Harley 483–4 for frequent references to sharp debates occurring alongside divisions.

four times in two days over propositions for Charles drafted by the Lords. On 5 August a joint conference of Lords and Commons was held in which the Lords presented their propositions. D'Ewes believed that the propositions were "full of honour, justice, and piety," indicating the role of status, political ideology, and confessional conflict in these deliberations. When Pym reported the conference in the Commons, D'Ewes moved that the propositions be read and debated in sections. At that point, according to D'Ewes, "some violent spirits, to divert the motion and debate of peace, began to object that there were some in the house who had not taken the Covenant." The Speaker replied that three of the four men these members named had in fact taken the Covenant. Sir John Maynard then "stood up and said that he did wonder that when the House was upon so great a business as this, which concerned the saving the kingdom from ruin, men should endeavor to put the House into unnecessary debates and divisions." The House then rejected the counter-motions concerning the Covenant. At this point some members resorted to speaking directly against considering peace propositions, and they faced rebuttals from D'Ewes and others in a lengthy debate.[5]

The House eventually agreed to put a question on whether to consider the propositions, but some members disputed the wording of the question. In D'Ewes' view, they were doing so only in order to consume more time and encourage the House to adjourn. Questions were finally put on the wording of the question and the suggested revisions accepted. Nevertheless, those who requested the revisions "all gave their negative voice against the said question and would have the house divided upon it." Those in favor of discussing the propositions won the forced vote. But the next motion debated was whether the discussion should occur on the following Monday, since the day was already coming to a close. Worried that this question would be carried against them, a few of D'Ewes' adversaries tried to begin a new debate about providing for the House's safety during the treaty negotiations. This "cunning bait" convinced thirty or forty members that the propositions had been laid aside for the day, thereby providing an opening to those who opposed them. Once the duped members had left for the day and were too far away to be called back, the opponents of peace suddenly motioned in favor of debating the propositions, "presuming strongly," D'Ewes observed, "that they should have cast them out of the house that very evening." The House then divided on whether or not to proceed with debate on the propositions, and the propositions' opponents won by two

[5] D'Ewes MS 165, ff. 137v.–141r. (741–50).

votes. The House proceeded to vote to approve the first set of propositions. Then Holles skillfully motioned for the House to be resolved into a committee, "seeing it grow late and desirous to let the violent party know ... that we meant to sit it out with them." With this credible threat of a filibuster, debate turned to the consideration of an adjournment, and the House was eventually adjourned.[6] The radicals may have been the first to use manipulative tactics on 5 August in hopes of timing votes to their advantage, but by the end of the day both sides of the conflict had indulged in the same set of practices.

That night, frustrated radical members worked with City militants to set the scene for the Monday, 7 August session, in which the rest of the propositions would be debated. They wrote, circulated, and posted in London and the suburbs a handbill that called for mass action before Parliament met on Monday and claimed that 20,000 Irish rebels were marching on London. The Speaker of the House was given a copy of the handbill and an account of what its distributors were saying, and he ordered the new lord mayor, Isaac Penington, to prevent the assembly. Penington, himself a radical member of the Commons who was likely involved in the original scheme, then organized a petition with the Common Council instead. Petitioning became from this moment on an effective weapon of City radicals, because the Common Council was now firmly parliamentarian in orientation.[7] A crowd still assembled Monday morning in support of the petition. As it was being presented and the Lords attempted to enter Parliament, they were harassed by demonstrators and forced to adjourn at midday after a conference with the Commons, because they could not work in freedom. D'Ewes believed that while most proponents of peace in the Commons had not been so intimidated that they refrained from attending the House, the privileges of parliament had been "shaken at the very root" by a "conspiracy." The crowd, he alleged, was meant "to overawe the members of the House of Commons that they might not consent to the propositions for peace."[8] The situation was similar to the troubles that befell Westminster in late 1641 and early 1642, with the crucial difference that parliamentarians were on both sides of the struggle.

In a Commons debate that day about those assembled outside the chamber, proponents of the peace propositions decided not to press for a declaration against the assembly as a tumult, because "the violent spirits were like to carry it against them." Accordingly, once a motion was made

---

[6] Ibid., ff. 141r.–143r. (750–4).
[7] Pearl, *London and the Outbreak of the Puritan Revolution*, 238.
[8] D'Ewes MS 165, ff. 145r. (756), 146r. (758–9).

to continue with debate on the propositions, "the violent spirits being now confident to carry it by the number of voices, opposed" the motion. Instead, they moved, "contrary to all order and the usual proceedings of the House," to "have a question put for the rejecting of these propositions before they had so much taken them into debate." Some debate did occur, however, and afterward the House divided again on whether to proceed with the propositions. Those against proceeding prevailed, 88 to 81. D'Ewes attributed the result to intimidation, corrupt reversals of votes from Saturday, and the presence of newcomers to the debate who had not been in attendance on Saturday. "No means was left unassayed," he observed grimly, "to procure suffrages."[9] These maneuvers are all the more remarkable because they did not occur in a situation where procedural means of avoiding a vote were unavailable. While both the committee system and conferencing were live options, the House never even reached a debate on the entirety of the propositions.

This was clearly a situation in which institutionalized consensual norms were at least competing with somewhat well-honed and self-conscious majoritarian tactics. This impression is strengthened by the fact that there were many other apparently majoritarian episodes in the late summer and fall of 1643 that did not result in divisions only because there happened to be a strong enough majority on one side of the question and the minority did not demand that the House be divided.[10] This suggests that the lower frequency of divisions in 1644 and 1645 relative to 1643 is not an entirely straightforward index of a drop in majoritarian decisions. It may be in part simply a record of war party dominance. D'Ewes reported lopsided voice votes in which he was in the minority often enough to give the impression that meaningfully majoritarian voice votes not followed by divisions were unusually common in this period.

Another suggestive aspect of Commons decision-making in the second half of 1643 is the incidence of majoritarian activity in situations dominated by religious conflict, following the creation of the Westminster Assembly and the entry of the Scots into the war. Decisions in the Commons related to these circumstances certainly brought fervently held

---

[9] Lindley, *Popular Politics and Religion in Civil War London*, 317–18; D'Ewes MS 165, ff. 145r.–148v. (756–66); BL MS Add 18778, ff. 9v.–12v. For evidence of the centrality of status to this struggle, see BL MS Add 18778, ff. 9r.–12v. For other forced, majoritarian divisions from this period, see D'Ewes MS 165, ff. 224v.–225r. (909), 229v. (922–3), 264v. (1014) (the final example was a minoritarian division).

[10] Aside from the examples described below, see D'Ewes MS 165, ff. 169r. (843–4), 173v. (854), 178v. (866), 224r. (907). For a majoritarian decision without a division from earlier in 1643, see ff. 97r.–v. (590–1).

beliefs to the table, but the role of status considerations is far less clear. This suggests that the employment of majoritarian decision-making may have moved, at least on some occasions, beyond situations in which it was unavoidable to the brazen waging of ideological and confessional conflict by majoritarian means. In other words, these were situations in which the status costs of dividing should have constrained majoritarian behavior because there were no countervailing status considerations involved. But such costs do not seem to have played a role.

On 1 September, for instance, the House continued a debate on the Covenant that had begun on 26 August. Their discussions focused on the question of whether the Covenant's *iure divino* clause should be placed in the main text or in the margins of the document. Opponents of the clause, who favored placing it in the margins, "perceiving they had much the greater number of voices," as D'Ewes understood situation, did not allow the question put to be whether the clarification should be placed in the main body of the text. Instead, "the other question being put for the placing of the said words in the margin, they carried it by so many voices that we never came to divide the house upon it." In general, that day, according to D'Ewes, "it was to little purpose to stay or speak because the violent spirits had the advantage of voices to carry what they listed." On this view of the situation, a majoritarian logic had completely displaced the logic of deliberation and consensus. On the following day, once many members had left the House with the expectation that debate on the Covenant would be postponed until the following Monday, "the violent spirits (who had numbers enough to have carried it upon a fair and parliamentary debate) took that advantage, when scarce any man was left in the house but honest Mr. John Maynard to oppose them." Abandoning conventions of thorough debate in a full House when according to D'Ewes it was not even necessary for victory, they "so finely handled the business that before five of the clock in the afternoon they were able to come to the fifth article of the same Covenant."[11] The clarity of this apparent example of religiously focused majoritarian behavior, however, should not be overestimated. Here again it is very likely that these debates, like similar ones before them on episcopacy, were closely related to the struggle over Scotland's role in the military and political affairs of the moment, which were in turn closely attached to a host of status considerations related to the ultimate outcome of the conflict. Debates over the Covenant were normally conducted in the shadow of Anglo-Scottish politics.

[11] D'Ewes MS 165, ff. 158v.–159r. (812-14), 162r.–163v. (826–9), 164r.–v. (831–2).

Understanding parliamentary decision-making over the eighteen months following these September 1643 debates requires some additional contextualization in terms of the ongoing dynamics of intra-parliamentarian conflict. In the wake of the Covenant and the Irish Cessation, factional alignments in Westminster shifted. The "peace party" grandees who clustered around the earl of Northumberland believed that Scottish intervention spelled disaster for England. At the same time, they saw no prospect of a negotiated settlement at a moment when royalists were being buoyed by the defection of peace-inclined peers in August 1643 and the king's cessation of hostilities with the Catholic Confederates in Ireland, both of which augured well for royalist military efforts in England. These grandees therefore aligned themselves with both Lord Saye and Oliver St. John, who replaced Pym as the leader of the pro-Scottish interest in the Commons after Pym's death in December 1643. The earl of Essex, meanwhile, became distanced from pro-Scots politicians in the Commons and sought to broker a peace with Charles I on the basis of his newfound military strength in late 1643. The Scots posed the primary obstacle to his negotiating power. In his desire for an English peace, Essex was joined by Holles and other allies in the Commons. They worked together to oppose Saye, St. John, and the Scots, who tried to weaken Essex and bolster the strength of both the Scottish forces and English commanders such as William Waller and the earl of Manchester, who favored military victory. Saye and St. John remained dominant in Westminster until autumn 1644, feeding off the series of parliamentarian victories that culminated at Marston Moor in July 1644 and benefiting from Essex's defeat at Lostwithiel in September.[12]

At that point, however, the Saye and St. John group grew distant from the Scots because of the Scots' aggressive religious and political demands in the Committee of Both Kingdoms and their apparent inability to secure a decisive military victory. In fall 1644, Saye and St. John came to center their military support and alliance-making on English warriors and they turned to an independent-minded religious policy. Essex's failures in the fall of 1644 allowed them to begin marshaling support for a New Model Army. At the same time, the Essex faction and the Scots began to form an alliance in favor of a negotiated settlement. Attention shifted to Westminster as the campaigning season ended in late 1644. Self-denial emerged as a policy counterpart to a New Model Army. The measure appealed to peaceniks worried about profiteering generals and to those who worried that the generals' infighting was

---

[12] Scott, *Politics and War in the Three Kingdoms*, 69–71.

hurting the war effort. But it was centrally an effort by Essex's opponents to strip him of power.[13]

This was the general context for struggles within the Commons in 1644 and early 1645. After August 1643, peace discussions proceeded informally, outside Parliament's purview.[14] Nevertheless, divisions in the Commons in 1644 centered on the same issues that had predominated the year before: negotiations, military affairs, and royalism. These issues were also addressed in familiar terms: members underlined both the necessity of ending the war and the need to vindicate the honor, authority, and legitimacy of Parliament, the Commons, and its members. On occasion, however, some of the struggles over military command and negotiations were so patently battles for control between two groups in the Commons that they seem to have been driven as much by sheer partisan competition, partly rooted in ideological and confessional differences, as by status considerations. There is some evidence of important decisions reached without a division on controversial issues. But once again, we cannot be absolutely sure that these were not meaningfully majoritarian votes. Examples include the 6 July 1644 vote for an ordinance to form a standing army from the southern and eastern counties, the votes on ministerial ordination in early September, and the 1 October vote on merging the armies of Essex, Manchester, and Waller.[15] The debates on self-denial and the creation of the New Model Army both featured numerous divisions. Decisions on these issues were more often made by means of voice votes, but many of these votes, too, could have been meaningfully majoritarian or the site of tactical concessions.

Indeed, as noted earlier, there is considerable evidence that the division count in this period masked a large number of majoritarian but

---

[13] Ibid., 84–7.

[14] The Uxbridge negotiations, which began in late 1644, were constructed in such a way as to require less regular input from the Commons. They resulted in divisions only during the pre-treaty phase. See CJ, 12/19/44, 12/28/44; Smith, *Constitutional Royalism and the Search for a Settlement*, 114–20.

[15] CJ, 7/6/1644, 7/12/1644, 9/7/1644, 9/9/1644, 9/13/1644, 10/1/1644; D'Ewes MS 165, f. 80r. (1345); D'Ewes MS 166, ff. 113r.–v. (1459, 1470), 127v. (1509); BL MS Add 31116, ff. 159r., 160r. There is also the interesting case of the 13 November vote on Laud's attainder. There is evidence of some sympathy for Laud (for example, D'Ewes MS 166, ff. 152r.–v. (1562–3)), and there was of course opposition in the Lords to the treason charge. While both the manuscript and printed Commons journals record a decision without division in favor of attainder, their account of the proceedings has a mid-sentence gap (with a large blank space left in the manuscript), and D'Ewes' diary has an ambiguous reference to what appears to be a division on the attainder, or at least a majoritarian voice vote in which many remained silent and D'Ewes could count votes. See CJ, 11/13/1644; PA HC/CL/JO/1/27 (unfoliated, entry for 11/13/1644); D'Ewes MS 166, f. 161v. (1579).

fairly lopsided voice votes. D'Ewes explicitly recorded a number of these. He also complained of the lopsided nature of partisan struggle at this juncture and took less interest in Commons business under these conditions.[16] Many of these meaningfully majoritarian voice votes were also preceded by aggressive or otherwise majoritarian tactics. These tended to be described by observers from a partisan viewpoint, of course, but D'Ewes occasionally implicated himself and his allies.[17] The diarist, for instance, sometimes left the House during debate and timed his return for votes. Here D'Ewes was responding with majoritarian behavior to an environment in which he believed deliberation had lost its significance as a means of consensus-building.[18] He described the majoritarian tactics of his opponents more matter-of-factly in these years than in previous ones, having seemingly accepted them as a fixture of parliamentary politics in civil war.

Some of these partisan tactics are evident in the struggle over the formation of the Committee of Both Kingdoms in early 1644, in the wake of the Covenant. Designed and promoted by Lord Saye, Northumberland, Sir Henry Vane junior, Oliver St. John, and their allies in the Lords and Commons, it threatened finally to eclipse Essex's political and military power and that of his supporters in the lower house. On 7 February, the Commons fell for a second time into debate about an ordinance for the appointment of a group of peers and members of the Commons who would meet as a standing committee with the Scots. The ordinance had been greeted with significant opposition and suspicion from members of the lower house on the 3rd, when a version of it that came down from the Lords was first read and debated. It had then been revised accordingly by its proponents. Debate on the 7th centered around who the members named to the committee should be and by what process they should be named. This was, in other words, a contest over who would control the committee.

When the ordinance originally came down from the Lords, its Commons members had already been named. This tactic of Vane and his allies in the Lords was taken to be a breach of Commons privilege. D'Ewes also alleged that passing a Commons draft of the bill with all names entered by the Commons would similarly violate the Lords'

---

[16] McGee, *An Industrious Mind*, 408. See, for instance, D'Ewes MS 166, ff. 3r.–v. (1078–81), 106r. (1412–13).

[17] Aside from the examples described below, see D'Ewes MS 166, ff. 32r.–v. (1141–2), 36r. (1156–7), 48v. (1201), 154v. (1228), 98r. (1364), 123v.–124r. (1486–8), 125r.–v. (1495–7), 160r. (1568), 181r. (1660), 196v. (1707) (the last two examples are from 1645).

[18] See, for example, ibid., f. 256v. (1911).

privileges. There was strategic coordination on both sides of the debate. Vane had colluded with the Lords on the original list, and D'Ewes, for instance, tried but failed to coordinate with Giles Green to add different names to it. The contest ended in a division, 65 to 51, in favor of retaining the original set of fourteen Commons names. The House also resolved with voice votes to name the seven lords in the ordinance. On the 8th the bill was sent to the Lords, who attempted to weaken the committee considerably by altering its directive from a charge to "order and direct" to a charge to "consult and advise." The Commons refused to back down when they considered the revised bill on the 10th, but the Lords would not budge either.[19]

On the 13th, Vane junior, who had moved after receipt of the Lords' most recent statement on the 12th to form a committee to draft a response to the Lords, was given permission for the committee to meet that morning. According to D'Ewes, Vane's return to the House to report on the work of the committee "was so sudden that I could easily guess that the reasons were prepared before he went out." In the rationale it had composed, the committee insisted that if "order and direct" did not appear in the ordinance, it would be of no efficient use. "As soon as Sir Henry Vane had finished it, diverse called out to have the question put, as if a business of this great weight might be determined upon the sudden." D'Ewes urged that the Lords' rationale be discussed by the House, "but the same men that called for the question before called for it still." The Speaker began to stand to have the question put when Sir Henry Mildmay rose and asked for debate with the same rationale as D'Ewes, adding that "the power which we were to give to this committee did exceed all former precedent." This successfully led to a debate. But according to D'Ewes "it was not arguments and reasons that would now prevail." Debate was cut short when "the solicitor St. John, [Edmond] Prideaux, and other violent spirits, knowing that they had the greater number of voices joined with them, called for the question to be put, and so carried it by vote that we should adhere to our former resolution that the words 'order and direct' should still continue in the ordinance." To D'Ewes' astonishment, when the Lords were urged again by the Commons after this vote, they "receded from their own unanswerable

---

[19] Ibid., f. 9 (1062–3); CJ, 2/7/1644; Notestein, "Establishment of the Committee of Both Kingdoms," 489–93; Adamson, "Triumph of Oligarchy" (for this and the previous paragraph). Typically, the division on the 7th was on the procedural question (essentially a previous question) of whether to read (and then vote on, in turn) the fourteen original names.

reasons" for declining to grant such considerable power to the committee. D'Ewes' adversaries had been successful in both Houses.[20]

The following year, 1645, divisions continued to center on similar issues, beginning with the struggle over the formation of the New Model Army. During this conflict, the independent and presbyterian factions in Parliament took shape. This was a crystallization of the divisions already present in the winter of 1643–4, which had emerged from debates within the Westminster Assembly. Politics in the Assembly, however, were structured differently from politics in Parliament. There were indeed a series of divisions on religious topics in the Commons over the course of 1645. Nearly all of them (six in total) were held between late August and early November, and they concerned church government and related mass petitioning by presbyterians. As usual, these divisions were also directly related to the politics of status. They were linked to the struggle over the terms of settlement (and related conflicts over the military) between the two factions, who did not themselves have strong allegiances to specific religious settlements. In this environment, the presbyterians were forced to satisfy the source of their military strength, the Covenanters, especially once Essex's and Manchester's armies had been absorbed into the New Model, the military anchor of independency in Parliament. With the failure of the Uxbridge negotiations, the presbyterians, not to mention advocates of peace, were seriously weakened, and the independents remained in control as the royalist forces were decimated at Naseby and Langport in June and July, and Holles and Bulstrode Whitelocke came under suspicion of treachery in the Savile affair.[21] The lower incidence of divisions in 1645 might easily be attributed to the movement of many important decisions into the Committee of Both Kingdoms, the partisan dominance of the independents in the House, and an environment in which an attempt at a negotiated "honorable peace" was not a realistic option.

The Collapse of Parliamentary Politics and the Minoritarian Revolution: 1646–1649

In the early weeks of 1646 up to 5 March, the Commons was still dividing only 6 percent of the time a question was put, or once every six days. For the remainder of the year, however, they divided 12.5 percent of the time, or every two days (Figures 4.1, 4.2, and 5.1). Both

---

[20] D'Ewes MS 166, ff. 1r. (1072), 2v.–3v. (1077–81).
[21] Scott, *Politics and War in the Three Stuart Kingdoms*, 89–92; Mahony, "Presbyterian Party in the Long Parliament," 174–7.

political controversy and the divisions themselves continued to revolve around Parliament's status, and parliamentary honor and privilege in particular. These issues were of course still closely linked to questions of war and peace. In 1646, as in 1643, a series of excruciating decisions related to the question of a political settlement laid waste to consensual patterns of politics in the Commons, because of the disputed issues of status and the competing partisan agendas they exposed. In particular, peace propositions with the king and the Scots, which were at issue in well over a quarter of the divisions in 1646, were once again at the core of an explosion in the frequency of divisions. Subsidiary issues that usually had clear status dimensions included the war in Ireland, the Great Seal, relations with the City, the church settlement, and interactions with the Lords.

On the surface, all of this seems familiar. But it is important to appreciate the unique gravity of the breakdown of consensual politics in the later 1640s. To an extent, this was simply a matter of the acceleration of dynamics familiar from previous years. As members continued to use divisions to defend parliamentary privilege and authority, the significance of divisions as dishonorable or illegitimate acts was being undermined. Indeed, the institution of consensual decision-making had become thoroughly self-undermining under revolutionary conditions. The practical logic of consensus politics was no longer being reinforced. And as the hold of consensual norms on members' conduct weakened, divisions became likely under a widening set of conditions, and therefore occurred even more often. As a result, the status-related norms governing members' behavior moved ever more rapidly toward the point where they would reach irrelevance. This was a spiraling dynamic of deinstitutionalization. What intermittently stepped into the institutional void was an instrumental logic in which the status significance of a division was wholly dependent on the ends for which it was employed.

This stage of self-undermining deinstitutionalization left signature traces in the record of decision-making in the Commons. First of all, the relevance of consensual norms had been so thoroughly weakened at this point, and the revolutionary crisis had become so acute, that groups in the Commons became more willing than ever to pursue their agendas with regular recourse to tactics that self-evidently threatened parliamentary privilege. In particular, members regularly allowed outside forces to impinge on decision-making in the Commons in hopes of fending off even greater threats to the status of Parliament. These violations of privilege, of course, provoked motions to respond to them. This naturally led, in turn, to divisions on how to address these violations of privilege, with those who had committed the violations in the first place on one side of the question! At this point, privilege itself had been thoroughly politicized. And in every such instance, consensual norms took another direct hit, and the tendency to disregard them intensified, making another round of the cycle more likely.[22]

This was the height of deinstitutionalization. The status-related norms that normally guided both the means *and* the ends of parliamentary decision-making were being thoroughly undermined, with the exception of attempts to defend the status of Parliament at the highest level of constitutional struggle and crisis, in the context of settlement negotiations and other emergencies that provoked desperate tactics by members of Parliament. This was still, however, probably not a moment in which majoritarian politics was becoming institutionalized as a replacement for consensual decision-making. Divisions on politically important issues that did not have a clear status component – the telltale sign that principled distaste for divisions had vanished and a new institution had emerged – remained rare.

Petitions and related attempts to influence the course of parliamentary business were the triggers for this new stage of institutional breakdown. What was peculiar if not unprecedented about these activities in 1646 and beyond was the aggressive nature of the petitions and the fact that eventually, many of them were apparently masterminded by members of Parliament and then set in motion by powerful individuals working outside it. Cooperation between the City and Scots' interests in London to empower the Scots' allies in Parliament had been a common political tactic at least since the Savile affair and the royalist storming of Leicester in the summer of 1645.[23] Petitions, which had already played a role in the breakdown of consensual decision-making in the early 1640s, soon became a crucial aspect of this cooperation. Perhaps the most important characteristic of petitions from the summer of 1645 onward was their formal origination with the City government.[24]

On the broadest level, the Commons' initial attitude toward such petitioning was inconsistent, indicating that norms regarding privilege were neither operating in the traditional way nor yet falling prey to utter politicization. In June 1645, the Common Council presented to the Commons a modified version of a petition sent to them. It raised alarm about an enemy advance on the capital, discussed the diplomatic and military situation more generally, and requested that Oliver Cromwell be named to command cavalry in the Eastern Association army. There

[22] Contrast Kishlansky, *Rise of the New Model Army*, 10, 19, 77–8, 108–9.
[23] Mahony, "Presbyterian Party in the Long Parliament," 183.
[24] Kishlansky, *Rise of the New Model Army*, 78–9.

ensued a "long and hot debate of near upon three hours' space" about how to respond to the petition. Members eventually concurred in their sense that the petition, in D'Ewes' words, "was a breach of the privilege of the House" because its recommendation regarding Cromwell was contrary to the self-denying ordinance, and because the petition seemed generally intended "to give rules to the House how to order their affairs." Nevertheless, in the end they also agreed, without a division, to accept the petition, to give thanks for it, and to indicate that they would take it into serious consideration. This was done simply because the petitioners concluded the petition by stating "that they would live and die with the parliament," and "because affairs of the parliament were now in a doubtful condition."[25] Whatever the hollowness of its explanation, the House had helped to legitimate the attempts of ordinary citizens to work through the Common Council to pressure Parliament.

Three months later, the Commons' approach was less lenient. In September citizens began organizing a large petition of all covenanted citizens in support of a presbyterian church settlement consistent with the wishes of the Westminster Assembly. D'Ewes reported that "the petition was so cunningly penned as that it was not doubted but some of the assembly had a hand in it." Laurence Whitaker reported in his diary that this was a "proceeding" that "the House much disliked." The Commons resolved on a voice vote that the petition contained "several matters scandalous to the proceedings of this House, and untrue." It then ordered London's Recorder and member of Parliament John Glynn to acquaint the Common Council with the vote, in order to preempt any presentation of the petition to the Commons by the Council, which was meeting that afternoon.[26]

Yet the mobilizations continued. In October, the Commons passed an ordinance on the election of elders and resurrected a committee for determining a church settlement palatable to both presbyterians and independents. The following month both clerical and lay figures began to organize responses and convince the Common Council to present petitions to Parliament for them. Alderman William Gibbs, the Council's representative in Parliament, presented petitions for both citizens and ministers on 19 November in the form of a single document. After a long debate, the House made a careful statement to the petitioners. They observed that the Commons' proceedings were "misrepresented and

---

[25] CJ, 6/4/1645; D'Ewes MS 166, f. 216r. (1810–11); BL MS Add 31116, f. 213v.; Kishlansky, *Rise of the New Model Army*, 79.

[26] CJ, 9/20/1645; D'Ewes MS 166, f. 265r. (1953); BL MS Add 31116, f. 233r.; Juxon, *Journal*, 85–6; Kishlansky, *Rise of the New Model Army*, 79.

mistaken" in the petition and made clear that the Commons' privileges were threatened by the prejudging, precipitating, or independent interpretation of their proceedings. In the future, they added, they expected conduct consistent with this interpretation of parliamentary privilege. At the same time, though, the Commons mollified the Council by registering their belief that the City acted with good intentions. The petition was presented to the Lords the next day. This audacity further disturbed the Commons. The lower house, according to the diarist Thomas Juxon, looked "upon it as that which might make the two houses clash." It also signified, members believed, that the petitioners "would have their wills one way or the other."[27]

Petitions from other sources were also causing divisions in the House. On 6 December, the House admitted some Northamptonshire gentlemen who presented a petition, part of which requested funds from delinquents' estates for the county committee and the payment of their garrison. With some members concerned about the legality of this move, the House divided on whether to put the question and then held a very close division – 77 to 75 – in favor of approving the use of funds. The tellers for the winning side in the divisions were the presbyterians Lord Wenman and Sir John Evelyn of Surrey.[28]

These petitions from 1645 were not extremely aggressive, nor were they clearly masterminded by members of the House. But they reflected tensions that would gradually escalate and then explode over the course of 1646. Despite the general concern of the House's members for the status of Parliament, the reliance of parliamentary presbyterians on the support of the Scots commissioners–influenced Common Council made them unable or unwilling fully to resist the Council's increasing inclination to pressure Parliament through petitions on matters that Parliament was currently considering or had even already resolved. On 15 January 1646 the City presented a petition from the Common Council and another from the ward of Farringdon Within. They did the same in the House of Lords the following day. They were given a warm reception in both houses. This may have been because the petition expressed regret for the Council's activities in November and acknowledged the independence of Parliament while still making clear requests on matters of church government and sectarianism. The House, prompted by the petition's rhetorical form, was apparently willing to

---

[27] CJ, 12/19/1645; BL MS Add 31116, ff. 243v.–244r.; Juxon, *Journal*, 95; Kishlansky, *Rise of the New Model Army*, 79–80; Lindley, *Popular Politics and Religion in Civil War London*, 358–9.

[28] CJ, 12/6/1645; BL MS Add 31116, f. 246v.

condone objectionable methods and substance if they were couched in terms favorable to Parliament's status claims.[29]

This may, however, have been only the majority opinion of the presbyterians, if they were already in a strong enough position to force through such a response without a division resulting. This would help explain why in February and March the House's reaction to petitioning was again different from its most recent reaction. On 20 February the City presented a petition against the House member and future independent Francis Allen for making false statements to the Commons about what happened at an 11 February Common Council meeting. At the meeting, the Scots commissioners had presented a letter from the Scottish parliament thanking the Council for its support and they had denounced the independents. The Commons had requested the Council to present the Scottish letter and an account of the event, but they responded only with the petition against Allen. After heated debate, according to Whitaker, "the consideration whereof was referred till tomorrow: the house resenting much the bringing in of such a petition against a member of the House and charging him with falsehood." The next day, 21 February, the House ruled that Allen had done nothing wrong, but his account of the Common Council meeting was expunged from the Commons journal on a technicality after the House divided on two related previous questions.[30]

Throughout late winter and early spring, petitions continued to be mired in partisan clashes. On 12 March the City presented to the Lords a petition against parliamentary legislation on the institution of lay commissioners to oversee expulsions of church members by ministers. This bill had already been passed by the Commons after a 5 March debate that involved a division on revisions. The petition successfully politicized the Lords' decision-making on the bill, and the Lords accordingly voted the petition a violation of privilege in a close vote that was later expunged from their journal. When the petition was taken to the Commons the following morning, John Glynn convinced the delegation not to present it because it would be voted a violation of privilege.[31] On the 14th the House received a report from twelve lords and twenty-four Commons members who had been charged with considering how the House should explain to the Common Council that their petition had, as Whitaker put it, "broken the privileges of Parliament," and that Parliament required

[29] Kishlansky, *Rise of the New Model Army*, 81–2; BL MS Add 31116, ff. 254r.–v.
[30] BL MS Add 31116, f. 256r.; Juxon, *Journal*, 103–4; Lindley, *Popular Politics and Religion in Civil War London*, 363–4; CJ, 2/20/1646, 2/21/1646.
[31] Kishlansky, *Rise of the New Model Army*, 82–5; Juxon, *Journal*, 108–10; CJ, 3/5/1646.

them "not to present any more petitions of that nature."[32] Two days later the committee delivered in person an admonishment to the Common Council, but the committee specified that it was the timing of the petition, not its content, that breached privilege. In return they received from the Council an apology that affirmed parliamentary privilege.[33] This petition primarily differed from earlier ones because it dealt with an ordinance already passed by the Commons.

This trend continued with the Westminster Assembly's 23 March petition to the Commons, which addressed the same ordinance opposed by the City earlier in the month. Discussion was postponed to the 27th, at which point the petition was debated at length; further discussion was then scheduled for a committee of the whole on 1 April. That day, after another extensive debate, the Commons agreed, according to Whitaker (who was in the chair for most of this discussion), that the Westminster divines "had exceeded the power given them by ordinance of Parliament." The diarist and member John Harington, however, noted that some (presumably presbyterian) members were instead "magnifying [the divines'] learning, piety and exceeding services for the Parliament" and arguing "that they ought not to be so charged for all the subjects may petition and show their reasons why freely." These members appear to have explicitly condoned petitions that commented aggressively on bills the Commons had already passed. Whatever the balance of opinion that day, the House took no formal action.[34]

A continuation of debate on 3 April was interrupted and the issue was rejoined on the 8th in a committee of the whole. This debate lasted the entire day without conclusion, and continued for another entire day on the 11th. That day the House deliberated on whether to even address the issue of privilege again. They at last divided along partisan lines on whether to do so. Independents, led by the tellers Arthur Haselrig and John Evelyn of Wiltshire, prevailed 106 to 85 over the presbyterians led by Holles and Stapleton, forcing the issue of privilege to be addressed. After another long round of debate, the Commons divided over the question of whether the petition was a breach of privilege. Again the independents secured a yes vote, 88 to 76. The House then postponed discussion of how to communicate their vote to the Assembly. This issue was taken up on the 16th and with no division a committee led by Marten and Haselrig was appointed to craft a statement and prepare questions for the Assembly on the topic of *iure divino* ecclesiastical authority. On the 18th a draft narrative and questions were read to the House by

[32] BL MS Add 31116, ff. 259v–260r.   [33] Juxon, *Journal*, 109–10.
[34] CJ, 3/23/1646, 3/27/1646, 4/1/1646; BL MS Add 31116, ff. 261v.–263r.; *Harington*, 15.

committee members and debated. Debate continued on the 21st, and the narrative was approved for presentation and enlargement by a select committee before the Assembly. The following day, the questions were voted, again without divisions, in the same manner. This was all, of course, a major triumph for independents.[35] The presbyterians had been unsuccessful here in their effort to have the Commons countenance aggressive petitioning that furthered their agenda.

The next conflict over perceived threats to parliamentary authority centered on Scottish public attacks on Parliament and its proceedings. This followed months of similar public appeals and private efforts aimed at merging the Scottish and City political programs. The Scots' actions were first taken under consideration on 13 and 14 April with some unanimity: the House condemned the attacks and resolved to publish a declaration vindicating Parliament.[36] The content of this declaration was debated at length on the 17th. In the course of a day-long debate, partisan divisions were held over two sections of the text, supported by independents, which implied that the Scots were working to overthrow the fundamental laws and government of England while accusing Parliament of doing the same thing. Both sections were in the end retained.[37] The final text was ordered to be printed, distributed to every county, and posted in every parish. The conflicts over the declaration, not to mention the text of the declaration itself, revealed a serious crisis of parliamentary authority. Even the most severe threats to parliamentary privilege could not be dealt with consensually because they had been subsumed within a partisan struggle.[38]

The following month the Common Council continued its aggressive tactics with two divisive remonstrances to Parliament, one delivered to each house on 26 May. The Commons, according to Whitaker, "much disliked" the Council's decision to proceed by remonstrance. It nevertheless spent the entire day debating whether to "give them thanks or a reproof" for their statement on a wide range of national issues. In two bitter divisions – unusually, one was held on a previous question and another on the question itself – the presbyterians carried a motion to simply tell the citizens that the remonstrance would be taken into consideration at a convenient time. While the remonstrance was never in fact considered, the House had failed to reject it on principle. Even worse for

---

[35] CJ, 4/3/1646, 4/8/1646, 4/11/1646, 4/16/1646, 4/18/1646, 4/21/1646, 4/22/1646; BL MS Add 31116, ff. 263r.–265v.

[36] CJ, 4/13/1646, 4/14/1646; *Harington*, 18–19.

[37] CJ, 4/17/1646; BL MS Add 31116, f. 265r.

[38] Cf. Kishlansky, *Rise of the New Model Army*, 101–2.

independents in the Commons, the shorter, less aggressive remonstrance sent to the Lords was greeted with thanks for its "respect to preserve the rights and privileges of the Parliament."[39]

Independents outside Parliament were also active at the time. On 2 June, a petition that had been rejected by the now obviously partisan Common Council (it was intended for submission to Parliament with the remonstrances of 26 May) was presented to Parliament by citizens and other inhabitants of London. According to Whitaker it contained six thousand signatures collected after the campaign had been condemned by the Common Council. In this case the petition was, according to Juxon, "only a long compliment" that did not include aggressive demands. Whatever the accuracy of this description of the petition, the Commons debated it for "many hours" and divided twice over whether to give thanks to the petitioners, with the independent tellers narrowly winning votes on the previous question and the question of thanks itself. This incident, featuring yet another highly unusual double division, only further confirms how the issue of privilege had been thoroughly politicized.[40] As violations of parliamentary privilege were condoned by friendly audiences in the Commons and made the subject of divisions by the opposite side, the underpinnings of consensual decision-making were being rapidly eroded.

For the remainder of the summer and on occasion throughout the closing months of 1646, petitions to the Commons continued to signify the destruction of consensus politics.[41] More generally, debate in the Commons was firmly structured by presbyterian partisan dominance: it was repeatedly ended abruptly in favor of easily won, partisan voice votes and harder-fought divisions, without eliciting much comment from diarists.[42] Even when the division frequency was at its highest, in the fall, there may have been a high number of meaningfully majoritarian voice votes in the Commons not followed by divisions and not described as majoritarian by contemporaries. Strictly speaking, however, it is impossible to know for sure if these decisions were further signs of presbyterian

[39] CJ, 5/26/1646; BL MS Add 31116, f. 271r.; Kishlansky, *Rise of the New Model Army*, 86–7.

[40] Kishlansky, *Rise of the New Model Army*, 88–9; CJ, 6/2/1646; BL MS Add 31116, f. 272r.; Juxon, *Journal*, 125.

[41] CJ, 7/3/1646, 8/28/1646, 12/22/1646; BL MS Add 31116, ff. 282r., 294r.; Lindley, *Popular Politics and Religion in Civil War London*, 369–70.

[42] For example, *Harington*, 22, 25, 34–6, 44.

dominance amid fierce partisan competition and not instead evidence of the partial persistence of consensual decision-making.[43]

Perhaps the best evidence for the eclipse of consensual politics in the Commons by 1646 is the long debate and extremely close double division on Sir John Clotworthy's ultimately unsuccessful motion of 10 October to charge a committee with considering the use of a ballot box for certain votes in the House. This debate had itself been prompted by a dispute over Sir William Brereton being given Eccleshall Castle as a reward for military service. According to Whitaker, the secret ballot was being considered for occasions "when any question should be put for giving of money or office," but the Commons journal itself did not mention this in the recorded wording of the question. Whether or not the question was put for these cases only or for all votes in the Commons, the narrow defeat of Clotworthy's motion confirmed a widespread awareness that the Commons' privileges – in this case, free speech and voting – were thought to be fundamentally threatened by the politics of civil war. It also confirmed that the ultimate effect of such threats would be to corrupt the core of parliamentary decision-making: the vote.[44]

In 1647 the frequency of divisions remained constant from 1646, occurring after 12 percent of questions put, or once every other day (Figures 4.1, 4.2, and 5.1). The basic underlying conditions for these divisions also remained constant. As with other divisions from the period following the first Civil War, enumerated votes in 1647 were subsumed by partisan conflict and driven in part by pressure from (and partisan

---

[43] For example, CJ, 9/16–17/1646, 10/15/1646; *Harington*, 36–7, 44. Contrast Kishlansky, *Rise of the New Model Army*, 137. Divisions rose to a frequency of 13.1 percent in the last four months of 1646, compared with 10.6 percent in earlier months.

[44] CJ, 10/10/1646; *Perfect Occurrences of Both Houses of Parliament* (10–16 October 1646; Nelson and Seccombe, *British Newspapers and Periodicals*, 465.4042), sig. Rr2; BL MS Add 31116, f. 285v.; *Harington*, 42; Kishlansky, *Rise of the New Model Army*, 137; Morrill, "Sir William Brereton and England's Wars of Religion." Debate over a ballot box reappeared during discussions of the proper procedure for naming a Council of State in 1654, and again in 1658. For 1654, see *Burton*, vol. I, cv–cvi. According to the diarist Guybon Goddard, the ballot box "was found to have much deceit, and to be capable of practice, and was called indeed no better than a juggler's box … that hath been found to have many inconveniences; every man being led by particular interest and affection." This judgment – based on an awareness of how the ballot box, too, can be manipulated to corrupt ends – evinces clear concern with the acceptance of voting on the basis of mere preference without a mechanism by which members would be held accountable by other members for their views and voting. In late 1658, John Thurloe, making much the same point, wrote to Henry Cromwell to report that commonwealthsmen hoped better to manage their work in Parliament by means of a motion for voting by ballot box, "judging that there will be many Nicodemites in the House, who would be of their party, if they durst" (*Collection of the State Papers of John Thurloe*, vol. VII, 550; thanks to Jason Peacey for this reference).

coordination with) political mobilization occurring outside Parliament. From the beginning of the year, the Commons regularly held divisions over matters that did not have major constitutional implications but were status-related decisions of some importance for securing a partisan advantage.[45] The House was usually able to maintain traditional patterns of decision-making only in their ongoing confrontation with the Lords.[46] By the spring, they had fallen into a pattern of divisions over petitions and pamphlets taken by presbyterians to threaten the House.[47] Divisions concerning the disbandment of the army quickly became the clearest indications of the utter dislocation of parliamentary practices and the end of parliamentary independence. These partisan decisions began with narrow 17 and 19 February divisions in a full House that in essence centered on whether the House would proceed with the disbandment of the New Model Army.[48]

The destruction of parliamentary legitimacy and the increasing hostility of the army were both furthered by the majoritarian patterns that had taken hold of decision-making in the Commons. As the presbyterians gained firm control of Parliament by the end of March 1647, they became subject to unprecedented aggression and opposition from the army – behavior that was, in effect, unprecedented action against Parliament itself. This culminated with Fairfax's 15 June presentation of the army's charges against eleven members to the parliamentary commissioners, and the army's constitutionally novel presentation of articles of impeachment on 6 July.[49] The employment of majoritarian tactics was an important element of these charges.

One of the members charged by the army, the presbyterian Walter Long, was specifically cited by Fairfax and the council of war as a master of majoritarian maneuver. In a letter drafted by John Rushworth, they alleged that Long "has for the space of two years last past usually pressed and urged several members to give their votes such ways as he pleased." To that end Long "does constantly place himself near the door of the House, [so] that when any debate is concerning any design wherein his party is engaged," he "used much tampering and violence to such of his

---

[45] For example, CJ, 1/5/1647, 1/7/1647, 1/8/1647, 1/12/1647.
[46] BL MS Add 31116, ff. 297v., 298v., 300r.; CJ, 1/15/1647, 1/16/1647, 1/18/1647, 1/19/1647, 1/21/1647, 2/2/1647.
[47] CJ, 4/1/1647, 4/27/1647, 5/4/1647, 5/20/1647, 6/2/1647; *Harington*, 50, 54; BL MS Add 31116, ff. 309r., 310r., 311v.
[48] CJ, 2/17/1647, 2/19/1647; BL MS Add 31116, f. 302v. For other related divisions and debate, see CJ, 2/23/1647, 2/25/1647, 2/26/1647, 3/3/1647, 3/5/1647, 3/13/1647; BL MS Add 31116, ff. 303r., 303v.
[49] Kishlansky, *Rise of the New Model Army*, 243–56, esp. 252–3; Braddick, *God's Fury, England's Fire*, 498–9.

own party as would go out of the House and has persuaded them to continue there for their votes." As for those who had already left the House, Long was "very inquisitive where they might be found, that so he may go for them when the business in debate comes near to be put to the vote." Moreover, "when they come not according to his expectation," Long "does ordinarily and speedily run out of the House himself to call them and drive them in again." Because of this activity, they concluded, "he hath been commonly called (by those that are without the House, and have taken notice of his actions) the Parliament Driver." The consequence of all this, of course, was disastrous: "[T]he freedom of the members is taken from them, the manner of the Parliament's proceedings much scandalized, and many times evil and dangerous designs drove on in a faction by votes, to the great prejudice of the commonwealth."[50] Long, remarkably, owned these charges.[51] The presbyterian William Prynne also defended him, charged the army with identical behavior, and suggested that Long's activities were common practice. "The army's friends (if this charge be a crime) are more guilty of it than M. Long," he argued, since they "will be sure upon all debates in the House and at Committees to keep their party together, and send up and down for recruits, if they see themselves likely to be over-voted."[52] While Prynne acknowledged traditional norms here, he appeared to be tacitly endorsing Long's actions (and the actions of his opponents) as ordinary practice.

By this point the army, in response to such perceived majoritarian behavior, had emerged as a profound threat to parliamentary authority and power that had been merged with popular pressure from independent elements in the City. Under these conditions, parliamentary privilege was thoroughly compromised, frequent divisions continued, and relations between the Lords and Commons reached a new low. From early June, when crowds of reformadoes at Westminster physically intimidated members, to later in the month, when presbyterian crowds invaded the House and coerced votes, and on to August, when the army itself entered London and did the same, there was hardly any parliamentary honor or independence left to protect – only desperate, partisan efforts to cobble together a semblance of parliamentary authority and legitimacy. These efforts utterly failed.[53] Once the independents seized control of the Commons in the summer, divisions fell back into another familiar

---

[50] Anon., *A Particular Charge or Impeachment*, 27–8.
[51] *Parliamentary or Constitutional History of England*, vol. XVI, 156–7.
[52] [Prynne], *Brief Iustification of the XI. Accused Members*, 10.
[53] Braddick, *God's Fury, England's Fire*, 496–502.

pattern, centering around conflict over the terms of negotiation with the king.[54] It was manifest by this point that the conventions of consensual decision-making had fallen completely out of practice.

If the ultimate question of the English Revolution is the question of why Parliament failed to "preserve its institutional prerogatives," the preceding account provides an answer.[55] Fairfax's famous excuse to the king for resistance, of course, was "necessity." It cannot be stressed enough that this was also the original reason why in 1643 the House of Commons began to discard its traditional mode of deciding and acting as the nation's representative. By 1648, the Commons had completely lost its bearings. In institutional terms, the climax of the English Revolution was an afterthought, the upshot of Parliament's precipitous loss of status as a result of the emergence of majoritarian politics.

From yet another angle, the moment of Pride's Purge and the trial and execution of Charles I simply continued what would turn out to be a period of deinstitutionalized decision-making in the Commons that out-lasted the Revolution itself. In 1648, before the Purge, the Commons divided 10.5 percent of the time, or about once every three days, slightly less frequently than in the previous two years (Figures 4.1, 4.2, and 5.1). In the spring, the independents fatefully split over the future political settlement, and popular mobilization continued apace on both sides. Presbyterians also regained strength over the summer. This set in motion the process that would lead to outright revolution, provoked by the commitment of a majority of the Commons to circumventing the wishes of the army and the radicals in Parliament. The conflict over a settlement dominated the persistence of majority voting in this period.[56]

Between 1 and 5 December 1648 the House divided six times over the king's answers to the propositions of Newport and the prospect of a settlement.[57] The last of these divisions was the fateful 129 to 83 previous question vote in favor of a settlement with the king on the basis of his answer to Parliament's propositions. This was the first step in a

---

[54] For example, CJ, 8/27/1647, 9/22/1647, 9/23/1647, 10/16/1647, 10/20/1647, 11/1/1647, 11/18/1647, 11/26/1647, 11/27/1647.

[55] This answer is fundamentally different from Kishlansky's description of a sudden perversion of parliamentary privilege after the end of the First Civil War. See Kishlansky, *Rise of the New Model Army*, 228.

[56] See Underdown, *Pride's Purge*, 97–142. Examples of consecutive divisions in a single day on the issue of the settlement before Pride's Purge include CJ, 2/11/1648 (three divisions), 2/26/1648 (seven divisions), 4/28/1648 (three divisions), 7/3/1648 (two divisions), 7/28/1648 (two divisions), 10/31/1648 (two divisions), 11/6/1648 (two divisions), 11/7/1648 (two divisions), 11/9/1648 (two divisions), 11/10/1648 (two divisions), and 12/4/1648 (three divisions).

[57] CJ, 12/1/1648, 12/4/1648, 12/5/1648.

revolutionary unraveling of parliamentary power based, in essence, on the perceived illegitimacy of majoritarian decision-making in the Commons.[58] This illegitimacy – founded on a conviction that Parliament was ruled by a faction and its signature political weapon, the division – was yet again met with a minoritarian response, just as it had been in November 1641, after votes on the Grand Remonstrance, and on so many other occasions over the course of the Civil War era. This time, however, the minority revolt would originate outside the House, and it would involve not protests, but armed force. As such it would prove far more effective than previous revolts: the minority would be coercively transformed into a majority. In this sense, Pride's Purge registered both the defeat of the House's half-hearted attempt to assert its status on the authority of majorities and the demise of parliamentary privilege and honor. All the dynamics conspiring in this final moment – including the rise of majority votes, minority resistance, and external threats – were nearly a decade in the making. They had been present at the initial deinstitutionalization of consensus politics. Now having taken recognizably new forms, they ushered in the final phase of the self-undermining of Parliament's decision-making tradition. Similar dynamics would drive English politics until the establishment of the Commonwealth.

The fundamental aspects of these developments are vividly clear in the basic record of divisions in the House. On 6 December 1648, after the Commons had been purged in favor of the previous day's minority, the Council of War presented proposals to the House. It demanded that the eleven members charged in June 1647, along with one other, be brought to justice. It insisted, too, that nearly one hundred other members be permanently excluded, that others who had voted against the army be suspended, that innocent members should declare their innocence, and that a dissolution of the parliament and new election dates should be settled on. On the following day, the House put a previous question for proceeding with the proposals, and the motion passed in a clearly majoritarian and relatively sparse division of 50 to 28. This was obviously to some degree a protest division: after the vote, some of the twenty-eight members in the minority promptly left the House in anger and frustration. They resolved not to return until the House and its excluded members were vindicated. The Commons' acquiescence to the army, now actively championed by radical members, was only partly mitigated by the next division, in which the House decided to confront the

---

[58] Ibid., 12/5/1648.

army about its conduct. On 14 December, after the lower house reached a quorum only by convincing the soldiers to admit six members they had detained in the lobby, the House voted 35 to 18 to send a committee to ask Fairfax why members had been restrained from entering the House. Two similar divisions were held on 20 December. In all of these votes, for which many members voluntarily stayed away from the House, the decimation of the Commons on multiple levels was clear. So too was the firmness of divisions within the Rump when under military domination, despite the purge. By this point the army was in firm control of the political process. The High Court, erected on 4 January, began the trial of Charles I on the 8th. There were only three more divisions between 20 December and the execution of the king on 30 January, all of them concerning fraught relations with the Lords.[59] The Commons was still defending its status where it could.

Chronic Instability in the Commonwealth and Protectorate

Over the course of 1649, following the regicide and the resolutions to abolish the House of Lords and the monarchy on 6 and 7 February, respectively, the Rump Parliament divided 8.6 percent of the time, or once every four days. The Rump was far from a purely revolutionary body, especially once – in its desperation for legitimacy and stability after declaring its sovereignty with a tiny minority of the Long Parliament membership present – it readmitted as many members as would dissent to the 5 December vote for a settlement and later take the Engagement. This expanded group, which still owed its existence to the coerced, minoritarian reversal of an earlier majority vote, included many members who had no enthusiasm for the Commonwealth. As a whole, the Parliament exhibited an unstable, dynamic factionalism. Unless pressured by the army, even radicals were generally unwilling to act aggressively for reform. The Rump's oscillation between activism and inclusion – a result of the fundamental weaknesses of minoritarian politics and the negative basis for unity within the revolutionary minority – eliminated the possibility that the purge of December 1648 would lead to either a smooth institutionalization of majority rule under the dominance of a forced plurality or a return to the conventions of consensus.[60]

---

[59] Underdown, *Pride's Purge*, 145, 151, 163; CJ, 12/7/1648, 12/14/1648, 12/20/1648, 1/9/1649, 1/18/1649.

[60] Underdown, *Pride's Purge*, 262–3; Worden, *Rump Parliament*, 26–32, 38, 42–3, 57–60, 88–9, 123, 170.

The Rump and Nominated parliaments were very thinly attended assemblies operating with limited legitimacy as single chambers. These factors in themselves made the lasting institutionalization of any practices – either novel or familiar – unlikely. In 1649 and 1650, the frequency of divisions in Parliament remained around 9 percent, and rose significantly only in 1651, when divisions occurred 15 percent of the time. The division frequency for the Rump between the Purge and the Rump's dissolution in April 1653 was 12.8 percent. This narrowly eclipsed the division frequency in any single year of the Long Parliament. The figure for the Nominated or Barebone's Parliament was a striking 17.8 percent, which matched the frequency of the Rump in its final sixteen months. On the basis of this evidence, we might indeed conclude that majoritarian politics had become institutionalized following the English Revolution. But this is difficult to confirm with any certainty. The sparsity of documentation for this period does not quite make it possible to assess whether this pattern of divisions had an institutional foundation.

The record of business in the Commons does confirm that the Rump and Nominated Parliaments were very commonly unable to resolve contentious issues without divisions. Most importantly, they often failed to do so when deliberating on issues that did not have a strong status component. They also very commonly divided on issues of minor political significance, especially from 1651 onward. This basic pattern matches that of the House soon after the Restoration, when as we will see majoritarian decision-making was certainly institutionalized. The most common general issue before the Commons in 1651 and 1652 was the question of delinquency and oblivion. In 1651, dozens of divisions concerned the treatment of delinquents, a matter that had public and status significance but no grave political import in any individual case.[61] Far less frequently, divisions were caused by politically serious issues, such as the formation of the Council of State and the possibility of electing a new parliament.[62] The year 1652 began with the House dividing a staggering twenty-three times on the Act of Oblivion alone, in January and February.[63] After this period, however, the Commons resettled into the pattern evident in 1651, dividing scores of times on

---

[61] If one were to emphasize the private nature of these votes, this too would explain the resort to divisions, but in accordance with a traditional justification that remained part of the new, majoritarian institution. Private matters would still lead to divisions in a majoritarian system, just as they had in a consensual system.

[62] These latter divisions were similar to another series of divisions held before the Rump was dissolved in April 1653.

[63] Similar episodes would again be common during the Protectorate.

delinquents and the forfeiture of their estates, including the property of Charles I. This pattern continued until the Rump was forcibly dissolved by Cromwell in April 1653, an event that confirmed its continuing lack of legitimacy and institutional standing.

The 144-member Nominated Parliament, which first met on 4 July 1653 and ended on 12 December, met more often than the Rump and was for about a month much better attended. The House admitted members from a wider ideological spectrum as well. The conflicts that eventually led to this parliament's demise were evident as early as mid-July, in a debate on tithes. From that point onward, the Parliament divided regularly on a variety of political, legal, and religious issues. Even though it appears to have conducted thorough debate on a number of controversial topics, it was clearly unable consistently to reach consensus on revolutionary reform. Here as elsewhere, though, it can often be difficult to tell if prolonged debate was aimed at the achievement of a consensus or simply at the securing of a majority. The Parliament had a factional makeup at numerous points, but it also divided along nonfactional lines. When conflict reached a climax in the final months before the dissolution, radicals were blamed for making reasoned debate impossible with their claims that God spoke through them and that their speech was to be evaluated accordingly.[64] The session ended with a close division that killed a committee report on the parochial ministry. The vote was divisive enough that the next day proponents of the motion began business by condemning the previous day's work as destructive. Then, supported by the Speaker, Francis Rous, these members simply walked out of the session without any debate or vote to do so, processed to Whitehall, and abdicated their power to Cromwell. The members who remained behind in the House could not make a quorum and were soon dispersed by officers from the army.[65]

Despite such obvious institutional failures, in the early 1650s and beyond traditional norms continued to be articulated – amid fear, of course, that they were not being followed anymore. In 1651 Isaac Penington, Jr., whose father was a member of the Rump, made a striking set of observations on this front. "And here I may not unfitly add one thing," he began, "concerning the way of managing affairs in Parliament so much in use, viz. by votes." Penington hinted that the practice had

---

[64] Woolrych, *Commonwealth to Protectorate*, esp. 157–8, 194, 236–50, 288–9, 328, 332.

[65] Ibid., 337, 339–45; Scott (ed.), *Collection of Scarce and Valuable Tracts*, VI, 282–3. There were also other occasional signs of a willingness to adopt majoritarian tactics before the dissolution. See ibid., VI, 274, 276, 280–1; Woolrych, *Commonwealth to Protectorate*, 308–10.

become habitual as the result of a series of crises and an onslaught of pressing business. "The necessity whereof in some cases, and the multitude of transactions," he wrote, "may have been an occasion to draw into more common use then is either fit or safe." Penington, in other words, was describing the piecemeal process by which majoritarian decisions had become too common an aspect of parliamentary affairs, largely as a result of Parliament's assumption of executive functions. He also registered the basis for his normative critique. "My ground of excepting against it is this," he wrote. "[T]he actions of the people (and so of the Parliament, who are the collective body of the people) should be very clear and evident to the eye of common sense, so as to bear down all opposition or gainsaying." Penington was connecting the legitimacy of parliamentary decisions to national consensus and the wisdom and truth it implied. "The people," he explained, "should desire the removal of nothing but what is evidently burdensome, the addition of no law but what is evidently good, the punishment of none but him who hath evidently been an offender." The frequency of divisions in the Rump made clear that such an environment no longer existed. "Putting things to vote," he explained, "is an argument against this clearness and evidence, and doth seem to whisper, if not to speak out, that things are doubtful, and that the determination is also doubtful, arising not necessarily from the strength of reason, but perhaps from the number of voices."[66] Penington continued to believe that sound deliberation and majoritarian decision-making were opposed. He had succinctly described the moment of deinstitutionalized decision-making in which he was living, one born of revolutionary circumstances.

The better-documented second half of the republican period presents different problems for assessing whether or not majoritarianism became institutionalized under the revolutionary regime. The Protectorate Commons divided nearly as often as Barebone's Parliament and the Rump in 1652–3: 16.3 percent of the time a question was put. But it did so overwhelmingly in the context of fundamental constitutional instability, outside pressure from petitions and other mechanisms, and extremely long and vigorous debate. This seems to reflect deinstitutionalized decision-making, but it cannot really be assessed with certainty one way or the other as evidence of institutionalized majoritarianism. Traditional norms continued to be regularly aired, if sometimes to partisan advantage, and thorough debate remained a priority. During this period, Parliament was generally understood more clearly than ever

---

[66] Penington, *Fundamental Right, Safety and Liberty of the People*, 28 (thanks to Markku Peltonen for this reference).

to be the sole, collective representative of the people of England and Wales, and this was thought to make the achievement of unity in decision-making extremely important.[67] But the constitutional uncertainty of this moment meant that nearly all of Parliament's important decisions had profound status implications, and deeply significant divisions were all too frequent occurrences. Whatever uncertainty remains about the ultimate question of institutionalization in the 1650s, it is worth making use of the superior documentation for this period to explore the nature of the apparently unmoored decision-making of the Protectorate House of Commons.

When it met in September 1654, the first Protectorate Parliament made efforts to work consensually while debating a series of core constitutional issues in the context of the Instrument of Government. Two divisions occurred on the 6th and 7th, the latter over whether the Instrument would be considered in a committee of the whole. But after the 141 to 136 vote in favor of a committee, against Cromwell's wishes, not another division occurred until 25 October, despite the profoundly divisive topics under consideration in committee of the whole.[68] On 29 September, for instance, the House turned to the issue of whether the Lord Protector and Council should have discretion in matters of war and peace, independent of Parliament. Members again debated the matter in a committee of the whole, which as we have seen was a traditional mechanism for working toward consensus decisions that were otherwise difficult to achieve. "The debate being long, and the House divided in opinion," according to the diarist member Guybon Goddard, the committee was adjourned. Debate apparently continued on 30 September and 2 October. On the 2nd the House confined debate to the question of war, which was itself controverted between members friendly to the court's agenda and their opponents, who claimed parliamentary right in this sphere. According to Goddard, at the end of the day (presumably in committee of the whole, since this decision was not recorded in the journal), "it was brought to the question, and resolved, without one negative," that war-making power lay with Protector and Parliament jointly, giving both a veto.[69] On the 3rd, debate turned from war to peace, and on the 4th, according to Goddard, the House (again in committee, it seems) resolved on joint peacemaking powers, with the

---

[67] Little and Smith, *Parliaments and Politics during the Cromwellian Protectorate*, 222–7. On petitioning, see esp. 227–9.

[68] CJ, 9/6/1654, 9/7/1654; Woolrych, *Britain in Revolution*, 605. On the use of committees of the whole to avoid divisions in this period, see *Burton*, vol. I, li, lix.

[69] CJ, 9/29/1654, 9/30/1654, 10/2/1654; *Burton*, vol. I, xliv, xlvi.

exception of cases when Parliament was not sitting. For these cases the House specified restrictions on independent action by the Protector and Council.[70] This series of events is in itself strong evidence that majoritarian politics had not been institutionalized at this point.[71] It is nevertheless possible that the continuance of debate was tactically promoted by members who wanted to postpone votes on decisions relating to the authority of the Lord Protector and Council that they were likely to lose at specific moments.

Whatever the underlying nature of prolonged debate in September and October, the House fell into very frequent divisions between November and the parliament's dissolution in January 1655. Divisions on the constitutional bill began on 9 November. This bill immediately became nearly the sole source of the sixty divisions that occurred in under three months prior to the dissolution. As one might expect, this situation provoked some reflection on partisan groupings in the House, roughly organized around a broad courtly interest and its largely presbyterian opponents.[72] Goddard repeatedly referred to an intransigent "Court party" and an "anti-court party" (as well as "courtiers," "soldiery," and "patriots") once the period of frequent divisions began. Of the 10 November vote to ordinarily deny the Protector a negative voice in legislation, "it was said by them," according to Goddard, "that this vote had destroyed the government ... We had, as much as vote could do, unmade the Protector."[73] From this point onward Goddard reflected frequently on partisan tactics.[74]

On 18 November, for instance, the House entered into debate on the question of whether after Cromwell's death standing military forces would be directed by the Council until Parliament assembled. "There did seem to be a general concurrence," Goddard wrote, "and the sense of the House was almost unanimous in it." Nevertheless, "the courtiers and soldiers were not pleased with it." They "pretended" various interpretations of the question, and then "pretended they were not yet ready for [the question to be put], although they had both voted before in the

---

[70] *Burton*, vol. I, xlvi.

[71] See also ibid., vol. I, lx, lxiii. Cf. Gaunt, "Oliver Cromwell and His Protectoral Parliaments." Little and Smith, in *Parliaments and Politics during the Cromwellian Protectorate*, esp. 103–4, somewhat overdraw the difference between their position and Gaunt's, although their account (to 126) is more informative.

[72] For an attempt to piece together partisan and factional groupings in the Protectorate Parliaments that makes extensive use of division teller names, see Little and Smith, *Parliaments and Politics during the Cromwellian Protectorate*, 105–26. For 1654–5, see 105, 114–15.

[73] *Burton*, vol. I, xxvi, xxvii, xxxv, lxvi–lxvii, lxx, lxxiv, lxxxi–lxxxii.

[74] For example, ibid., vol. I, lxviii.

grand committee." Debate continued to the end of the day. "The House being very strong and desirous to have the question put, the Court party moved that this debate be adjourned ... which, to satisfy their importunity, was granted." On 6 December, which Goddard called "a day of the greatest dispute of business that I had known in the whole parliament," one motion "gave great offense to the Court party, some of which were heard to say, that they cared not ever to come into the Parliament House again."[75] On Goddard's account, at least, court supporters came to the House with fixed views. They pretended to adhere to consensual norms and assailed Parliament's legitimacy when they faced resistance.

The second Protectorate Parliament – purged by the Council of over a hundred men who won elections with the added loss of fifty to sixty who, in protest, refused to sit – exhibited similar dynamics to the first. To complicate matters, an emerging division between "civilian" and "army" interests drawn from the old courtier grouping made parliamentary management even more difficult than in the previous session. Civilian courtiers looked to presbyterian members, perhaps the largest single (if also a very diverse) grouping in the House, while the army interest looked to build coalitions with outright enemies of the regime.[76] Again an apparently strong commitment to debate was accompanied by frequent divisions that very often decided matters of basic constitutional importance. There do not appear to have been fixed partisan groupings in these divisions.[77] Majoritarian decisions began on 22 September 1656, five days after the opening of the session. That day featured two divisions, including a minoritarian vote in which twenty-nine members voiced opposition to the 125 in the majority, civilians and army officers among them, who wanted to get on with business and leave excluded members who desired admission to the House to fend for themselves with the Council.[78] This was a clear protest against the perceived illegitimacy of the session from a large contingent of members, clearly evincing the institutional instability of the Commons at this point.

The first major controversy of the second Protectorate Parliament began on 5 December, when the House began to debate the case of the Quaker James Nayler after a committee reported on the matter. This triggered numerous divisions, nearly all of them ostensibly procedural but in fact extremely substantive, dealing with a host of issues that

---

[75] Ibid., vol. I, lxxx, lxxxii, cxii; CJ, 11/18/1654.

[76] Little and Smith, *Parliaments and Politics during the Cromwellian Protectorate*, 106–13, 115–17.

[77] Roots, "Lawmaking in the Second Protectorate Parliament," 136–7.

[78] CJ, 9/22/1656; Little and Smith, *Parliaments and Politics during the Cromwellian Protectorate*, 106.

included the jurisdiction of Parliament in such a case. The struggle over how to proceed with Nayler, which played out for months, seems a clear case of a body committed to consensual decision-making despite its impossibility amid the constitutional ambiguities of the revolutionary regime.[79] According to the diarist member Thomas Burton, it was argued on the 5th that "it is very considerable that you should be unanimous in this debate."[80] Others urged the House to follow related traditional norms, such as deciding matters of importance in a full House and using committees to forge compromises.[81]

Between 5 and 11 December, the date of the first division on the Nayler problem, the House reached important decisions by means of voice votes. Militating against the considerations favoring consensus politics, of course, were both the difficulty of the general issue and members' increasing impatience with the House's inability to resolve it at a time when it was widely feared that the session might soon end.[82] The close, 87 to 84 division on the 11th over whether simply to adjourn debate for two hours or adjourn until the next day reflected these pressures, as did the 13 December division on adjournment carried against a minority pushing a vote on Nayler's punishment.[83] By the 15th, members were even advocating for divisions with reference to these conditions. The Speaker urged that the question be switched to a higher punishment for Nayler, so that a "no" vote did not set him free. The Speaker was clearly expecting and accepting a division. Others argued that some question simply had to be put "for your honour abroad." This was an early instance of what would become during the Restoration period a standard inversion of pre–Civil War norms concerning the honor stakes of divisions, especially in cases where, as one member argued on the 15th, "the House is full enough to put the question."[84] Honor was to be secured in the decision made, not the manner in which it was made. Others, however, countered that debate had to be totally exhausted – every member given an opportunity to speak – before the question could be put. They also reiterated other traditional norms.[85] This, again, could have been tactical at many points, in the same way that

---

[79] For the legal questions involved, see Little and Smith, *Parliaments and Politics during the Cromwellian Protectorate*, 183–5.

[80] *Burton*, vol. I, 37; see also vol. I, 96–7, 118.

[81] Ibid., vol. I, 50, 51, 137. From December, see also vol. I, 253.   [82] Ibid., vol. I, 104.

[83] Ibid., vol. I, 130–1; CJ, 12/11/1656, 12/13/1656.

[84] *Burton*, vol. I, 143, 146; see also 255–6. For further concern about a thin House later in the month, see vol. I, 190–5, 234. For other evidence of the prominent role of considerations of the House's honor in the Nayler controversy, see 261–4.

[85] Ibid., vol. I, 147, 234–5, 258–9.

pushing *for* the question could be. On the following day, the House finally divided 96 to 82 against a previous question on drafting a bill to have Nayler executed. They then agreed by means of a voice vote on an elaborate series of corporal punishments short of death.[86] This result was secured by a successful effort simply to end the interminable debate and vote. The notion apparently accepted by the House was that, as the member Francis White put it, "there has been enough said in this business."[87]

The Nayler case continued to cause divisions for the rest of the month, and opposed sets of norms continued to be aired.[88] On 27 December Lord Fleetwood introduced his speech during a long debate by saying that "if I thought you were fit for a question, I should not trouble you." The Speaker eventually tried to put the question to move the debate into a committee, but was derailed by a dispute over whether the Commons should "go a slow a pace as may be, in this business, fully to debate the business" and perhaps adjourn for the day. Here again, gestures to traditional norms may have been tactical in nature. Whatever the motivations behind it, this sentiment was met with the argument that "it is not for your honour to part without coming to some resolution in this business."[89] As this example shows, it was still common for members to associate the honor of the House with consensual decisions and full debate, either as an expression of a continuing commitment or as a tactic in a fundamentally majoritarian environment. At the same time, it was becoming common for members to adopt the rather novel position that resolute action supported by a forced division was the best means of protecting the House's honor. This position was slightly ambiguous, but it may have implied the view that *divisions themselves* could be considered honorable – the opposite of the traditional view. This open conflict vividly demonstrates from yet another angle that deinstitutionalized decision-making appears to have persisted into the later 1650s.

In the new year, 1657, the House behaved similarly. It turned to a series of new questions with profound significance for the constitution and the military and financial settlement of the regime. At the same time, members made clear their commitment to thorough debate and engaged a variety in familiar tactics aimed at avoiding divisions, including frequent deliberation in committees of the whole.[90] Divisions nevertheless became remarkably common during the six months of 1657 in which the House was in session. They occurred after one out of every five questions

---

[86] CJ, 12/16/1656.   [87] *Burton*, vol. I, 152.
[88] CJ, 12/17/1656, 12/23/1656, 12/27/1656.   [89] *Burton*, vol. I, 253, 255, 256.
[90] For other tactics, see, for example, *Burton* vol. I, 294, 303; vol. II, 173, 194, 208.

put and on three out of every four days in session. From late February to June, the House was simply overwhelmed with conflicts over the Remonstrance and Humble Petition and Advice, which caused about a quarter of the 101 divisions held that year. The question of Cromwell's status and title was a particularly common source of many of these enumerated majority votes.

The mixed approaches to parliamentary decision-making evident in this period again suggest structural dislocation, although it is hard to rule out the possibility that references to traditional norms and engagement in what had once been consensual practices were now merely tactics in a majoritarian game. On 11 March an initiative presumably aimed at bolstering the legitimacy of divisions on important issues – raising the quorum from twenty-one to thirty-one, during a period in which attendance was very low – was soundly defeated 96 to 53. Numerous votes in 1657, like this one, were forced by minorities. The House nevertheless remained generally committed not only to debate but to reaching a consensus on formally substantive questions. On 23 April, the House conducted a voice vote with only one negative to approve their committee's work with the Protector on the Petition and Advice. A dispute then arose about whether anyone voted "no," and the Speaker was criticized for challenging members' freedom of speech by raising the issue. At other points, members discussed how given the large volume of important legislation under consideration in the session, endless debate had somehow to be curbed. Such considerations might themselves have led to some divisions. The Speaker's verdict in voice votes also appears to have been regularly incorrect or partisan in the period. He was frequently forced to call divisions and often overruled by the tallies. On occasion the House also continued to witness the expression of apparently majoritarian views. On 9 June, when members moved to leave behind the catechism bill, which was the subject of numerous divisions in the session, they noted that the bill would "discontent many godly persons" and "it would not be handsome to have a negative upon it." But others opposed this traditional insistence on consensus. They observed the importance of the bill and justified bringing it to a vote with the claim that "more godly men rejoice at it than any that are against it."[91] This was a remarkably majoritarian justification for continuing to pursue the bill's passage.

[91] Ibid., vol. II, 9, 50, 58, 90, 107, 114, 116, 173, 202–3, 212, 245, 260; CJ, 3/11/1657, 4/23/1657.

During the Commons' brief sitting between 20 January and 4 February 1658, the "civilian" interest worked ineffectively on behalf of Cromwell.[92] This effort triggered an even higher level of conflict and uncertainty. So too did the readmission of relatively radical members excluded in 1656 and the controversy over the status of the Other House, which was sitting concurrently with the Commons under the terms of the Petition and Advice. Divisions occurred on one out of every three questions put, or once every other day. On the third day of the session, members explicitly addressed the problem of forced divisions. A question was put on whether messengers from the Other House would be called into the Commons in order to see if the messengers referred to the Other House as the House of Lords. According to Burton, after the voice vote, in which the yeas appeared to have the advantage, "Mr. Mildmay moved to divide the House for the noes." He was stopped in his tracks by the Speaker, who argued that "to divide the House without a reason, is without all reason. He ought to lay his hand on his breast, and say, on his conscience or judgment, he is not satisfied."[93] The Speaker was attempting to curb perceived abuses of the House's voting system, abuses that implied a blithe attitude toward the incidence of divisions.

Richard Cromwell's short-lived Commons, once again consumed by constitutional issues debated by members drawn from a wide ideological spectrum, was even more graphically divided. Its deliberations were dominated by a variety of important constitutional debates. The presence of "commonwealthsmen," or supporters of the Rump in this parliament, ensured constant and effective resistance to infringement by either the Protector or the Other House on the Commons' authority. The commonwealthsmen, who never themselves managed to win a single division, were joined by some crypto-royalists and army officers on specific issues. They were opposed by presbyterians, who increasingly set and enforced their own agenda in alliance with courtiers. This bloated and unproductive parliament, which was dissolved by force in favor of the Rump, divided nearly 40 percent of the time and once every other day. Here again, members argued over how best to make collective decisions. In this situation, especially early in the session, it was partly in the interest of commonwealthsmen to refer to traditional, consensual norms in order to impede speedy progress on legislation, and it was partly in the interest of courtiers to speed up the process of decision-making and, if necessary, force questions to be put. The use of both delaying tactics and initiatives to speed up the process was commonplace, and the use of these tactics

---

[92] Little and Smith, *Parliaments and Politics during the Cromwellian Protectorate*, 108.
[93] *Burton*, vol. II, 340.

was not completely correlated with factional alignments. Indeed, there is, in general, only incomplete evidence of simple partisan organization in this parliament.[94]

All signs, then, point to the persistence of deinstitutionalized decision-making under what were still fundamentally revolutionary conditions. The most important phenomena evident in early 1659 were an evidently strong commitment to thorough debate – not simply among obstructionist republicans – and the continual airing of traditional norms. But these efforts were stymied by the presence of a series of extremely complex, controverted items on the agenda. As a result, the House had extremely frequent recourse to divisions.[95] By 1 February, Goddard was reporting that "by this time it began plainly to appear that the commonwealth party," led by Sir Arthur Haselrig, "and His Protector's or court party began to vie stakes and pocked at one another in their light skirmishes."[96]

A week later, as controversy over recognizing Richard Cromwell as Protector continued, Thomas St. Nicholas attempted to delegitimate the passage of the Humble Petition and Advice in Oliver's second Parliament by saying it was "carried but by three, and in a precipitant and unparliamentary way." This was a reiteration of basic consensual norms, and St. Nicholas' historical reference was meant to apply to the present situation. He was asserting that the legitimacy of parliamentary decisions was limited by rushed, narrow divisions. Haselrig, in turn, arguing against a hasty vote on Richard's status even when the extremely unstable political environment encouraged expedition, urged that "it is against the orders of the House, to move us by arguments of fear, or any other arguments without doors." He also cautioned later on in the debate that the House should "not pass a question that the wisdom of the nation shall say we had not thought on." The presbyterian Lambert Godfrey concurred: "Take caution," he said, "against all the mischiefs that may follow, if it pass barely, and I shall freely concur with the question." Another member later added that "for the honour of your House, I would have you not to pop off the question; but do it unanimously, and in a full House." Sir Henry Vane junior agreed: "[T]here is much to

[94] Hirst, "Concord and Discord in Richard Cromwell's House of Commons"; Little and Smith, *Parliaments and Politics during the Cromwellian Protectorate*, 104, 112, 117–24. Hirst's account is more measured than Little and Smith suggest. On the profound constitutional ambiguities that bore on the session, see Peacey, "The Protector Humbled."

[95] Many of debates in this moment were nevertheless resolved through compromise after extensive debate. See, for example, *Burton*, vol. III, 286–7, 444–5, 472; vol. IV, 106–7, 111, 142.

[96] BL MS Add 5138, ff. 59v., 60r.

be said to the whole matter," he said, "before a question is propounded. You will surprise men that have not spoken to it. It becomes not the gravity of this House." John Barton made the same point another way: "[I]t is against a fundamental order that any man should have his liberty of speech taken from him."[97]

In the following days, other members made similar arguments. On 9 February one related that he "was never of that opinion, that a minor part should supplant a major part by force or fraud ... I have observed that a packing of Parliament, or a packing in Parliament, can never have good success." Thomas Scot observed that "there is not a word in the question but what is controverted, every iota. We are not ripe for any question." And on the 10th, in a long procedural debate, it was argued that the House should "not lose our ingenuity in surprising one another into a question. The debate has been soberly carried on hitherto."[98] The possibility of divisions was clearly still being considered in terms of a costly division of the nation's representatives.[99] At the same time, the House was, in fact, holding divisions constantly, and opponents of what seemed to be obstruction were often driven implicitly to endorse the high frequency of divisions by urging questions to be put.[100] The Commons' constitutional paralysis was keeping it in a state of institutional confusion.

The end of the republican period graphically illustrated how Parliament had fundamentally failed to reestablish its legitimacy after the Revolution. It remained ultimately subject to coercion from without. In late April, Richard Cromwell submitted to army demands for the dissolution of his parliament and thereafter effectively fell from power. On 7 May the army restored the Rump Parliament and the Commonwealth, but the Rump fared no better than the assembly it had replaced.[101] The severely undermanned body had only forty-two members at its first sitting and recognized the right of only seventy-eight to sit. It met until October 1659, when it, too, was interrupted by the army, whose needs and demands it had neglected. Amid the deepening political chaos, it met a second time – again with only forty-two members on the first day – from December 1659 to March 1660, at which point it dissolved itself. George Monck's army had begun its march across the Tweed to London on the first of the new year and thus set in motion the restoration of the monarchy. The secluded members

---

[97] *Burton*, vol. III, 119, 123, 141, 144, 149, 150; see also 180. For other insistence on extended debate and bill amendment being necessary to achieve consensus, see 359.
[98] Ibid., vol. III, 158, 192, 198; see also 171.
[99] See also Schilling (ed.), "Parliamentary Diary of Sir John Gell," 75.
[100] *Burton*, vol. III, 151, 328; vol. IV, 138, 219.
[101] Smith and Little, *Parliaments and Politics during the Cromwellian Protectorate*, 168–9.

were returned to the Rump on 20 February and a vote for new elections and a 16 March dissolution followed soon after.[102] Over both periods in session, the Rump divided only 7 percent of the time.

The House of Commons had apparently gone through the entirety of the revolutionary and republican periods of its history without firmly establishing an institutional alternative to the consensual system of decision-making it had failed to preserve in the early 1640s. To an extent, this has to remain a tentative conclusion, because under political conditions dominated by fundamental constitutional problems, the House had little opportunity consistently to divide on the sorts of politically significant issues unrelated to status considerations that would clearly demonstrate the institutionalization of majoritarian politics. In addition, it is often hard to determine when the invocation of consensual norms and engagement in traditional behavior was merely tactical. The evidence available, however, points strongly to persistent structural dislocation. The frequency of divisions in the House was inconsistent, and debate in the Commons clearly evinced a situation of institutional indeterminacy. Members continually politicized the question of parliamentary decision-making, offering at different times both consensualist and majoritarian arguments that were normally consistent with their tactical and ideological objectives.

The reasons why this situation persisted for so long cannot be established with great precision either, because of both the limitations of the evidence and the inherent difficulty of studying disorganization. On a general level, the extreme constitutional and logistical chaos of this period was unsuitable to the establishment of a new set of routine decision-making practices. It certainly provided no opportunity for the reestablishment of a consensual institution. On a more precise level, it was difficult, in these conditions, for a majoritarian practice to secure the sorts of benefits that had previously been secured by consensual decision-making. From this perspective, the key fact of the period, again, was the extremely fragile and limited legitimacy and status of Parliament. Under these conditions, the status benefits to majoritarian government remained unclear. This meant, in turn, that the incentives to practice it were few. At the same time, the prolonged crisis of parliamentary legitimacy was a prime environment for the resuscitation of appeals to the need to make unanimous or consensual decisions, whose wisdom could be trusted by a skeptical public as a result of the manner in which those decisions had been reached.

---

[102] For a summary narrative, see Woolrych, *Britain in Revolution*, 727–69.

Whatever its causes, this prolonged period of deinstitutionalization meant that the experience of consistent consensus decision-making was now a rather distant political memory, and the experience of majoritarian decision-making was perhaps more familiar than its predecessor. Commitment to the ideal of consensus nevertheless remained strong. Would the reestablishment of the monarchy, which reestablished the essential organizational environment that existed before the destruction of consensus politics, provide an environment in which consensual traditions could be successfully recovered? Or would the king in Parliament finally provide the essential, basic level of legitimacy for the Commons that would allow political actors to recognize a connection between secure status claims for the House and decision-making by majority vote?

6   The Majority Institutionalized, 1660–1800

The explosion of majoritarian decision-making in the House of Commons after the outbreak of the Civil War in 1642 was more than a temporary symptom of unrest. It was the beginning of an institutional transformation of the greatest significance. Decision-making in the Commons was deinstitutionalized for nearly two decades following the outbreak of hostilities. This itself suggests that mid-century was a point of no return. But the institutionalization of a fundamentally novel form of political practice in the wake of the English Revolution can be fully appreciated and demonstrated only by examining the nature of parliamentary decision-making in the restored monarchy. The Restoration was the ultimate test of whether the majoritarian behavior of the revolutionary era was more than a transient side effect of severe constitutional conflict. It established relative constitutional stability and reintroduced a series of institutional elements that had helped to maintain consensus decision-making prior to the Civil War. Yet despite the return of these institutional supports, the consensual tradition was never restored along with the monarchy. Neither the return of the Stuarts and the House of Lords nor the Commons' retreat from executive government could resuscitate a moribund practice. Instead, the opposite happened: a true institutional change was completed. Majority decision-making became habitual.

Between 1660 and 1699 the Commons divided 17 percent of the time a question was put (Figure 4.1). This was comparable to the 1650s, but it dwarfed the overall frequency of divisions in the revolutionary period as a whole (1643–59), which was 12.2 percent. Divisions were already routine as early as 1660 and 1662, if not in 1661. For these three years the usual frequency measure is somewhat misleading, because the high number of simple motions put to the question in July 1660 and at other points in this early period masks the striking daily frequency of meaningfully majoritarian votes (Figure 4.2). Divisions were held on nearly half the days on which the Commons met in 1660 and 1662, making divisions in these years, considered in terms of daily frequency, more common than divisions in 1646 and about equal in frequency to divisions in 1647.

The divisions of 1660 and 1662 also centered on many of the crucial political and religious problems of the moment. Finally, while previous questions – a crucial index of deinstitutionalized decision-making – were still used very frequently in 1660, they fell completely out of use in 1661 and 1662. They were replaced by explicit conflict on substantive issues. For all these reasons the first three years of the Restoration era marked an important turning point in the history of majority decision-making in the Commons.

The overwhelmingly royalist Convention that began meeting on 25 April 1660 and completed its business on 29 December divided 8.4 percent of the time a question was put. The relatively low division frequency during this period indicates that majoritarian decision-making had not yet been institutionalized. Yet there is evidence of assertive management techniques that proceeded from majoritarian assumptions.[1] In May 1660, Sir Alan Broderick, Sir Edward Hyde's agent in the Convention Commons, wrote to Hyde about Broderick's organizational efforts. "I daily confer with the best men before the House sits," he reported, "and deliver out notes of directions, contrived by Mr. Palmer and the ablest lawyers and perused by my Lord Southampton ... and the soberest statesmen, by which all with whom I had any correspondence, and many new men, direct their votes." To an extent this effort to count and direct predetermined votes was complemented, Broderick explained, by a retreat from deliberative practices and a rejection of debate as a source of truth, persuasion, and consensus. "I speak seldom," he said, "taking to myself and giving this maxim, that if any of our enemies or half friends move anything desired in my notes, that it be presently seconded and brought to the question, our number being much superior."[2] On Broderick's reading, genuine deliberation had no inherent value in the Convention Commons. The tactic he described here deflected attention from his initiation and organization of a partisan agenda and rested on predetermined conclusions. It even implied that while cross-factional consensus might emerge in the House on a particular issue, its emergence would have nothing to do with a genuine commitment to employing debate as a means of fostering agreement and unity.

In 1661 the Cavalier Parliament divided only 5.7 percent of the time (Figure 6.1 below). This was the lowest annual frequency of the

---

[1] See Jones, "Political Groups and Tactics in the Convention of 1660," esp. 170; Bodl. MS Dep. f. 9.

[2] Scrope and Monkhouse (eds.), *State Papers Collected by Edward, Earl of Clarendon*, vol. III, 747–9.

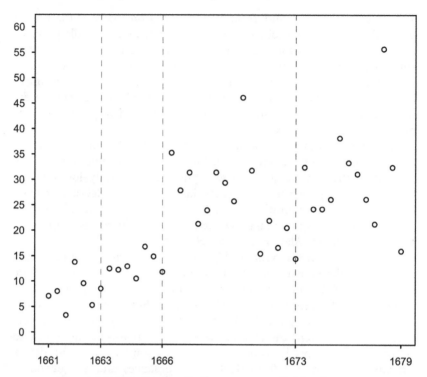

Figure 6.1 The Cavalier Parliament: mean division frequency as percentage of all questions put. Tick marks are located on the thirty-day unit that includes the beginning of each year.

Restoration period and only about one third of the mean frequency in the Cavalier Parliament as a whole (17.6 percent). This is another clear sign that majority voting had not yet been institutionalized. The Commons reached many decisions on politically important bills in this session after voice votes and without previous divisions on any aspect of the bill. These included votes to pass bills for securing religious uniformity, punishing regicides, punishing Quakers, arranging a voluntary grant to the king, and confronting tumultuary petitions.[3] The Commons journal also specifically noted *nemine contradicente* votes on burning and rejecting Interregnum legislation, declaring Arthur Haselrig guilty of high treason, and punishing regicides.[4] It is of course difficult to tell whether there were significant differences of opinion in the voice votes not described as

[3] CJ, 5/17/1661, 5/21/1661, 6/13/1661, 7/1/1661, 7/9/1661, 7/11/1661, 7/19/1661.
[4] Ibid., 5/27/1661, 5/30/1661, 7/1/1661, 7/11/1661.

nemine contradicente; they cannot be taken, on an individual basis, as clear evidence of the persistence of consensual decision-making.

In any case, the occurrence of divisions in this opening session was more meaningfully elevated than the basic data suggest. An unusually high number of routine questions were put in this early period of regime reconstruction; this artificially depressed the division frequency. Divisions occurred about every four days in session, making them a regular experience. Indeed, the nature of the divisions in the first session of the Parliament, which lasted from May to July, partly indicates institutionalized majoritarianism. The Commons divided on public issues of significant political import that nevertheless did not, for the most part, clearly touch on the status of the Commons in particular or Parliament in general. Often divisions from this period concerned central aspects of both Parliament's management of the legacy of the English Revolution and the Restoration regime's plan for achieving unity and stability.

The first division of the Cavalier Parliament was over a procedural aspect of the House's management of Charles II's main priority: the ratification of the acts of the Convention. The House divided over whether nonmembers of the committee for confirming these acts would be able to vote in the committee's meetings. The vote, 209 to 129 against, was fairly lopsided with a strong turnout. While we have very little information on this division (as is the case for most divisions in the early 1660s), it was clearly forced by one side after what must have been an obvious voice vote. It is also clear that this vote was part of a straight-forward power struggle over the Commons' eventual decisions on this central aspect of the "second" Restoration settlement.[5] The next division of the Parliament, which took place three days later on 17 May after a long debate, was on a previous question about whether to publicly burn the Solemn League and Covenant. Again this was an ostensibly proced-ural decision that in fact had profound ideological import, and again it was resolved through a forced, open acknowledgment of conflict. The vote was 228 to 103 in favor of putting the question, and the following vote was easily carried in favor of burning the Covenant.[6]

The vote on the Covenant was the first major act in a vocal struggle between conformist, royalist Anglicans and their opponents in the Cavalier Commons. This struggle continued throughout the 1661 ses-sions and beyond. The next acts were the 26 May vote requiring all who desired a seat in Parliament to receive the sacrament according to Anglican rites and the 30 May introduction of a bill to restore bishops

---

[5] Ibid., 5/14/1661.   [6] Ibid., 5/17/1661; BL MS Egerton 2043, f. 8r.

184 The Majority Institutionalized, 1660–1800

to their places in the Lords.[7] Divisions on religious and other central aspects of the Restoration settlement accounted for over half the divisions in the session. They included two divisions on the Act of Oblivion, six divisions on what became the Corporation Act, two divisions on the militia bill, and a division on the bill for regulating the press. Each one of these pieces of legislation was central to the unifying agenda of the regime but nevertheless revealed conflict. The third division of the session, by contrast with the first two, was only slightly over the mean division vote differential of 16 percent – in other words, the voice vote was likely close enough that the division was not forced by the minority. This division, 192 to 135 against accepting a Lords amendment to the bill for securing and preserving the king's person, allowed exceptions to some of the bill's provisions for the peerage.[8] This was a division on an ostensibly substantive and politically relevant but by no means central issue. Other divisions from this first session, especially those dealing with election returns, which became politicized in rather clearly partisan ways, demonstrated how even relatively minor political struggles were being resolved by division.[9] This was a strong indication of majoritarian inclinations and behavior among members.

In the second session of 1661, the House divided only 3.8 percent of the time. Presumably in agreement about the necessity of solidifying the regime's finances, the Commons began the session by speedily passing a large vote of supply by assessment without a division after a series of drafting periods and debates. The session also featured numerous revisions to bills eventually approved by voice votes. Despite these possible signs of consensual decision-making, the House's unity frequently fell apart when it considered issues of partisan if not profound significance. The Commons divided early in the session on whether to lay aside the bill for executing regicides after some of those named in the bill had pled their cases at the bar. Their pleas were rejected 124 to 109. A few weeks later, the House held a clearly minoritarian division of 117 to 64 on whether to lay aside a series of proposed provisoes for a stridently anti-presbyterian bill on ministerial office that had emerged from what were ostensibly attempts to ratify the Convention's act for confirming and restoring ministers. The following day the Commons divided 108 to 85 on whether William Russell, son of the earl of Bedford and associate of

---

[7] Bosher, *Making of the Restoration Settlement*, 222.

[8] CJ, 5/28/1661, 6/15/1661, 6/20/1661, 7/5/1661, 7/17/1661, 7/19/1661, 7/24/1661, 7/25/1661.

[9] Ibid., 5/31/1661, 6/13/1661, 7/3/1661; see also 6/5/1661. Since nearly all election return disputes at the opening of the Cavalier Parliament were resolved by voice votes, it was clearly not the case that the House simply thought such issues were unworthy of debate.

the Catholic earl of Bristol, had been duly elected. Finally, two days later, the House divided on the superficially procedural matter of how to name the Commons members of a committee charged with meeting during the recess to investigate and propose remedies for a suspected republican conspiracy against the regime. This was poised to be an incredibly important body in a moment of perceived crisis, and the question was resolved by a minoritarian division of 142 to 92. Many believed that the king would use this committee to secure a standing military force, so it was probably "country" members who opposed the measure. In all these instances, the House divided on politically significant issues that were nevertheless neither pivotal nor clearly related to the House's status.[10]

In 1662 the House divided 7.5 percent of the time, not much more frequently than in the late spring and summer of 1661 before the Parliament's first recess (when it divided 6.6 percent of the time) (Figure 6.1). Once again, the session that year, which ran from January to May with an Easter recess, featured a high volume of questions on individual revisions to bills. Indeed, the average number of questions put per day in session in the Cavalier Parliament in 1661 and 1662 was 5.3, two and a half times the mean frequency for the 1663–77 period. This continued artificially to depress the division frequency per questions put, occluding the more revealing fact that in 1662 the House divided once every other day in session. By this measure, the 1662 sessions set the norm for the day-to-day frequency of divisions in the rest of the Cavalier Parliament. The House predictably moved more smoothly on less divisive issues, such as the regicides and Quaker bills. But even a series of bills with much less obvious political centrality and status significance could not be processed without divisions resulting.[11]

Indeed, most divisions in 1662 centered on politically pivotal issues that concerned the status of the House only indirectly if at all. On 11 January 1662 the House resolved to focus its work on the militia and the settlement of the king's revenue until these matters were concluded. Both issues were politically significant, of course, and both could be related to fears of the king's intent to rule in an absolutist fashion. But the need for a militia bill had been reinforced by the revelation of two

[10] CJ, 11/21–23/1661, 11/26/1661, 11/27/1661, 12/4/1661, 12/6/1661, 12/10/1661, 12/16/1661, 12/17/1661, 12/19/1661; Seaward, *Cavalier Parliament*, 144–5, 172–3, 219; Bosher, *Making of the Restoration Settlement*, 240; BL MS Egerton 2043, f. 21r. The only exception might be the joint committee, which could have been understood as an "unparliamentary" proceeding.

[11] CJ, 1/21/1662, 1/27/1662, 1/29/1662, 2/6/1662, 2/8/1662, 2/17/1662, 2/18/1662, 2/18/1662, 3/3/1662, 3/11/1662, 3/15/1662, 3/22/1662, 4/7/1662, 4/10/1662, 5/12/1662, 5/13/1662, 5/14/1662, 5/15/1662.

conspiracies against the regime during the late summer and fall 1661 recess, and the revelation of another on 19 December. In the new year the House debated the militia bill in a committee of the whole on no fewer than nine occasions before the bill was voice-voted on 7 March to be engrossed. On 13 March, before a series of revisions and the passage of the bill by voice vote, there was a minoritarian division on whether to read a new proviso to the bill, and the motion was rejected 116 to 51. John Fowke was disciplined after this vote for a "factious" speech likely made in favor of the motion. The bill was then sent up to the Lords, who made a series of changes that many in the Commons, when the bill was returned to them, considered attempts effectively to convert the militias into a standing army. The House divided five more times on the bill between its return to the Commons and its passage on 17 May.[12]

The revenue agenda was more complicated. On 18 February the House rejected a motion to consider the court's initiative for a beer and ale excise in a 70 to 63 division.[13] This reversal and similar failures on related issues encouraged the court to pursue a hearth tax after the king's speech on 1 March. The hearth tax bill was completed in a series of committees of the whole; on the 10th, before the bill was engrossed, the court won a fairly close division over the threshold of the tax amid fears that the bill would lessen the king's need for parliaments.[14]

The tension between the regime's commitment to indemnity and the need to vindicate and compensate royalists and punish radical republicans also continued to cause divisions. On 13 January the House divided along minoritarian lines, 110 to 56, voting against hearing another day of testimony with regard to a Lords bill on unjust delinquency fines. This was a case in which lawyers in the Commons feared that vacating a fine threatened the authority of the common law.[15] The case was debated on two other occasions before a marathon debate of over eight hours on 28 January, which included two lopsided votes on continuing deliberation and a final, late-night vote in which the bill was passed. The Commons journal listed this as a voice vote, but the diarist Reymes claimed that the

---

[12] Seaward, *Cavalier Parliament*, 143–4, 147–8; CJ, 1/14/1662, 1/16/1662, 1/22/1662, 1/31/1662, 2/3/1662 (closely related to the 3/13/1662 division), 2/13/1662, 2/22/1662, 2/26/1662, 3/1/1662, 3/4/1662, 3/7/1662, 3/13/1662, 5/3/1662, 5/5/1662, 5/7/1662, 5/17/1662.

[13] CJ, 2/18/1662, 3/15/1662, 3/21/1662; Seaward, *Cavalier Parliament*, 110. For related divisions, see CJ, 2/27/1662, 2/28/1662, 3/11/1662, 3/19/1662, 3/21/1662. Another bill for improving excise revenue was brought to the House in mid-March but rejected after its second reading on the 21st in a 66 to 61 division.

[14] CJ, 3/1/1662, 3/10/1662; Seaward, *Cavalier Parlament*, 111.

[15] CJ, 1/13/1662; Seaward, *Cavalier Parliament*, 204. For other examples, see CJ, 2/25/1662, 2/26/1662, 4/11/1662, 4/16/1662; Seaward, *Cavalier Parliament*, 74.

bill "cost the House three dividings, two about bringing in of candles, and the last for passing the bill."[16] The final major issue to elicit divisions was the bill of uniformity, which was passed by the Lords on 9 April and sent down to the Commons. The struggle over the revised bill, which had originated in the Commons in the summer of 1661, resulted in four divisions on crucial details before an aggressively conformist version of it was accepted by the Lords.[17]

By 1662, then, there were already strong (if not perfectly clear) signs that majoritarianism had, somewhat ironically, been institutionalized alongside the restoration of the Stuarts, the dynasty that had once presided over a stable, consensual decision-making regime in the Commons, even amid serious political conflict. Divisions were an every-day experience in the early days of the Cavalier Parliament. And even more importantly, the Commons was frequently dividing over politically important issues that had little direct significance for the status of the House. This indicates that its members were perhaps no longer taking seriously the notion that divisions were dishonorable acts whose normal status costs had to be weighed against the possible status gains from other effects of the particular decision at hand.

Majoritarian Politics Institutionalized: The Cavalier Parliament, 1663–1671

Unambiguous signs of the institutionalization of majoritarian politics emerged over the course of the next decade. Between 1663 and 1677 the Commons divided 23.6 percent of the time a question was put (Figure 6.1). This striking figure approaches modern standards for majoritarian assemblies. In the 1663–5 period alone, divisions became significantly more frequent than in the opening years of the Restoration era: the House divided 13 percent of the time (as opposed to 7.5 percent in 1662), or every two or three days. Division frequency, however, jumped massively in 1666, to 30 percent, or every other day. Between September 1666 and the end of the reign of Charles II the House divided 27 percent of the time.[18] These facts alone are probably enough to establish that the Commons was from this point onward working in thoroughly majoritarian mode.

In order to confirm the existence and better understand the workings of this new institution, it will be helpful to describe it in more detail and

[16] CJ, 1/28/1662, BL MS Egerton 2043, f. 44r.
[17] Seaward, *Cavalier Parliament*, 177–8.
[18] Up to the end of the Cavalier Parliament, the figure was 26.9 percent.

move out of a narrative framework, focusing on the 1666–71 period as a whole. Ample source material beyond the Commons journal survives for this period; this makes the study of it unusually illuminating.[19] Pausing the analysis at the end of the 1671 session also makes it possible to see that majoritarian politics was institutionalized before the long succession crisis of the 1670s. This periodization is important because most historians agree that the emergence of Whig and Tory party politics – often touted as the world's first party system – accompanied or followed this crisis. Dating majoritarian politics to the 1660s clearly establishes that this institution predated and was a precondition for the first English party system. The next section accordingly explores how the institutionalization of majoritarian decision-making triggered the emergence of partisan forms of political coordination.

Perhaps the central index of the institutionalization of majoritarian decision-making in this period is the commonplace resort to divisions on politically important but hardly irresolvable, grave, or status-related issues. These divisions, which also occurred with some frequency in the early 1660s, imply disregard among the House's members for the status significance of the manner in which decisions were made. This disregard for the status consequences of dividing was a new development. Divisions on a wide variety of politically important issues certainly became common in the 1650s. But these divisions, like many of the divisions of the early 1660s, typically concerned fundamental constitutional conflicts and uncertainties. When looking at these situations, in which the politics of status were to an extent always in play, one cannot rule out the possibility that majoritarian decisions were still deemed dishonorable and occurred only because countervailing status considerations were present. There is no such difficulty when looking beyond the mid-1660s. Between 1666 and 1671, divisions on politically important but nonfundamental issues occurred hundreds of times, and they were treated as utterly unremarkable by commentators. Divisions over elections, which had import for the balance of power among factions in the House, may reflect most clearly how resort to divisions had become a factional weapon.[20] These votes were, in essence, majoritarian contests

---

[19] Since John Milward's diary begins in September 1666 and overlaps with the beginning of Anchitell Grey's *Debates*, which begins in October 1667, the following study of revealing cases and patterns begins in fall 1666 and eventually incorporates the diary of Sir Edward Dering, which begins in 1670.

[20] CJ, 10/4/1666, 10/6/1666, 10/23/66, 11/26/1667, 1/10/1667, 1/11/1667, 11/22/1669, 12/7/1669; *Milward*, 16, 29. Divisions over parliamentary attacks on Clarendon and other courtiers were also a frequent and nakedly political source of divisions. See, for example, Witcombe, *Charles II and the Cavalier House of Commons*, 93–5.

over the means of winning future majoritarian contests, uninhibited by any concern about the status costs of dividing.

The fundamental gulf between this period and preceding eras of parliamentary history is perhaps best seen, however, in Commons votes on supply. This was traditionally the area of Commons business in which consensus was most highly prized, primarily because of the need to project unity in matters of national defense and secure the consent of the entire political nation. The reversal here was dramatic: while in the early Stuart period divisions on supply were extremely rare despite supply often sparking controversy, in the later 1660s votes on supply were the main stage for majoritarian decision-making. Divisions on taxation were commonplace, regularly determining the initiation of debate on it, its amount, the method of its collection, and its passage in bill form. Scores of these divisions occurred in the House itself and many others in committees of the whole, which after 18 February 1668 became obligatory for motions on taxation.[21]

These divisions on supply did not simply result from failures of earnest deliberation. A primary indication of this is that like many of the votes on the earl of Clarendon's impeachment and their famous antecedent, the minority protest division on Strafford's attainder in 1641, votes on supply were very commonly lopsided. As John Nicholas put it to his father, Sir Edward, in the fall of 1667, after reporting the lopsided vote of 9 November on whether to label Clarendon's impeachment an impeachment for treason, "it was the parallel case of my lord of Strafford and I much fear we are acting that tragedy over again."[22] Similarly lopsided divisions on supply imply, as with the Strafford vote, the intentional forcing of divisions after an obvious voice vote. This was presumably done to publicly signify division and incomplete support, to dissociate minority voters from the decision, and to allow fellow members to identify which individuals took which side. These divisions were then very commonly communicated outside the walls of the chamber in newsletters. In an environment like this, where supply legislation was the subject of publicized, factional struggle, debate gradually ceased to be aimed at the achievement of consensus through persuasion. Instead, it was meant to isolate points of disagreement and persuade the uncommitted – a large and crucial group – in order to secure a majority. As a

---

[21] CJ, 2/18/1668. *Dering* includes many examples of divisions in committee, which occurred almost daily in 1670 and 1671. Divisions in committee were, of course, a means of avoiding divisions in the House proper, but their regularity is significant when paired with the regularity of formal divisions of the House.

[22] BL MS Egerton 2539, f. 135r.

result, consensual decisions on matters of political significance were a rarer achievement in this period than ever before.[23]

The fall of 1666 and winter of 1666–7 debates on supply during the second Anglo-Dutch War are a clear example of this new pattern of decision-making. These discussions quickly mutated into a broader conflict over whether to do the king's wartime business without delay or not. A wide range of issues and legislation became entangled in the struggle. This resulted in dozens of divisions.[24] Early on, in October 1666, the diarist member John Milward wrote that "it will be the great contest whether the land tax (which is the opinion of the Presbyterian party) or a general excise (which the Court party proposeth) should be resolved on as the best way to raise the £1,800,000." Milward assumed that this contest would be resolved in a majoritarian fashion but hoped, instead, that "a medium between both may be found out."[25] His hopes were dashed. In another session four years later, despite the fact that the court was firmly in control of the Commons, the House could reach unanimity – and did so without debate, according to the member Andrew Marvell – only on the rather hollow assertion "that the king be supplied, proportionable to his present occasions."[26] When supply was under consideration, even unanimity was not necessarily the result of earnest debate.

Indeed, when any politically important issue was under consideration in late 1666 and early 1667, parliamentary speech was apparently pitched to the uncommitted, not directed to the entire chamber.[27] This was the product of an active majoritarian calculus. Already in October 1665, Sir Alan Broderick was busy counting likely votes for "us" among his and the duke of Ormond's "friends." Broderick apparently even viewed debate as a possible obstacle to the winning of votes when he and his "friends" had secured a majority among the House's membership, because debate could cause that majority to slip away. He expressed dismay, for instance, when on one occasion his "friends" left the House before important votes. They had done so, he believed, because they were "wearied" over the "length of a dispute wherein noise only prevailed."[28] Here debate was described not as a prized route to consensus but as an unproductive waste of time that risked attrition among one's factional allies. Had

---

[23] On the importance of the "unconnected center" in the Restoration period, see Montaño, *Courting the Moderates*, esp. 27.

[24] See Seaward, *Cavalier Parliament*, 292–8; Witcombe, *Charles II and the Cavalier House of Commons*, 49–60.

[25] *Milward*, 25.   [26] CJ, 10/27/1670; Marvell, *Poems and Letters*, vol. II, 108.

[27] For descriptions of such debating and voting, see *Milward*, 22, 58.

[28] Bodl. MS Carte 34, f. 448r.

Broderick conceived that his opponents purposely prolonged the debate, he would not have hesitated to describe the debate itself as a tactic for the manipulation of voting.

In the following years, Broderick continued to report to Ormond on the ups and downs of their factional activities and those of their opponents. In November 1666 he registered the fact that those "who depend upon the king" were in ideal circumstances "able to carry any vote (we firmly resolve) within those walls" by strength of numbers. He admitted, however, that the House had thus far made limited progress on supply because of disorganization: "[W]e are not directed as formerly," he wrote, "and being left to the accident of wind and tide, in a popular assembly, drive at random." Since "the consequence will be fatal if not timely prevented," Broderick hoped to "fix the councils" himself for the next day in session. In mid-December, he again disparaged "debates continuing in a circle." He noted that the "country gentlemen with more than ordinary vehemence moved that all members that had not attended the House should be sent for by the sergeant" and that all who were "departed with license should be immediately summoned, and the House to be again called over the second of January." The courtiers' opponents were doing this, he surmised, because they had a "great apprehension that we who depended on the king and resided in or near the town being about 140 might pass what we pleased in the interval," while members from the country were away for Christmas. Another court-aligned member, John Nicholas, was at the same time observing other anti-court tactics at work. Again depicting debate as nothing more than a factional weapon, he told his father that "it's a very shameful thing to observe how some who have great influence in the House of Commons catch at every trifle that can spin out time and long debates on purpose to delay the business of the supply." Here debate, like the introduction of various impeachment proceedings, was functioning "only for delay" and the avoidance of granting supply.[29]

Early in the new year, 1667, Broderick observed frequent divisions occurring amid the continuing tactical manipulation of majorities. "We make slow progress in raising money," he wrote, "and do dissent from the Lords and divide amongst our selves on every trifle." Delay that was aimed at the eventual achievement of a majority remained the order of the day for "country" politicians. In late January, under "country" management, a bill was read twice "to oblige all members to a continued attendance under severe penalty, lest the court party, as they call us in

[29] Bodl. MS Carte 35, ff. 118r., 171r. (see also 238v.); BL MS Egerton 2539, f. 77r. (see also ff. 77v., 162r., 172v., 206r.).

private, should any time over-vote them, which we hope to throw out, at least to bury with the Lords."[30] As the year progressed, other observers commented on debate clearly not aimed at achieving consensus. "The whole day's debate was carried on," wrote John Swinfen during deliberations concerning the earl of Clarendon in November, "each side enforcing their arguments but no endeavor made to answer each other."[31] As Nicholas noted at the same time, "The Duke of Buckingham is the great man who carries all before him." Nicholas had assured the king he would use "his interest in the House of Commons" to "make them do whatever he shall desire."[32]

In this environment, debates on important issues that ended *without* a division became worthy of notice.[33] In the Restoration period the Commons recorded *nemine contradicente* votes in its journal five times more often than it had in the entire period prior to the Restoration.[34] Members and other observers were clearly assuming that differences over politically salient issues would be resolved by a majoritarian calculus; they accordingly made note of occasions when this calculus somehow proved consistent with unanimity. Commentary on parliamentary politics regularly implied that the House was more or less full of men with positions predetermined by self-interest.[35] Observers took it for granted that parliamentary debate was a game of numbers in which factional leaders combined committed followers with those attracted in debate to their side in order to win divisions.[36] At the same time, division counts themselves continued to reflect majoritarian behavior. More than 10 percent of divisions over the course of the period were so lopsided that the winning side outnumbered the losing side by at least two to one. Each session was filled with minoritarian divisions that had clearly been forced.

The prevalence of majoritarian calculus among members led to the rapid development of appropriate tactics. It became imperative to get like-minded members in the House for votes, to avoid occasions when opponents were thick on the ground, and to debate effectively for the votes of the many uncommitted "country gentlemen." These demands were met by a tactical repertoire that extended well beyond speechmaking. Most common was the timing of votes for moments in which one's side had a numerical advantage.[37] In this period, "court"

---

[30] Bodl. MS Carte 35, ff. 238v., 271v.   [31] *Milward*, 334.

[32] BL MS Egerton 2539, f. 140r.

[33] For example, *Milward*, 86; Marvell, *Poems and Letters*, vol. II, 49.

[34] Such votes were recorded 101 times in the Restoration period.

[35] BL MS Add 36916, ff. 91r., 159r.   [36] Seaward, *Cavalier Parliament*, 258–9.

[37] For other majoritarian tactics not highlighted here, see *Milward*, 282–3; BL MS Add 36916, f. 199r.; *Dering*, 50, 67, 82.

politicians were friends of thin houses and, in particular, Houses that had just begun to meet again after a recess, adjournment, or prorogation. Alternatively, they preferred Houses that were about to stop sitting. In these situations, "country" members had either not yet arrived in London or left the metropolis.[38]

There are a number of important examples of these tactics from the later 1660s. The bill for Clarendon's banishment, according to the newsletter writer John Starkey, was purposely read and committed in a thin House shortly before Christmas in 1667.[39] And during a supply debate in February 1668, according to Milward, opponents of supply "seemed prevailing for a great while." This situation required careful timing by "court" members. "The House being thin at one time," Milward observed, "if it had been put to the vote would have gone near to have carried it." But opponents of supply lost their opportunity. "The House filling and members that were going out coming in again, the royal party prevailed."[40] The struggle went in the opposite direction three days later in committee of the whole. "The House growing thin," Milward noted, opponents of the court won a vote to ban supply raised on foreign commodities via excise (the court's preferred policy). Milward explained that this vote was possible only "by taking advantage of a thin House, which in the full House they could not have done."[41] Calls of the House themselves, as we have already seen, became a crucial means of managing attendance. On 27 March 1668, for instance, a very thin House had two tied divisions broken by the Speaker in favor of waiting to discuss a fen drainage project until after the House had been called. On the following day, members involved in the project, who wanted it discussed in a thin House, tried to reverse the earlier votes on the argument that they had been made in a thin House![42] Similarly, but more generally, during this period the House regularly divided over its schedule of business, to which members attributed great tactical significance.[43]

Observers and participants often commented on thin House voting in ways that implied that it was a commonplace tactic. Reporting at the end of the 1669 session, Starkey observed that "at their next meeting it may be hoped that a greater sum of money may be given, possibly before the country gentlemen come up." Sure enough, at the beginning of the following session on Monday, 14 February 1670, the Commons "sat

[38] For examples not discussed below, see Witcombe, *Charles II and the Cavalier House of Commons*, 53–4.
[39] BL MS Add 36916, f. 47r.   [40] *Milward*, 198.   [41] Ibid., 202–3.
[42] CJ, 3/27/1668; *Milward*, 238.   [43] For example, CJ, 3/30/1668.

three hours" on the first day, "and had smart debates whether they should adjourn till Thursday or Monday next and then take the king's speech into consideration." But numbers were already determining process. "At last the courtiers by reason of the absence of many country gentlemen (who are much blamed for their neglect at this time) carried it by seven voices for Thursday." The rush was on. "If the country gentlemen do not come up," Starkey predicted, "the others may give what they please."[44]

On Thursday, the court, securing the advantage, began to proceed with supply. By Saturday, they had passed a series of votes on the contours of a seven-year wine duty. Before the final two votes, which led to an order to draw up a bill, the "country" members present grew desperate. "Several of the country gentlemen," Starkey reported, "having desired to know how much the king was in debt, and what this duty would arise to, they could not obtain any satisfaction but were run down with calling to the question." Forcing divisions by loudly rejecting calls for further debate and inquiry was itself an important tactic, but one deemed especially aggressive. In response to the courtiers' behavior, about eighty of the "country" members simply "arose and went out of the House in discontent, and left the rest to vote as they pleased, who immediately voted it for seven years." This angry minority protest again recalled crucial moments in 1641 when majority power was met by challenges to its legitimacy as the voice of the whole. But this episode also suggested a lack of poised coordination in opposition, which Starkey condemned in January 1671 after a narrowly lost division. He thereby revealed his own assumptions about the majoritarian nature of the House and the demands it made on members. "So negligent are the country gentlemen of their own concerns," he reported, "as not to sit out a debate until it come to a question, there being then about 100 out of the House that were in town."[45]

This incident also suggests, however, that more traditional norms did continue to be articulated and defended in the later 1660s and early 1670s. On 12 November 1666, for instance, the House decided not to allow the second reading of a bill in a thin House because parts of the bill were likely to be controversial. Yet even these actions in favor of traditional norms were very often taken in the service of fundamentally majoritarian ends or modes of practice. They had been at least partially transformed from normatively endorsed practices into parliamentary

---

[44] BL MS Add 36916, ff. 159r., 165r., 166r. See also 201r. and *Dering*, 82.
[45] BL MS Add 36916, ff. 167r., 207r. For a similar Restoration-era incident, see Marvell, *Poems and Letters*, vol. II, 94.

tactics. On 6 February 1668, for instance, the House voted not to do new business until the House was called so that "the House may be full before any new business to be debated." According to Milward, a religious conformist, "this vote was passed to prevent the bringing in the bill of comprehension, which will be brought in and countenanced by very great persons."[46] By the 10th, this tactic had apparently succeeded in positive form: the House had resolved to petition the king to enforce the Act of Uniformity.[47] Similarly, opponents of supply or other court agenda items were keen to insist (supported by the 1668 standing order referenced earlier) on thorough debate in committees of the whole. Debate in these committees could serve as a form of filibustering when more obvious forms of resistance to the royal agenda might result in a dissolution.[48] Debate remained a sign of legitimate decision-making, but it was more and more often subject to tactical manipulation.

Full houses do appear to have often been a genuine normative commitment at this time, as they had been earlier in the century. But in the Restoration period, even when older norms prevailed, their significance was transformed, because they prevailed within the context of a new relationship between decision-making and status considerations. In particular, it became common for members to evaluate the honorability of a decision in the Commons not in terms of whether it had been reached by means of consensus, but rather in terms of how many members had participated in the vote. This was an expansion and foregrounding of the sentiments likely underpinning the establishment of a quorum in 1641. First heard occasionally in the 1640s, this advocation of full houses was fundamentally majoritarian in nature. It was an adaptation of traditional norms to majoritarian realities.

In a 16 February 1671 debate about doubly assessing members not in attendance in a subsidy bill, for instance, a series of speakers expressed this sentiment. Sir Thomas Lee argued that "when you come to a division of eightscore, rarely three hundred, this shews the world that you take it to be your interest to have a full House; and this will carry on the weighty affairs of the kingdom." Sir Thomas Clifford responded by agreeing "that the honour of the nation is a full House." Sir Thomas Meres later concurred that "the greatest evil in the world is a thin House." After debate the House, appropriately, divided on the issue with a moderate turnout, as 213 members voted, 115 of them agreeing to add the amendment to the subsidy bill that penalized nonattenders.[49]

---

[46] *Milward*, 40, 179; Witcombe, *Charles II and the Cavalier House of Commons*, 79.
[47] CJ, 2/10/1668.   [48] BL MS Add 36916, f. 74r.; *Dering*, 18, 28.
[49] Grey, 2/16/1671; CJ, 2/16/1671.

If majoritarian decisions were most legitimate when the greatest number of members possible were on the winning side of the question, then the more divisive the issue, the more important a full House became. When nearly half of the members present were in the minority, it was likely that the winning side would be only a small minority of the House's total membership. The implicit norm that may have been in play here was the idea that the House ought to aim for full houses that could make decisions supported by an absolute majority of the members (even if in practice this remained rare) because the decisions of an absolute majority were more legitimate than the decisions of a mere majority of the members present.

Majoritarian Politics and Party Organization, 1673–1685

By the early 1670s, at the latest, the institutionalization of majoritarian politics was complete. Between 1673 and 1685 the division rate in the Commons was a spectacular 29 percent of questions put (Figure 4.1). Members seeking particular political outcomes no longer attempted to secure them by achieving consensus. This was ultimately because the easiest means of securing these outcomes – a simple majority vote – no longer had negative status implications. In fact, majority votes had increasingly acquired positive status associations with respect to both ends and means. Since the 1640s, the effects of many majority votes had enhanced or protected the status of Parliament, the Commons, its members, and the political nation. At the same time, the sense members had of an honorable *means* of deciding was changing in a manner that also had roots in the 1640s. Votes in full houses that followed considerable debate could be deemed honorable even when they required the House to be divided. But the fundamental, necessary characteristic of this new institution was the lack of any status barriers to seeking one's desired result in a decision before the House with recourse to nonconsensual votes. This is what was required to make majority votes a pattern of political transaction under conditions of disagreement on politically significant issues.

With this new institution in place, political practice became organized around the securing of majorities. This led in turn to the emergence and eventual institutionalization of party politics in Parliament, because party politics was the form of coordination best suited to securing those majorities.[50] Even in the 1640s and 1650s, when majoritarian decisions were

---

[50] On partisan politics outside of Parliament, see Halliday, *Dismembering the Body Politic*.

frequently being made but had not quite been institutionalized, basic partisan tactics and coordination quickly materialized. Political parties are a common organizational response to the assumption that important political decisions will be made on the basis of two-sided, enumerated votes. They coordinate political activity within and without majoritarian representative assemblies with the ultimate goal of securing majority votes within those assemblies. Partisan practices rationally prompted by majoritarian conditions include advance planning among leaders; the publication of consistently articulated ideological and policy positions or agendas, eventually in the form of platforms; self-conscious and avowed membership; electioneering; and, finally, incentivization, discipline, and other tactics for securing votes.[51] All of these practices, at least in their specifically modern forms, follow only on the assumption that the optimal strategy for securing specific outcomes in Parliament is to secure vote commitments before debate begins. They render debate a political practice of declining and fundamentally altered importance. It becomes primarily useful for reinforcing prior commitments and convincing the unaligned.

It is therefore no surprise to see that in England, the elaboration of partisan politics followed somewhat quickly on what may have been the first institutionalization of majoritarian practices in a national, elected, representative institution. We have already seen evidence that a majoritarian tactical repertoire began to emerge in the 1666–71 period. Historians have understandably been keen to pinpoint the precise point at which modern political parties first appeared in England (and thus the world). While some argue that groupings from the 1640s and 1650s are properly understood as parties and a few refer to party politics in the 1660s, the historiographical mainstream argues for the advent of modern parties and a party system at some point after the beginning of the succession crisis in 1673, in keeping with Roger North's seminal 1740 commentary on the issue. The precise point a historian identifies usually has less to do with the recovery of new information than with standards of definition and measurement. As a result, the English or

---

[51] For an introduction to parties in the social-scientific literature, see Lipset and Rokkan, *Party Systems and Voter Alignments*; Aldrich, "Political Parties in and out of Legislatures"; Aldrich, *Why Parties?*; Cox and McCubbins, *Legislative Leviathan*. The question of motivation, which is often taken by historians to distinguish party from faction, is largely unanswerable and in fact dispensable. Parties organize around ideologies, principles, and policy objectives, but answering the question of whether these sincerely motivate their members is unnecessary for our purposes here.

British party system's emergence is in fact dated to a variety of different points between the Long Parliament and the later nineteenth century.[52]

Arguments for the existence of parties in the Restoration era before the Exclusion Crisis are easily challenged on the basis of comparison with Elizabethan and early Stuart parliamentary management.[53] The best way of distinguishing between early modern "factional" politics and modern partisan politics might be the rooting of the latter in a basic characteristic of post–Civil War political practice: majoritarian decision-making. In other words, it is unlikely that group coordination in political decision-making would be the same after this institutional change, and very likely that such coordination would be creatively adapted to majoritarian voting practices. After all, nearly anyone would agree that modern party organization is founded on the existence of pre-debate commitments both in favor of and in opposition to specific policy or legislative agendas, and the attendant need to secure not consensus but numerical victory. Historians of late seventeenth-century partisan politics have missed this clear way of distinguishing between traditional political coordination and partisan coordination precisely because they have assumed, in different ways, that majoritarianism is a constant in the parliamentary realm. The goal of this section of the chapter is therefore to identify the late seventeenth- and early eighteenth-century elaboration of forms of coordination that rested on majoritarian foundations, while keeping in mind the fact that many of these tactics had precedents in the revolutionary period of mid-century. This section thereby completes this book's account of the emergence of majoritarian politics in early modern England while also reshaping existing understandings of the emergence of party politics.

Before 1673 political groupings in the Commons were clearly unstable, internally conflicted, and complex. From the winter of 1666–7 onward diarists regularly linked majoritarian activity with conflicts between "parties" in the House. Most frequently, they mentioned "court" and "country" groupings; they also spoke of "undertakers," "nonconformists and courtiers," "sectaries," the "old Parliament gang,"

---

[52] See, for example, Kishlansky, "Emergence of Adversary Politics"; Browning, "Parties and Party Organization"; Harris, *Politics under the Later Stuarts*; Jones (ed.), *Britain in the First Age of Party*; O'Gorman, *The Rise of Party in England*; O'Gorman, *Emergence of the British Two-Party System*; Stewart, *Party and Politics*; Cox, *Efficient Secret*; Hanham, *Elections and Party Management*; Lawrence and Taylor (eds.), *Party, State, and Society*.

[53] See, for example, Graves, "Managing Elizabethan Parliaments." The same goes for a definition of party or partisan politics that is focused on shared ideology and sharply distinguishes it from faction on this basis. See Halliday, *Dismembering the Body Politic*, esp. 9–12, for a trenchant critique of such conceptualizations. If one opts for the thesis that party politics began in the 1640s or 1650s, Chapters 2 and 3 make clear that this beginning too was preceded by a majoritarian shift.

"the Royal party," "the presbyterian party," and "the country party."[54] Yet there is very little evidence of large-scale, centralized coordination of action in the Commons by groups meeting outside the chamber and working independently of court parliamentary management. Very occasionally, some politicians, such as Alan Broderick in 1660, seem to have adapted their coordination activities to majoritarian assumptions. But the larger-scale management described and practiced by Clarendon and his associates in the 1660s is hard to distinguish clearly from Elizabethan and early Stuart precedents in theory and practice. Clarendonian management was rooted in the assumption of a shared interest between "court" and "country" and maladapted to majoritarian practices. In accordance with its guiding assumptions, it emphasized coordinated speechmaking by the most credible agents of royal initiatives along with the rest of the familiar repertoire of consensus politics. These tactics were somewhat awkwardly combined with a willingness to pursue royal policy with routine recourse to divisions. It is less clear whether the more aggressive tactics espoused and pursued by Henry Bennett and later parliamentary managers before 1673, first in competition with Clarendon and then after his fall, were still essentially factional and traditional in nature.[55]

Perhaps the clearest early indicators of majoritarian assumptions prompting party-political planning are the remarkable lists of confirmed supporters of different groups that were first drafted during the late 1660s and proliferated in the later 1670s. These lists often explicitly tallied the individuals identified, allowing for the securing and computation of probable majorities before debate began.[56] In 1675 Thomas Osborne, earl of Danby, was the first to make extensive use of such information and planning. In advance of the October session of Parliament, he attempted to ensure that his identified supporters attended regularly and voted predictably. Adopting tactics that would soon be condemned in Parliament for "making faction," he formed a basic core of supporters who would automatically follow his directions. He expanded his following by means of excise pensions. And he sent

---

[54] *Milward*, 16, 20, 21, 23–5, 189–91, 206, 230, 282; BL MS Add 36916, f. 202r. See also Seaward, *Cavalier Parliament*, 298–300; Witcombe, *Charles II and the Cavalier House of Commons*, 58–60; CJ, November and December 1669.

[55] Seaward, *Cavalier Parliament*, 78–99; Witcombe, *Charles II and the Cavalier House of Commons*, 78, 92, 95, 98, 100, 128, 180–1. See also Montaño, *Courting the Moderates*, 255; and Sir Richard Temple's 1668 planning tract, which appears to have had majoritarian premises (Roberts (ed.), "Sir Richard Temple's Discourse on the Parliament of 1667–1668").

[56] Browning, *Thomas Osborne*, vol. III, 33–44, 56–120. See also Reresby, *Memoirs*, 103; De Beer, "Members of the Court Party in the House of Commons."

letters to a larger group of likely supporters to ensure their attendance.[57] During this period, at least one newsletter writer took to referring to Danby's opponents as the "anti-Treasurists," "the angry party," "the hot men," "the angry Commons," and "the opposition party." Both groups were thought to delay final decisions, "hoping for strong recruits" and thereby manipulating majoritarian assumptions. The "Treasurists" were openly suspected in the newsletter and in the Commons of offering money or office to members in order to suddenly change their voting on crucial issues. They also used divisions to assess their current strength in numbers and worked to avoid decision-making in committees of the whole so that the Speaker could aid the "Treasurists" and mitigate their disadvantage in debating skill.[58]

Before the parliamentary session that opened in February 1677, Danby dangled the prospect of dissolution before members unlikely to be reelected, and he dangled government resources – including titles, pensions, places, and local offices – before others. He focused attention on probable supporters outside government circles, and he or his agents personally approached just under 200 members he placed in this category. Danby also worked to destroy the organizational operation of the opposition. He increasingly had recourse to money payments in 1677–8 and continued other familiar tactics, trying to bring up voters for important divisions, entertaining and instructing important supporters, and carefully timing votes. He also worked aggressively to win by-elections.[59] It is here that Danby's activities connected with the electoral dynamics that also strengthened the majoritarian character of decision-making in the Commons. From at least the 1670s, increasingly contested, politicized elections arguably encouraged the pre-commitment of members to more or less specific stances on policies, in an agreement with their constituents. Those constituents' own partisan understanding of decision-making in Parliament was in turn furthered by an emergent public politics in which knowledge of parliamentary proceedings was

---

[57] Browning, *Thomas Osborne*, vol. I, 167–73; Montaño, *Courting the Moderates*, 277. Sir Joseph Williamson defended Danby's letters in the Commons as simply a means of achieving a full House: Grey, 10/27/1675.

[58] Morrison (ed.), *Collection of Autograph Letters and Historical Documents*, 316, 320, 322, 323, 324.

[59] Browning, *Thomas Osborne*, vol. I, 191–7, 206, 207, 274–5, 277; Montaño, *Courting the Moderates*, 277 (for additional commentary on Danby's organization, see 256–7, 261–2, 265–72, 275–8, 283–5). For the emergence of party organization in the Lords over the same period and into the succession crisis, see Swatland, *House of Lords in the Reign of Charles II*, 211–59.

becoming more available, and partisan categories and logics were beginning to take hold.[60]

With respect to all of these partisan elaborations on majoritarian politics, it is difficult to see the Exclusion Crisis as a terribly pivotal moment. The opposition groupings of 1679–81 have traditionally been aggregated and labeled by historians as the first political party, the Whigs. But the available evidence suggests that these groupings actually exhibited much less of an ability to harness majoritarian politics than Danby's group had in the earlier years of the decade. There were, nevertheless, strong signs of continued partisan organization in the politics of the House of Commons. An observer in June 1679 bemoaned the "caballing" that dominated parliamentary sessions. "The leading men do busy themselves in making their court to such as they would bring over to their party," with the result that there existed "but little freedom in the votes of the House of Commons, men bringing their opinions along with them stiff and unalterable by debate and reason." Others claimed that "all transactions of Parliament are first designed and hammered, collections made, [and] a common purse managed."[61] These are striking descriptions of partisan discipline that resulted in the utter nullification of traditional parliamentary privilege and an attendant rejection of debate as a means of building wisdom and consensus. If they have any basis in reality, they were related to the detailed opposition agenda for the 1679 session crafted by Lord Holles, who of course had been a central perpetuator of majoritarian politics in the 1640s. Another detailed agenda was drawn up after the dissolution of this Parliament. The opposition agenda (not to mention its enforcement) was, however, not particularly well organized before the Commons met in October 1680. None of the personal appeals and incentivizing seen under the Danby regime was present, and the opposition remained diverse and pluralistic in any organization it had.[62] It is, finally, also unclear that members were given precise voting instructions in 1681, despite the survival of a strongly worded draft to this effect in the earl of Shaftesbury's papers.[63]

The distinctive force of both opposition and loyalist politics in this moment is better understood in terms of a basic ideological or sentimental affinity with a regularly shifting and complex personal basis than in terms of partisan organization. Whig and Tory politics was really an

---

[60] See, for example, Knights, *Politics and Opinion in Crisis*; Knights, *Representation and Misrepresentation in Later Stuart Britain*; De Krey, *London and the Restoration*; Kishlansky, *Parliamentary Selection*. But for precursors, see Peacey, *Print and Public Politics in the English Revolution*, esp. 364–93.

[61] Quoted in Knights, *Politics and Opinion in Crisis*, 128.   [62] Ibid., 134–5.

[63] Ibid., 291–2; Browning (ed.), *English Historical Documents 1660–1714*, 256, 258.

effect of the succession crisis.[64] Accordingly, the so-called Exclusion Crisis was more important in terms of the use of public politics to influence action in Parliament than in terms of any clear response to majoritarian decision-making within the House. Nevertheless, by 1681, opponents of partisan domination of the political scene could distinguish themselves by *rejecting* majoritarian tactics. Thus the "trimming" marquess of Halifax told Gilbert Burnet on 5 March that members ought to assemble in Parliament "with no schemes ready drawn, nor resolutions taken beforehand."[65] Charles II's parliaments had left an important if somewhat notorious practical legacy. Not until after the Glorious Revolution would members of the Commons embrace the fuller possibilities and strategic dictates of majority rule.[66]

James II's brief parliament in 1685 only accentuated the limited extent to which the majoritarianism of the House of Commons had been fully subsumed within partisan organization. The nomenclature of "Whig" and "Tory" had by then become a prevalent means of classification and identification in the wider political environment. Yet this was a parliamentary session dominated by Tories that featured not the harmony we might expect in a party-political system controlled by one party but a division rate of 28 percent of questions put. This is comparable to any degree of dissension experienced during the reign of Charles II or indeed after the Glorious Revolution. Majoritarian decision-making remained far more essential to parliamentary politics than parties, and remarkably independent of them. In 1685, members otherwise united were divided over their attitudes toward James II's religious policies and, in particular, his employment of Catholic officers in the army. The climax of this struggle was the epic division James lost 183 to 182 the day after his opening speech in the November session. This was the usual stuff of Commons divisions under majoritarian conditions. But it was utterly divorced from clear partisan loyalties, and instead centered, as usual in the Restoration period, on attitudes to the king's agenda, and the tug between grievances and supply.[67]

Accordingly, the parliaments of the 1670s and 1680s are most revealing as an additional source of insights into the characteristics of a majoritarian parliamentary system – one only slowly and sporadically

[64] Knights, *Politics and Opinion in Crisis*, 143, 354–6.
[65] Quoted in ibid., 112. For a similar sentiment expressed in 1676, see Reresby, *Memoirs*, 110–11.
[66] See, for example, Hayton, *House of Commons 1690–1715*; Harris, *Politics under the Later Stuarts*; Speck, *Tory and Whig*; Speck, "House of Commons 1702–1714"; Holmes, *British Politics in the Age of Anne*.
[67] On this understudied parliament, see Sowerby, "Tories in the Whig Corner."

organized along party lines. In this period, members casually referred on
numerous occasions to majorities as a legitimate guide to decision-
making in the House.[68] In addition, by the late 1670s, there were further
indications that the traditional honor politics of Commons decision-
making had been turned upside down. On 1 June 1678 Sir William
Coventry complained: "What will the censure be abroad, when the
question is to justify the House, that after so many hours debate, we
should not come to a question! For our honour's sake let us come to a
question."[69] This was a glaring reversal of the attitudes characteristic of
pre-revolutionary England. In Coventry's view, situations in which the
status of the House was at stake were not at all ones in which divisions
sometimes regrettably occurred because they not could be avoided. They
were instead situations in which divisions might have to be *actively
pursued* as a means of forcing Parliament to take action necessary to
maintaining its status. This was especially appropriate, Coventry suggested, once a matter had been debated at length. In an extension of this
logic, members continued to suggest in passing that a full House con-
ferred legitimacy on debates and votes on important matters, while the
opposite was true of thin houses.[70]

In crucial moments, it appears, putting the question, not answering it
consensually, was considered to be the point of honor. There are even
indications at this point that some members believed that as a *means* of
deciding, not simply as an instrument, divisions had intrinsically positive
status implications. A few months after Coventry's remarks, during the
4 November 1678 debate on Parliament's address regarding the Popish
Plot, Samuel Pepys offered this line of thinking to his fellow members.
"Will you have it said abroad," he asked, "that the House of Commons is
afraid to put this address to the question, which if you carry not, you will
hazard our prince's life and safety, and all you have?" The necessity of
voting in this situation, whether or not it led to a division, was obvious.
Avoiding the question was cowardly, and therefore dishonorable, while
hazarding a division was honorable, because it projected bravery and
fortitude. "Put the question," Pepys continued, "and I doubt not but
all good Protestants, and good Christians, will be for it."[71] The House's
status and legitimacy was now being lodged not in unity but in great

[68] For example, Grey, 10/26–7/1675, 11/6/1675, 5/2–3/1678, 11/1–5/1678, 11/21/1678, 4/
21–30/1679, 1/7/1681.
[69] Ibid., 6/1/1678.
[70] Ibid., 3/21/1673, 4/4/1677, 11/22/1678, 12/4/1678, 1/10/1690 (on thin houses); 1/27/
1674, 2/7/1674, 5/11/1675, 6/3/1675, 2/14/1678, 5/7/1678, 3/26/1679, 5/15/1679, 1/
22/1689, 3/20/1689 (on full houses); Sowerby, "Tories in the Whig Corner," 197.
[71] Grey, 11/4/1678.

numbers. And at many junctures, its honor was best preserved and enhanced by the confident acts of a majority.

At the same time, while members continued to register traditional aspirations to consensus, the significance of these aspirations had been transformed. "Nothing does the king more honour," Anthony Irby said hopefully in a supply debate on 3 November 1675, "than an unanimous sound from hence."[72] Irby's statement was greeted with nine divisions on supply in the next seven days in session. Utterances like his were now comparable in sentiment to mentions of *nemine contradicente* votes in the Commons journal. They described as exceptional and ideal what had once been normal and necessary. Pleas for unanimity, in particular, were usually confined to desperate moments when unity was taken to be particularly necessary in conveying a message on matters of the highest importance, and the absence of unity was thought to promote factionalism.[73]

Accordingly, pleas for consensus and unanimity were particularly common during the Popish Plot and succession crisis. In a debate on foreign policy and the army in May 1678, Sir Robert Sawyer addressed a dispute on the wording of a resolution to be communicated to the king by saying that he "would not divide the House upon the word 'immediately'" because "unanimity is worth a thousand 'immediatelies.'" Months later, in early November, after a unanimous resolution on the existence of the Popish Plot, multiple members similarly discussed the disastrous consequences of dividing on the House's public actions in the middle of the controversy. In the following year, during the 11 May 1679 debate on competing approaches to dealing with the question of the succession, Sir Francis Winnington said that "if the House divide upon this great thing, you give the greatest blow to the Protestant religion imaginable; therefore, whatever we do, let it be with unanimity, as Protestants." Unanimity was itself a projection of power in moments like these. "If we divide upon the question, the papists will have more encouragement than the duke ever gave them," Winnington continued. Finally, during the 2 November debate on exclusion, Sir Edward Seymour remarked: "I have often reminded myself, since this debate, that this question is of the last concernment to the kingdom; and whatever resolutions are of the last importance, we ought to be unanimous in; since gentlemen come here not with resolutions, but to take upon them clear debate of things."[74]

---

[72] Ibid., 11/3/1675; see also 5/25/1677.
[73] For example, ibid., 1/10/1671, 2/26/1673, 11/17/1680.
[74] Ibid., 5/27/1678, 11/1/1678, 11/4/1678, 5/11/1679, 11/2/1679.

In these moments, consensus, unanimity, and other apparently traditional gestures had in fact come to acquire the same sort of significance
they would have in the rigorously majoritarian legislative systems of the
modern world. These sorts of appeals are typical even to the present day,
but they are deemed appropriate only to a very small subset of issues or
situations. They reflect a fundamental unease with the effects of majoritarian government that endures and continues to fuel critiques of representative democracy. In the late seventeenth century, much of this same
unease was expressed in the context of party politics, at the core of which
lay majoritarian decision-making in Parliament and at the hustings.
While the present study is focused on practice, it is important to register
these changes in norms and discourse as related but in many ways
separate developments. Strong expressions of distaste for majority
decision-making and partisanship continued for a very long time after
majoritarianism had been institutionalized in practice. In this sense there
was a correspondence between public discourse on partisanship and
discussions within the House of Commons. Most fundamentally, perhaps, various political publics were coming to associate partisanship with
an epistemological crisis that threatened the entire foundation of government in the public interest. Within the Commons, sentiments were very
similar. Truth – once the shared, acknowledged goal of rational, patient
parliamentary deliberation – had in the view of many members been
subordinated to the securing of majorities by any linguistic means necessary. In public and in Parliament, it seemed that the appearance of truth,
which functioned to secure partisan allegiance, was all that mattered.[75]

Indeed, most invocations of traditional norms in the Commons during
this period were merely means of registering regret at the fact that these
norms had in practice been utterly rejected. In November 1679, for
instance, during a debate on a proviso for the bill disabling Catholics
from sitting in Parliament, which was added by the Lords in an attempt
to exempt York from taking oaths of allegiance and supremacy, the now
common practice of calling for the question without ample debate was
greeted with both criticism and resignation. Observing silence from those
against the proviso, Anchitell Grey heard the earl of Ancram comment
that "this debate looks as if it was not upon good ground and reason, but
a resolved business," thus pointing to the role of the politics of resolution
in destroying the politics of consensus. "Nobody," he continued, "opens
his mouth to answer any thing that is said, but only to call for the

---

[75] Knights, *Representation and Misrepresentation in Later Stuart Britain*, 208–18, 238–48,
272–348.

question. If so, put it to the common fate of aye and no."[76] Ancram saw no point in the pretense of continuing debate in an atmosphere of firm majoritarian commitments. There was no denying that the most important parliamentary decisions were now being regularly subjected not to genuine deliberation but "to the common fate of aye and no."

The Post-Revolutionary Institution

By the end of the Stuart period, majoritarian politics was firmly in the grip of partisan coordination. In the reign of William III, the House divided 19.2 percent of the time, nearly every other day (Figures 4.1 and 4.2). During the reign of Anne, the height of partisan rancor, the House divided 20.7 percent of the time and again nearly every other day. The Whig and Tory parties were hardly monolithic in this period, and "court" and "country" identifications and interests were often quite powerful. But a partisan structure of voting began to be imposed on majoritarian politics beginning in the later 1690s. The parties (especially the Whigs) came to exhibit clear leadership, remarkably complex organization and discipline, consistent if not formal membership, and identifiable ideology and policy. On a conservative interpretation, of the 1,875 members who served between 1690 and 1715, only 200, or 10.7 percent, cannot be classified as Whig or Tory with reference to their behavior in elections or in the House. This percentage dwindles as one moves forward in time, from 11.2 percent in the 1690–5 period to a mere 3.7 percent in 1713–14.[77]

Majoritarian decision-making nevertheless remained more fundamental to the political process in the Commons than party did. It persisted through the Whig dominance of the early Hanoverian period and the partisan vicissitudes of the later eighteenth century and beyond. During the reign of George I, the House divided 21.4 percent of the time, or once every four days. This demonstrates remarkable continuity over a thirty-eight-year period following the Glorious Revolution. The only notable change in division frequency patterns in George I's reign was the drop in the average number of divisions per day in session. This, juxtaposed with the frequency of divisions per question put during the reign, implies that fewer questions were being put each day in session. From the end of the reign of Anne to the end of the reign of George II (1714–60), the House divided 17.7 percent of the time, or about every four days. Remarkably, while the daily frequency of divisions dipped in

---

[76] Grey, 11/21/1678. See also the speech of Sir Winston Churchill on the same day.
[77] Hayton, *House of Commons 1690–1715*, 434–44, 462–79.

this period, the frequency of divisions per question put in this period was identical to the mean frequency for the entire century of institutionalized majoritarian politics between 1660 and 1760.

The frequency of divisions did fall in the later eighteenth century, but this did not indicate any weakening of the institution of majoritarian decision-making. Between 1760 and 1800 the House divided only 10 per cent of the time a question was put. This difference from the mid-eighteenth century onward is attributable to a massive rise in the volume of fairly routine parliamentary business and the more consistent notation of such business in the Commons journal. The best-studied index of such business – legislation – shows that between 1714 and 1760 Parliament dealt on average with one piece of legislation per day in session. In the later period, it considered more than two acts per day in session. This alone probably accounts for the differential in division frequencies per question put because the additional measures under consideration in the later period were overwhelmingly unimportant in political terms. Bills with relatively specific coverage took over a larger and larger percentage of parliamentary business. In other words, in order to compare across the entire eighteenth century, the secondary index of division frequency used on occasion in earlier chapters – divisions per day in session – is the most meaningful. If we turn to this measure, the frequency of divisions per day in session remained remarkably constant between 1714 and 1800, at one division every four days in session (0.26 divisions per day between 1714 and 1760, and 0.27 per day between 1760 and 1800).[78] Divisions therefore remained a commonplace experience, even under conditions of uneven partisan power. However we measure or date it, the basic modern conditions of political decision-making in representative assemblies were locked in place long before Britain's party system had reached maturity.

---

[78] Data in this paragraph were computed by combining Commons journal voting data with the legislative data available in Hoppit (ed.), *Failed Legislation*, 4. For a convenient and compatible account of legislation patterns in the eighteenth century, see Hoppit, *Britain's Political Economies*, 38–65, esp. 41, 50–1.

7 Little Parliaments in the Atlantic Colonies, 1613–1789

Colonial lower assemblies were created under conditions fundamentally different from those that prevailed in the Westminster House of Commons. Some were part of corporations and proprietorships, not royal colonies; and some initially admitted all freemen, not simply elected representatives. These factors led to distinctive institutional trajectories. In general and over the long run, these factors appear to have reinforced a tendency for the colonial lower assemblies to be or become majoritarian. But the institutional implications of the English precedents on which colonial governments drew were mixed. The early modern English corporate tradition also prized consensus and unanimity. As we have seen, the exact nature of decision-making in many English corporate bodies before the English Revolution cannot be determined with any certainty.[1] But there is plenty of evidence to suggest that in many corporate environments, consensual norms prevailed. Proprietors were of course less influenced by corporate precedents. Instead, they turned to the parliamentary tradition for guidance in creating their own assemblies. There is therefore some reason to believe that consensual decision-making would have been the default option for proprietary assemblies before the English Revolution and majority decision-making the dominant practice in assemblies erected after the restoration of the monarchy and the institutionalization of majority rule in the English House of Commons.

But the situation was not quite as straightforward as this series of generalizations might suggest. English trading corporations – from the East India and Levant Companies to those, like the Virginia, Somers Islands, and Massachusetts Bay Companies, which quickly took on a colonial dimension – were both private and public entities. They were organizations of merchants and investors who sought profit for themselves, but they were also state agents authorized, privileged, and

---

[1] See above, 16, n. 35.

protected by the monarch to engage in a trade thought to raise revenue for the Crown and efficiently procure goods for the commonwealth. At the core of this dual existence was the translation of individual private gain into public benefit on a voluntary basis. This fundamentally distinguished the nature of participation in corporations from participation in government assemblies, which was automatically open to the entire political nation. This difference probably tended to reduce the extent to which investors were as hostile to majority voting as members of the House of Commons. A division among investors could never be taken to imply a division in the political nation. In addition, when company assemblies voted, the role of private interest was to some degree taken for granted. In the Commons it was generally abhorred. The companies certainly practiced representative government to varying extents, but the representative bodies they created were, in essence, mechanisms for the representation of private interest. The Commons admitted private interest in its proceedings only when considering private bills. As noted earlier, these bills could easily be subject to divisions without adverse consequences. There is reason to think that analogous decisions in the companies would be made in a similar manner.

It is also important to appreciate the colonial assemblies from the opposite angle, by considering the extent to which these assemblies did not initially exhibit the institutional elements that in the first place accounted for the consensualism of the pre-revolutionary English House of Commons. When colonial popular assemblies, whether corporate or proprietary in nature, became representative assemblies, they often did so for practical, not principled reasons. This tended to encourage a delegatory understanding of representation, in stark contrast to the discretionary norms that prevailed in Parliament. In these colonial assemblies the represented tended to bind their representatives – whom they often meaningfully called "deputies" – to fixed positions. To the extent that this delegatory conception of representation prevailed, it prevented the emergence of consensus in colonial assemblies when that consensus did not already exist prior to the onset of deliberations.

Second, it is important to appreciate the specific sense in which colonial assemblies were bodies politic, and why the colonies of which they were a part were sometimes referred to as "states." While the assemblies were in many ways public, self-governing, and representative organizations deeply concerned about their status, they did not represent a fully autonomous and sovereign entity connected to the entirety of a nation or country, as Parliament (monarch, Lords, and Commons) did. Every colonial assembly ultimately enjoyed its existence and authority at the pleasure of the monarch. This limited the extent to which a division in these assemblies could be viewed as a dishonorable division of a body politic that was both national and popular in nature. Third, these assemblies did not exhibit in their infancy the high level of rhetorical and dialectical training among members that in the House of Commons helped make the cultivation of consensus possible under conditions of severe conflict. The extent to which the colonial lower assemblies were harmonious in this period was due to a relative absence of the sort of sophisticated ideological conflict characteristic of national politics. In other words, to the extent that consensual decision-making was institutionalized for a time in some colonial lower assemblies, the underpinning of that institution was some combination of triviality and ideological concord. Consensual decision-making in the colonies, to the extent that it ever existed, was necessarily a fundamentally different institution from the one that prevailed in Tudor and early Stuart England.[2]

These general tendencies are important to outline not only because they serve as a rough synthesis of the descriptions of individual cases that constitute this chapter, but also because remarks on these tendencies must often stand in for a detailed reconstruction of decision-making in individual lower assemblies that are thinly and fragmentarily documented. In many cases it is simply impossible to tell when lower assemblies became majoritarian and for what reasons. In these situations it is important at least to be able to venture tentative conclusions based on the likely consequences of a panoply of structural factors and on what we know about better-documented cases that exhibit similar structural conditions. Applying the appropriate method and standard of certainty to each case, this chapter considers the development of decision-making in twenty-seven colonies in Ireland, mainland North America, and the Caribbean, treating them in the chronological order of their original creation.[3]

---

[2] For a broader introduction to the relationship between English traditions of polity and colonial political institutions in North America, see Man, "English Colonization and the Formation of Anglo-American Polities."

[3] Georgia's assembly is the latest creation considered here. Later, pre-1776 creations that were apparently majoritarian from their inception – including Nova Scotia, Dominica, Grenada, St. Vincent, Tobago, and the Virgin Islands – have been excluded from explicit consideration because they were created after majoritarian decision-making had clearly been institutionalized throughout the lower assemblies of Britain's empire. There is no evidence in any of these cases of a departure from what had become a dominant tradition.

The Earliest Colonial Assemblies: Ireland, Virginia, and Bermuda

The earliest evidence on decision-making in the colonial assemblies suggests that majoritarianism was by no means the automatic result of structural forces in these environments. The oldest colonial lower assembly, the Irish House of Commons, was of course in many ways sui generis, not least in its status as the representative body of a separate kingdom. The Irish Parliament's history can in fact be traced to the thirteenth century, long before the Tudors began to place it firmly under the authority of the regime in England. In these ways, Ireland's elected assembly was more akin to the Westminster Commons, the Scottish Parliament, or even continental national assemblies than to American colonial assemblies. Despite its status as the parliament of a kingdom, however, Ireland's early modern representative body was a recognizably colonial institution. The Irish House of Commons' procedures very closely mimicked those of its English counterpart. And because of Poynings' Law, Ireland's proximity to England, and a series of other formal institutions and conventions, the Irish Commons had a relatively close, direct, and strictly subordinate relationship with the English monarch and Privy Council.

Perhaps unsurprisingly, then, the first Irish parliament for which there survives a journal, that of 1613–15, was a strongly consensual affair governed by roughly the same regime of debate, committee work, voice voting, and formal divisions that prevailed in England at the same time. Indeed, throughout the seventeenth-century parliaments, divisions remained rare events.[4] Only five divisions were held in the entire period prior to 1641, only about eighteen in the entire revolutionary period, only slightly more over the course of the 1661–6 parliament, and only about thirty over the course of the 1690s. Divisions very slowly grew more commonplace in the eighteenth century, but only in the 1770s, just prior to the emergence of legislative independence in 1782, do divisions obviously appear to have become institutionalized.[5]

While firm conclusions on the causes of this trajectory would be premature, it is useful to consider the Irish case in light of some of the institutional elements it shared with both English and other colonial assemblies. Despite the variation in its interpretation and enforcement

---

[4] Dennehy, *The Irish Parliament, 1613–89*. On divisions, see 84–5.
[5] These are tentative (but for the present purposes sufficiently accurate) figures drawn from manual and digital searching and counting in *Journals of the House of Commons of the Kingdom of Ireland*.

over the course of the early modern period, Poynings' Law originally implied that the English and Irish executives exerted a strong degree of direct and indirect agenda control over parliamentary business. Regime agents also dominated parliamentary sessions. These structural realities probably limited the possibility of irresolvable conflict. From the Restoration parliament of 1661–6 onward, however, the Irish Parliament slowly gained the ability effectively to initiate legislation on its own. This could have heightened the possibility for conflict by loosening agenda control.[6] In fact, it is clear that matters on which the Irish House of Commons divided after the Restoration were matters arising from their own initiatives and internal affairs. The most clear rise in the incidence of divisions over the course of the seventeenth century occurred after the 1690s' institutionalization of the "heads of bills" process, which effectively allowed Parliament to originate legislation. Moreover, the upsurge of divisions in the 1770s roughly corresponds with the increasing desire among members of the Irish Commons to weaken the restrictions of Poynings' Law in more fundamental ways.[7] Finally, like other colonies, Ireland may have simply followed earlier developments in Westminster. This would be in keeping with the Irish House's close emulation of English practices over the course of the early modern period.

In contrast to Ireland, the first two representative assemblies in America and the second and third oldest in the empire, the Virginia and Bermuda General Assemblies, were extensions of corporate enterprises. Virginia's assembly first met in 1619, more than two decades before the shift to majoritarian decision-making in the English House of Commons. The General Assembly had been created as part of a wide-ranging reform of the Virginia Company's operations carried out in 1618. The Company's aim was to create the proper governmental conditions for economic prosperity. Developed to suit corporate goals, the Assembly nevertheless incorporated institutional features and traditions from both the Company and Parliament.[8]

Immediately prior to the creation of Virginia's assembly, decision-making in the Virginia Company appears to have been remarkably consensual, despite the role of private interest and internal conflict in its proceedings. In 1619 the Company's quarter court, to which all

---

[6] Kelly, *Poynings' Law and the Making of Law in Ireland*; Clarke, "History of Poynings' Law."

[7] *Journals of the House of Commons of the Kingdom of Ireland*, vol. I, 410, 435, 451, 507, 509, 531, 545, 559, 582, 584, 638, 664, 680, 685, 686, 709; Kelly, *Poynings' Law and the Making of Law in Ireland*, esp. 17–112, 241–309.

[8] Craven, *Dissolution of the Virginia Company*, 67–71.

adventurers were admitted, was making decisions by the putting of questions and the "erection of hands." On nearly all occasions this seems to have been a form of acclamation or "general consent" (the hands were not counted).[9] These patterns indicate a largely consensual decision-making body that dealt with all important matters of Company policy. None of this meant, of course, that the Company's deliberations were devoid of factional conflict.[10] Moreover, from the summer of 1622 onward, the Company experienced multiple incidents of majority decision-making on important matters.[11] A clear division procedure was used at least once, and on that occasion the votes of all adventurers present were officially recorded.[12] Finally, by 1623 the two factions in the Company had developed a series of tactics for maximizing the vote count on their side.[13]

While the Company had clearly embraced majoritarianism in practice by the early 1620s, the use of plurality voting remained controversial.[14] As a result, the Company's majoritarianism itself became a central point of contention and helped to trigger the Company's dissolution. The most prominent internal critics of the Company on this front were John Bargrave, Sir Thomas Smith, and the earl of Warwick, who (among others) argued that the government of the company was a factionally engineered democracy. Bargrave contended that the Company's majoritarian decision-making was the mainstay of the partisan tyranny that plagued its operations. According to Bargrave, even under the treasurership of Sir Thomas Smith, which had ended in 1619 after the creation of the Assembly in Virginia, the Company leadership had "carried" decisions in the courts by "private packings." It had "by practice and action ... framed a Company which being able by most voices to carry government as they list" was able to make "a monopoly of the plantation." Even after Smith's tenure, Bargrave claimed, there remained "no course taken to

---

[9] Kingsbury (ed.), *Records of the Virginia Company*, vol. I, 212 (this entry is for 28 April 1619; the court records are available only for the period beginning in spring 1619). For other examples of this practice prior to the first General Assembly's meeting, see vol. I, 216, 221, 225, 227, 231, 238, 242 (a variant: "it was by most voices affirmed"), 252 (a variant in one decision: "ratified by general consent"). In a small unit, the raising of hands was a convenient alternative to voice votes, which could be unreliable indicators. Later records confirm that raising hands remained the practice, although phrasing is sometimes more vague; the only specific language still describes erection of hands and "general" consent, agreement, or assent. For elections the court used a balloting box with balls, an obviously majoritarian procedure (vol. I, 212, 385, 468, 471, 474, 489).

[10] See Craven, *Dissolution of the Virginia Company*, esp. 105–47.

[11] Kingsbury (ed.), *Records of the Virginia Company*, vol. II, 72, 84, 258, 295, 320, 474, 490, 494.

[12] Ibid., vol. II, 159–60.   [13] Craven, *Dissolution of the Virginia Company*, 241–2, 246.

[14] See Kingsbury (ed.), *Records of the Virginia Company*, vol. III, 638; vol. IV, 42, 55, 149.

prevent oppression of single planters or small bodies of adventurers by plurality of voices of great numbers interested in any differences." Bargrave was also apparently concerned that similar tendencies to popular government and majoritarian tyranny might be present in Virginia's General Assembly.[15] Smith and Warwick likewise dubbed the current government of the Company "democratical and tumultuous."[16]

In April 1623, Lord Cavendish penned a defense of both the Virginia and Somers Islands Companies that was endorsed by the Company's quarter court. It included the paradoxical claim that by allowing for the possibility of votes by plurality, the court was able to maximize consensus. "To discern what is the judgment of a company if there not be unanimity," Cavendish wrote, "there is no way but by plurality of voices," as any member of the House of Commons would have also conceded. "If plurality of voices were not" an option, he continued, "there would scarce at any time in any point be unanimity in any assembly." This was because unanimity so often proceeded "from despair of prevailing in their private opinions, or from shame to discover opposition to public good."[17] Cavendish seems to have been arguing that a system in which plurality voting was always an option made unanimity possible. Members in such an assembly would normally capitulate before the vote when they recognized they were in the minority, and on many occasions, they would also be afraid of identifying themselves with a private faction in the voting process and revealing opposition to the public good within the corporate body. In a system without a majority voting option, each member would have veto power and be unlikely to relinquish it. One important corollary of this view was that in such an assembly, majority decisions, when they occurred, would normally be the products of practical necessity, not faction. From this perspective, again, plurality voting was a mechanism of *identifying* and *preventing* faction, not a means of enabling it.

Whatever the precise nature of decision-making in the Company, majority voting was certainly a frequent occurrence in its later years, and there was widespread concern over majority voting's consequences. In fact the perception of majoritarian tyranny even appears to have played a role in the Company's dissolution by James I in 1624. Charles I began his 1625 proclamation for the settling of Virginia as a royal colony with the observation that Virginia "has not hitherto prospered so happily, as

[15] Craven, *Dissolution of the Virginia Company*, 279–82; Kingsbury (ed.), *Records of the Virginia Company*, vol. III, 605, 638.
[16] Craven, *Dissolution of the Virginia Company*, 283.
[17] *Records of the Virginia Company*, vol. II, 359; see also 355.

was hoped and desired." A primary reason for this, he asserted, was "that the government of that colony was committed to the Company of Virginia, incorporated of a multitude of persons of several dispositions, amongst whom the affairs of the greatest moment were and must be ruled by the greater number of votes and voices."[18] On Charles' account, Company rule in Virginia had to be ended precisely because of the majority voting practiced by the Virginia Company and the rooting of that convention in the private interests of "a multitude" of adventurers.[19]

The corporate body that created Virginia's General Assembly was therefore ambiguous in its institutional implications: the Company was apparently largely consensual at the time of the Assembly's creation, but it made numerous majoritarian decisions of great import in its later years and was attacked for doing so. The nature of decision-making in the Assembly at Jamestown under Company rule is equally ambiguous. It met in 1619, 1621, and 1624, if not in other years for which no records survive. In the summer of 1619 it made a series of decisions. One was explicitly described in speaker John Pory's account of the meeting as a question put: it "had both the general assent and the applause of the whole Assembly." This suggests a strongly consensual decision.[20] Another resolution was made "by voices" and by "all the General Assembly," Pory said, and another "by voices united" and by "the whole court."[21] These descriptions also indicate consensual decision-making and suggest that the General Assembly employed House of Commons-style voice voting instead of the raising of hands typical in the Company's courts. Most decisions made by the Assembly in this period, however, were not recorded in such revealing ways, so it is difficult to reach a firm conclusion about their overall character. There are also no clear descriptions of other Assembly decisions prior to the Company's dissolution.

When Virginia became a royal colony, of course, the General Assembly's procedures may have been further altered more closely to follow those of the House of Commons. Over the long term, the Assembly certainly took on a parliamentarian identity and procedures.[22] It also eventually turned to majoritarian practices. An account of its October 1629 meeting recorded a decision with regard to aggression against Indians that was "the opinion of the whole body of the assembly." But when two questions were formally put on the regulation of tobacco

---

[18] Larkin (ed.), *Stuart Royal Proclamations*, 27.
[19] See also Craven, *Dissolution of the Virginia Company*, 327. The term "multitude" often had negative, democratic connotations in this period.
[20] McIlwaine (ed.), *Journals of the House of Burgesses of Virginia*, vol. I, 7.
[21] Ibid., vol. I, 11, 15.   [22] In general, see Billings, *Little Parliament*.

cultivation, "the maior part" decided one and "the opinion of the most voices" the other.[23] This indicates at least some meaningfully majoritarian decisions on politically salient topics fairly soon after the dissolution of the Company and before majoritarian decisions became common in the English House of Commons. In general, though, we have no revealing, comprehensive evidence of the nature of the Assembly's decisions in any period before 1680, when the Assembly began to keep a formal journal of its proceedings. It is therefore entirely possible, even likely, that the advent of majority rule in the General Assembly followed the deinstitutionalization of consensus decision-making in the English Parliament.

Scattered records from the 1650s describe Assembly decisions in various ways, but almost always as unanimous or at least consensual. A 30 April 1652 decision on colonial office-holding was, for instance, "unanimously voted and concluded" by burgesses and parliamentary commissioners. A week later it was "generally voted" that the governor and Council should remain members of the General Assembly along with the burgesses. A description of decisions taken by the General Assembly in November 1652 described them as "the votes of the whole Assembly." On 1 December 1656, a judicial verdict was reached "by the general and unanimous assent and vote of both houses without any contradiction." On 1 April 1658 the Assembly "voted unanimously" on measures taken against absent members. Part of the vote was an order "that Mr. Speaker sign nothing without the consent of the major part of the House."[24] From 1659 onward, Assembly decisions were recorded in vaguer terms, usually in descriptions of House orders or documents called journals whose contents were nevertheless very similar to lists of orders. There is no telling what procedures prevailed in this period or what the frequency of meaningfully majoritarian decisions was. It is therefore unclear whether Virginia had turned away from consensual decision-making prior to the Restoration, when majoritarian politics became institutionalized in the English House of Commons. The Assembly may have become majoritarian only after its parent institution had.

The Assembly began to record vote tallies in 1680, the year the burgesses began to send detailed journals to London. At this point majoritarian votes were being recorded with great frequency. This suggests that majoritarian decisions may have been common before this date

[23] McIlwaine (ed.), *Journals of the House of Burgesses of Virginia*, vol. I, 52, 53.
[24] Ibid., vol. I, 76, 78, 82, 83, 84, 88, 94, 99, 102, 110, 114 (an election). See also "resolved by a general consent" (107), "resolved by the first vote" (107, 108).

but not recorded as such. It does not, however, tell us when such a practice would have begun.[25] The 1680 records also contain the first detailed description of how the House of Burgesses made decisions. In this period the House clerk seems to have used the language of "questions" to identify formal decisions put to the House. He then noted how the question was "resolved." He often described questions as resolved "in the negative" or "in the affirmative," and very occasionally he noted unanimous resolutions or bill passages. All of these conventions extended beyond 1680. But the crucial convention adopted in this year did not. The clerk appears to have observed enumerated votes by describing questions as resolved "by plurality of voices" or, on a few occasions, by a "majority of voices" or "the major votes." Many of the "plurality" votes were certainly enumerated votes, because they were accompanied by a tally in the journal. The most probable assumption here is that when the clerk labeled a vote as resolved by "plurality," the House had held a form of division, while in other cases they were holding largely consensual voice votes or acclamations by raising of hands. On this measure, in 1680 if not earlier, the House of Burgesses was operating as a meaningfully majoritarian assembly. Assuming that majoritarian decisions occurred only when they were explicitly noted, the House held meaningfully majoritarian votes after 17.9 percent of all questions put in 1680, or in seven out of thirty-nine cases.[26]

The Assembly journals compiled after 1680 and before 1720 give no clear indication of how often enumerated votes occurred. On 2 December 1720, when a division was explicitly mentioned for the first time, the clerk employed phrasing similar to that used in the journal of the English House of Commons.[27] This practice continued for the rest of the colonial period. If we took the clerks' records from 1720 onward to be accurate, we would be led to conclude that the frequency of divisions per questions put to the House of Burgesses was very low – only 4.2 percent. But a burgess' diary from mid-century makes clear that this figure is probably a vast underestimate of the frequency of divisions in the eighteenth-century House. Colonel Landon Carter's record of proceedings between 1752 and 1755 shows that a very large proportion of decisions simply described in the journal as orders and resolutions (with no question put) were in fact made by formal divisions of the House. In Carter's experience, divisions were a completely mundane and

---

[25] Only a few journals survive from the earlier Restoration period.
[26] McIlwaine (ed.), *Journals of the House of Burgesses of Virginia*, vol. II, 119–53.
[27] Ibid., vol. V, 286.

ever-present aspect of the fierce political contests fought in Virginia's legislature.[28]

Because he was new to the House when he began this diary, Carter also recorded the division procedure that prevailed at the time. He noticed early on that "upon a division, the ayes [were] on the left of the [speaker's] chair, the noes on the right."[29] He later clarified that the House had two separate division procedures. "When a division happens, if it is relating to things entirely in the House, vizt., about clerks, etc., ayes on one side noes on the other. But, if it is about any matter in the House that some are against and some for," he wrote, "those against the resolution in the House, such as the reports of any committee, go out of the House on the division. Tellers are appointed of each party. One going out is stopped and counteth those within. Another from within counteth those who went out as they come in."[30] Still later he wrote that "as a rule the opposers to any thing in the House go out."[31] The House was approximating House of Commons practices. By the 1750s, then, Virginia's lower assembly was certainly majoritarian. Indeed, it was almost certainly majoritarian by 1680, and probably from an even earlier point in time. This all points to the conclusion that Virginia simply mimicked the practices of the House of Commons as they evolved. Alternatively, if the Assembly did in fact make regularly majoritarian decisions during the early Stuart period, this can probably be attributed to the initial creation of the Assembly not as a royal institution but as an organ of the Virginia Company.

An offshoot of that company, the Somers Islands Company, was chartered in June 1615. It erected an assembly in Bermuda in 1620, just months after Virginia, in basic accordance with letters patent from James I.[32] One might expect such a company, nearly all of whose founding investors were Virginia Company shareholders, to have had an institutional character similar to that of its parent company.[33] In fact, both the company's courts and the colonial assembly seem to have been similar to those of Virginia. On his arrival in October 1619, Bermuda's first governor, Nathaniel Butler, was required to assemble his "counsel and as many of the ablest and best understanding men in the islands, both of the clergy and laity" in a unicameral body that would meet at least annually. He was told "rather to take too many than too few" men into

---

[28] Greene (ed.), *Diary of Colonel Landon Carter*, vol. I, 65–124. Carter also explicitly observed that some divisions were left unrecorded (vol. I, 73).

[29] Ibid., vol. I, 68.   [30] Ibid., vol. I, 69–70.   [31] Ibid., vol. I, 72.

[32] Lefroy (ed.), *Memorials of the Discovery and Early Settlement of the Bermudas*, vol. I, 89–90.

[33] Jarvis, *In the Eye of all Trade*, 19 (on shareholders).

the assembly "both because every man will more willingly obey laws to which he has yielded his consent as likewise because you shall the better discover things as have need of redress by many than by few."[34] This statement suggested that the company did not see much representative legitimacy in the assembly, but other official statements from the time, we will see, suggest the opposite.

The Company's orders left undetermined how decisions would be made by those who did attend. "What in assembly shall, by the major or better part, be agreed upon," Butler was told, "we would have you distinctly to advertise us of by the return of the next ship." This implied that Butler could adopt a majoritarian procedure but was also permitted have decisions ultimately made by the "better part." The instructions went on to say that during the time in which the assembly waited for the company courts to ratify their decisions, the governor could "put in execution any such wholesome orders or constitutions as shall by the major part in the said assemblies be agreed upon."[35] This was a stronger indication that the Assembly would ordinarily be majoritarian, at least in the formal sense that majority votes would be permissible.

Direct evidence of how the Bermuda Assembly actually made decisions over time is, however, sparse, ambiguous, and conflicting. When the Assembly met in August 1620, the secretary was sworn to read all bills three times over three separate days "before they were put to the question, and came to be decided by plurality of voices."[36] In his speech to the assembly, the governor did not explicitly emphasize consensus, but rather open-minded debate. Members were to come to St. George's church "without all prejudication," with "equal minds," and "without having our minds so preoccupied and taken up before, as no room is left for justice and right." If members gave "attention and diligent ear to such reasons as we shall hear delivered, either for or against any bill," they would be able to "be ruled, swayed, and led by the truth, force, and reason of those reasons, and so accordingly give our votes."[37] Free deliberation was here described as consistent with enumerated voting, but not in a manner that would have alarmed anyone in England. It certainly does not imply the early institutionalization of majoritarianism.

Indeed, the one surviving account of the first meeting of the General Assembly in Bermuda described a procedure very close to that of the early Stuart House of Commons:

[34] Lefroy (ed.), *Historye of the Bermudaes*, 190.   [35] Ibid., 190–1.   [36] Ibid., 193.
[37] Ibid., 196–7.

After a bill was read three several days, and sufficiently disputed upon, the secretary was to demand whether it should be put to voices or no, the which being granted, the said secretary to hold up the bill in his hand and to say, "All you that will have this bill to pass for a law let them say so; as many as will not let them say the contrary"; if the [sic] then cry affirmatively yea, were found apparently greater than the negative no, the bill was passed for a law, if on the contrary, it was dashed. If it proved doubtful which cry was the greater, the secretary was to say thus: "As many as allow the bill, stand up on your feet; you that refuse sit still"; and then both the numbers being counted, the most carried it. And, in this fashion, all the bills were decided during the whole session of the Assembly.[38]

This familiar process was apparently employed in a consensual manner, again in keeping with contemporary House of Commons practice. The same account stated that all fifteen acts passed in this first session were approved "with a very great and general unanimity."[39] In 1622, the Company laws specified that both the governor and a unanimous council had a negative voice in the Assembly. This may have been the colony's interpretation of the "better part" clause in Butler's original instructions. Otherwise, the laws specified, "all things shall be established by plurality of voices."[40] This is a basic if by no means conclusive suggestion that the Assembly may have already adopted majority voting. Contrary to Butler's original instructions, the 1622 warrant of assembly suggested that delegates from Bermuda's "tribes" were to be treated as local representatives. They were commanded "to speak and answer for the body of the whole tribe."[41] But it is unclear whether their role was primarily delegatory or discretionary in nature. Beyond these glimpses of procedure, there are no additional, informative records of the General Assembly's decision-making for the period when it was under the control of the Somers Islands Company or for the period after it became a royal colony in 1684.[42]

---

[38] Ibid., 198; see also 309–10, 311, 312. On at least one occasion (in 1627), the Assembly "or most part of them" voted "by holding up their hands" (Lefroy (ed.), *Memorials of the Discovery and Early Settlement of the Bermudas*, vol. I, 425).

[39] Lefroy (ed.), *Historye of the Bermudaes*, 199.

[40] Lefroy (ed.), *Memorials of the Discovery and Early Settlement of the Bermudas*, vol. I, 209.

[41] Ibid., vol. I, 267; see also vol. II, 382, 399, 537.

[42] For mentions of individual decisions in the Company period, all of which were described as unanimous or consensual, see ibid., vol. I, 362, 369, 372, 427, 428–9, 432. In 1686, early in the period of royal control, the Privy Council ordered the governor to produce and send to England a journal of proceedings in the Assembly. The Assembly met in 1687, but records of proceedings in the Assembly do not survive for any year prior to 1696. Even the journals for the period from 1696 do not provide any information on the frequency of majoritarian decisions in the General Assembly, preventing us from giving Bermuda a clear place in the narrative of majoritarian decision-making's emergence in

While the evidence for decision-making in the two oldest representative assemblies in English North America is frustratingly incomplete, it suggests, overall, that despite a mixed institutional heritage of corporate governance and parliamentary procedure, Virginia and Bermuda followed the practices and trajectory of what quickly became their archetypical institution in England, the House of Commons. The oldest colonial lower assembly, the Irish House of Commons, did the same.

Delegate Representation: New England and Maryland

The only early colonial lower assemblies in which basic English precedents were especially unlikely to be followed were either assemblies that did not begin, like the House of Commons, as representative bodies, or assemblies that imitated other originally nonrepresentative assemblies. The second set of popular assemblies to emerge in England's empire prior to the Civil War typically fit into one of these two categories. Each assembly was an outgrowth of a corporate or proprietary mode of colonization. In the 1630s some of these colonies instituted what were originally meetings of all freemen acting in an essentially private, nonrepresentative capacity. This arrangement tended to encourage majoritarianism by curtailing its negative significance, just as it did in the English House of Lords. These assemblies quickly became representative bodies, but they did so out of practical necessity. This tended to imply that representation was more a form of delegation than it was a discretionary trusteeship. This, in turn, tended to encourage majoritarian tactics, because representatives were given marching orders by their constituents. Indeed, representatives very often received formal instructions. A strictly delegatory understanding of their role would have left them unable to form a consensus with other representatives unless that consensus already existed prior to their meeting. Other lower assemblies created at the time imitated these delegatory assemblies and thereby acquired the same characteristics, even if they were representative in form from the beginning.

Before 1640 there were four colonial assemblies in New England, at Massachusetts Bay, Plymouth, Connecticut, and New Haven. In the Massachusetts Bay Colony, there was a very clear continuity between corporate governing practices and the initially unicameral assembly because the charter and the government of the company were simply moved to New England in 1630 with the first settlers. In August 1629,

the American colonies. See ibid., vol. II, 565, 568; *Ancient Journals of the House of Assembly of Bermuda.*

when the London-based General Court decided to move the government and patent to New England, those present raised hands for and against the motion after considerable debate, and it "appeared" that there was "general assent" for the move. Like the Virginia Company's quarter courts, the General Court was using "the erection of hands" as a form of acclamation. It would presumably have used the counting of hands or another method when enumeration became necessary.[43] Once the Court moved to New England, however, its decision-making procedures were not clearly recorded. While we might assume that basic procedures remained the same, doing so tells us nothing about the frequency of consensual and majoritarian outcomes.[44]

In 1634 the Massachusetts General Court supplanted the Court of Assistants as the central unit of government in the Massachusetts Bay Colony. It was composed of elected freemen acting as representatives along with the governor, lieutenant governor, and assistants (who were now elected by freemen). The records of the Court's decision-making, however, remained opaque. By 1644 the General Court had become formally bicameral and had ended the practice of allowing freemen to vote independently by proxy. In this way a fully representative body, the House of Deputies, was established for practical reasons.[45] As a result, and as its name implied, this body was strongly influenced by the understanding that representatives were *deputed* by local freemen. They acted on behalf and by the direction of the freemen who elected them, exerting minimal discretion. This expectation was reinforced by the use of instructions to representatives, a practice that became widespread in Massachusetts over the course of the eighteenth century.[46] These dynamics, in turn, made majoritarian decision-making more likely. The House of Deputies was therefore probably a majoritarian institution around the same time that the English House of Commons first began to exhibit regular majority voting. But England's Commons and Massachusetts' House likely became majoritarian for fundamentally different reasons. In the Massachusetts Bay Colony it was not status considerations, but the deputed, practical mode and origin of representation that would have been crucial.

---

[43] Shurtleff (ed.), *Records of the Governor and Company of the Massachusetts Bay*, vol. I, 51; see also 67.

[44] Twenty-seven were present at the session in London where the vote to move to New England occurred, while nine were present at the 23 August 1630 Court of Assistants, the first meeting in the colony, and twelve were present at the second meeting (ibid., vol. I, 73, 75). Later meetings usually had fewer than ten in attendance.

[45] On developments in the early period, see in general Wall, Jr., *Massachusetts Bay*.

[46] Squire, *Rise of the Representative*, 14–15, 236–49.

The House of Deputies did, to some extent, record its voting practices in more detail in the House records that survive for the years 1644–57. Initially, the House simply used phrases like "it is ordered" to describe nearly all its actions. Notation was occasionally expanded to the phrase "it is voted and ordered."[47] On 16 June 1645 the House recorded a decision on the Speaker's power to resolve tied votes by noting that "it was resolved upon the question by vote" and that two deputies were "contra dicentes." This implied a minimally majoritarian resolution. Another decision from the same day, described as "resolved, upon the question," was in fact a tie vote of 16 to 16, settled by the vote of the Speaker. The next vote to occur that day was decided by a margin of 18 to 12.[48] Both decisions were clearly majoritarian in nature. Five "contra dicentes," presumably deputies, were similarly identified in an 18 June 1645 order of the House.[49] Such lists of dissenters continued to be recorded occasionally until the end point of this more informative string of records in 1657.[50] The overall impression here, despite the lack of standardized recording procedures, is one of frequent enumerated votes in the House of Deputies and a willingness to publicly acknowledge dissent by individual representatives. Such practices were beyond the pale in contemporary English representative government, even during the 1640s. There are, then, some indications that Massachusetts had institutionalized a fairly strong form of majoritarian decision-making at mid-century, in a partial divergence from practice in the English House of Commons. Again, this likely occurred as a result of the Massachusetts Bay Colony's strongly delegatory understanding of representation, which was itself a practical outgrowth of a corporate tradition that permitted the participation of all freemen as individuals in the governance of the General Court.

After mid-century the relevant Massachusetts records go silent. And because the records of the House of Deputies' post-1715 successor, the House of Representatives, were published soon after each session, making an impression of unity in the journal more important, the House did not record decisions in a manner that reveals specific decision-making procedures, the frequency of majoritarian decisions, or even the frequency of formal votes.[51] One is, however, left with the assumption that majoritarian decision-making continued and perhaps intensified in this period. Roll call votes were held if there was a motion

---

[47] See, for example, Shurtleff (ed.), *Records of the Governor and Company of the Massachusetts Bay*, vol. III, 4.
[48] Ibid., vol. III, 19.   [49] Ibid., vol. III, 29.   [50] See, for example, ibid., vol. III, 250.
[51] Zemsky, *Merchants, Farmers, and River Gods*, 239–40.

from the floor and majority consent, but unrecorded, enumerated votes were very likely also held. Only seventeen roll calls were published, all of them between 1740 and 1756. These more public admissions of division, equivalent to a division list in the English context, amounted to a very small percentage of questions put that were noted in the journals for that period.[52] This provided only a very limited way for representatives to be precisely accountable to the electorate, which worked against the delegatory conception of representation. The House was not a very tactically complex terrain, and certainly not one with a partisan organization, in part because attendance was inconsistent and whipping mechanisms unavailable. As a result, debate was vigorous and a premium was placed on persuasion.[53] In the end, we can say that while Massachusetts was likely majoritarian from an early date, it is impossible to tell for sure whether or not this majoritarianism predated the English Revolution. Nor can we rule out the possibility that there were post-1650s moments of largely consensual decision-making.

There is, unfortunately, less to be said about the other early New England assemblies. The Connecticut General Court, closely modeled on Massachusetts, first met in the spring of 1637 and codified its practices in the colony's 1639 Fundamental Orders. The Court was immediately representative in nature and from 1639 comprised deputies from each town and magistrates elected by the deputies.[54] By this time it also had a procedure for enumerated votes and the resolution of ties by the governor or moderator, but it is unclear how often these procedures were used.[55] From the beginning, the Court's records, which were carefully constructed to give the impression of a unified decision-making body, do not provide information on how specific decisions were made. Deputies were also permitted to meet separately in advance of the General Court, but they did not meet as a formally separate body until 1698, when the General Court was reconstituted as the General Assembly.[56] In 1667, one matter before the Court was clearly resolved in corporate fashion through the raising of hands, but formal notation of questions put in the records did not commence until 1698. Even then, the precise manner of voting was not recorded.[57]

---

[52] Ibid., 21, 72, 240–2, 312–17. For examples, see *Journals of the House of Representatives of Massachusetts*, vol. XXVII, 195–6.

[53] Zemsky, *Merchants, Farmers, and River Gods*, 17–23.

[54] For details, see Jones, *Congregational Commonwealth*, 31–2, 65–98.

[55] Trumbull (ed.), *Public Records of the Colony of Connecticut*, vol. I, 25. Majority decisions in the General Assembly were also endorsed in the royal charter of 1662.

[56] Ibid., vol. I, 24.   [57] Ibid., vol. II, 79.

The separate journal of the Connecticut General Assembly's lower house survives only for the period between 1708 and 1738. On multiple occasions the lower house recorded a vote margin or tally.[58] It sometimes recorded enumerated votes simply as a "resolve." A personal journal from 1757 reveals that "a poll" was conducted on some voting occasions, and that this was in fact a House of Commons–style procedure in which the Connecticut lower house would "divide." This journal also recorded that the lower house initially raised hands for a nonenumerated vote. Apparently, corporate traditions remained intact and had been merged with parliamentary practice. The private journal recorded at least seven divisions for proceedings that lasted less than a month. This suggests that by at least 1757 the lower house of the General Assembly was a majoritarian body.[59] Indeed, the case of Connecticut appears to be similar to that of Virginia: the Connecticut journals may have concealed a tradition of institutionalized majoritarianism that long predated the 1750s.

The records available for the other pre-1640 corporately organized colonies of New England, Plymouth and New Haven, are insufficient for describing their decision-making in any detail.[60] Both formed representative bodies in the late 1630s. Plymouth's government – organized into a General Court, a Court of Assistants, and a Court of Freemen – originally insisted on all freemen attending. But it took on a representative character, for logistical reasons, from 1638.[61] This in itself suggests that the institution may have been majoritarian from the outset. The records of the Plymouth Court are more lists of orders and acts than journals of proceedings. Fragmentary evidence from 1649 at least suggests the legitimacy of majority decision-making, but the frequency of such decisions remains unknown.[62]

New Haven's General Court, in contrast to those of its neighbors, quickly became a strongly representative body built on a trustee or discretionary model.[63] This gave it more potential for consensual decisions than Plymouth or Massachusetts. When New Haven's freemen met to form a government in June 1639, they voted in corporate fashion by raising hands. The votes were unanimous, although on one occasion a freeman waited until after the vote, which he claimed to accept, before

---

[58] Connecticut State Library, Hartford, Connecticut General Assembly, Journals of the Lower House, entries for 10/31/1717 (unpaginated). In October 1717 a secret, written ballot was used for a particularly controversial vote; this method was not mentioned when the other margins and tallies were recorded. See entries for 10/29/1717 and May 1718 (unpaginated).

[59] Turner (ed.), *Journal Kept by William Williams*, 32, 35, 39, 42, 55.

[60] Plymouth's joint stock company was dissolved in 1627. See Langdon, *Pilgrim Colony*, 29.

[61] Ibid., 85–6.   [62] Ibid., 94–5.   [63] Squire, *Rise of the Representative*, 16–17.

registering his dissent.[64] In the 1640s New Haven's elected magistrate and deputies (what would be called governor and assistants in other similar colonies) met as a "court," but most important business was conducted by "general courts" of all freemen.[65] By 1643 neighboring towns had been brought under a colonial government that adopted a structure and nomenclature even closer to that of Massachusetts and Connecticut, and at this point New Haven's General Courts became representative in practice, with two deputies from each locality attending.[66] Later recorded votes seem to have consensual, in keeping with the record of early practices, but the Court records also regularly implied a basic majority standard for legitimate votes.[67] In general, the Court did not record the details of individual decisions.

The next General Court or Assembly formed in New England was that of Rhode Island. It first met in 1647 after the securing of a charter from Parliament in 1644 and some public meetings of freemen.[68] In May 1647 a General Court of Election legitimated its transactions on the basis of a majority of freemen being present and defined its "democratical" government in terms of "the consent of all or the greater part of the free inhabitants." The colony immediately adopted a representative format for meetings of the General Court between elections, but they also experimented with majoritarian procedures for law-making meant to preserve the power of all freemen to exercise direct control.[69] This again suggests majoritarian decision-making in the context of a delegatory understanding of representation. The corporate nature of the colony and its institutions was confirmed in its 1663 charter under the restored monarchy, but the government was partly altered to look more like Massachusetts and Connecticut and be more thoroughly representative, with weaker provisions for town power and direct democracy. An oligarchically inflected, qualified form of majority voting in the General Assembly was also confirmed.[70] The Assembly became bicameral in 1696.[71] The records for the Assembly are largely uninformative about its decision-making from its founding to the Revolution, including the period for which House of Deputies journal records survive.[72] The colony's democratic form and delegatory conception of representation,

---

[64] Hoadly (ed.), *Records of the Colony and Plantation of New Haven*, 12–16. See also 57.
[65] Calder, *New Haven Colony*, 107.   [66] Ibid., 118–20.
[67] Hoadly (ed.), *Records of the Colony and Plantation of New Haven*, 111, 117, 118, 192.
[68] James, *Colonial Metamorphoses in Rhode Island*, 42.   [69] Ibid., 43, 46–8.
[70] Ibid., 49–51.   [71] Ibid., 117.
[72] This is from 1728, around the time the House acquired a clerk and formal rules. See ibid., 117.

however, strongly suggest that it proceeded in a majoritarian manner from a very early date.[73]

Maryland, of course, was a proprietary and not originally a corporate colony like the early New England settlements, but many of its salient characteristics were nevertheless similar. Again the fundamental factor here was the late advent of representation and the practical rationale behind it. The charter granted by Charles I to Lord Baltimore specified an assembly of freemen or delegates. The Calverts initially modeled this and their general scheme of government on the Durham palatinate in England, which in the fourteenth century had brought together barons and freemen in an unelected, unicameral body. When the Maryland assemblies began to meet, however, parliamentary norms and traditions were quickly implemented. The first assembly met in February 1635 and the second in 1638. The second assembly, for which there survives detailed evidence, was a combination of freemen, elected representatives, and specially summoned councillors and manor lords. All freemen were permitted to appear personally or have representatives act as their proxies. In 1642, the vagaries of this setup were dramatically exposed when nineteen men cast proxy votes for at least 138 eligible freemen.

In such an environment, there were no clear costs to majority voting, and nonenumerated, consensual voting was extremely unlikely, if not impossible, for logistical reasons. Those voting by proxy could be gathered effectively under a consensus only if they entrusted decision-making to the discretion of their proxies. The practical difficulties of attendance by all freemen soon necessitated some form of representation, which had always been permitted by the charter. By 1650 the Assembly had gradually assumed a more clearly elected, representative character, and in April of that year Lord Baltimore formalized the change. Throughout this period the assemblies were very small. This too would have encouraged the enumeration of votes: individual voice differences could make the outcome of a voice vote suspect, and an estimate of raised hands would have had no clear advantages over other forms of counting. Over the course of the 1640s the Assembly also slowly assumed a bicameral orientation. In 1646 elected members sat separately from unelected members for the first time and styled themselves a "house of Commons." The bicameral format was officially recognized in the 1650 meeting of the Assembly, and unicameral bodies met on only a few occasions in later years.[74]

---

[73] Squire, *Rise of the Representative*, 17.

[74] Jordan, *Foundations of Representative Government in Maryland*, 1–3, 19–21, 26–32 (this and the previous paragraph). See also Morgan, *Inventing the People*, 39–40.

By 1650 majoritarian practices appear to have already been institution-alized. The Assembly's first decisions were made on 29 January 1638 by means of enumerated votes in which the tallies and individuals on each side of the question were identified.[75] On 8 February, the next day in session, questions were formally put to the House; the votes were enumerated and meaningfully majoritarian.[76] From this point onward in the early years of the Assembly, the official record was often more cursory and incomplete, so it is impossible to compile data on the frequency or closeness of enumerated votes. Nor is it possible to ascertain precisely how voting was conducted at this time. But the information available strongly suggests that decision-making in Maryland's Assembly was blithely majoritarian from the outset. Although the Assembly was not bicameral in the late 1630s, it is significant that the majoritarian pattern in Maryland predates the advent of such a pattern in the English House of Commons by a few years. Rules of the Assembly ratified in later sessions reinforce the impression that the Assembly's conduct in early 1638 continued uninterrupted.[77]

The Assembly records also continued in later years to take no notice of nonenumerated forms of voting. They simply noted tersely that bills had been "passed"; eventually, they also often specified who voted on which side. They did so by using the language of "consent" and "dissent," which recalled language used in the House of Lords. Indeed, in these descriptions of Maryland voting, "no" voters were completely disassociated from the passage of a bill. On 23 October 1640, for instance, a bill on religious liberty was "passed by all," but a bill on the proprietor's prerogatives was "not passed by all but the President and Secretary." A third bill was "passed by" nine men identified individually. In the rest of that day's voting, the recorded proceedings tended to identify only those by whom the bill was "not passed."[78] This apparently individual-istic practice and recording of voting would have of course been anathema in the English House of Commons. Here again, an instance of precocious majoritarianism in the colonies was the result of both the way in which lower assemblies drew on nonparliamentary traditions and the logistical aspects of decision-making and representation.

In the earliest separate lower house journal for Maryland, which dates to 1666, the clerk did not transparently describe the house's decision-making. But his description does provide strong evidence that majoritar-ian practices continued in the separate chamber once it was stabilized

[75] *Archives of Maryland*, vol. I, 8–9.   [76] Ibid., vol. I, 11.   [77] Ibid., vol. I, 33, 91–2.
[78] Ibid., vol. I, 93–4. For other early evidence of enumerated voting and the identification of those in the minority, see 107, 136, 173, 239, 282–3.

following the restoration of the monarchy. At this point, of course, the English House of Commons was itself settling into a majoritarian mode of decision-making. The first formal decision of the Maryland lower house's session in April 1666, on whether it was necessary to draw up a bill concerning outlaws and coroners, was "put to the vote" and resolved "in the affirmative by all (except those of the committee)." This notation of majority and minority voices, familiar from the Assembly's early years, was compressed in notation dating from later in 1666. From that point many decisions were described as being made by "the maior vote." This phrase was used in combination with descriptive phrases in use in earlier periods, such as "passed by all" and "voted in the affirmative."[79] After 1666, the phrasing in the journals switched to a language of "voted that" for the rest of the Restoration period. In the early eighteenth century one finds a similarly uninformative language of votes "carried."[80] A slightly clearer language of "carried by a majority" appeared in the journal starting in 1698 and continued to 1727.[81] However uninformative this laconic notation might be, there is no evidence to suggest that the House's originally majoritarian practices were somehow abandoned in the early eighteenth century.

From 1732, the majoritarian practices of Maryland's lower house were elaborated and recorded in detail. On the second day of the session beginning 11 July, the question was put and carried that "on each vote of this House the names of the persons that vote for and against any question or bill be inserted in the journal in order for printing." The roll call was taken on this vote itself.[82] This order indicated both a comfort with majoritarian decision-making and a willingness to publicize individual members' voting. The publication of majority voting had a series of important consequences because it made possible a strong tie between voter behavior and representative behavior in the House. In part, it must have merely reinforced the delegatory understanding of representation that appears to have always prevailed in Maryland. Over the rest of the colonial period this roll call voting and recording procedure was followed over 800 times. Even if we assume that only on such occasions was a meaningfully majoritarian decision being made, this indicates an extremely majoritarian assembly. On this measure, questions put resulted in enumerated votes (occasionally called "divisions" in the

[79] Ibid., vol. II, 66.
[80] See, for example, ibid., vol. II, 443, 532. On occasion there was an explicitly majoritarian description (for example, vol. II, 535; vol. VII, 10).
[81] Ibid., vol. XXII, 122 (the first instance).   [82] Ibid., vol. XXXVII, 447–8.

230 Little Parliaments in the Atlantic Colonies, 1613–1789

records) about three quarters of the time.[83] Maryland is unusually well documented. But on the basis of what we can know about this and other colonies, it was the earliest majoritarian lower assembly, possibly predating even the English House of Commons itself. The extent of its majoritarianism in the eighteenth century also appears to have been unique. But the origins of its early turn to majority voting are familiar from other colonies in early colonial North America. They embraced delegatory understandings of representation, often in the wake of a practically motivated turn away from direct, nonrepresentative decision-making.

Other Island Colonies: Barbados, the Leeward Islands, Jamaica, and the Bahamas

The other early island colonies cannot be studied with anything approaching the precision possible for some of the early colonies of mainland North America. Barbados and the Leeward Islands were originally established as proprietary colonies in 1627 on the Durham model also used in Maryland, but their assemblies postdated their mainland counterparts. Under the patent granted to the earl of Carlisle, the proprietor could pass laws with the assent of the majority of freeholders. Despite this provision, however, the early government of the islands was committed only to a governor and council.[84]

The small representative Assembly of Barbados was not created until 1639. It met with some frequency, assembling separately from the council at an early date, and its procedures were becoming regularized by the 1650s.[85] No detailed record of its proceedings survives, however, until the 1670s, when it was sitting separately from the Council.[86] It is probable that by this time the Assembly was solidly majoritarian. The frequent notation of unanimous votes in the journal suggests that the nonunanimous votes were routinely nonconsensual. This impression is strengthened by the survival of vote tallies from the early eighteenth

---

[83] For examples of explicit use of the term "division," see ibid., vol. L, 230, 415; vol. LXIII, 136.

[84] Williamson, *Caribbee Islands under the Proprietary Patents*, 40–1, 88.

[85] Harlow, *History of Barbados*, 18–19, 25–6; Williamson, *Caribbee Islands under the Proprietary Patents*, 144; Gragg, *Englishmen Transplanted*, 63; Shilstone, "Evolution of the General Assembly of Barbados," 188–91; Davis, *Cavaliers and Roundheads of Barbados*, passim; Spurdle, *Early West Indian Government*, 29. There were earlier meetings of all freeholders as well. Even in the early eighteenth century there were usually fewer than twenty members present in the Assembly. See, for example, NA CO 31/13.

[86] But see Shilstone (ed.), "Records of the House of Assembly of Barbados." On bicameralism, see Davis, *Cavaliers and Roundheads of Barbados*, 166.

century onward. These tallies came to be regularly recorded for nonunanimous votes in addition to what was already the commonplace language used in the journals for describing Assembly decisions. This permits the tentative conclusion that the earlier nonunanimous votes were probably also enumerated votes.[87]

We know less about the assemblies of the individual Leeward Islands – St. Christopher, Nevis, Montserrat, and Antigua – which were first settled by the English in the 1620s and 1630s. The islands were embroiled in the politics of mid-seventeenth-century England, and both their legal status in England and their local political order were regularly in flux. At least two of them, Antigua and St. Christopher, appear to have formed assemblies in the 1640s. Nevis had an assembly by 1658. Montserrat likely did not have representative institutions until after the Restoration.[88] These Caribbean assemblies do not seem to have met separately from councils until late in Charles II's reign (and Montserrat's not until 1696).[89] No journals or other detailed procedural information survive for these colonies until the eighteenth century, and that material itself is largely uninformative on the precise nature of decision-making.[90]

In 1671 the Leeward Islands as a whole became independent of Barbados. The Islands were arranged into a federated unit with a governor, a Council, and an Assembly of the Islands. The individual island assemblies remained. The Assembly of the Islands was active in some form between 1674 and 1711. It was greeted with wariness and on occasion hostility by the individual islands. Early meetings were consultative, and starting at least with a documented example from 1682, two representatives from each island were chosen by their councils and assemblies to attend the Assembly meetings.[91] Rules established in 1692 established a majority vote for decisions binding on all islands, but individual islands could be exempt from an Assembly decision if a majority of their (now) five representatives (three of whom were elected by the island freemen) dissented. This rule implies that enumerated votes

---

[87] NA CO 31/2, 127–30 (rules adopted in December 1674). For the earliest recorded tallies, see CO 31/6, 11/18/1701 (unpaginated); CO 31/7, 6/8/1703 (unpaginated).

[88] Bennett, "English Caribbees in the Period of the Civil War," 363; Williamson, *Caribbee Islands under the Proprietary Patents*, 185; Spurdle, *Early West Indian Government*, 11.

[89] Spurdle, *Early West Indian Government*, 29.

[90] See, for example, NA CO 177/2, 177/13 (Montserrat, both ends of the period); CO 9/1, 9/2, 9/37 (Antigua, both ends of the period); CO 241/1, 241/3, 241/15 (St. Christopher, both ends of the period); CO 186/1, 186/2 (Nevis). CO 241/1, assembly journal entry for 9/19/1704 (unfoliated), mentions a decision "by plurality of votes," but of course this does not inform us about the frequency of enumerated voting.

[91] Higham, *Development of the Leeward Islands under the Restoration*, 229, 231.

would have been held in these meetings. In 1701 the rule was changed to require unanimous dissent from an island's five representatives.[92] In general, however, the records of the Assembly's proceedings were extremely scanty until the eighteenth century, and after that, uninformative.[93] There is nevertheless no reason to suspect that the Leeward Islands rejected the majoritarian practices of the other American colonies and the post-revolutionary English House of Commons.

Jamaica, the next Caribbean colony to be founded, was taken by the English in 1655. A civil government did not begin to form until 1661, when the royal colony's governor was empowered to call assemblies.[94] At this point, the Assembly was predictably and clearly modeled on the House of Commons.[95] It first met in 1663, separately from the Council, and it immediately recorded proceedings in its journal, which unfortunately does not provide clear information on how decisions were made.[96] The Assembly met only once more before 1671, in 1664 or 1665.[97] Little detailed content appeared in the Assembly journal before 1675, when true minutes began to be recorded. The rules for the House approved on 3 September 1678 included the stipulation that "in all votes the major party carry it, wherein the Speaker is to have his casting voice." This suggests a blithe attitude to enumerated majority voting.[98] The phrasing of the rule is not conclusive, but nothing else in the journals contradicts the impression it gives, and the apparently consistent but rare recording of unanimous votes in the Assembly journal reinforces the impression of majoritarianism.[99] By the 1750s, as an unofficial account of a session beginning in September 1755 makes clear, observers were thinking about Assembly politics in strongly majoritarian and partisan terms. The author of the account recorded in exquisite detail what appears to have been remarkably sophisticated and aggressive

---

[92] Higham, "General Assembly of the Leeward Islands," 197–8.

[93] See, for example, NA CO 155/1, 155/8 (both ends of the period).

[94] Whitson, *Constitutional Development of Jamaica*, 10–12, 20–38; BL MS Add 12428, f. 25r.

[95] Whitson, *Constitutional Development of Jamaica*, 44–5. See also BL MS Add 12430, f. 41r. For contemporary awareness of colonial assemblies as little parliaments, see *Interesting Tracts Relating to the Island of Jamaica*, 110, 112; BL MS Add 12430.

[96] Pestana, *English Conquest of Jamaica*, 235–6. See also BL MS Egerton 2395, ff. 576–583, which contains information on proceedings in 1678.

[97] Whitson, *Constitutional Development of Jamaica*, 39; BL MS Add 12428, f. 25v.

[98] *Journals of the Assembly of Jamaica*, vol. I, 24. See also NA CO 140/5, assembly journal entry for 9/22/1682 (unfoliated); Long, *History of Jamaica*, vol. I, 56.

[99] For recordings of *nemine contradicente* votes, see, for example, *Journals of the Assembly of Jamaica*, vol. I, 30. The manuscript journals are slightly more complete than the printed editions but do not include important additional information. See BL MS Add 12426; NA CO 140/5, 140/7.

majoritarian maneuver throughout the session.[100] Much of the detail of this account also suggests that enumerated votes were the regular means of resolving questions put to the House.[101] But no clear conclusions are admissible for Jamaica with respect to the period before the 1750s.

The remaining seventeenth-century island colony, the Bahamas, became a proprietary holding in 1670. It was held by a group similar to the one that was granted Carolina. Originally named Eleutheria by settlers from Bermuda, the Bahamas became in 1647 the concern of the Company of Eleutherian Adventurers, and in 1649 the colony was apparently recognized by a parliamentary ordinance. The Bahamas fell under the control of the Carolina proprietors in 1670, in a separate charter, and 1671 instructions for the colony included provision for a "Parliament" and an elected assembly modeled on the House of Commons. But the colony remained disorganized, underfunded, and a center for piracy into the eighteenth century, and there is no specific information on the meeting of assemblies in the proprietary period. The Bahamas came under royal control in 1718 and piracy had been mostly eradicated by 1725. A legislature for the royal colony first assembled in 1729.[102] The records of the lower house of Assembly date from its first meeting, but they are uninformative on the way in which the chamber made decisions.[103] The Assembly did record some vote tallies in its earliest meetings, but refrained from doing so soon thereafter. This makes it probable that the Assembly was majoritarian, but it is impossible to be certain.[104] As with the other Caribbean colonies, while the records of the Bahamas do not permit precise conclusions about the emergence of majoritarian institutions, the dominant impression is one of strong cultural and temporal connections to the evolving nature of decision-making in the English House of Commons.

Post-Restoration Proprietaries: New Jersey, Carolina, Pennsylvania, and New York

Leaders of later proprietary colonies, of course, could look to a fully majoritarian House of Commons for guidance, and although the

---

[100] *Historical Account of the Sessions of Assembly.* See also Long, *History of Jamaica*, vol. II, 38.

[101] See, for example, *Historical Account of the Sessions of Assembly*, 13.

[102] Craton and Saunders, *Islanders in the Stream*, vol. I, 74, 76, 93–4, 105, 113, 126; Malcolm, *History of the Bahamas House of Assembly*, 1–44.

[103] Bahamas Department of Archives, *Journal of the Lower House of Assembly.*

[104] Ibid., vol. I (1729 session), 10, 23. There are also very occasional *nemine contradicente* notations in the journal – another weak sign of majoritarianism.

evidence is spotty, they appear to have done so. Some even eventually developed a more strongly majoritarian institution than their English equivalent did. One of the two oldest post-Restoration colonies to do so was New Jersey. An assembly for the joint proprietorship of New Jersey that was in place from 1664 to 1674 met four times between 1668 and 1671.[105] After England retook New Jersey from the Dutch in 1674, the separate provinces of East and West New Jersey were established. East New Jersey held its first assembly under the new arrangement in 1675, and the assembly met with some frequency until the establishment of the single royal province of New Jersey in 1702.[106] Unfortunately, the records for the East New Jersey assemblies do not provide information on how it made decisions.[107] The West New Jersey Assembly met for the first time in 1681, but here again there is no record of the nature of its decision-making aside from the rules approved when it was established.[108] These rules are, however, somewhat illuminating. The assembly endorsed a strongly delegatory conception of representation for its 100 members from ten localities, thus encouraging majoritarianism. It also allowed individual members to request both roll calls and the entrance of formal protests and reasons for votes in the formal record. The only countervailing rule was the requirement of a supermajority for passing legislation.[109] Most questions put to the Assembly by the "chairman," with the exception of those for the passage of legislation, were to be "determined by plurality of votes." In addition, once debate had ended and a question had been put, "the doors of the house" were "to be set open, and the people have liberty to come in and hear, and be witnesses of the votes, and the inclinations of the persons voting."[110] This all suggests a broadly majoritarian environment.

These rules for West New Jersey also accord well with the better documented, twenty-four-member New Jersey House of Representatives, which met for the first time in November 1703. This connection supports the tentative conclusion that the New Jersey assemblies were strongly majoritarian (or in West Jersey, partly majoritarian and partly supermajoritarian) from the beginning. The early journals of the New Jersey House did not record the specific manner of decision-

---

[105] Pomfret, *Province of East New Jersey*, 83.   [106] Ibid., 107.
[107] See Leaming and Spicer, *Grants, Concessions, and Original Constitutions of New Jersey*, 77–140, 227–381; Whitehead (ed.), *Documents Relating to the Colonial History of the State of New Jersey*, 299–315, 354–63.
[108] See Leaming and Spicer, *Grants, Concessions, and Original Constitutions of New Jersey*, 423–587.
[109] Pomfret, *Province of West New Jersey*, 96.
[110] Leaming and Spicer, *Grants, Concessions and Original Constitutions of New Jersey*, 406–7.

making, but they apparently recorded unanimous votes with enough consistency to render it probable that voting was regularly majoritarian. Beginning in 1738 the House regularly used the roll calls mentioned in the original rules for West Jersey. Two years later it decided to allow roll calls at the request of any three members. The frequency of the roll calls from this point onward – nearly 500 of them between 1738 and 1775 – confirm that the House was strongly majoritarian by at least the 1740s.[111] From 1745 onward the House was dividing over one third of the time a question was put.[112]

While Carolina's general institutional path was in a sense the reverse of New Jersey's – it was established near the same time as a single proprietary colony but later divided into two – the development of its decision-making procedures appears to have been similar. The unicameral Carolina Parliament, obviously constructed on an English parliamentary model, first met in 1671. But no detailed record of its proceedings survives until the South Carolina Commons House of Assembly first met separately from the Council in 1692 and immediately set down proceedings in a journal.[113] On its fourth day in session the Commons approved rules that included a near replica of English Commons voting procedure: "in the assembly they are to vote by yeas and nays and if it be doubtful which of them is the greater number then the yeas to draw forth the noes are to stand still."[114] A rule from 1696, repeated in 1698 and in later years, suggests that when the question was put there may not have been a voice vote, but rather "the yeas are to stand up and the nays to sit down."[115] This was apparently almost always sufficient for the Speaker to determine the question by roughly enumerating votes, even when a vote was meaningfully majoritarian. We know this because while divisions were held on occasion from 1743, they were held only on extremely close votes, which almost always were ties decided by the Speaker or the vote of a single, ordinary member. In a small chamber, having the yeas stand was probably sufficient for confident enumeration

---

[111] Purvis, *Proprietors, Patronage, and Paper Money*, 112.

[112] This very conservative estimate was derived from the roll call total cited in Purvis, *Proprietors, Patronage, and Paper Money*, a manual removal of pre-1745 roll calls from that total, and a digital count of questions put drawn from explicit mentions of questions put in the House journals. Purvis' roll call total is itself a conservative figure; see the higher counts in Batinski, *New Jersey Assembly* and Newcomb, *Political Partisanship in the American Middle Colonies*.

[113] For the first parliament, see Cheves (ed.), *Shaftesbury Papers*, 337–8.

[114] Salley, Jr. (ed.), *Journal of the Commons House of Assembly of South Carolina … October 15, 1692*, 7.

[115] Ibid., 9; Salley, Jr. (ed.), *Journal of the Commons House of Assembly of South Carolina … 1698*, 9. See also a visitor's observation from 1773: Quincy, "A Journal," 452.

on nearly all occasions.[116] In part because of the nature of the procedure followed by the Commons, its journals are too ambiguous to permit precise estimates of the frequency of meaningfully majoritarian votes. It is nevertheless clear that South Carolina's lower assembly was accustomed to enumerating votes from its founding and did not use divisions in quite the same way as its English counterpart did.

The North Carolina General Assembly emerged from the Albemarle County Assembly. The Albemarle body met regularly from 1665, but detailed records of its proceedings have not survived. A lower house did not meet separately from the governor and council until the 1690s. The journal of North Carolina's lower house survives from 1725, shortly before it became a royal colony in 1728. The journal does not include detailed information on decision-making. In 1740 the journal noted the establishment of a rule of the House for divisions and recorded an enumerated vote.[117] An entry from 1754, concerning an election for speaker, strongly suggests that the House followed something close to English House of Commons procedure. "The question was put," the clerk wrote, "and on the House dividing there appeared an equality of votes," at which point one candidate conceded to the other. Another vote in 1754 was described as "carried by a majority," and such notation became common from this point onward.[118] In 1771 numerous roll calls were taken after motions by individual members; this occurred again in 1774.[119]

In January 1771 rules adopted by the House required that "on any motion being made and carried for putting the question on any bill or other matter, Mr. President shall immediately proceed to put the question and collect the suffrages of the House beginning with the junior members."[120] This suggests that all votes at this point would have been meaningfully majoritarian, or at least individualistic. The procedure specified here was similar to that followed by the British House of Lords. A division from 1774 clarifies that at least at this point, roll calls were sometimes requested after divisions. They were not, in other words, automatically conducted as a part of the voting procedure.[121] Only a small minority of decisions in the House were described as the result of questions put, and the most likely interpretation of this (aside from the conclusion that the journal was simply inconsistent) is that it was on

---

[116] For the first two divisions in 1743, see Easterby (ed.), *Colonial Records of South Carolina*, 197, 239.

[117] Saunders (ed.), *Colonial Records of North Carolina*, vol. IV, 504, 569.

[118] Ibid., vol. V, 233, 245; see also vol. V, 283; vol. VI, 389, 507.

[119] Ibid., vol. VIII, 422, 454; vol. IX, 144, 901–2, 930.   [120] Ibid., vol. VIII, 479a.

[121] Ibid., vol. IX, 930.

these occasions (and perhaps others) that there were enumerated major-ity votes.[122] This is confirmed by the fact that 87 percent of recorded questions put are followed by notation of a division or another major-itarian vote. On that index, the House divided 7 percent of the time it voted, or 8 percent of the time if one ignores sessions in which no questions put were noted. More probably, however, there is a great deal of inconsistent reporting at work here. The tentative conclusion for North Carolina, as for other colonies, has to be the very limited one that it had a majoritarian lower assembly before the American Revolution. Little else can be said on the chronological front.

The New York and Pennsylvania assemblies met for the first time almost concurrently, years after Carolina, in a second wave of post-Restoration, proprietary establishments. Elected delegates from Pennsylvania first gathered briefly in December 1682.[123] The assembly immediately adopted a detailed procedure closely modeled on the English House of Commons. On 4 December the assembly voted that when a question was put and there was a "diversity of votes arising in the House," two members were to "be elected to inspect which party carried it by the major votes." Another vote that day implied that this would be done according to an English-style division procedure. But without a clear provision for a voice vote in advance of the division, one has to assume that votes in this body were to be enumerated whenever a vote was not unanimous. The first formal General Assembly meeting (i.e., the Council and Assembly meeting concurrently) as specified in Pennsylvania's First Frame of Government began in March 1683. In the session that began on 12 March, during an early vote on whether to accept a request for a conference with the governor, "the number of votes was decided by beans, put into the balloting-box."[124] After this use of a secret ballot, in April, the Assembly approved the Second Frame of Government, and met under its provisions in May 1684. While the Assembly apparently continued to experiment in the 1680s with how to administer enumerated majority votes, it does seem to have already been committed to majoritarian decision-making, in keeping with practices that had become institutionalized in the English institution on which it was modeled.

---

[122] But see ibid., vol. IX, 144, where a decision was described simply as a resolution and then a roll call was made.

[123] Bronner, Penn's "Holy Experiment", 33–4.

[124] MacKinney and Hoban (eds.), Pennsylvania Archives, vol. I, 3, 15, 17; Bronner, Penn's "Holy Experiment", 33–4.

Whatever the Pennsylvania Assembly's precise decision-making procedures in the brief sessions of the seventeenth century, telling rules were adopted in 1703, after a powerful, unicameral, elected body, the House of Representatives, had been created in 1701. The rules clarified the House's commitment to enumerated majorities. "Upon debates, and passing of bills," read the rules, "the majority of votes shall govern." When the question was put, members were to stand and say "yea" or "nay." This appears to have been a switch to a more Lords-style procedure, which would of course have ensured enumerated voting.[125] That automatic enumeration was in fact already the practice seems confirmed by two unusual entries in the Assembly journal from 1700. In May, when a bill for extending the length of the session was "put to the vote," it was "carried in the affirmative, thirty-three yeas, three noes."[126] Roll calls recorded in 1754 also give the impression that enumerated votes were automatic.[127] This impression also corresponds to a January 1762 diary description of two successive votes. On the first, "the question being put ... the whole house arose to it except two members of Chester County," and then on the second vote, "the question being put ... the House was equally divided and the Speaker gave it a cast in the negative."[128] Here, however, the custom had changed slightly, since only members voting in the affirmative stood; they therefore had no need of voicing their votes. This practice was later codified in 1767 and 1774 statements of House rules.[129]

---

[125] MacKinney and Hoban (eds.), *Pennsylvania Archives*, vol. I, 405. For later confirmations of this rule, see, for example, vol. II, 1228 (in 1717), 1344 (in 1721).

[126] Ibid., vol. I, 234, 248 (a second example).

[127] Ibid., vol. V, 3690, 3692, 3693, 3694, 3701, 3726, 3727, 3728. Roll calls were also conducted on occasion in 1761, 1764, 1765, and, more commonly, between 1773 and 1776. For the first formal approval of this procedure as initiated on the request of any member, from January 1773, see vol. VIII, 6906 (this journal entry also included approval for weekly publishing of the "minutes of the proceedings of this Assembly"). In 1745 the Assembly was petitioned to publish roll calls for all votes, so "that [members'] constituents may be acquainted with their conduct." The petition was ordered to lie on the table (vol. IV, 3030).

[128] Foulke, "Pennsylvania Assembly in 1761–2," 411; see also 412, 413. None of these proceedings was noted the official journal, which is unusually sparse in this period.

[129] MacKinney and Hoban (eds.), *Pennsylvania Archives*, vol. VII, 6067; vol. VIII, 7156. The Assembly of the Lower Counties on the Delaware, which began to meet separately in 1704, left records that survive only from 1739 onward. This was a very small assembly in which counting votes was probably logistically automatic. Even though we have no detailed information on the frequency of majoritarian decisions, it is very likely that the House proceeded in a majoritarian fashion at least from the time that a journal was kept, because as early as 1740 rules agreed for the House specified that on every question put the names of all affirmatives and negatives were to be recorded. See *Minutes of the House of Assembly of the Three Counties upon Delaware*, entry for 10/21/ 1740. This is telling evidence even though this practice was not apparently always

The majoritarianism of the Pennsylvania General Assembly was not without its critics. In 1708 the Assembly was in conflict with the governor over the clause in the 1701 Charter of Privileges that required a meeting of the General Assembly to have two thirds of the possible number of representatives present in order to have full power of assembly. The Assembly claimed that this clause was superseded by the royal charter, which gave the colony power to enact legislation with the assent of the greater part of the freeholders' delegates. "By this clause," they claimed, "the law of majority is absolutely settled, as is usual in all such assemblies." In any case, they argued, "by the law which requires two thirds to make an Assembly, it has been generally understood, that a lesser number could not act legislatively; but never doubted till of late, that such as met were a House to adjourn from day to day till they had a quorum."[130] The concern here, in part, was with the majoritarian dominance of anti-governor (anti-proprietary, Quaker) elements in the Assembly. In a message to the House, the governor, George Thomas, wrote in August 1740 with regard to the question of war and the provision of armed defense for the colony that "though the majority of your House oppose all these things, I know there are some few of the same religious persuasion in it, and many out of it, who dislike all your proceedings." The Quaker party was guilty of working with constituents to "obtain an uncommon majority in this Assembly, to oppose my endeavors for the security of this part of his Majesty's dominions." He added that the Assembly's "own minutes will show the rest" of the Quaker party's majoritarian machinations.[131]

We have no information on decision-making in the early years of New York's Assembly, which first met soon after Pennsylvania's, in 1683. It met again in 1684 and 1685 before New York became part of the Dominion of New England. The main achievement of the Assembly's first session, the Charter of Liberties and Privileges, specified that "all persons chosen and assembled in manner aforesaid or the major part of them shall be deemed and accounted the representatives of this province." To this quorum provision the Charter added the stipulation that "all bills agreed upon by the said representatives or the major part of them shall be presented unto the Governor and his Council for their approbation and consent."[132] This probably reflects at least some initial comfort with majoritarian decision-making. The General Assembly next

---

followed in future sittings. The assembly very likely always enumerated votes when questions were put but recorded roll calls only on the request of members.

[130] MacKinney and Hoban (eds.), *Pennsylvania Archives*, vol. II, 1087–8.
[131] Ibid., vol. III, 2637.   [132] *Colonial Laws of New York*, vol. I, 112–13.

met in 1691, following the Glorious Revolution, Leisler's Rebellion, and the dissolution of James II's Dominion of New England. From this point onward the Assembly kept a journal that described its decision-making in only bare form. The only important early indicator of the General Assembly's procedures at that time is an April 1691 order "that upon all debates arising in this House, upon any matter or thing whatever, the determination thereof shall be concluded by majority of votes of the members present at the time of debate."[133]

In later years, the New York Assembly's journal recorded a number of explicitly majoritarian votes and, on occasion, vote tallies.[134] But none of this information allows for an estimate of the frequency of meaningfully majoritarian decisions. Beginning in 1737 the Assembly began to record roll calls. It did so ninety-nine times between 1737 and 1745, and 510 times over the course of the entire colonial period.[135] Perhaps because the Assembly journals were available to the public, the recording of roll calls was inconsistent in the period after 1745. But roll calls were frequent enough that majoritarian decision-making was clearly a familiar experience. The chamber itself was open to the public from 1769, and from then onward a large volume of roll call votes appeared in the journal: 216 in all between 1769 and 1775, some of which were explicitly linked to what the journal described as divisions.[136] The New York Assembly was thus clearly majoritarian on the eve of the Revolution and probably long before. Like the rest of the post-Restoration lower assemblies, its majoritarianism was very likely a foregone conclusion once its dominant institutional model, the English House of Commons, had itself become majoritarian.[137]

Later Arrivals: New Hampshire and Georgia

While New Hampshire's royal commission of 1679 established a separate lower assembly on its separation from Massachusetts, journal records of the assembly date only from 1711, and detailed records only from 1722. Orders of the House from 1699 for what were usually tiny, joint meetings of the council and assembly included a measure for allowing any member

---

[133] *Journal of the Votes and Proceedings of … New-York*, vol. I, 5.
[134] See, for instance, ibid., vol. I, 32, 33.
[135] Ibid., vol. I, 711 (first two roll calls); Squire, *Rise of the Representative*, 227; Newcomb, *Political Partisanship in the American Middle Colonies*, 217.
[136] Countryman, *People in Revolution*, 76; Squire, *Rise of the Representative*, 228.
[137] For a broader account of imitation of English traditions as the source of eighteenth-century legislative cultures in the colonies (albeit one focused on an English tradition of struggle between prerogative and liberty), see Greene, "Political Mimesis."

to register dissent from a vote without giving reasons for it. Such dissent occasionally appeared in the records.[138] While this indicates some comfort with majoritarian decision-making, the full lower house journal that dates from 1722 does not permit firm conclusions on the nature of the lower assembly's decision-making. There were usually fewer than twenty members in attendance. There are certainly frequent mentions of meaningfully majoritarian votes and some notation of unanimous votes, but the records are neither clear nor consistent enough to generalize about the frequency of majoritarian decisions. The language of "passed" and "voted" that dominated the text of the journal was, as we have seen, generally characteristic of the records of majoritarian bodies, and there is certainly no reason to think this assembly was an outlying, consensual body, especially given its origins in the government of Massachusetts.

The other major late addition to the constellation of legislatures in North America before the era of the American Revolution was Georgia's assembly. Originally a unicameral body, it first met in 1751, at the end of its proprietary period.[139] Georgia became a royal colony in 1754, and its first Commons House of Assembly met in January 1755. This was an institutionally weak body whose members were largely inexperienced in representative government. Originally an extension of the South Carolina Lowcountry, Georgia seems to have followed South Carolina in adopting a decision-making procedure very similar to that of the English House of Commons.[140] In 1755, however, because of problems with attendance, the House resolved to make decisions only with the unanimous consent of ten members – a majority of those entitled to sit in the House.[141] From late 1772 onward the House conducted some roll calls and published its minutes weekly. Roll calls were included in the minutes either on the demand of members who had made the motion under consideration or on the demand of a majority of the members.[142] From the time roll calls and other divisions were recorded, the House appears to have divided about 11 percent of the time per (recorded) question put between December 1772 and March 1774. It was by that time a somewhat weakly majoritarian institution, assuming that all its majoritarian decisions were being recorded. Before this point the journal's language is too imprecise to ascertain how decisions were being made.

---

[138] For the orders and examples, see Bouton (ed.), *Documents and Records Relating to the Province of New-Hampshire*, vol. III, 2, 19, 26, 68.

[139] Candler (ed.), *Colonial Records of the State of Georgia*, vol. I, 547, 557–60.

[140] For mentions of divisions, see, for example, ibid., vol. XV, 333.

[141] Ibid., vol. XIII, 24; see also 93, 481.

[142] Ibid., vol. XV, 345; for roll calls, see, for example, 350, 355–6.

The Rise of the Majority in America

As is perhaps most obvious in the cases of New Hampshire and Georgia, there are many gaps in our understanding of the development of decision-making in the lower assemblies of colonial America. Yet by scrutinizing the available evidence one is left with the overwhelming impression of a total embrace of majoritarian politics before the American Revolution, and in most cases, long before that time. Indeed, there is no definitive evidence that these colonial assemblies ever rejected majoritarian decision-making. Certainly, in none of the twenty-six American colonies under examination here is there any strong evidence of the persistence of consensual decision-making. To the extent that any majoritarianism in North America preceded that of the English House of Commons, it can be explained by the peculiarities of those lower assemblies with respect to the procedures and organization of their English counterpart. In particular, we have seen that the most likely source of precocious majoritarianism was a delegatory understanding of representation, which was itself the practical outgrowth of originally nonrepresentative bodies in which all freemen acted as individuals and governed directly. In this sense, apparently precocious assemblies such as Maryland's had more in common with the long-majoritarian English House of Lords than with the House of Commons.

In the late eighteenth century, as the colonial lower assemblies of North America became provincial congresses and then state lower assemblies, they predictably continued their majoritarian practices. The heightened constitutional and political status of these bodies could not in itself reverse what were now thoroughly institutionalized practices. Nor is there any indication that the primacy of unity under revolutionary and early national conditions prompted the deinstitutionalization of majority decision-making. The prevalence of majority rule in the many provincial congresses and early state conventions is clear from existing records.[143]

---

[143] See, for example, Bushman et al. (eds.), *Proceedings of the Assembly of the Lower Counties on Delaware 1770–1776*, 202–31; *Proceedings of the Conventions of the Province of Maryland*, 167–378. Many journals do not provide clear evidence but also offer no reasons to doubt the continuation of majority rule. See, for example, *Journal of the Proceedings of the Provincial Congress of North-Carolina*; Candler (ed.), *Revolutionary Records of the State of Georgia*, vol. I, 229–82; *Journals of the Provincial Congress of Massachusetts in 1774 and 1775*; Bouton (ed.), *Documents and Records Relating to the Province of New-Hampshire*, vol. VII; Bouton (ed.), *Documents and Records Relating to the State of New-Hampshire during the Period of the American Revolution*; *Minutes of the Provincial Congress and the Council of Safety of the State of New Jersey*, 169–255 (New Jersey's congress apparently voted by county: see 206–7, 231–2); *Journals of the Provincial Congress ... State of New-York*, vol. I (New York also apparently voted by

State legislatures, too, used the colonial assemblies as their institutional models.[144] They all predictably embraced majoritarian decision-making in the process.[145]

The most important final chapter of the American branch of the story of the rise of majority rule concerns the emergence of national representative assemblies comparable to the British House of Commons, and, eventually, the emergence of the US House of Representatives. By the mid-eighteenth century, once the colonial lower assemblies had all apparently become majoritarian in nature, the first intercolonial assemblies – from the Albany Congress of 1754 to the Stamp Act Congress of 1765 – were launched as novel experiments in political representation. At the Stamp Act Congress, the fact that there were unequal numbers of representatives from each colony led the delegates to vote as whole colonies on all occasions, with the exception of the choice of a chairman. Voting proceeded from the north to the south after each colony's delegation had deliberated internally on what the colony's single vote would be. It is unclear how delegates from an individual colony determined that colony's vote. In formal terms, at least, the procedure embraced by these congresses was a revival of the dominant form of voting in the republican assemblies of ancient Rome. But it is not clear that the delegates thought of their experiment in this way.[146]

The Continental Congress adopted a largely identical procedure under the initial assumption that its duration, like that of the Stamp Act Congress, would be brief. Decisions were made by the vote of a majority of the colonies, and the vote of each individual colony was determined by the votes of a majority among its delegates. If a colony had a tie vote, this was noted in the journal, and the colony did not have a

county: see, for example, vol. I, 8); *Minutes of the Proceedings of the Convention of the State of Pennsylvania; Extracts from the Journals of the Provincial Congress of South-Carolina.*

[144] Squire, *Evolution of American Legislatures*, 87.

[145] See, for example, *Journal of the House of Commons. State of North Carolina; Votes and Proceedings of the House of Delegates of the State of Maryland; Votes and Proceedings of the General Assembly of the State of New-Jersey; Votes and Proceedings of the Assembly of the State of New-York ... 1779; Votes and Proceedings of the Assembly of the State of New-York ... 1780.* More ambiguous examples include *A Journal of the Honorable House of Representatives of the Commonwealth of Massachusetts;* Bouton (ed.), *Documents and Records Relating to the State of New-Hampshire; Early State Papers of New Hampshire; Minutes of the First Session of the Fourth General Assembly of the Commonwealth of Pennsylvania* (this does, however, include roll calls; it is simply unclear if some votes were nonenumerated when no roll call was included); *At the General Assembly of the Governor and Company of the State of Rhode-Island and Providence Plantations;* Bushman et al. (eds.), *Journal of the House of Delegates of Virginia ... 1776; Proceedings of the House of Assembly of the Delaware State,* 94–185.

[146] Weslager, *The Stamp Act Congress,* 124–5, 198. Historians of neither the Stamp Act Congress nor the Continental Congress have remarked on this similarity.

role in the intercolonial vote. Again, delegates voted by colony and north to south; and within each colony, they voted in order of seniority. Individuals voted by voice and then their votes were tallied. The Continental Congress was not, of course, a sovereign or national body, so there is no reason to suspect, on the basis of what we know about the House of Commons, that a new barrier to majoritarian procedures would have developed here in any case. The procedures used predictably reflected deference to the already majoritarian individual colonies from which the delegates came.

Despite the fact that the Congress was kept in being by the outbreak of an international conflict, the delegates never reconsidered the body's basic institutional procedures. This meant that the procedures of the Congress remained fundamentally different from the procedures of both the colonial lower assemblies and the British House of Commons. As was the case in the Stamp Act Congress, the "one colony, one vote" procedure of the Congress was decided on after some voice votes on preliminary matters partly because individual colonies had varying numbers of delegates.[147] The Congress also lacked the information necessary to weight each colony's voting according to population and wealth. Aside from this crucial aspect of procedure, an adapted form of House of Commons rules prevailed, as it had in the colonial lower assemblies. These rules were readopted at the meeting of the second Congress in 1775. The votes of the Congress from 1777, when roll calls were recorded for the first time, were also, as one might expect, meaningfully majoritarian. A quarter of the votes were decided by a single state, and individual colony votes decided by a single delegate occurred even more frequently than they occurred at the intercolonial level.[148]

The majoritarianism of the Stamp Act, Continental, and Confederation Congresses was in the end overdetermined, dictated by the practices of its two main sources of precedent: the colonial (and state) lower assemblies and the British House of Commons. The majoritarianism of these early Congresses was perpetuated in the federal House of Representatives, established by the constitution ratified in 1789.[149] Here, however, there was a clear return to more familiarly British practices. In the House's first session, business began to be conducted in earnest in April 1789, and on 7 April, a committee named to draft standing rules

[147] Delegate numbers had not been determined in advance of the Congress meeting.
[148] Jillson and Wilson, *Congressional Dynamics*, esp. 43–4, 46, 51–3, 56–8, 63, 65, 142–5. Two supermajority standards for state votes (seven votes and nine votes) were adopted in 1781 (143).
[149] For an introduction, see Bowling and Kennon (eds.), *Inventing Congress*, 29–105, 138–65.

and orders made a report. The committee's draft rules and orders opened with directions for the Speaker, which included a procedure for voice votes and divisions that was nearly identical to traditional House of Commons procedure in Britain.[150] The House of Representatives retained this procedure in the following century, and its majoritarian commitments only deepened. In 1811, for instance, a rule was established that allowed majorities to use the previous question as a means of ending debate. This opened the door to further rule changes forced by a majority in order to solidify its control over the House. At this point, majority decision-making and party politics were in a relationship of mutual augmentation. By the early nineteenth century, the US House of Representatives was well on its way to establishing itself as a fiercely majoritarian and partisan body, in keeping with the character of its uniquely influential predecessor in Britain.[151] The ferociously partisan politics of the antebellum United States, like the precociously partisan politics of the British House of Commons, were made possible by the institution of majority voting – a prior and more fundamental reality of American political practice that took shape in particular circumstances over the course of the seventeenth and eighteenth centuries.[152]

[150] Claussen (ed.), *Journal of the House of Representatives*, vol. I, 9–10. From May, voters on each side of the question were individually identified when a division occurred and a count was called for by a fifth of the members present (45).

[151] Binder, "Partisanship and Procedural Choice"; Fink, "Representation by Deliberation."

[152] The massive literature on factional, partisan, and party politics in colonial, revolutionary, and antebellum American politics does not consider the fact that majority decision-making was a historically specific precondition for the institutionalization of party politics. For the earlier periods, see, for example, Tully, *Forming American Politics*; Main, *Political Parties before the Constitution*.

8   Conclusion

The rise of the majority in early modern England's House of Commons was a fundamental and apparently permanent transformation of the way the representatives of the people made decisions for the nation. Nearly the only scholars even partly aware of this transformation to date have been political theorists, who have been struck and fascinated for decades by the "adversary revolution" in later seventeenth-century political thought.[1] What has gone unnoticed by theorists, historians, and scientists alike, however, is that this intellectual revolution appears to have mostly been a republication and ratification of a revolution in practice. The strands of normatively majoritarian discourse that can be found in later seventeenth-century political writing, while hardly unimportant, mostly recorded, schematized, and reduced to universals what began as complex and historically specific transformations in particular practices and institutions.[2]

In the winter of late 1679 and early 1680, for instance, when John Locke wrote the *Second Treatise on Government*, he simply accepted what was already evident in the parliamentary politics of the present.[3] "When any number of men have so consented to make one community or

---

[1] Mansbridge, *Beyond Adversary Democracy*, 3–16, quotation on 8.

[2] For analogous findings on the relationship between political practice and political thinking in midcentury on other fronts, see Peacey, *Print and Public Politics in the English Revolution*; Zaret, *Origins of Democratic Culture*, esp. 266–70.

[3] Thomas Hobbes' 1642 commentary on majority decision-making in *De Cive* registered its practical necessity as an available procedure for making decisions affecting the entire *civitas* while denying that it was a natural practice. See Hobbes, *On the Citizen*, 77–8, 89 (VI.2–3, 20). This was consistent with traditional practice and norms in the House of Commons. It did not address the crucial points at issue over the course of the seventeenth century with regard to consensual norms. *Leviathan* (1651) addressed majority decisions only in the context of the institution of a sovereign power, but made essentially the same point as Hobbes had made in *De Cive*. See Hobbes, *Leviathan*, vol. II, 264, 265, 268, 269. Hobbes also discussed majority rule in the context of democracy, but this was not of course related to English practice. Hobbes may nevertheless have been influenced by contemporary developments in practice in all of his discussions of majority decision-making.

government," he explained, "they are thereby presently incorporated, and make one body politic, wherein the majority have a right to act and conclude the rest."[4] Majority rule was for Locke not the result of a structural transformation that had begun when he was a child, but rather the essence of any government once formed. Knowingly or not, he had transformed a historical peculiarity into an inevitability.

When men made a political community, Locke claimed, they automatically subjected themselves to majority rule. To deny this was to ensure the immediate paralysis and destruction of that community. Elaborating on the hallowed discourse of the body politic, Locke contended that those who institute a political community "have thereby made that community one body, with a power to act as one body, which is only by the will and determination of the majority." Locke hereby overturned the traditional identification of unity with consensus or unanimity. He asserted instead that only by being ruled by the majority could a political body remain whole. He supported this assertion with an analogy to corporeal mechanics. "For that which acts any community," he continued, "being only the consent of the individuals of it, and it being necessary to that which is one body to move one way; it is necessary the body should move that way whither the greater force carries it, which is the consent of the majority." Otherwise, he reiterated, it was "impossible it should act or continue one body, one community, which the consent of every that united into it, agreed that it should; and so every one is bound by that consent to be concluded by the majority." In other words, the association between unity and majority rule was so strong that by consenting to acting as one body, each member of the community had consented to majority rule. This general reality, Locke insisted, was evident in historical particulars. "Therefore we see," he observed, "that in assemblies empowered to act by positive laws where no number is set by that positive law which impowers them, the act of the majority passes for the act of the whole, and of course determines, as having by the law of nature and reason, the power of the whole."[5]

Up to this point in his discussion, Locke had merely sought to establish the necessity of majority decisions for the basic integrity of the polity. But he went on to specify how the nature of political deliberation ensured the ubiquity of majoritarian decisions. "If the consent of the majority shall not in reason, be received, as the act of the whole, and conclude every individual; nothing but the consent of every individual can make any thing to be the act of the whole." Such consensus, however, was for

---

[4] Locke, *Two Treatises of Government*, 349 (§95).   [5] Ibid., 349–50 (§96).

Locke "next impossible ever to be had, if we consider the infirmities of health, and avocations of business, which in a number, though much less than that of a common-wealth, will necessarily keep many away from the public assembly." Attendance aside, however, the consent of each individual was in practice still impossible to procure because of "the variety of opinions and contrariety of interests, which unavoidably happen in all collections of men." A constitution that required universal consent "would make the mighty Leviathan of a shorter duration, than the feeblest creatures."[6]

A relatively sanguine observer of the parliamentary politics of his day, Locke expressed confidence that the acceptance of political division and recourse to majority rule was the precondition for both unity and the very survival of the state. His entire argument was based on a specific definition of consensus, the false dilemma between majority rule and unanimity that definition implied, and, it seems, more than a little historical amnesia. Locke's discussion erased more than a century of recent English political history. Only thirty years earlier, it had been the emergence of *majority* decision-making that had quite clearly led to the mighty Leviathan's temporary demise. And in the century before the English Revolution, an insistence on the achievement of basic consensus and the presence of a majority voting procedure for moments when consensus either failed or was deemed unnecessary had helped keep the English polity in being. Locke's argument entirely ignored the possibility of such a subtle arrangement. In the face of his country's honored traditions and history, he simply accepted and took for granted the deliberative conditions of the Exclusion Crisis–era House of Commons. If parliamentary debate was no longer capable of shaping the "opinions" and thereby forming, unifying, or sidelining the "interests" of members, plurality in preferences and majoritarian decisions would indeed "unavoidably" result. By skillfully rendering the particularity of his day a universal and wrapping this maneuver in an updated version of the traditional metaphor of the body politic, Locke helped to begin the process by which the modern world would come to assume that there was something natural about majority decision-making in politics.

In this book I have tried to resist Locke's false dilemmas and historical erasures and reintroduce majority rule as a historical problem. Doing so also recasts majority rule as a political problem. The partly contingent transformation of parliamentary decision-making in the early modern British empire was an event of world-historical importance. Largely because

---

[6] Ibid., 350–1 (§98). For a somewhat different and more extended discussion, see Kendall, *John Locke and the Doctrine of Majority-Rule*, esp. 112–19.

of the institutional continuity and global dominance of the governments of Britain and the United States in the nineteenth and twentieth centuries, most democracies in the modern world have inherited the English empire's majoritarian revolution along with the theoretical naturalization and myth-making that accompanied it. This revolution was not the only European development in the history of majority rule to have momentous global consequences in the modern era. A comprehensive global history of major-ity decisions in national, representative institutions has yet to be written. But the basic outlines of that history are clear enough, and they confirm the centrality of developments in early modern Britain and its empire.

France and Spain, in particular, also had profound effects on the modern history of representative government. More than a century after Britain, both countries acquired their own majoritarian representative institutions. These emergent traditions were then transferred in varying proportions to a series of postcolonial polities during the protracted breakup of the Spanish and French empires. The primary catalyst for all this, of course, was the French Revolution. Majority decision-making in French popular assemblies began suddenly with the meeting of the Estates General and the formation of the National Assembly in June 1789. In the Estates General, the third estate, like the nobility and clergy, immediately adopted routine, enumerated majority voting, and this practice continued in the National Assembly.[7] Similar regimes of repre-sentative decision-making appeared elsewhere across the continent under the influence of French aggression and expansion from the 1790s onward. Over the course of the late eighteenth, nineteenth, and twentieth centuries, the former colonies and dependencies of the British, French, and Iberian empires all embraced majority decision-making in representative assemblies.[8]

Largely as a result of these developments and the broader influence of Britain and the United States in twentieth-century geopolitics, the twenty-first century world lives with the legacy of a seventeenth-century transformation. For this reason, among many others, the rise of the majority in early modern England and America merits serious appreci-ation and consideration from students of modern politics. Today major-itarian institutions and the party systems founded on them are associated with a series of grave political maladies, from governmental gridlock to the oppression of minorities. Nearly all of these maladies worried

---

[7] Mavidal and Laurent (eds.), *Archives parlementaires de 1787 à 1860*, ser. 1, vol. VIII, passim. See also Gueniffey, "Les assemblées et la représentation."

[8] For an introduction to salient developments in nineteenth-century Latin America, see Posada-Carbó (ed.), "Congresses versus *Caudillos.*"

observers of majoritarian politics from its infancy. In particular, early moderns experienced and identified the threat that majority rule posed to the role of rational, informed argument and inclusion in national decision-making. These are the same essential threats associated with the populist variant of majority rule today, and with the corruption of representative democracies more generally.[9]

At the same time, we face the strange irony that paralysis and persecution were also to a large extent the primary *causes* of the majority vote's initial emergence as a common practice in the English House of Commons. In 1641, majority votes became a more familiar experience partly because minorities saw forced divisions as a way of registering their dissent from what they believed were the disastrous decisions of a desperate majority faction. And two years later, majoritarian decisions became utterly commonplace because members of the House could not agree on how to shoulder the excruciating burden of both executive action and negotiation with an anointed monarch who had declared war on them.

This initially puzzling relationship between the pitfalls of modern majoritarian government and the character of its predecessor can be sorted out only with a precise analysis of the transition from one institution to the other. It is only on a finer level of detail, made visible by the slow-motion account of the 1640s at the core of this book, that the exact significance of this transformation becomes discernible. In the House of Commons, majority decision-making replaced a deliberative, disputative, honor-bound regime of decision-making defended with recourse to the traditional metaphors of the body politic. This was a fundamentally consensual institution, but not in the sense that it eliminated political conflict or rested on the existence of an ideological consensus. Its workings were more subtle. Under this regime of decision-making, political conflict was channeled, displaced, sometimes hidden, and often resolved. This was a system of deliberation in which truth was to be discerned through the application of learning and wisdom in rhetoric and disputation, and through the utilization of mechanisms – such as conferences and committees – by which the search for truth could be prolonged or a confrontation with division delayed.

However laudable we might find some of the ideals and fictions of pre-revolutionary, consensual decision-making, the preceding analysis makes clear that we would be mistaken in adopting a nostalgic attitude toward the predecessor to majority rule, if only because of the similarities

---

[9] See, e.g., Rosenfeld, *Democracy and Truth*; Urbinati, *Democracy Disfigured*; Urbinati, *Me the People*; Mounk, *The People vs. Democracy*.

between the two institutions. The distinguishing norms and practices of the pre-revolutionary House of Commons certainly merit the interest of today's students of politics, many of whom are trying to imagine more deliberative forms of democracy as alternatives to the adversarial, majoritarian, and discursively deficient politics of so many contemporary representative democracies.[10] But it is equally important to recognize that when majority decision-making displaced consensus decision-making in the representative assemblies of England and its empire, what occurred was the substitution of an institution characterized by inequality, conflict, coercion, hierarchy, and exclusion for another, fundamentally different institution that nonetheless exhibited these same general characteristics.

It is also important to keep in mind that the transition between the two institutions hardly required a quantum intellectual leap. In the traditional regime of Commons practice, majority decision-making, like democracy, was easily conceivable but eminently undesirable. This is what explains the resonance of both ancient and early modern commentaries on majority rule with contemporary critiques of democratic government. Early moderns took majoritarian decisions as signs of the failure of debate, the absence of the wisdom (and for some, at least, the divine grace) that enabled consensus, and the tyranny of faction or party. These decisions reflected poorly upon the deliberative abilities of the assembly and its members, and threw suspicion upon the Commons' commitment to the public good. Every meaningfully majoritarian vote in the pre-revolutionary House of Commons made a mockery of the claim of the House and its members to represent a single people, nation, and commonwealth. Divisions, in particular, ritualized this mockery and the impotence and illegitimacy it suggested. And yet the early modern critique of majority decision-making is not an adequate guide to its emergence. The key to explaining its emergence, as we have seen, is an appreciation of the intense and vigilant status consciousness of the early modern British political elite. The convulsions of the 1640s regularly led to situations in which the Commons was confronting perceived (and normally external) threats to the honor and privileges of the House and its members that far outweighed the undesirable status consequences of the division procedure itself. It was in these moments that the House was forced into majority decisions by the same logic that usually prevented them. That logic was a logic of status.

As these moments proliferated during the Civil Wars and Revolution, the resulting flurry of majoritarian decisions destroyed the status and

---

[10] For an introduction, see Fishkin and Mansbridge (eds.), "The Prospects and Limits of Deliberative Democracy."

legitimacy of the Commons and Parliament more generally, insofar as that status and legitimacy had been based on consensus decision-making. This resulted in another series of developments with modern resonances. The institution of consensus decision-making became self-undermining under the conditions of the early 1640s. It gradually became less and less important, in general, for members to continue to help the House maintain what had become a Sisyphean struggle to act as a united body. To the extent that this occurred, and the status significance of consensus decreased, consensus politics was likely to fail in a still wider set of situations in the future. Eventually, it was the effects of a particular decision that came to matter most, not how that decision was reached. This instrumental perspective would ultimately prevail even in political moments when the status of Parliament and its members was not obviously at issue. It was at this point, when consensual decisions had mostly lost their normative significance, that majoritarian decision-making had clearly become institutionalized.

In the medium term, however, the majoritarian takeover of Parliament triggered what appear in retrospect to have been a series of modern objections to majority rule gone wrong. Most important among these was what eventually amounted to a *minoritarian* revolution against the perceived illegitimacy of the new, disturbing pattern in national decision-making. What had begun in the early 1640s with protests against crucial divisions such as the vote on Strafford's attainder culminated in late 1648 with what is now a familiar spectacle: the armed takeover of a representative institution by agents of a minority faction who had come to see the majoritarian domination of the assembly as tyrannical and viewed themselves as the true representatives of the people. Despite its immediate production of minoritarian revolts, however, majoritarian politics outlasted the resistance it triggered. The pattern of purging Parliament that began in the late 1640s and continued into the 1650s led, of course, neither to minority decision-making nor to the reestablishment of consensus politics, but to a series of doomed experiments in using purges to turn parliamentary minorities into parliamentary majorities supposedly acting in the true interest of the commonwealth. In this way the practice of majority voting continued and even gained traction during a succession of protests and armed revolts against it, revolts that culminated in the restoration of the monarchy.

As majority voting persisted, members of the Commons gradually developed a broader majoritarian repertoire. The dismantling of consensus politics opened the door to a series of tactical innovations that had a series of extremely important consequences, including the remaking of parliamentary legitimacy along majoritarian lines. On an organizational level, the institutionalization of majority decision-making removed normative barriers to the development of an array of coordination tactics aimed at the securing of majorities. These tactics transformed the deliberative environment in the Commons. Debate was aimed no longer at securing a wide consensus but rather a narrower majority. This transformed the relationship between Commons debate and provision for the common good, because that common good no longer had to be specified with appeal to as wide a spectrum of opinion. The continued elaboration of such tactics eventually gave rise to party politics. It is crucial to recognize that both the institutionalization of majoritarian decision-making and its elaboration in an embryonic party politics occurred during the reigns of Charles II and James II. On this fundamental political terrain, at least, the Restoration era was a crucial moment. Yet as such this period was neither a stark break from a revolutionary past nor fundamentally different in character from the revolutionary future. Instead, it witnessed the continuation and consolidation of Civil War–era transformations of practical politics and the creative extension of these transformations into the forms of party-political organization typically associated with British politics in the wake of the Glorious Revolution.[11]

As England took its majoritarian turn, the miniature Houses of Commons in England's colonies found themselves in much the same position. On the other side of the Atlantic, the rise of majority rule occurred more quickly and quietly, because, in terms of both conventional practices and political status, less was at stake in the transition. This was true in a variety of senses, and the details are dependent on the historical particulars of the colony in question. Most American assemblies and their procedures became institutionalized, of course, after Parliament itself had abandoned consensual decision-making. Any American assembly in this position that was eager to emulate Westminster was unlikely to invite controversy when it embraced majority voting. The assemblies that predated the English Civil Wars or the Restoration-era institutionalization of majority voting in the House of Commons were similarly inclined to quickly embrace majoritarianism, but for different reasons. In general, the corporate or proprietary tradition of governance according to which these assemblies were originally instituted was far more conducive to majority decision-making than the Tudor and early Stuart parliamentary tradition.

---

[11] For a similar conclusion about the relationship between the English Revolution and the Restoration era on different topical terrain, see Peacey, *Print and Public Politics in the English Revolution*, 394–413.

In particular, the corporate and proprietary traditions did not normally foster a strong commitment to discretionary representation. Representatives strongly beholden to the initial wishes of their constituents were poorly positioned to engage in the consensus-building, compromise, and capitulation that could result in nonmajoritarian decisions. The nonparliamentary traditions from which these colonies often drew are also closely related to the second major factor that conduced to majority decision-making in the colonial assemblies: their original impotence and relative lack of symbolic significance. The public matters decided in the infancy of the American lower assemblies were in general more akin to the private bills that had always been subject to enumerated majority votes in Parliament than they were to public bills. They had no clear relation to a sovereign national unity, even if they were the work of a body politic. Finally, even to the extent that parliamentary traditions governed the early practices of these assemblies, as they very often did, the members of these assemblies were generally not, especially in the seventeenth century, the same sorts of men who populated the House of Commons. Consensus decision-making in the Commons was made possible in part by the rhetorical and dialectical skill of the members, qualities that were relatively rare in the colonies. Thus the practical repertoire of consensus decision-making was relatively absent in America as well.

By the later eighteenth century, the colonial lower assemblies of North America had acquired significant political power, symbolic gravity, and deliberative sophistication. It was these assemblies that provided part of the template for creating the national lower assembly of the United States. Under different circumstances the characteristics acquired by these assemblies before the American Revolution might in themselves have helped sustain and strengthen consensual decision-making, as had been the case with the House of Commons in early Stuart England. But American elected assemblies had generally adopted majority rule long before their rise to political significance, and they were entirely unlikely to turn back the institutional clock, especially in a moment when parliamentarian notions of virtual and discretionary representation had become so troubling to them.

What had emerged in both Britain's House of Commons and the US House of Representatives by the early nineteenth century, and what would emerge over the following two centuries in scores of other national assemblies across the globe, was a new way of acting and deciding as a nation. The institution of majority rule quickly acquired fictions of unity and public interest to address its imperfections and contradictions, just as its predecessor had. These even included the occasional unanimous decision in grave political circumstances, and widespread provisions for supermajorities in the case of constitutional amendments and a variety of other important decisions. These practices are themselves evidence that the dilemmas readily identified at the infancy of majoritarian politics by concerned seventeenth-century observers persist. These dilemmas are often most visible and most troubling, of course, in the very spaces where it has proven necessary for democratic polities occasionally to succumb to the persistent impulse to employ fictions of unity. These latter-day fictions range from the willing reconciliation of majority and minority to an implicit faith in the wisdom of a major part that, from the moment it becomes the major part, has no need to defend its preferences or its actions, unless an attentive electorate stands ready to pass judgment.

Bibliography

Manuscripts and Other Archival Materials Cited

Bahamas Department of Archives, Nassau

The Journal of the Lower House of Assembly of the Bahama Islands, 6 vols. (Nassau: Nassau Guardian, 1910–13).

Bodleian Library, Oxford

MSS Carte 34–5	Correspondence and papers of the duke of Ormond
MS Dep.f.9	Parliamentary diary of Seymour Bowman
MS Rawl.D.932	Parliamentary diary of Sir John Holland
MS Tanner 66	Letters and papers, 1641

British Library, London

IOR B/13	East India Company Court Minutes
MS Add 4180	Papers of Sir Edward Nicholas
MS Add 5138	Parliamentary diary of Guybon Goddard
MS Add 11045	Newsletters
MS Add 12426	Jamaica assembly minutes (extracts)
MS Add 12428	Account of the constitution of the Jamaica Assembly
MS Add 12430	Jamaica journal of William Beeston
MSS Add 18777–80	Parliamentary diary of Walter Yonge
MS Add 24667	Satirical poem on Parliament, 1646
MS Add 26644	Henry Elsynge tract on passage of bills in Parliament
MS Add 31116	Parliamentary diary of Laurence Whitaker
MS Add 31954	History of the Long Parliament by Sir Edward Nicholas
MS Add 33468	Parliamentary diurnal
MS Add 36856	Treatise on parliamentary procedure
MS Add 36916	John Starkey newsletters
MS Add 47145	Parliamentary diurnal
MS Add 64807	Parliamentary journal
MS Add 64922	Papers of Sir John Coke
MS Egerton 2043	Parliamentary diary of Bullen Reymes

MS Egerton 2395	Papers on English colonies in America, West Indies
MS Egerton 2539	Correspondence and papers of Sir Edward Nicholas
MSS Harley 164–6	Parliamentary diary of Sir Simonds D'Ewes
MS Harley 390	Newsletters
MSS Harley 483–4	Latin diary of Sir Simonds D'Ewes
MS Harley 1058	Papers on parliamentary affairs
MS Sloane 1467	Parliamentary proceedings

Connecticut State Library, Hartford

Connecticut General Assembly, Journals of the Lower House

Durham University Library, Durham

| MS MSP 30 | Parliamentary diurnal |

London Metropolitan Archives, London

Microfilm X109/072	London Court of Common Council
Ms 5257/4–5	Barber-Surgeons Court Minutes
Ms 16967/4	Ironmongers Company Court Minutes

National Archives, Kew

CO 9	Antigua assembly records
CO 31	Barbados assembly records
CO 140	Jamaica assembly records
CO 155	Leeward Islands assembly records
CO 177	Montserrat assembly records
CO 186	Nevis assembly records
CO 241	St. Christopher assembly records
SP 105/148	Levant Company General Court Minutes

Parliamentary Archives, London

| HC/CL/JO/1 | Manuscript journals of the House of Commons |

Yale University Archives, New Haven

| MS 1987 | Partial transcript of British Library MSS Harley 163–6 |

Printed and Digital Primary Sources Cited

Ancient Journals of the House of Assembly of Bermuda from 1691 to 1785, 4 vols. (Bermuda: Gregory V. Lee, Waterlow and Sons, 1890–1906).

Archives of Maryland, 72 vols. (Baltimore: Maryland Historical Society, 1888–1972).

Anon., *The Declaration of the Lords and Commons of Parliament Assembled at Oxford* (Oxford: Leonard Lichfield, 1643 [March 1644]; Wing E1356B).

The Heads of Severall Proceedings in This Present Parliament from the 22 of November, to the 29. 1641 (London: John Thomas, 1641).

A Particular Charge or Impeachment in the Name of His Excellency Sir Thomas Fairfax and the Army under His Command (London: George Whittington, 1647).

A Test, Offered to the Consideration of the Electors of Great Britain (London: F. Burleigh, 1714).

Baker, Philip (ed.), *Proceedings in Parliament 1624: The House of Commons* (British History Online, 2015–18), *British History Online*, www.british-history.ac.uk/no-series/proceedings-1624-par.

Bateson, Mary (ed.), *Records of the Borough of Leicester*, 4 vols. (Cambridge: Cambridge University Press, 1905–23), vol. III (1905).

Bidwell, William B., and Maija Jansson (eds.), *Proceedings in Parliament 1626*, 4 vols. (New Haven: Yale University Press, 1991–6).

Birch, Thomas (ed.), *A Collection of the State Papers of John Thurloe, Esq.*, 7 vols. (London: Thomas Woodward, Charles Davis, et al., 1742).

Bouton, Nathaniel (ed.), *Documents and Records Relating to the Province of New-Hampshire*, 7 vols. (Concord: State Printers, 1867–73).

Documents and Records Relating to the State of New-Hampshire during the Period of the American Revolution (Concord: Edward A. Jenks, 1874).

Browning, Andrew (ed.), *English Historical Documents 1660–1714* (New York: Oxford University Press, 1953).

Bruce, John (ed.), *Verney Papers* (London: Camden Society, 1845).

Bushman, Claudia L., Harold B. Hancock, and Elizabeth Moyne Homsey (eds.), *Proceedings of the Assembly of the Lower Counties on Delaware 1770–1776, of the Constitutional Convention of 1776, and of the House of the Assembly of the Delaware State, 1776–1781* (Newark: University of Delaware Press, 1986).

Proceedings of the House of Assembly of the Delaware State 1781–1792 and of the Constitutional Convention of 1792 (Newark: University of Delaware Press, 1988).

Candler, Allen D. (ed.), *Colonial Records of the State of Georgia*, 25 vols. (Atlanta: Franklin, 1904–16).

The Revolutionary Records of the State of Georgia, 3 vols. (Atlanta: Franklin-Turner Company, 1908).

Charles I, *His Majesties Answer, to a Book, Intituled, The Declaration, or Remonstrance of the Lords and Commons, the 19 of May 1642* (Cambridge: Roger Daniel, 1642).

[Chestlin, Robert], *Persecutio Undecima* (London: s.n., 1648; Wing 3785).

Cheves, Langdon (ed.), *The Shaftesbury Papers* (Charleston: South Carolina Historical Society, 1897).

Cicero, Marcus Tullius, *On the Republic and On the Laws*, David Fott (ed.) (Ithaca: Cornell University Press, 2014).

Clarendon, Edward, Earl of, *History of the Rebellion and Civil Wars in England*, William Dunn Macray (ed.), 6 vols. (Oxford: Oxford University Press, 1888).

Claussen, Martin P. (ed.), *The Journal of the House of Representatives: George Washington Administration 1789–1797* (Wilmington, DE: Michael Glazier, 1977).

Coates, Wilson H. (ed.), *The Journal of Sir Simonds D'Ewes from the First Recess of the Long Parliament* ... (New Haven: Yale University Press, 1942).

Coates, Wilson H., Anne Steele Young, and Vernon F. Snow (eds.), *The Private Journals of the Long Parliament*, 3 vols. (New Haven: Yale University Press, 1982–92).

Colonial Laws of New York from the Year 1664 to the Revolution, 5 vols. (Albany: James B. Lyon, 1896).

Cope, Esther, and Wilson Coates (eds.), *Proceedings of the Short Parliament of 1640*, Camden 4th Series (London: Royal Historical Society, 1977).

Dewar, Mary (ed.), *De Republica Anglorum by Sir Thomas Smith* (Cambridge: Cambridge University Press, 1982).

D'Ewes, Simonds (ed.), *The Journals of All the Parliaments during the Reign of Queen Elizabeth* (London: Paul Bowes and John Starkey, 1682).

Early State Papers of New Hampshire, Including the Constitution of 1784 ... (Manchester: John B. Clarke, 1891).

Easterby, J. H. (ed.), *The Colonial Records of South Carolina: The Journal of the Commons House of Assembly: September 14, 1742–January 27, 1744* (Columbia: South Carolina Archives Department, 1954).

Extracts from the Journals of the Provincial Congress of South-Carolina ... *1775* (Charleston: Peter Timothy, 1776).

Foster, Elizabeth Read (ed.), *Proceedings in Parliament 1610*, 2 vols. (New Haven: Yale University Press, 1966), vol. I.

Foulke, Samuel, "The Pennsylvania Assembly in 1761–2," *Pennsylvania Magazine of History and Biography*, 8 (1884), 407–13.

Gardiner, S. R. (ed.), *The Constitutional Documents of the Puritan Revolution 1625–1660*, 3rd ed. (Oxford: Clarendon Press, 1951).

At the General Assembly of the Governor and Company of the State of Rhode-Island and Providence Plantations (n.p., 1776).

Greene, Jack (ed.), *The Diary of Colonel Landon Carter of Sabine Hall, 1752–1778*, 2 vols. (Charlottesville: University Press of Virginia, 1965).

Grey, Anchitell, *Debates of the House of Commons, from 1667 to 1694*, 10 vols. (London: T. Beckett and P. A. De Hondt, 1769).

Hakewill, William, *The Manner How Statutes Are Enacted in Parliament by Passing of Bills* (London: John Benson, 1641).

Hartley, T. E. (ed.), *Proceedings in the Parliaments of Elizabeth I*, 2 vols. (Leicester: Leicester University Press, 1995).

Henning, B. D. (ed.), *The Parliamentary Diary of Sir Edward Dering, 1670–1673* (New Haven: Yale University Press, 1940).

An Historical Account of the Sessions of Assembly ... *Which Began on Tuesday the 23rd of September 1755* (London: n.p., 1757).

Hoadly, Charles J. (ed.), *Records of the Colony and Plantation of New Haven, from 1638 to 1649* (Hartford: Case, Tiffany and Company, 1857–8).

Hobbes, Thomas, *Leviathan*, 3 vols., Noel Malcolm (ed.) (Oxford: Oxford University Press, 2012).

On the Citizen, Richard Tuck and Michael Silverthorne (eds.) (Cambridge: Cambridge University Press, 1998).

Hobson, M. G., and H. E. Salter (eds.), *Oxford Council Acts 1626–1665* (Oxford: Oxford University Press, 1933).

House of Commons, *Journals*, 17 vols. (London: H. M. Stationery Office, 1742).

House of Lords, *Journals*, 19 vols. (London: H. M. Stationery Office, 1767).

[Hyde, Edward], *A Complaint to the House of Commons, and Resolution Taken up by the Free Protestant Subjects of the Cities of London and Westminster, and the Counties Adjacent* (Oxford: Leonard Lichfield, 1642; Wing C5623A).

Interesting Tracts Relating to the Island of Jamaica (St. Jago de la Vega: Lewis, Lunan, and Jones, 1800).

Jansson, Maija (ed.), *Proceedings in Parliament 1614* (Philadelphia: American Philosophical Society, 1988).

Proceedings in the Opening Session of the Long Parliament, 7 vols. (Rochester: University of Rochester Press, 2000–7).

Jansson, Maija, and William B. Bidwell (eds.), *Proceedings in Parliament 1625* (New Haven: Yale University Press, 1987).

Johnson, Robert, Mary Frear Keeler, Maija Jansson Cole, and William B. Bidwell (eds.), *Proceedings in Parliament 1628*, 6 vols. (New Haven: Yale University Press, 1977–83).

A Journal of the Honorable House of Representatives of the Commonwealth of Massachusetts … Twenty-Sixth Day of May, Anno Domini, 1784 (Boston: Adams and Nourse, 1784).

Journal of the House of Commons. State of North Carolina … 14th Day of April, in the Year of Our Lord 1778 (n.p., 1778).

Journal of the House of Delegates of Virginia … 1776 (Williamsburg: Alexander Prudie, 1779).

The Journal of the Proceedings of the Provincial Congress of North-Carolina … 1776 (New Bern: James Davis, 1776).

Journal of the Votes and Proceedings of the General Assembly of the Colony of New-York, 2 vols. (New York: Hugh Gaine, 1744–6).

Journals of the Assembly of Jamaica, 14 vols. (Jamaica: A. Aikman and John Lunan, 1811–29).

The Journals of the House of Commons of the Kingdom of Ireland, 19 vols. (Dublin: House of Commons, 1796–1800).

Journals of the House of Representatives of Massachusetts, 55 vols. (Boston: Massachusetts Historical Society, 1919–90).

The Journals of the Provincial Congress of Massachusetts in 1774 and 1775 … (Boston: Dutton and Wentworth, 1838).

Journals of the Provincial Congress … State of New-York (Albany: Thurlow Tweed, 1842).

Juxon, Thomas, *Journal*, Keith Lindley and David Scott (eds.), Camden 5th Series (Cambridge: Cambridge University Press, 1999), vol. XIII.

Kingsbury, Susan M. (ed.), *Records of the Virginia Company of London*, 4 vols. (Washington, DC: Government Printing Office, 1906–35).

Larkin, James F. (ed.), *Stuart Royal Proclamations, vol. II: Royal Proclamations of King Charles I 1625–1646* (Oxford: Oxford University Press, 1983).

Leaming, Aaron, and Jacob Spicer, *The Grants, Concessions, and Original Constitutions of New Jersey* (Philadelphia: W. Bradford, 1758).

Lefroy, J. Henry (ed.), *The Historye of the Bermudaes or Summer Islands* (London: Hakluyt Society, 1882).

Memorials of the Discovery and Early Settlement of the Bermudas or Somers Islands 1511–1687, 2 vols. (London: Longmans, Green, 1877–9).

Locke, John, *Two Treatises of Government*, 2nd ed., Peter Laslett (ed.) (Cambridge: Cambridge University Press, 1967).

Long, Edward, *The History of Jamaica*, 3 vols. (London: T. Lowndes, 1774).

MacKinney, Gertrude, and Charles F. Hoban (eds.), *Pennsylvania Archives*, 8th ser., 8 vols. (1931–5).

Maltby, Judith M. (ed.), *The Short Parliament Diary (1640) of Sir Thomas Aston*, Camden 4th Series (London: Royal Historical Society, 1988), vol. XXXV.

Marvell, Andrew, *Poems and Letters*, H. M. Margoliouth (ed.), 2 vols. (Oxford: Oxford University Press, 1927).

Mavidal, Jérôme, and Emile Laurent (eds.), *Archives parlementaires de 1787 à 1860*, 82 vols. (Paris: Librairie Administrative de Paul Dupont, 1867–1913).

McIlwaine, H. R. (ed.), *Journals of the House of Burgesses of Virginia, 1619–1776*, 13 vols. (Richmond: Colonial Press, 1905–15).

Mercurius Aulicus (Oxford: William Webb, 1643–5).

Minutes of the First Session of the Fourth General Assembly of the Commonwealth of Pennsylvania (n.p., 1779).

Minutes of the House of Assembly of the Three Counties upon Delaware at Sessions Held at New Castle in the Years 1740–1742 (Wilmington: Public Archives Commission of Delaware, 1929).

Minutes of the Proceedings of the Convention of the State of Pennsylvania ... 1776 (Philadelphia: Henry Miller, 1776).

Minutes of the Provincial Congress and the Council of Safety of the State of New Jersey (Trenton: Naar, Day and Naar, 1879).

Morrison, Alfred (ed.), *Collection of Autograph Letters and Historical Documents*, Second Series (1882–93), the Bulstrode Papers, vol. I (1667–75) (privately published, 1897).

Notestein, Wallace, and Frances Helen Relf (eds.), *Commons Debates for 1629* (Minneapolis: University of Minnesota Press, 1921).

The Parliamentary or Constitutional History of England, 24 vols. (London: Thomas Osborne and William Sandby, 1751–61).

Perfect Occurrences of Both Houses of Parliament (London: Jane Coe, 1644– 7).

Penington, Isaac, Jr., *The Fundamental Right, Safety and Liberty of the People* (London: Giles Calvert, 1651).

Proceedings of the Conventions of the Province of Maryland ... 1774, 1775, 1776 (Baltimore: James Lucas and E. K. Deaver, 1836).

[Prynne, William], *A Brief Iustification of the XI. Accused Members* (London: s.n., 1647; Wing 2nd P3908).

Quincy, Josiah, Jr., "A Journal," *Proceedings of the Massachusetts Historical Society*, 3rd ser., 49 (1915–16), 424–81.

Records of the Parliaments of Scotland, www.rps.ac.uk.

Reresby, Sir John, *Memoirs*, Andrew Browning (ed.) (Glasgow: Jackson, Son, 1936).

Robbins, Caroline (ed.), *The Diary of John Milward* (Cambridge: Cambridge University Press, 1938).

Roberts, Clayton (ed.), "Sir Richard Temple's Discourse on the Parliament of 1667–1668," *Huntington Library Quarterly*, 20 (1957), 137–44.

Rutt, John Towill (ed.), *Diary of Thomas Burton*, 4 vols. (London: H. Colburn, 1828).

Salley, A.S., Jr. (ed.), *Journal of the Commons House of Assembly of South Carolina for the Session Beginning September 20, 1692, and Ending October 15, 1692* (Columbia: Historical Commission of South Carolina, 1907).

   Journal of the Commons House of Assembly of South Carolina for the Two Sessions of 1698 (Columbia: Historical Commission of South Carolina, 1914).

Salter, H. E. (ed.), *Oxford Council Acts 1583–1626* (Oxford: Oxford University Press, 1928).

Saunders, William L. (ed.), *The Colonial Records of North Carolina*, 26 vols. (Raleigh: Trustees of the Public Libraries, 1886–1907).

Schilling, W. A. H. (ed.), "The Parliamentary Diary of Sir John Gell, 5 February–21 March 1659," MA thesis, Vanderbilt University (1961).

Scott, Walter (ed.), *A Collection of Scarce and Valuable Tracts*, 13 vols. (London: T. Cadell et al., 1809–15).

Scrope, R., and T. Monkhouse (eds.), *State Papers Collected by Edward, Earl of Clarendon*, 3 vols. (Oxford: Clarendon Printing House, 1767–86).

Shilstone, E. M. (ed.), "Some Records of the House of Assembly of Barbados," *Journal of the Barbados Museum and Historical Society*, 10 (1943), 173–87.

Shurtleff, Nathaniel B. (ed.), *Records of the Governor and Company of the Massachusetts Bay in New England*, 5 vols. (Boston: William White, 1853–4).

Sims, Catherine (ed.), "'Policies in Parliaments': An Early Seventeenth-Century Tractate on House of Commons Procedure," *Huntington Library Quarterly*, 15 (1951), 45–58.

   "The Speaker of the House of Commons," *American Historical Review* 45 (1939), 90–5.

Snow, Vernon F. (ed.), *Parliament in Elizabethan England: John Hooker's* Order and Usage (New Haven: Yale University Press, 1977).

Steig, Margaret (ed.), *The Diary of John Harington, M.P., 1646–53* (Yeovil: Somerset Record Society, 1977).

Stevenson, W. H. (ed.), *Records of the Borough of Nottingham*, 8 vols. (Nottingham: Thomas Forman and Sons, 1882–1952), vol. IV (1889).

Stocks, Helen (ed.), *Records of the Borough of Leicester*, 4 vols. (Cambridge: Cambridge University Press, 1905–23), vol. IV (1923).

Thucydides, *The War of the Peloponnesians and the Athenians*, Jeremy Mynott (ed. and trans.) (Cambridge: Cambridge University Press, 2013).

Townshend, Heywood (ed.), *Historical Collections, or, An Exact Account of the Proceedings of the Four Last Parliaments of Q. Elizabeth* (London: T. Basset, W. Crooke, and W. Cademan, 1680).

Trumbull, J. Hammond (ed.), *The Public Records of the Colony of Connecticut*, 15 vols. (Hartford: Brown and Parsons, 1850–85).

Turner, Silvie J. (ed.), *Journal Kept by William Williams of the Proceedings of the Lower House of the Connecticut General Assembly May 1757 Session* (Hartford: Connecticut Historical Society, 1975).

Vinaya Texts Translated from the Pali: The Kullavagga, IV–XII, T. W. Rhys Davids and Hermann Oldenberg (trans.), in F. Max Müller (ed.), *The Sacred Books of the East*, 50 vols. (Oxford: Clarendon Press, 1885), vol. XX.

Votes and Proceedings of the Assembly of the State of New-York … 1779 (Fish-Kill: Samuel Loudon, 1779).

Votes and Proceedings of the Assembly of the State of New-York … 1780 (Fish-Kill: Samuel Loudon, 1780).

Votes and Proceedings of the General Assembly of the State of New-Jersey (Trenton: Isaac Collins, 1779).

Votes and Proceedings of the House of Delegates of the State of Maryland … June Session, 1777 (n.p., 1777).

Weslager, C. A. (ed.), *The Stamp Act Congress: With an Exact Copy of the Complete Journal* (Newark: University of Delaware Press, 1976).

Whitehad, William A. (ed.), *Documents Relating to the Colonial History of the State of New Jersey*, 10 vols. (Newark, NJ: Daily Advertiser Printing House, 1880), vol. I.

Wilson, David Harriss (ed.), *The Parliamentary Diary of Robert Bowyer, 1606–1607* (Minneapolis: University of Minnesota Press, 1931).

Secondary Sources Cited

Achen, Christopher, and Larry Bartels, *Democracy for Realists: Why Elections Do Not Produce Responsive Government* (Princeton: Princeton University Press, 2016).

Adamson, John, *The Noble Revolt: The Overthrow of Charles I* (London: Weidenfeld and Nicolson, 2007).

"The Triumph of Oligarchy: The Management of War and the Committee of Both Kingdoms, 1644–1645," in Chris R. Kyle and Jason Peacey (eds.), *Parliament at Work: Parliamentary Committees, Political Power and Public Access in Early Modern England* (Woodbridge: Boydell, 2002), 101–27.

Aldrich, John H., "Political Parties in and out of Legislatures," in R. A. W. Rhodes, Sarah A. Binder, and Bert A. Rockman (eds.), *The Oxford Handbook of Political Institutions* (Oxford: Oxford University Press, 2006), 555–76.

Why Parties? A Second Look (Chicago: University of Chicago Press, 2011).

Armitage, David, and Jo Guldi, *The History Manifesto* (Cambridge: Cambridge University Press, 2014).

Bailyn, Bernard, *The Origins of American Politics* (New York: Vintage, 1967).

Baker, Nicholas Scott, "Discursive Republicanism in Renaissance Florence: Deliberation and Representation in the Early Sixteenth Century," *Past and Present*, 225 (2014), 47–77.

Batinski, Michael C., *The New Jersey Assembly, 1738–1775: The Making of a Legislative Community* (Lanham, MD: University Press of America, 1987).

Baty, Thomas, "The History of Majority Rule," *Quarterly Review*, 430 (1912), 1–28.

Baydal Sala, Vicent, "Voting in the Parliaments of the Crown of Aragon, c. 1300–1716," in Serena Ferente, Lovro Kunčević, and Miles Pattenden (eds.), *Cultures of Voting in Pre-Modern Europe* (New York: Routledge, 2018), 274–89.

Beeman, Richard R. *The Varieties of Political Experience in Eighteenth-Century America* (Philadelphia: University of Pennsylvania Press, 2004).

Bellany, Alastair, and Thomas Cogswell, *The Murder of King James I* (New Haven: Yale University Press, 2015).

Bennett, J. H., "The English Caribbees in the Period of the Civil War, 1642–1646," *William and Mary Quarterly* 24 (1967), 359–77.

Billings, Warren M., *A Little Parliament: The Virginia General Assembly in the Seventeenth Century* (Richmond: Library of Virginia, 2004).

Binder, Sarah A., "Partisanship and Procedural Choice: Institutional Change in the Early Congress, 1789–1823," *The Journal of Politics*, 57 (1995), 1093–118.

Borah, Woodrow, "Representative Institutions in the Spanish Empire of the Sixteenth Century: The New World," *The Americas*, 12 (1956), 246–57.

Bosher, Robert S., *The Making of the Restoration Settlement: The Influence of the Laudians, 1649–1662* (New York: Oxford University Press, 1951).

Bourdieu, Pierre, *The Logic of Practice*, Richard Nice (trans.) (Stanford: Stanford University Press, 1990).

  Outline of a Theory of Practice, Richard Nice (trans) (Cambridge: Cambridge University Press, 1977).

  Practical Reason: On the Theory of Action (Stanford: Stanford University Press, 1998).

Bourdieu, Pierre, and Loïc Wacquant, *An Invitation to Reflexive Sociology* (Chicago: University of Chicago Press, 1992).

Bourke, Richard, and Quentin Skinner (eds.), *Popular Sovereignty in Historical Perspective* (Cambridge: Cambridge University Press, 2016).

Bowling, Kenneth R., and Donald R. Kennon (eds.), *Inventing Congress: Origins and Establishment of the First Federal Congress* (Athens: Ohio University Press, 1999).

Braddick, Michael J., *God's Fury, England's Fire: A New History of the English Civil Wars* (London: Allen Lane, 2008).

Brenner, Robert, *Merchants and Revolution: Commercial Change, Political Conflict, and London's Overseas Traders, 1550–1653* (Cambridge: Cambridge University Press, 1993).

Bronner, Edwin B., *William Penn's "Holy Experiment": The Founding of Pennsylvania, 1681–1701* (New York: Columbia University Press, 1961).

Brown, Keith M., and Alan R. MacDonald (eds.), *The History of the Scottish Parliament: Parliament in Context, 1235–1707* (Edinburgh: Edinburgh University Press, 2010).

Brown, Keith M., and Alastair J. Mann (eds.), *Parliament and Politics in Scotland, 1567–1707* (Edinburgh: Edinburgh University Press, 2005).

Browning, Andrew, "Parties and Party Organization in the Reign of Charles II," *Transactions of the Royal Historical Society*, 30 (1948), 21–36.

Thomas Osborne, Earl of Danby and Duke of Leeds, 1632–1712, 3 vols. (Glasgow: Jackson, Son, 1951).

Bulman, William J., "Consensual Conflict in the Early Stuart House of Commons," in William J. Bulman and Freddy Dominguez (eds.), *Political and Religious Practice in the Early Modern British World* (Manchester: Manchester University Press, forthcoming).

"The Practice of Politics: The English Civil War and the 'Resolution' of Henrietta Maria and Charles I," *Past and Present* 206 (February 2010), 43–79.

Bulman, William J., with Freddy Dominguez, "Introduction," in William J. Bulman and Freddy Dominguez (eds.), *Political and Religious Practice in the Early Modern British World* (Manchester: Manchester University Press, forthcoming).

Burgess, Glenn, *The Politics of the Ancient Constitution: An Introduction to English Political Thought, 1603–1642* (University Park: Pennsylvania State University Press, 1992).

Calder, Isabel MacBeath, *The New Haven Colony* (New Haven: Yale University Press, 1943).

Carsten, F. L., *Princes and Parliaments in Germany: From the Fifteenth to the Eighteenth Century* (Oxford: Oxford University Press, 1959).

Casey, James, *The Kingdom of Valencia in the Seventeenth Century* (Cambridge: Cambridge University Press, 1979).

Clarke, Aidan, "The History of Poynings' Law, 1615–41," *Irish Historical Studies*, 18 (1972–1973), 207–22.

Cogswell, Thomas, "The Canterbury Election of 1626 and *Parliamentary Selection* Revisited," *Historical Journal* 63 (2020), 291–315.

Como, David R., *Radical Parliamentarians and the English Civil War* (Oxford: Oxford University Press, 2018).

Countryman, Edward, *People in Revolution: The American Revolution and Political Society in New York, 1760–1790* (Baltimore: Johns Hopkins University Press, 1981).

Cox, Gary W., *The Efficient Secret: The Cabinet and the Development of Political Parties in Victorian England* (Cambridge: Cambridge University Press, 1987).

Cox, Gary W., and Matthew D. McCubbins, *Legislative Leviathan: Party Government in the House*, 2nd ed. (Cambridge: Cambridge University Press, 2007).

Craton, Michael, and Gail Saunders, *Islanders in the Stream: A History of the Bahamian People* (Athens: University of Georgia Press, 1999).

Craven, Wesley Frank, *Dissolution of the Virginia Company: The Failure of a Colonial Experiment* (Oxford: Oxford University Press, 1932).

Cust, Richard, "Politics and the Electorate in the 1620s," in Richard Cust and Ann Hughes (eds.), *Conflict in Early Stuart England: Studies in Religion and Politics 1603–1642* (London: Longman, 1989), 134–67.

Cuttica, Cesare, and Markku Peltonen (eds.), *Democracy and Anti-Democracy in Early Modern England 1603–1689* (Leiden: Brill, 2019).

Davies, Godfrey, and Edith Lucile Klotz, "List of Members Expelled from the Long Parliament," *Huntington Library Quarterly*, 2 (1939), 479–88.

Davis, Nicholas Darnell, *The Cavaliers and Roundheads of Barbados* (Demerara: Argosy Press, 1883).

De Beer, E., "Members of the Court Party in the House of Commons, 1670–1678," *Bulletin of the Institute of Historical Research*, 11 (1933–4), 1–23.

De Dios, Salustanio, "El funcionamiento interno de las Cortes de Castilla durante los siglos XVI y XVII. Las ordenanzas de votar (primera parte)," *Revista de las Cortes Generales*, 24 (1991), 185–274.

De Krey, Gary S., *London and the Restoration 1659–1683* (Cambridge: Cambridge University Press, 2005).

Dennehy, Coleman A., *The Irish Parliament, 1613–89: The Evolution of a Colonial Institution* (Manchester: Manchester University Press, 2019).

Downs, Jordan, "The Attempt on the Seven Londoners," *English Historical Review*, 135 (2020), 541–71.

Edwards, Goronwy, "The Emergence of Majority Rule in the Procedure of the House of Commons," *Transactions of the Royal Historical Society*, 5th series, 14 (1964), 175–96.

Elliott, J. H., *The Revolt of the Catalans: A Study in the Decline of Spain (1598–1640)* (Cambridge: Cambridge University Press, 1963).

Elton, G. R., *The Parliament of England 1559–1581* (Cambridge: Cambridge University Press, 1986).

Studies in Tudor and Stuart Politics and Government, 2 vols. (Cambridge: Cambridge University Press, 1977).

Ermakoff, Ivan, "Theory of Practice, Rational Choice, and Historical Change," *Theory and Society*, 39 (2010), 527–53.

Evans, Geoffrey, "Ancient Mesopotamian Assemblies," *Journal of the American Oriental Society*, 78 (1958), 1–11.

"Ancient Mesopotamian Assemblies: An Addendum," *Journal of the American Oriental Society*, 78 (1958), 114–15.

Ferejohn, John, "Rationality and Interpretation: Parliamentary Elections in Early Stuart England," in Kristen Renwick Monroe (ed.), *The Economic Approach to Politics: A Critical Reassessment of the Theory of Rational Action* (New York: HarperCollins, 1991), 279–305.

Fink, Evelyn C., "Representation by Deliberation: Changes in the Rules of Deliberation in the U.S. House of Representatives, 1789–1844," *The Journal of Politics*, 62 (2000), 1109–25.

Fishkin, James S., and Jane Mansbridge (eds.), "The Prospects and Limits of Deliberative Democracy," *Daedalus*, 146 (2017), 6–166.

Fletcher, Anthony, *The Outbreak of the English Civil War* (London: Edward Arnold, 1981).

Gaunt, Peter, "Oliver Cromwell and His Protectoral Parliaments: Co-operation, Conflict, and Control," in Ivan Roots (ed.), *"Into Another Mould": Aspects of the Interregnum*, 2nd ed. (Exeter: University of Exeter Press, 1998), 70–100.

Gil, Xavier, "Crown and Cortes in Early Modern Aragon: Reassessing Revisionisms," *Parliaments, Estates and Representation*, 13 (1993), 109–22.

Glow, Lotte, "The Committee of Safety," *English Historical Review*, 80 (1965), 289–313.

"The Manipulation of Committees in the Long Parliament," *Journal of British Studies*, 5 (1965), 31–52.

Goody, Jack, *The Theft of History* (Cambridge: Cambridge University Press, 2006).

Gragg, Larry, *Englishmen Transplanted: The English Colonization of Barbados, 1627–1660* (Oxford: Oxford University Press, 2003).

Graves, Michael A. R., *The House of Lords in the Parliaments of Edward VI and Mary I* (Cambridge: Cambridge University Press, 1981).

"Managing Elizabethan Parliaments," in David M. Dean and Norman L. Jones (eds.), *The Parliaments of Elizabethan England* (Oxford: Blackwell, 1990), 37–63.

Greene, Jack P., "Political Mimesis: A Consideration of the Historical and Cultural Roots of Legislative Behavior in the British Colonies in the Eighteenth Century," *American Historical Review*, 75 (1969), 337–60.

The Quest for Power: The Lower Houses of Assembly in the Southern Royal Colonies 1689–1776 (Chapel Hill: University of North Carolina Press, 1963).

Greif, Avner, *Institutions and the Path to the Modern Economy: Lessons from Medieval Trade* (Cambridge: Cambridge University Press, 2006).

Greif, Avner, and Christopher Kingston, "Institutions: Rules or Equilibria?," in N. Schofield and G. Caballero (eds.), *The Political Economy of Institutions, Democracy and Voting* (Berlin: Springer Berlin Heidelberg, 2011), 13–43.

Greif, Avner, and David Laitin, "A Theory of Endogenous Institutional Change," *American Political Science Review*, 98 (2004), 633–52.

Grever, John H., "Committees and Deputations in the Assemblies of the Dutch Republic, 1600–1668," *Parliaments, Estates and Representation*, 1 (1981), 13–33.

"The Structure of Decision-Making in the States General of the Dutch Republic, 1660–68," *Parliaments, Estates and Representation*, 2 (1982), 125–53.

Gueniffey, Patrice, "Les assemblées et la représentation," in Colin Lucas (ed.), *The French Revolution and the Creation of Modern Political Culture, vol. II: The Political Culture of the French Revolution* (Oxford: Pergamon, 1988), 233–57.

Halliday, Paul, *Dismembering the Body Politic: Partisan Politics in England's Towns, 1650–1730* (Cambridge: Cambridge University Press, 1998).

Hanham, H. J., *Elections and Party Management: Politics in the Time of Disraeli and Gladstone* (London: Longmans, Green, 1959).

Harlow, Vincent T., *A History of Barbados, 1625–1685* (Oxford: Oxford University Press, 1926).

Harris, Tim, *Politics under the Later Stuarts: Party Conflict in a Divided Society 1660–1715* (London: Longman, 1993).

Hayden, J. Michael, "Deputies and *Qualités*: The Estates General of 1614," *French Historical Studies*, 3 (1964), 507–24.

Hayton, David, *The House of Commons 1690–1715*, 5 vols. (Cambridge: Cambridge University Press, 2002), vol. I.

Hayward, Alasdair, *The House of Commons 1509–1558: Personnel, Procedure, Precedent and Change* (Oxford: Wiley-Blackwell, 2016).

Hébert, Michel, *Parlementer: Assemblées représentatives et échange politique en Europe occidentale à la fin du Moyen Age* (Paris: Éditions de Boccard, 2014).

Heinberg, John Gilbert, "History of the Majority Principle," *The American Political Science Review* 20 (1926), 52–68.

Henning, Basil Duke, *The House of Commons 1660–1690*, 3 vols. (London: Secker and Warburg, 1983), vol. I.

Hexter, J. H., *The Reign of King Pym* (Cambridge, MA: Harvard University Press, 1941).

Higham, C. S. S., *The Development of the Leeward Islands under the Restoration, 1660–1688: A Study of the Foundations of the Old Colonial System* (Cambridge: Cambridge University Press, 1921).

"The General Assembly of the Leeward Islands," *English Historical Review*, 41 (1926), 190–209.

Hirst, Derek, "Concord and Discord in Richard Cromwell's House of Commons," *English Historical Review*, 103 (1988), 339–58.

The Representative of the People? Voters and Voting under the Early Stuarts (Cambridge: Cambridge University Press, 1975).

Hodges, Vivienne Jill, "The Electoral Influence of the Aristocracy, 1604–1641," PhD dissertation, Columbia University (1977).

Holmes, Geoffrey, *British Politics in the Age of Anne*, 2nd ed. (London: Hambledon, 1987).

Hoppit, Julian, *Britain's Political Economies: Parliament and Economic Life, 1660–1800* (Cambridge: Cambridge University Press, 2017).

(ed.), *Failed Legislation 1660–1800* (London: Hambledon Press, 1997).

Hoyle, David, "A Commons Investigation of Arminianism and Popery in Cambridge on the Eve of the Civil War," *Historical Journal*, 29 (1986), 419–25.

Isakhan, Benjamin, and Stephen Stockwell (eds.), *The Edinburgh Companion to the History of Democracy* (Edinburgh: Edinburgh University Press, 2012).

The Secret History of Democracy (Houndmills, Basingstoke: Palgrave, 2011).

Jacobsen, Thorkild, *Toward the Image of Tammuz and Other Essays on Mesopotamian History and Culture*, William L. Moran (ed.) (Cambridge, MA: Harvard University Press, 1970).

James, Mervyn, *Society, Politics and Culture: Studies in Early Modern England* (Cambridge: Cambridge University Press, 1986).

James, Sydney V., *The Colonial Metamorphoses in Rhode Island: A Study of Institutions in Change* (Hanover, NH: University Press of New England, 2000).

Jarvis, Michael, *In the Eye of All Trade: Bermuda, Bermudians, and the Maritime Atlantic World* (Chapel Hill: University of North Carolina Press, 2012).

Jillson, Calvin, and Rick K. Wilson, *Congressional Dynamics: Structure, Coordination, and Choice in the First American Congress, 1774–1789* (Stanford: Stanford University Press, 1994).

Jones, Clyve (ed.), *Britain in the First Age of Party 1680–1750: Essays Presented to Geoffrey Holmes* (London: Hambledon Press, 1987).

Jones, J. R., "Political Groups and Tactics in the Convention of 1660," *Historical Journal*, 6 (1963), 159–77.

Jones, Mary Jeanne Anderson, *Congregational Commonwealth: Connecticut 1636–1662* (Middletown, CT: Wesleyan University Press, 1968).

Jordan, David W., *Foundations of Representative Government in Maryland, 1632–1775* (Cambridge: Cambridge University Press, 1987).

Kane, Brendan, *The Politics and Culture of Honour in Britain and Ireland, 1541–1641* (Cambridge: Cambridge University Press, 2010).

Keeler, Mary Frear, *The Long Parliament, 1640–1641: A Biographical Study of Its Members* (Philadelphia: American Philosophical Society, 1954).

Kelly, James, *Poynings' Law and the Making of Law in Ireland, 1660–1800* (Dublin: Four Courts Press, 2007).

Kelly, Paul, "Constituents' Instructions to Members of Parliament in the Eighteenth Century," in Clyve Jones (ed.), *Party and Management in Parliament, 1660–1784* (New York: St. Martin's Press, 1984), 169–89.

Kendall, Willmoore, *John Locke and the Doctrine of Majority-Rule* (Urbana: University of Illinois Press, 1965).

Kenyon, J. P. (ed.), *The Stuart Constitution: Documents and Commentary* (Cambridge: Cambridge University Press, 1966).

Kershaw, R. N., "The Recruiting of the Long Parliament, 1645–7," *History*, 8 (1923), 169–79.

Kishlansky, Mark, "Consensus Politics and the Structure of Debate at Putney," *Journal of British Studies*, 20 (1981), 50–69.

"The Emergence of Adversary Politics in the Long Parliament," *Journal of Modern History*, 49 (1977), 617–40.

Parliamentary Selection: Social and Political Choice in Early Modern England (Cambridge: Cambridge University Press, 1986).

The Rise of the New Model Army (Cambridge: Cambridge University Press, 1979).

Kloppenberg, James, *Toward Democracy: The Struggle for Self-Rule in European and American Thought* (Oxford: Oxford University Press, 2016).

Knights, Mark, *Politics and Opinion in Crisis, 1678–81* (Cambridge: Cambridge University Press, 1994).

Representation and Misrepresentation in Later Stuart Britain: Partisanship and Political Culture (Oxford: Oxford University Press, 2005).

Koenigsberger, H. G., *Estates and Revolutions: Essays in Early Modern European History* (Ithaca: Cornell University Press, 1971).

Politicians and Virtuosi: Essays in Early Modern History (London: Hambledon, 1986).

Kyle, Chris, *Theater of State: Parliament and Political Culture in Early Stuart England* (Stanford: Stanford University Press, 2012).

Lake, Peter, and Steve Pincus (eds.), *The Politics of the Public Sphere in Early Modern England* (Manchester: Manchester University Press, 2007).

"Rethinking the Public Sphere in Early Modern England," *Journal of British Studies*, 45 (2006), 270–92.

Lambert, Sheila, "The Opening of the Long Parliament," *Historical Journal* 27 (1984), 265–87.

Langdon, George D., *Pilgrim Colony: A History of New Plymouth* (New Haven: Yale University Press, 1974).

Larsen, Mogens Trolle, *The Old Assyrian City-State and Its Colonies* (Akademisk Forlag: Copenhagen, 1976).

Lawrence, Jon, and Miles Taylor (eds.), *Party, State and Society: Electoral Behaviour in Britain since 1820* (Aldershot: Scolar Press, 1997).

Leng, Tom, "'Citizens at the Door': Mobilizing against the Enemy in Civil War London," *Journal of Historical Sociology*, 81 (2015), 26–48.

Lindley, Keith, *Popular Politics and Religion in Civil War London* (Aldershot: Scolar Press, 1997).

Lipset, Seymour Martin, and Stein Rokkan (eds.), *Party Systems and Voter Alignments: Cross-National Perspectives* (New York: Free Press, 1987).

Little, Patrick, and David L. Smith, *Parliaments and Politics during the Cromwellian Protectorate* (Cambridge: Cambridge University Press, 2007).

Lorenzana de la Puente, Felipe, *La representación política en el Antiguo Régimen: Las Cortes de Castilla, 1655–1834* (Madrid: Congreso de los Diputados, 2013).

Macdonald, Alan, "Deliberative Processes in Parliament c. 1567–1639: Multicameralism and the Lords of the Articles," *Scottish Historical Review*, 81 (2002), 23–51.

"Voting in the Scottish Parliament before 1639," *Parliaments, Estates and Representation*, 30 (2010), 150–61.

MacIntosh, Gillian, *The Scottish Parliament under Charles II, 1660–1685* (Edinburgh: Edinburgh University Press, 2007).

Mack, Peter, *Elizabethan Rhetoric: Theory and Practice* (Cambridge: Cambridge University Press, 2002).

Madan, Falconer, *Oxford Books*, 3 vols. (Oxford: Oxford University Press, 1895–1931).

Maddicott, J. R., *The Origins of the English Parliament, 924–1327* (Oxford: Oxford University Press, 2010).

Mahony, Michael P., "The Presbyterian Party in the Long Parliament, 2 July 1644– 3 June 1647," D.Phil. thesis, University of Oxford (1973).

Main, Jackson Turner, *Political Parties before the Constitution* (Chapel Hill: University of North Carolina Press, 1973).

Maitland, F. W., *Township and Borough* (Cambridge: Cambridge University Press, 1898).

Major, J. Russell, *The Deputies to the Estates General in Renaissance France* (Madison: University of Wisconsin Press, 1960).

Representative Government in Early Modern France (New Haven: Yale University Press, 1980).

Representative Institutions in Renaissance France 1421–1559 (Madison: University of Wisconsin Press, 1960).

Malcolm, Harcourt Gladstone, *A History of the Bahamas House of Assembly* (Nassau: Nassau Guardian, 1921).

Maloy, J. S., *The Colonial American Origins of Modern Democratic Thought* (Cambridge: Cambridge University Press, 2008).

Man, Yunlong, "English Colonization and the Formation of Anglo-American Polities, 1606–1664," PhD dissertation, Johns Hopkins University (1994).

Mansbridge, Jane, *Beyond Adversary Democracy* (Chicago: University of Chicago Press, 1983).

Manuel de Bernardo Ares, José, "Parliament or City Councils: The Representation of the Kingdom of the Crown of Castile (1665–1700)," *Parliaments, Estates and Representation*, 25 (2005), 33–54.

Martin, Matthew III, and Daniel C. Snell, "Democracy and Freedom," in Daniel C. Snell (ed.), *A Companion to the Ancient Near East* (Malden, MA: Blackwell, 2005), 397–407.

McGee, Sears, *An Industrious Mind: The Worlds of Sir Simonds D'Ewes* (Stanford: Stanford University Press, 2015).

Millstone, Noah, *The Circulation of Manuscripts and the Invention of Politics in Early Stuart England* (Cambridge: Cambridge University Press, 2016).

"Seeing like a Statesman in Early Stuart England," *Past and Present*, 223 (2014), 77–127.

Mishra, Rupali, *A Business of State: Commerce, Politics, and the Birth of the East India Company* (Cambridge, MA: Harvard University Press, 2018).

Montaño, John Patrick, *Courting the Moderates: Ideology, Propaganda, and the Emergence of Party, 1660–1678* (Newark: University of Delaware Press, 2002).

Morgan, Edmund, *Inventing the People: The Rise of Popular Sovereignty in England and America* (New York: W. W. Norton, 1988).

Morrill, John, "Sir William Brereton and England's Wars of Religion," *Journal of British Studies*, 24 (1985), 311–32.

Mounk, Yascha, *The People vs. Democracy: Why Our Freedom Is in Danger and How to Save It* (Cambridge, MA: Harvard University Press, 2018).

Muhlberger, Steven, "Republics and Quasi-Democratic Institutions in Ancient India," in Benjamin Isakhan and Stephen Stockwell (eds.), *The Secret History of Democracy* (Houndmills, Basingstoke: Palgrave, 2011), 49–59.

Myers, A. R., *Parliaments and Estates in Europe to 1789* (New York: Harcourt, Brace and Jovanovich, 1975).

Neale, J. E., *Elizabeth I and Her Parliaments* (London: Jonathan Cape, 1953).

Nelson, Carolyn, and Matthew Seccombe, *British Newspapers and Periodicals 1641–1700* (New York: Modern Language Association of America, 1987).

Neu, Tim, "Rhetoric and Representation: Reassessing Territorial Diets in Early Modern Germany," *Central European History*, 43 (2010), 1–24.

Newcomb, Benjamin H., *Political Partisanship in the American Middle Colonies: 1700–1776* (Baton Rouge: Louisiana State University Press, 1995).

Notestein, Wallace, "The Establishment of the Committee of Both Kingdoms," *American Historical Review*, 17 (1912), 477–95.

Novak, Stéphanie, and Jon Elster (eds.), *Majority Decisions: Principles and Practice* (Cambridge: Cambridge University Press, 2014).

O'Gorman, Frank, *The Emergence of the British Two-Party System, 1760–1832* (New York: Holmes and Meier, 1982).

The Rise of Party in England: The Rockingham Whigs, 1760–1782 (London: Allen and Unwin, 1975).

Peacey, Jason, "'Fiery Spirits' and Political Propaganda: Uncovering a Radical Press Campaign of 1642," *Publishing History*, 55 (2004), 5–36.

Politicians and Pamphleteers: Propaganda during the English Civil Wars and Interregnum (Aldershot: Ashgate, 2004).

Print and Public Politics in the English Revolution (Cambridge: Cambridge University Press, 2013).

"The Protector Humbled: Richard Cromwell and the Constitution," in Patrick Little (ed.), *The Cromwellian Protectorate* (Woodbridge: Boydell, 2007), 32–52.

"Sir Edward Dering, Popularity, and the Public, 1640–1644," *Historical Journal*, 54 (2011), 955–83.

Pearl, Valerie, *London and the Outbreak of the Puritan Revolution* (Oxford: Oxford University Press, 1961).

Peltonen, Markku, *Rhetoric, Politics and Popularity in Pre-Revolutionary England* (Cambridge: Cambridge University Press, 2013).

Perl-Rosenthal, Nathan, "Atlantic Cultures in the Age of Revolution," *William and Mary Quarterly*, 74 (2017), 667–96.

Pestana, Carla Gardina, *The English Conquest of Jamaica: Oliver Cromwell's Bid for Empire* (Cambridge, MA: Harvard University Press, 2017).

Pincus, Steve, and James Robinson, "What Really Happened during the Glorious Revolution?," in S. Galiani and I. Sened (eds.), *Institutions, Property Rights, and Economic Growth* (Cambridge: Cambridge University Press, 2014), 192–222.

Pomfret, John E., *The Province of East New Jersey* (Princeton: Princeton University Press, 1962).

The Province of West New Jersey (Princeton: Princeton University Press, 1956).

Popper, Nicholas S., "An Information State for Elizabethan England," *The Journal of Modern History*, 90 (2018), 503–35.

Posada-Carbó, Eduardo (ed.), "Congresses versus *Caudillos*: The Untold History of Democracy in Latin America, c. 1810–1910," *Parliaments, Estates and Representations*, 37 (2017), 119–234.

Purvis, Thomas L., *Proprietors, Patronage, and Paper Money: Legislative Politics in New Jersey, 1703–1776* (New Brunswick, NJ: Rutgers University Press, 1986).

Puy Huici Goñi, Maria, *Las Cortes de Navarra durante la edad moderna* (Madrid: Ediciones Rialp, 1963).

Rait, Robert S., *The Parliaments of Scotland* (Glasgow: Maclehose, Jackson, 1924).

Raymond, Joad, *The Invention of the Newspaper* (Oxford: Oxford University Press, 1996).

Pamphlets and Pamphleteering in Early Modern England (Cambridge: Cambridge University Press, 2003).

Reuter, Timothy, *Medieval Polities and Modern Mentalities*, Janet L. Nelson (ed.) (Cambridge: Cambridge University Press, 2006).

Reynolds, Susan, *Kingdoms and Communities in Western Europe 900–1300*, 2nd ed. (Oxford: Oxford University Press, 1997).

Roebuck, Graham, *Clarendon and Cultural Continuity: A Bibliographical Study* (New York: Garland, 1981).

Roney, Jessica, *Governed by a Spirit of Opposition: The Origins of American Political Practice in Colonial Philadelphia* (Baltimore: Johns Hopkins University Press, 2014).

Roots, Ivan, "Lawmaking in the Second Protectorate Parliament," in H. Hearder and H. R. Lyon (eds.), *British Government and Administration: Studies Presented to S. B. Chrimes* (Cardiff: University of Wales Press, 1974), 132–43.

Rosenfeld, Sophia, *Democracy and Truth: A Short History* (Philadelphia: University of Pennsylvania Press, 2018).

Rothrock, George A., "Officials and King's Men: A Note on the Possibilities of Royal Control in the Estates General," *French Historical Studies*, 2 (1962), 504–10.

Runciman, David, *How Democracy Ends* (London: Profile Books, 2018).

Russell, Conrad, *The Fall of the British Monarchies, 1637–1642* (Oxford: Oxford University Press, 1991).

 King James VI and I and His English Parliaments, Richard Cust and Andrew Thrush (eds.) (Oxford: Oxford University Press, 2011).

 Parliaments and English Politics 1621–1629 (Oxford: Clarendon Press, 1979).

Russocki, Stanislaw, "De l'accord commun au vote unanime: Les activités de la Diète nobiliaire de Pologne, XVIème–XVIIIème siècles," *Parliaments, Estates and Representation*, 3 (1983), 7–21.

Schulze, Winfried, "Majority Decision in the Imperial Diets of the Sixteenth and Seventeenth Centuries," *Journal of Modern History*, 58, Supplement: Politics and Society in the Holy Roman Empire, 1500–1806 (1986), S46–S63.

Schwartzberg, Melissa, *Counting the Many: The Origins and Limits of Supermajority Rule* (Cambridge: Cambridge University Press, 2014).

Scott, David, *Politics and War in the Three Stuart Kingdoms, 1637–49* (Basingstoke: Palgrave Macmillan, 2003).

Seaward, Paul, *The Cavalier Parliament and the Reconstruction of the Old Regime, 1661–1667* (Cambridge: Cambridge University Press, 1989).

Sewell, William H., Jr., *Logics of History: Social Theory and Social Transformation* (Chicago: University of Chicago Press, 2005).

Sharma, J. P., *Republics in Ancient India c. 1500 B.C.–c. 500 B.C.* (Leiden: Brill, 1968).

Sharples, Jason T., "Discovering Slave Conspiracies: New Fears of Rebellion and Old Paradigms of Plotting in Seventeenth-Century Barbados," *American Historical Review*, 120 (June 2015), 811–43.

Shilstone, E. M., "The Evolution of the General Assembly of Barbados," *Journal of the Barbados Museum and Historical Society*, 1 (1934), 187–91.

Smith, David L., *Constitutional Royalism and the Search for a Settlement, c. 1640–1649* (Cambridge: Cambridge University Press, 1994).

Smolenski, John, *Friends and Strangers: The Making of a Creole Culture in Colonial Pennsylvania* (Philadelphia: University of Pennsylvania Press, 2010).

Smuts, R. Malcolm, *Culture and Power in England, 1585–1685* (New York: St. Martin's Press, 1999).

Snow, Vernon, "Attendance Trends and Absenteeism in the Long Parliament," *Huntington Library Quarterly*, 18 (1955), 301–6.

Sommerville, Johann, "Parliament, Privilege, and the Liberties of the Subject," in J. H. Hexter (ed.), *Parliament and Liberty from the Reign of Elizabeth to the English Civil War* (Stanford: Stanford University Press, 1992), 56–84.

Sowerby, Scott, "Tories in the Whig Corner: Daniel Fleming's Journal of the 1685 Parliament," *Parliamentary History*, 24 (2005), 157–201.

Speck, W. A., "The House of Commons 1702–1714: A Study in Political Organization," PhD dissertation, University of Oxford (1965).

    Tory and Whig: The Struggle in the Constituencies, 1701–1715 (New York: St. Martin's Press, 1970).

Spurdle, Frederick G., *Early West Indian Government: Showing the Progress of Government in Barbados, Jamaica, and the Leeward Islands, 1660–1783* (Palmerston North: the author, 1963).

Squire, Peverill, *Evolution of American Legislatures: Colonies, Territories, and States, 1619–2009* (Ann Arbor: University of Michigan Press, 2012).

    The Rise of the Representative: Lawmakers and Constituents in Colonial America (Ann Arbor: University of Michigan Press, 2017).

Staveley, E. S., *Greek and Roman Voting and Elections* (Ithaca: Cornell University Press, 1972).

Sternberg, Giora, *Status Interaction during the Reign of Louis XIV* (Oxford: Oxford University Press, 2014).

Stewart, Robert, *Party and Politics 1830–1852* (London: Macmillan, 1989).

Swatland, Andrew, *The House of Lords in the Reign of Charles II* (Cambridge: Cambridge University Press, 1996).

Thomas, Courtney, *If I Lose Mine Honour, I Lose Myself: Honour among the Early Modern English Elite* (Toronto: University of Toronto Press, 2017).

Thomas, P. G., *The House of Commons in the Eighteenth Century* (Oxford: Clarendon Press, 1971).

Thompson, I. A. A., *Crown and Cortes: Government, Institutions and Representation in Early-Modern Castile* (Aldershot: Variorum/Ashgate, 1993).

Thomson, Edith E. B., *The Parliament of Scotland, 1690–1702* (Oxford: Oxford University Press, 1929).

Thrush, Andrew, and John P. Ferris (eds.), *The House of Commons 1604–1629*, 6 vols. (Cambridge: Cambridge University Press, 2010).

Tully, Alan, *Forming American Politics: Ideas, Interests, and Institutions in Colonial New York and Pennsylvania* (Baltimore: Johns Hopkins University Press, 1994).

Underdown, David, *Pride's Purge: Politics in the Puritan Revolution* (Oxford: Oxford University Press, 1971).

Urbinati, Nadia, *Democracy Disfigured: Opinion, Truth, and the People* (Cambridge, MA: Harvard University Press, 2014).

    Me the People: How Populism Transforms Democracy (Cambridge, MA: Harvard University Press, 2019).

Urfalino, Philippe, "La décision par consensus apparent," *Revue Européenne des Sciences Sociales*, 45 (2007), 47–70.

Van Reybrouck, David, *Against Elections: The Case for Democracy* (New York: Random House, 2016).

Vázquez de Prada, Valentin, and Alfredo Floristán, "The Relationship of the Kingdom of Navarre to Central Government in the Eighteenth Century: The Struggle for Legislative Power," *Parliaments, Estates and Representation*, 9 (1989), 123–35.

Wall, Robert Emmet, Jr., *Massachusetts Bay: The Crucial Decade, 1640–1650* (New Haven: Yale University Press, 1972).

Walter, John, *Covenanting Citizens: The Protestation Oath and Popular Political Culture in the English Revolution* (Oxford: Oxford University Press, 2017).

Understanding Popular Violence in the English Revolution: The Colchester Plunderers (Cambridge: Cambridge University Press, 1999).

Weil, Rachel, *A Plague of Informers: Conspiracy and Political Trust in William III's England* (New Haven: Yale University Press, 2013).

Whitson, Agnes Mary, *The Constitutional Development of Jamaica 1660–1729* (Manchester: Manchester University Press, 1929).

Williamson, James Alexander, *The Caribbee Islands under the Proprietary Patents* (Oxford: Oxford University Press, 1926).

Witcombe, D. T., *Charles II and the Cavalier House of Commons* (Manchester: Manchester University Press, 1966).

Woolrych, Austin, *Britain in Revolution, 1625–1660* (Oxford: Oxford University Press, 2002).

Commonwealth to Protectorate (Oxford: Oxford University Press, 1982).

Wootton, David, "From Rebellion to Revolution: The Crisis of 1642/3 and the Origins of Civil War Radicalism," *English Historical Review*, 105 (1990), 654–69.

Worden, Blair, *The Rump Parliament 1648–53* (Cambridge: Cambridge University Press, 1977).

Zaller, Robert, *The Parliament of 1621: A Study in Constitutional Conflict* (Berkeley: University of California Press, 1971).

Zaret, David, *Origins of Democratic Culture: Printing, Petitions, and the Public Sphere in Early-Modern England* (Princeton: Princeton University Press, 2000).

Zemsky, Robert, *Merchants, Farmers, and River Gods: An Essay on Eighteenth-Century American Politics* (Boston: Gambit, 1971).

Index

acclamation. *See* voting, consensus
Act of Oblivion (1652), 166
Act of Oblivion (1660), 184
Albany Congress, 243
Allen, Francis, 156
Antigua. *See* Leeward Islands
Aragon. *See* Spain
assemblies, colonial. *See* colonial lower
    assemblies
Athens, 7–9

Bahamas, 233
ballot box, 16, 160, 213
Barbados, 230–1
Barebone's Parliament. *See* Nominated
    Parliament
Bargrave, John, 213–14
Beale, William, 50, 60, 70
Bennet, Henry, 1st Earl of Arlington, 199
Bermuda, 212, 218–21
Bourdieu, Pierre, 23
Broderick, Sir Alan, 181, 190–2, 199
Butler, Nathaniel, 218

Calvert, Cecil, 2nd Baron Baltimore, 227
Caribbean. *See* individual colonies
Carolina, 235–7
Carter, Landon, 217–18
Cary, Lucius, 2nd Viscount Falkland, 107
Castile. *See* Spain
Catalonia. *See* Spain
catechism bill (1657), 174
Cavalier Parliament, 183–201
Cavendish, William, 2nd Earl of
    Devonshire, 214
Chaffin, Thomas, 73
Charles I, 65, 115–16, 123–4, 129, 142,
    165, 167, 214–15
    Personal Rule, 63, 66–7
Civil War, English
    peace negotiations, 123–30, 133, 142–5,
        147–8, 151, 163

Coke, Sir Edward, 51, 56, 107
Coke, Sir John, 43
colonial lower assemblies, 208–10, 242,
    253–4
colonies. *See* individual colonies
Committee of Both Kingdoms, 147, 149,
    151
Commons, House of (England and
    Britain), 7, 10, 12, 18–19, 244–6;
    see also entries under voting
    agenda control, 32, 76, 212
    committees, 38–9, 64–5, 71, 250
    committees of the whole, 36–8, 78, 169,
        173, 189, 195, 200
    conferences, 38–9, 64–5, 71,
        250
    early Stuart period, 26–62
    journal, 4
    private bills, 32, 47, 76
    procedure, 21–3, 32, 34–5
    Speaker, 21–2, 30, 37, 39, 41, 44, 49, 56,
        64, 69, 88, 90, 94–5, 172, 174–5,
        200
    Tudor period, 25–6
Connecticut, 224–6
consensus, 1–2; *see also* voting, consensus
    as political tactic, 65
    as sign of truth, 49, 250
Continental Congresses, 243–4
Convention Parliament (1660), 181
Cooper, Anthony Ashley, 3rd Earl of
    Shaftesbury, 201
Corporation Act (1661), 184
corporations, 16, 208–9, 221, 253
Covenant, Solemn League and, *See* Solemn
    League and Covenant
Coventry, Sir William, 203
Cromwell, Oliver, 153, 167, 169,
    174–5
Cromwell, Richard, 175–7
Culpepper, Sir John, 86, 100, 102–3,
    108–9, 113, 118–19

276

CPSIA information can be obtained
at www.ICGtesting.com
Printed in the USA
LVHW080601190422
716593LV00005B/317